WELCOME TO THE BROADCAST

A Memoir

DON NEWMAN

HarperCollins*Publishers*Ltd

Published by HarperCollins Publishers Ltd.

First Edition

HarperCollins books may be purchased for educational, business,
or sales promotional use through our Special Markets Department.

HarperCollins Publishers Ltd
2 Bloor Street East, 20th Floor
Toronto, Ontario, Canada
M4W 1A8

www.harpercollins.ca

Library and Archives Canada Cataloguing in Publication

Newman, Don
Welcome to the Broadcast / Don Newman.

ISBN 978-1-44341-682-5

Printed and bound in the United States
RRD 9 8 7 6 5 4 3 2 1

To Shannon

CONTENTS

WELCOME TO THE BROADCAST

1

No Time-Outs in Politics

O UTRAGE COMES NATURALLY to him. But on the morning of Thursday, December 6, 2008, John Baird was ready to outdo himself.

"We will go over the heads of MPs, we will go over the head of the Governor General . . . We will go to the people," Baird fumed, telling me this face to face, one on one, on live television across the country.

The transport minister and I were in the foyer of the House of Commons, inside a small rectangle marked off by CBC camera crews and set up as an area for interviewing and reporting live to the CBC News Network. The atmosphere was electric. The foyer was full of reporters, camera crews and politicians.

Over the years, at different times, I had hosted a weekly and a daily political program from the foyer, and broadcast throne speeches, budgets and other big events from right outside the House of Commons chamber. But never had the atmosphere been like this. Because that morning, history seemed about to be made: for the second time since

Confederation, it was likely that a government was going to be replaced after a non-confidence vote in the House of Commons without there first being a general election. And if that did happen, the new government was going to be in office for at least a year and a half. Only one thing could prevent that: the agreement of Governor General Michaëlle Jean to a request by Prime Minister Stephen Harper to end a session of Parliament that had only been running for two weeks, and leave a break before starting a new session.

"We need a time-out," Baird said, and then claimed that was what Canadians in general wanted.

"You get time-outs in football," I challenged him. "This is politics, not football. There are no time-outs in politics."

While Baird and I were talking in the foyer, Stephen Harper was a couple of miles away at Rideau Hall, the Governor General's residence, making his case for why, after beginning a new, first session of Parliament, he now wanted to end the session and take a break of almost two months.

How had we suddenly reached such a curious state of affairs? Harper and his Conservatives had blundered. In a financial update a few days earlier, Finance Minister Jim Flaherty had not only painted a financial scenario everyone knew was much too optimistic, but the Harper government had also announced it was planning to end public funding for political parties. The Conservatives could prosper without public funds. The Liberals, New Democrats and Bloc Québécois could not.

Pretending that their own financial future was not their primary concern, the Opposition claimed it was concern for the economy that forced them to band together, agree to defeat the government in a non-confidence vote a few days later, and then present to the Governor General a signed agreement creating a Liberal–NDP coalition government. The separatist Bloc Québécois would not be in the government, but would support it on confidence votes for at least eighteen months, meaning the coalition would last at least a year and a half.

Only once before, in 1926, when Britain still sent governors general to Canada, had a request for an election coming from a prime minster defeated on a confidence vote in the House of Commons been refused. Lord Byng thought it proper that he first invite the Conservatives, led by Arthur Meighen, to try and win the confidence of the House, and said no to Liberal prime minister Mackenzie King's election request. At the time, the Conservatives had more seats in the House of Commons than the Liberals, and King had been abandoned by his voting partners, the Progressives.

Byng's decision created a constitutional crisis in 1926. Now it seemed Canada was on the edge of another one. Would Michaëlle Jean agree to Harper's request to end the parliamentary session (known as proroga-tion)? And if she did not, and the Conservatives were defeated on a con-fidence vote, would she agree to the new election that Harper would obviously ask for? Or would she give the coalition the government?

All that was on the line as John Baird and I began our conversation, seen live across the country.

Baird was then—and still is—the government's designated hitter. Over six feet tall, burly, with a shock of hair cut short that apparently used to be red enough to earn him the nickname "Rusty," his belli-cose, loud and aggressive style of answering questions in the House of Commons has some reporters referring to him as "Bombastic Bushkin." Away from the House, he is more genial. A bachelor, he often escorts the prime minister's wife, Laureen, to the National Arts Centre or other events in Ottawa.

In the foyer of the House that December 4, he was neither genial nor bombastic. He was determined. On a repetitive message track obviously worked out with the Prime Minister's Office, he kept pushing the idea that, in minority governments, coalitions are somehow illegitimate, and saying the Conservatives would go over the heads of Parliament and the Governor General, calling for a campaign of civil disobedience.

I was so amazed at this approach that at one point I told him: "I can't believe it. You are a Conservative, in the British parliamentary system, and you want to go over the heads of MPs . . . You are saying that MPs and the Governor General aren't important."

"Of course they are important. They are elected to come here and represent their constituencies," Baird responded, knowing full well that MPs come to Ottawa to vote their party's instructions and that the Governor General is appointed to exercise constitutional powers, not represent any constituents.

"But they are not important if they don't do what you want them to?" I inquired.

Baird then turned on what the Conservatives thought was the weakness of the coalition deal—the agreement of the Bloc Québécois to support the Liberal–NDP coalition on confidence votes—although he claimed incorrectly, as others in his party did, that the "separatists" were actually going to be part of the government.

This, of course was wrong, and Baird knew it. Still, he said it because it was an argument that resonated with many Canadians outside of Quebec, even though it flew in the face of two facts. First, as Opposition leader following the 2004 election that put the Paul Martin Liberals into a minority, Stephen Harper had signed a similar letter with the same leaders of the Bloc and the NDP to make an arrangement for a coalition government after a Liberal confidence defeat. And second, as a minority government, the Conservatives had a number of times stayed in power only because they were supported in confidence votes by the Bloc Québécois.

So, with that in mind, I asked Baird, "Does that mean if your government remains in power and you bring in a budget, and if that budget passes, but only with the votes of the NDP supporting you, it will be an illegitimate budget?"

"It will be a budget with a maple leaf on it," he quickly countered, completely ignoring the point because he couldn't answer it.

Baird also obfuscated on how the Conservatives "would go over the heads of Parliament and over the head of the Governor General." But since government supporters were already demonstrating outside of Rideau Hall while Harper was meeting inside, I had some idea of what he had in mind. I recalled demonstrations in Ukraine a few years earlier that had overturned the results of an election.

"Will it be like Kiev a few years ago? Will you go around marching with different-coloured scarves?" Protesters in the Ukrainian capital had worn either blue or orange scarves during the demonstrations to show which side they supported. He ignored my question and continued on his message track.

I'd had no sense of how our conversation would evolve when it began, but the longer it went on, the more dogged Baird became. Talking quickly, he pushed out more and more ideas that demanded that I challenge him either for accuracy or common sense.

I knew that what was going out on TV screens was going to be controversial. As I kept Baird to account, I finally told him, "If you think I am being unfair, you can always complain to the CBC ombudsman." Then, thinking he was overly aggressive but not necessarily accountable, I asked, "Do you have an ombudsman?"

"The voters of Ottawa West–Nepean," he shot back, naming his constituency.

Since all of this was happening in mid-morning, and not on my regular *Politics* broadcast, as our exchange went on I kept waiting for a voice in my earpiece to interrupt—a producer telling me I had gone way over my usual time, that other guests were waiting to be interviewed by someone else and that I had to wind up the conversation. Early on, I would have ignored the instructions, but as the minutes ticked by, that would have been harder to do. But the producers apparently found the minister's complete misrepresentation of the parliamentary system and how minority governments are meant to work as mind-boggling and outrageous as I did.

Finally, after about fifteen minutes, my senior producer, Sharon Musgrave, listening in from the CBC's studio across from Parliament Hill, told me, "You can wind it up whenever you want to."

And by then I did want to. The conversation was starting to go around in circles. Baird was still babbling on like the Energizer Bunny, but I thought enough was enough.

Shortly after, Harper emerged from Rideau Hall to say that the Governor General had acceded to his request. What could have been a crisis had quickly passed. The immediate fallout from my exchange with John Baird did not. Back in my office, I found my email and voicemail both jammed with messages. Predictably, the partisan ones were divided between those who liked or disliked John Baird, Stephen Harper and the Conservative government.

One, from CBC ombudsman Vince Carlin, joked, "Thanks for making me more work."

Other complimentary messages came from journalistic colleagues— many at the CBC, but also from other, competing organizations that had been watching in. The one that sticks in my mind the most came from a young reporter at the Global TV station in Halifax.

"Seeing the kind of thing you were able to do today," the email said, "is the reason I got into journalism."

As I wrote back a short email of appreciation, I thought to myself, "That's why I got into journalism too."

2

The Path to Journalism

BEING A JOURNALIST was not my boyhood ambition. I became one because of the adult measles.

In April of 1960, the measles made me so ill I had to postpone my university exams at United College in Winnipeg and delay looking for a summer job. By mid-May I had recovered and was feeling fine, but by then all the good summer jobs were taken—particularly the best-paying and easiest one, the job I coveted: cutting grass for the City of Winnipeg.

When I lamented my out-of-work situation to my brother, Roger, he came up with an idea, as all good older brothers should. Five and a half years my senior, he was working at the *Winnipeg Free Press,* already establishing himself in a journalism career he had planned on since he was twelve years old. He thought that having his kid brother working at the same place could turn out to be embarrassing. So he proposed that I go to the *Free Press*'s competitor, the *Winnipeg Tribune,* and see if they had an opening for a copy boy.

I didn't know exactly what a copy boy did, but I figured if my brother thought I could do it, I probably could. So, with considerable bravado and some trepidation, on a Friday afternoon, I took the elevator to the fifth floor of the Tribune Building and asked to see the managing editor.

I took that elevator in search of a sixteen-week summer job. It led to a career in journalism that has lasted more than fifty years, and isn't over yet. It was a life-changing day that set me on a course that, looking back, I can see that many of my life experiences to that time had been preparing me for.

I BEGAN MY summer job at the *Tribune* five months shy of my twentieth birthday. And those almost twenty years had been divided up into four almost equal, but quite distinct segments.

I was born in Winnipeg on October 28, 1940, just over a year after the Second World War began. My father's name was Lincoln Rosser Newman, and he was a banker with the Royal Bank of Canada. My mother's maiden name was Doris Angelina Arnett, and she and my father met when she went to work at the Royal Bank after graduating from United College.

When the war began, my father was thirty-five years old, with a wife and a four-year-old son. Not exactly the eighteen-to-twenty-two-year-olds for whom the army was looking. In early 1941 he was thirty-six, with a wife and two sons, when the bank transferred him to the main branch in Calgary. The war had intensified and my father joined the 2nd Battalion of the Calgary Highlanders, in the so-called Reserve Army. While continuing to work full time at the bank, he apparently trained every weekend and holiday. My first vague memory of him is in his lieutenant's uniform, a kilt and Scots wedge cap with a ribbon down the back.

In 1943 we were on the move again, this time to Toronto, where my father was to be a Royal Bank branch inspector working out of the main Ontario office on King Street, near Bay. But in high school and as a young man in Winnipeg, he had won public-speaking contests and been successful as an amateur actor. Somehow these talents were recognized, and my father was seconded to the group that travelled to towns and cities across Ontario selling Victory Bonds for the government to help finance the war. He wasn't home much, and the only thing I really remember about Toronto is that, after being away for a week, Dad would come home Saturday afternoon in the car that came with his job. He became very good at his work, becoming one of the bank's top bond salesmen. Having a car wasn't all that common then, particularly during the war. Sometimes we would get a drive around the block. But no further—gas was rationed and the car was for selling bonds to win the war.

My only other memory of Toronto is the day the war ended. Streetcar drivers on Yonge Street, near where we lived in North Toronto, opened the doors of their cars and threw transfers out in celebration—a sort of makeshift ticker-tape parade of their own.

The war over, we were on the move again. Although he was just forty-one, my father's career took a huge leap forward when he was named manager of the Royal Bank branch in London, England, on Cockspur Street, next to Canada House on Trafalgar Square.

The war was a very recent memory in England when we arrived in 1946. The rubble had been cleared away, but there were gaping holes in many city blocks throughout central London where the German bombs had hit their marks. We lived in the leafy suburb of Mill Hill in northwest London, between Hendon and Edgware. There was no visible damage there, but in spacious Mill Hill Park nearby, there were bomb shelters of reinforced concrete dug into the ground where our new neighbours had scurried for five years of bomber raids and buzz-bomb attacks.

The house in Mill Hill seemed fine to me. My mother wasn't quite so sure. It was built before the First World War, a two-storey brick structure with a low brick wall around the front and rose bushes filling the area between the wall and the house. A side drive led through a high wooden gate into a small courtyard in front of a garage. As a five-year-old I was really impressed with all the rooms and all the space. During the war, we had lived on the main floor of a two-storey house in North Toronto that had been duplexed to help deal with the wartime housing shortage. For six months after my father had gone ahead to London, my mother, brother and I lived with my grandparents in Winnipeg. Nice, but a bit cramped. Now I had my own bedroom and lots of space around the house, plus a big staircase to run up and down.

But with the kitchen sink in one room, the stove in another and no refrigerator, you can understand why my mother didn't find the house so attractive. There was also no basement and no central heating. Each room had a fireplace, and in most, the fireplace had been filled in and replaced with a gas heater. The heaters didn't throw much heat. You had to sit next to them on a winter evening. I remember getting dressed on cold mornings, turning slowly around in front of the heater, trying to warm both my back and front as I put on my clothes.

I began school in London. First at St. George's school in Mill Hill, and then, after a year, joined my brother at Highgate School. It was there that I spent the formative years from seven to ten, and they were good years. The academic side was rigorous. When we were eight, we were studying English, French, Latin, algebra, geometry, art and music appreciation and were acting in a school play. Every day ended with an hour and a half of games: soccer in the autumn and winter; cricket, track and field and swimming in the spring and early summer.

It was in London that I first saw the technology that years later would come to shape my life: television. The BBC was broadcasting on one channel in the London area. We did not have a TV, but our neighbours across the road in Mill Hill, Roy and Joan Smart, did. Roy was a high-ranking engineer at English Electric, and he had one of the first experimental commercial sets. He invited us over for a look. We watched the tennis at Wimbledon, and then that evening a musical program with "Two Ton" Tessie O'Shay. I was seven and remember thinking it was a miracle. I didn't guess that it was where my future lay.

SCHOOL HAD JUST begun in the fall of 1950 when suddenly our family was on the move again. This time, my father had been transferred to Montreal. We set sail for Canada in November on the Canadian Pacific liner *Empress of Scotland,* after a final night in London staying at the Savoy Hotel.

The late-November crossing from Greenock, near Glasgow, to Quebec City was rough. We were glad to go ashore, where I saw something I had rarely seen in England: snow. More of it that evening in Montreal, where we checked into the Windsor Hotel. I was wearing my English schoolboy uniform, rain coat, cap and short pants. The first thing next morning, my mother and I were at Eaton's, where I was properly outfitted in breeches, a parka and a toque.

Life in Montreal was certainly different. We moved into a duplex apartment in Notre-Dame-de-Grace, an English-speaking suburb near Westmount. It lacked the grandeur of the house in Mill Hill and didn't have the rose bushes, apple trees or greenhouse. But it was newly built, we were the first family to live in it, it was centrally heated of course, for the cold Canadian winter, with a modern kitchen complete with the latest in refrigerators, and the bathroom contained a shower. My mother thought it was terrific.

Going to school was different, too. No more the boys-only private school, with the uniform and a long commute. Our home was across the street from Willingdon Public School. Sports were also new. No more soccer and cricket; now there were hockey, baseball and football. The first two were pretty straightforward, but football was a little more obtuse. Soon, though, I enjoyed them all, and without many friends when I first arrived in Montreal, I spent every afternoon after school and every Saturday at an outdoor rink a block away run by the YMCA, first learning how to skate, and then perfecting my technique. My second winter in Montreal, I was as good a skater as anyone else, and I made a competitive hockey team.

Going to school with girls was different, too. At first it seemed just an anomaly, but by the time I was in junior high at Westward School two years later it had become a distraction, and after I started high school at West Hill High, the Friday night dances sometimes clashed with hockey games.

Family holidays were in the Eastern Townships. We spent the first two summers on Lake Memphremagog and the next on Brome Lake near Knowlton. Those holidays gave me a lot of time to spend with my father, whose work in Montreal seemed just about as busy as it had been in London. That was great for me; I idolized my father. My brother, Roger, who was a very good athlete and my sports hero, would some-times show up from his summer jobs on weekends, but when he had jobs at resorts in the Laurentians I hardly saw him at all.

In 1952 I had my second exposure to what was to become my life. That summer, the CBC began television broadcasting in both Toronto and Montreal. On a hot evening on the first day of broadcasting, I stood in a crowd in front of an electrical appliance store on Monkland Avenue, not far from our home. The store had a television in the window, and that television was broadcasting pictures of the Montreal Royals baseball game taking place at Delorimier Stadium in the heart of the city. I was twelve. I thought the TV was interesting, but I was more interested in seeing the game than I was impressed by how I was seeing it.

As a young teenager in Montreal, there was a challenge to life that was not present elsewhere in Canada. That was going to a movie. A horrific theatre fire that claimed young lives in the 1920s had created a provincial law that said no one under sixteen years of age could go to a theatre, movie or otherwise, even accompanied by an adult. Obviously, the trick became to look sixteen. Luckily for me, I grew to be about five feet ten before my fourteenth birthday and was rarely turned away at the box office. Still, it was really a drag when a group of kids would go to a movie and most would get tickets, but one or more would be rejected and left outside. It was really a grim fate if you invited a girl to a movie, and then were turned down at the cashier and couldn't get tickets.

In the fall of 1955, life seemed to proceed as normal. When we returned from our Brome Lake holiday on the Labour Day weekend, my father had a bad attack of indigestion. But the next day, he was fine and resumed his daily routine, including an early-October business trip to Chicago.

I was at West Hill High School, doing enough work to get by, playing pickup football after school, going to Friday night dances and following the fortunes of the Montreal Alouettes and Canadiens in the newspapers and on the radio. We lived only a block and a half from West Hill, and I came home each day for lunch. On Wednesday, October 19, 1955, I had just finished my sandwich when the telephone rang. I answered, and I will never forget what I heard.

It was my father's secretary. "Something has happened to your father. He's been taken to the Queen Elizabeth Hospital. Tell your mother to come right away."

I couldn't believe my ears. I called my mother and gave her the phone. She understood. She immediately called a taxi, and then told me to go back to school and come home right after classes.

It was bad. My father was in a coma. The next evening, my grandmother arrived from Winnipeg; the morning after, two of my father's brothers, my uncle Ross and my uncle Ed, also arrived. They and my mother went to the hospital. My grandmother stayed home with me. After midnight, early in the morning of October 22, the phone rang. My mother took the call. I could hear her speak in a muffled voice and then hang up. She came into my room.

"Are you awake?" she asked.

"Yes," I said.

"Daddy has died."

It was a week before my fifteenth birthday. It was the end of the world as I had known it.

It was also the end of my time in Montreal. Without my father's job, there was nothing to keep my mother or me in the city, and Mother wanted to move to Winnipeg as quickly as possible to live near her mother, sister, two brothers and my father's four siblings.

My brother, Roger, was already planning to live outside the family home, but when my father died he dropped his plans and moved to Winnipeg to be with Mother and me. For the next two years, he would be the most important role model in my life.

My grandmother, my mother's sister Frances, her husband, Richard Bowles, and their four children quickly became the closest part of our extended family. Their eldest son, Sheldon, a year and a half younger than me, became like a younger brother. Other aunts and uncles were also around, particularly my father's sister, Renee Newman. As for many women of her generation, the First World War had diminished her opportunities to marry. She owned her own millinery business and became good friends with my mother.

In January of 1956 I started at Kelvin High School. Counting back to Highgate in England, it was the fifth school I had attended in seven years. High school is the worst time for a change of schools. Changing schools, cities and, in many ways, cultures is even harder. I started Kelvin in mid-year. Not only had everyone else in the class been together since September, but many of them throughout the school had been together all the way through elementary and junior high before getting to Kelvin at the same time.

Hockey was my main interest during my years at Kelvin. When we moved from Montreal, I made the competitive team at the Sir John Franklin Community Club, and it was a pretty good team. The first year I played, we went to the city championships, only to lose a two-game, total-goals series 14–7. The second year, we were one game away from the championship again, but we lost the opportunity when half the team stayed out on a Saturday night partying before a Sunday afternoon game we had to win. I was pretty annoyed, but it was a lesson learned for the future: if you are going to be involved with other people in any endeavour, try to make sure you all share the same commitment; otherwise, don't get involved.

Given that I had lost my father and then moved to a new and unknown city fifteen hundred miles away, things went pretty well at Kelvin. But there were no nostalgic regrets as I left high school there. Still, life seemed to really pick up when, that fall, I enrolled at United College in downtown Winnipeg.

Most Kelvin students went on to postsecondary studies at the more prestigious University of Manitoba. I didn't want to follow them there. My mother suggested United. She had gone there in the 1920s when her family had moved to Winnipeg from Souris, Manitoba. The college was then named after John Wesley, the founder of the Methodist Church. (It was renamed United in 1938 following a merger with Manitoba

College.) She had enjoyed her time there and thought I might too. And she was right. I loved it.

At United, students came from a wide variety of backgrounds, from areas all over Winnipeg and from rural Manitoba towns and villages to live at the college in residence. There were a few scholarship students from the Caribbean. At United, you could meet people from the ethnically diverse North End of the city. People from the suburbs of St. Vital and Fort Garry. People from MacGregor, Manitoba and Dryden in northwestern Ontario. If you didn't keep up with lectures, your reading and your reports, you were in trouble. I liked the responsibility and I liked the more sophisticated social scene where you could go on a date without a whole gang going with you, like at Kelvin.

My first summer at United, my uncle Sheldon Arnett gave me a job working on the factory floor of the Arnett family's manufacturing business, which made industrial kitchen equipment. Uncle Shel was my mother's younger brother. It was hot and hard work, but it paid union wages and I made more money that summer than I had ever before. However, the job convinced me to stay in university for fear I might have to work that hard all the time.

The next summer, I worked for another uncle, Richard Bowles. He was married to my mother's sister Frances, and I saw a lot of him, since Mother and Frances were not just sisters but also best friends.

Rich Bowles was one of the top lawyers in Winnipeg. Well respected, very successful. He would later become chancellor of the University of Manitoba and Lieutenant-Governor of Manitoba. But that summer I thought I might like to be a lawyer and, true to his generous nature, he created a summer job for me in his office. It was pleasant working there, and some of the secretaries were cute, but I wasn't sure the law was for me. So the next summer, I tried my father's career. The Royal Bank of Canada gave me a summer job as a junior at the branch at Main Street and Logan Avenue in a tough section of Winnipeg's North End. At the end of the summer, the Royal offered me a deal: drop out of university, take a full-time job with the bank, and over the next few years take the special banking courses arranged through the University of Western Ontario. This was the way my father had joined the bank, and I think my mother secretly wanted me to follow in his footsteps. But I had already realized what a charmed career my father had had, and that most of banking, even at a high level, didn't compare with the jobs he'd had in London and Montreal. So I went back to United College.

Early the next April, I was studying one evening in the library at the College for the upcoming final exams. I felt as though I was coming down with a cold, so I skipped going for coffee as I usually did and caught the bus home. By the time I arrived at our house, I was running a fever. My mother sent me to bed with two Aspirin. The next morning, I was much worse—aching, no appetite, feeling terribly weak. We called our doctor—back in the 1960s, doctors still made house calls. He said it must be a virus that would run its course. Just keep taking the Aspirins. But three days later, I was no better, and my mother took matters into her own hands. She ran a hot bath for me, then had me drag myself out of bed and into the hot water. I can still remember the feeling; the water was boiling hot and very uncomfortable. But suddenly, I felt better. I looked down, and my body was covered with a bright red, blotchy rash. So were my hands. So, it turned out, was my face. I might have looked terrible, but I felt enormously better, so much so that after eating nothing for almost a week, I was suddenly hungry.

The doctor returned for an examination, and his verdict was both a relief and chilling. He said I had contacted adult measles, and if the rash had not come out on my body within the next day or so, it would have come out internally in my stomach and on my liver and other organs. An internal adult measles rash was usually fatal.

It took three weeks to recuperate, during which time I wore sunglasses to protect my eyes during the day and when I watched television in the evening. Those three weeks meant I couldn't write my exams, couldn't get out and find a summer job. But because of my mother's hot bath treatment, I was recuperating and getting my strength back, to get on with the next stage of my life, one that determined who I am and what I would be. And it started with that cold-call trip to the *Winnipeg Tribune*.

When I got off the elevator that afternoon, I asked for Eric Wells, who my brother had told me was the managing editor. But he was too busy to deal with copy-boy applicants, so he handed me off to his deputy, news editor Alan Rogers. Rogers was someone who would pop up again in the first decade of my career, but neither of us knew that as we sat across from each other in the imposing *Tribune* boardroom while he asked me why I wanted to work on a newspaper, and I tried to give the sort of answers that I thought my reporter brother, Roger, would give.

Rogers was friendly enough, but said there were no openings for copy boys, although he would keep me in mind if one came up. I am not sure what happened next at the newspaper, but I left the *Tribune* and took the bus home. When I got there, my mother was waiting with a message: call a Mr. Rogers at the *Tribune*. Quickly, I did.

"Things have changed," Alan Rogers told me. "Can you start Monday morning at eight?"

"Yessir, thanks, I'll be there."

3

Getting Started

THE *WINNIPEG TRIBUNE* was at the corner of Graham Avenue and Smith Street, across from the main post office, one block south of Portage Avenue and three blocks east and a block and a half south from its bigger rival, the *Winnipeg Free Press*. Equally as important, it was on the Corydon bus line, which went by the end of my street in the River Heights area. That was a bonus. At United College, I had worked my schedule around so that I had only one class a week that started at eight-thirty. Beginning work half an hour earlier, on a route that required one or more bus transfers, would have been a challenge for someone who liked to sleep in.

But the morning of Monday, May 16, 1960, I was up bright and early and arrived before the eight-o'clock start time on the fifth floor of the Tribune Building to find out what it was that a copy boy did, and then to do it.

Quickly, I realized the job was very interesting. The copy boy was the first person to see much of the news that might go into that day's paper. News from across Canada and around the world rolled into the *Tribune*—and newspapers everywhere—on teletype machines. The machines were rather like large electric typewriters, standing on four legs, but with no keyboards. The letters were moved electronically by an operator typing, often hundreds or even thousands of miles away, at the headquarters of the news service that provided the teletype, sending the stories at the same time to every subscribing newspaper.

The incoming stories were printed on special rolls of newsprint. Actually, three rolls in one: a roll of white newsprint and a roll of green, separated by a carbon paper roll, all pressed together to pass through the teletype as a single unit while the news story was being typed on the top page.

The teletype machines all had plastic covers over them, to muffle at least some of the noise from their incessantly clacking keys. Even so, they were noisy and so were located in a separate room at the rear of the newsroom—known, not surprisingly, as the wire room.

Clearing the stories off the teletype, hanging the green carbon copy on a nail, throwing the carbon paper in the garbage and then taking the top printed copy to the appropriate editor was one of the two main tasks of a copy boy. The stories could go to the international editor, the national editor, the sports editor or the business editor, depending on what they were about. If the editor wanted the story to go in the paper, he either typed a headline for it himself or handed it off to a sub-editor to read and edit it and write the headline. All of the editors (except the business editor) sat around a horseshoe-shaped desk. The sub-editors sat at the round part of the horseshoe and were known as rim men.

When the story had been edited and the headline typed on a square piece of newsprint attached to the copy with a paper clip, it landed in a metal tray in the middle of the desk. Then came the copy boy's next important job: to take the story, roll it up and put into a thick plastic tube.

The tube was then inserted into a pneumatic metal pipe, and pulled by air pressure up one floor to the composing room, where the story was set into type, locked in a page frame and sent to the printers in the *Tribune* basement for that day's paper.

It might all sound a bit routine, but I loved it. I loved seeing the news first, loved watching how the editors handled it, loved working with people who were smart and serious about what they did, but who were not too serious about themselves or each other.

And every day was fast-paced. Like most Canadian dailies in 1960, including the competing *Free Press,* the *Tribune* was an afternoon paper. That meant most of the action each day happened between eight and noon. The paper was on the street by 1 p.m. Every day, there was a rush to deadline—not only for the editors I was bringing the copy to, but for the city editor, his assistant and the reporters who covered the news of the city each day and either rushed back to the newsroom to write their stories or phoned them in to reporters on the rewrite desk, who acted as stenographers and took down the reports dictated over the phone.

There was a real sense of competition each day with the *Free Press,* and the reporting of local news was where the competition lay. Both papers subscribed to and were members of the *Canadian Press* wire service, where much of the national and international news came from, but the local news was covered competitively by each paper's reporters. "Scoops"—stories that were exclusive to a reporter and paper—were coveted by everyone.

While fierce competitors, the *Tribune* and *Free Press* had a deal to exchange ten copies of their papers as soon as they came off the press each day. A copy boy from the *Free Press* was sent to the *Tribune* to pick up the ten papers, and I was usually the copy boy sent to the *Free Press* for the *Tribune*'s ten. And this could be exciting. As soon as I grabbed my copies of the *Free Press* and headed for the door, I was scanning the headlines on the front page. If there was a big headline claiming a *Free Press* exclusive, I would run the four blocks back to the *Tribune,* race up to the fifth floor, slam the papers down on the horseshoe desk and, with almost no breath left, wheeze out, "They have a scoop."

The editors would then yell for reporters to get on the phone and try to match at least some of the details in the *Free Press* exclusive. The presses would stop until at least the rudiments of a matching story had been pulled together quickly and inserted into a page frame. Then the press run would start again, with *Tribune* faces not quite as red as they might have been. Luckily, roles were reversed when the *Tribune* had the scoop, which it often did.

Quite often, the *Tribune* would have a national scoop the *Free Press* could not match. That's because the paper was owned by the Southam group of newspapers, put together by the heirs of William Southam, who had bought the *Hamilton Spectator* from its original owner in 1877. By 1960 the Southam chain contained the Montreal *Gazette,* the *Ottawa Citizen,* the *Spectator* and the *Tribune,* as well as the *Calgary Herald, Edmonton Journal, Lethbridge Herald* and *Vancouver Province.* It also had built up the Southam News Service, with a large and talented bureau of reporters in Ottawa and correspondents in Washington, London and other places where news was likely to break out. The Southam News Service had its own teletype in the *Tribune* wire room, and clearing it was a particular pleasure when the Ottawa stories would start rolling in—well written, well researched and sometimes exclusive. The *Tribune* also subscribed to the *New York Times* news service. The *Times* was then and still generally is the best newspaper in the world, and I read all of its coverage and columns. It was an election year in the United States. I had taken an American history course at United College, but watching the *Times*'s coverage that summer of the presidential race that would culminate in the election of John F. Kennedy was the best course I could have in contemporary American politics.

I learned a lot just watching the people at the paper, and enjoyed working for and with them. Some would reappear in my life, like Nick Hills, who was from England and would later become a friend in Ottawa, when we were both posted there on two occasions, ten years apart. Martin O'Malley was quiet, a year older than me and spent a lot of time on the police desk. He worked his way up through the system at the *Tribune* for a number of years, then left to join *The Globe and Mail* in Toronto. We became colleagues again when I went to the *Globe,* and yet again, thirty-five years later, when he turned up as a writer at CBC.ca, the network's website. Alan Rogers, who as news editor gave me the copy-boy job, would do almost as much for my career six years later when he rehired me at the *Tribune* to be the top reporter covering the provincial legislature. And Bill Macpherson, the city editor, gave me confidence and the experience of seeing something I had written actually appear in print. That, as much as anything, probably, got me hooked on journalism.

But the man who, in both the short term and the longer term, did more to help me with my career was the international editor of the *Winnipeg Tribune.* Louis Ralph (Bud) Sherman was thirty-three years old in 1960. He was friendly, funny, fast at his work and liked by every-one in the newsroom. I didn't really know him—I just brought him copy and took away the edited stories—but he was always easy to get along with and often showed a wry sense of humour and had a way with puns.

In 1960, the Progressive Conservative government of John Diefenbaker was in power in Ottawa. Part of its agenda was to open up television broadcasting in the country's biggest cities. Until then in Canada there had been only one television station in each city, no matter the size. There were some privately owned stations in smaller cities, but they were all affiliates of the CBC and carried much of the same programming available on CBC-owned stations in Toronto, Montreal,

Winnipeg and elsewhere. The Diefenbaker government had created something called the Board of Broadcast Governors, a forerunner of the CRTC, to award second licences for privately owned stations in Halifax, Toronto, Montreal, Winnipeg and Vancouver. Not surprisingly, the bidding for the licences was furious. And not surprisingly, the licences went to people who had good Conservative connections.

In Winnipeg, the licence went to a group headed by the Misener family, who had more experience in Great Lakes grain shipping than in broadcasting, but who had ties to the Moffat family, owners of the powerful Winnipeg radio station CKY. The new TV station would broadcast on Channel 7 and be known as CJAY-TV. The goal was to be on the air in late fall, but no one knew who would be working there—until, that is, a warm summer day in mid-August. On that day, people were standing around Bud Sherman's desk, shaking his hand. I didn't know what was going on, but upon asking found out that he had just been named the news director, the top journalist, at the new station. As fate would have it, as he was leaving for lunch later, I got on the elevator with him. We were the only two people on the ride down.

"Congratulations," I said. Then, without any planning, I added, "If you ever need a copy boy there, keep me in mind."

"Thanks," Sherman replied. "I'll do that."

A few days later, Bud Sherman was gone from the *Tribune,* and a few weeks later, so was I. I was back at United College, trying to interest myself in retaking some of the same courses I had done the year before but had not written the exams for, owing to having had the measles. I kept up my connection with the *Tribune;* I was the overnight copy boy on Friday evenings, starting at midnight and finishing at 8 a.m. Through my brother, I got a small job covering junior football in the Manitoba-Saskatchewan league for United Press International, and I wrote some sports stories for the University of Manitoba newspaper where Marty

O'Malley, fresh from his *Tribune* summer job, was the sports editor and Peter Herrndorf, whom I had known at Kelvin High School and would meet many times again, was the editor–in–chief.

I was busy, but not very engaged and not very interested. But then things changed, and again because of a phone call. This time not from an editor at the *Tribune,* but from Bud Sherman, the news director of the soon-to-be-on-the-air Channel 7.

"I remember what you told me in the elevator. I won't have any copy-boy jobs, but I do have an opening for a junior reporter. It pays fifty dollars a week. Do you want to try it?" he asked.

I was momentarily stunned. "I'm back doing courses at United," I said, "but I like the idea of the job."

"You can always finish your courses later. This is a pretty good chance to get in on the ground floor in television."

"You're right," I said. "Thanks. When do I start?"

When I told my mother what I had done, she was concerned that I was leaving United without a degree.

"Don't worry, I'll get a degree," I told her. (Years later, after United College became the University of Winnipeg, I received an honorary doctor of laws degree, which was followed by another from Queen's University in Kingston.)

That October evening in 1960, I didn't have a degree, but I had a full-time job as a journalist.

4

The Sixties and CJAY-TV

C ANADA WAS CHANGING as the 1960s began. Some of the changes were apparent, some weren't. A lot of them had to do with television.

Television arrived in Canada in 1952. Like all broadcasting at that time, it was controlled by the Canadian Broadcasting Corporation and its board of governors. Since 1936, the CBC had owned its own network of radio stations, but was also tasked with licensing private broadcasters, sometimes to compete openly with CBC stations in larger cities, and sometimes to carry CBC network programs in smaller centres where the corporation had no station of its own.

This public-private arrangement was in place with the arrival of TV. The CBC built and operated stations in the big cities like Toronto, Montreal, Winnipeg and Vancouver. Private broadcasters were licensed to build and operate stations in smaller cities, like Regina, Saskatoon, Red Deer and Victoria, and in some that weren't so small, like Calgary, Edmonton and Hamilton, Ontario. But whether owned by the CBC or by a private broadcaster, what Canadians saw on their local TV stations was pretty much the same: CBC network programming for most of the day; local news, weather and sports; and perhaps a children's program or afternoon programming aimed at women who, in those days, almost all worked at home.

Television had a unifying effect on the country. By the end of the fifties, Canadians almost everywhere could see the Grey Cup, watch the Stanley Cup finals, and enjoy the comedy of the *Wayne and Shuster Hour*. For the first time, a leadership convention to select a national party leader was televised—John Diefenbaker defeated Donald Fleming and Davie Fulton for the Progressive Conservative Party leadership. Two years later, Lester Pearson won the Liberal leadership, defeating Paul Martin Sr. By 1960, two national elections had been reported on TV: in 1957, when Diefenbaker ended twenty-one years of Liberal rule with a PC minority government, and a year later, when he swept back into power with a record-breaking majority.

And if they could stay up until eleven each night, Canadians could watch the CBC News on TV. Even by 1960, it wasn't much more than radio with pictures. Following the tradition of the British Broadcasting Corporation, a presenter in a studio with just a curtain behind him, who had nothing to do with the preparation of the news, read a script of news stories written by the news writers somewhere else at the network headquarters in Toronto. Just as it had during the Second World War, the CBC had a fine crew of foreign correspondents: Knowlton Nash and James M. Minifie, based in Washington, and Donald Gordon, based in London, were among the regular contributors. But the CBC had few domestic reporters. It was all right to have Canadian eyes reporting on events abroad, but not on events in Canada—too political and too open to controversy.

There was one exception. Norman Depoe was making a name and a reputation both for himself and for the CBC with his strong, tough, sometimes opinionated reporting from Ottawa. He usually did his reports live from Parliament Hill into the newscast, making it very hard to edit what he said. And what he said often tended to prove the concern about domestic reporting being too political and too controversial. At least that is what John Diefenbaker and a lot of Conservatives seemed to think as their government started to get into trouble.

So in 1960, television in Canada meant the CBC, whether you lived in one of the big cities with a CBC station, or someplace where a privately owned television station carried the CBC's network programming. Either way, the CBC had the audience all to itself. But that was about to change as the private stations licensed by the new controlling agency, the Board of Broadcast Governors, were about to sign onto the air. And in Winnipeg, CJAY-TV on Channel 7 was one of those stations.

WHEN I REPORTED for work in the middle of October, there was no TV station to report to. It was still under construction in the near west end of the city, north of Portage Avenue, between the Polo Park Shopping Centre and the Winnipeg Arena and Stadium. I was the greenest of green rookies, and some other newly hired people were also trying television for the first time. Most of the people with television experience came from contract jobs they had held at the CBC in Toronto, or from the private station that already served Calgary.

And Winnipeg was an attractive location for them. In 1960, it was still the fourth-biggest city in the country, the hub and gateway to the Prairie West. It was then a communications centre in a way it no longer is, with two good-quality competing newspapers and three strong private radio stations that attracted talent from across the Prairie provinces—much of that talent hoping Winnipeg was a way station en route to the big time in

Toronto. And Winnipeg was the home of the only CBC-owned TV station between Toronto and Vancouver, with a big production facility that turned out shows like *Red River Jamboree* for the entire network as well as a large, well-staffed newsroom. Over the years, a number of well-known personalities who worked at CBC Winnipeg went on to have national careers—people like Warren Davis, Don Wittman and Bob Moir. Later there was Peter Mansbridge and Diana Swain.

Upon arriving from Montreal in December 1955, the first face I saw when I turned on the TV in Winnipeg was a very young-looking announcer who said his name was Lloyd Robertson. Lloyd had moved on to Toronto by the end of 1960, but it was still a formidable and experienced staff at the CBC that those of us at CJAY faced as we tried to get the station up and running and on the air.

With the station still under construction, the assembling news staff gathered across the street, in what was usually a storage room under the stands of the Winnipeg Arena. It wasn't very impressive. The roof slanted downward from the door to the wall, the way the seats above were sloped upward from the ice. There wasn't much to do, but there were the newspapers and a coffee urn.

Within two weeks, we were inside the new building, practising how to put TV news on the air. I had never been inside a television station before; it was like a magical place. The cameras and studios where programs went to air were, of course, nothing like they appeared on television at home. But even more amazing to me were the places at the nerve centre of the broadcasting operations: master control, where everything—programs, commercials, slides or news film—was controlled and passed through before it went to air; and the control rooms for each studio, where the directors, script assistants, audio people and the people who switched the cameras did their magic to make programs come together seamlessly.

News was just a part of the overall operation. And not a very big part, at that. The newsroom was in the basement of the building—windowless, but close to the coffee shop, which made up for some of its other shortcomings.

As news director, Bud Sherman had assembled a diverse staff with different experiences. His deputy was Al Vickery, a veteran of Canadian Press with the ability to grasp the importance of just about any story. The only reporter with previous television experience was Don Hoskins, who had worked in small television stations in both Brandon, 120 miles west of Winnipeg, and in Swift Current, Saskatchewan. Jim Farrell came from Winnipeg radio station CKRC; Wes Rowson came from the only radio station in Kenora, Ontario; and Bruce Ogilvy was an older man who seemed to have worked as a reporter and news writer in radio in both Canada and the United States. There were two women in the newsroom. Lois Parkhill was a member of the prominent Winnipeg Parkhill family, whose mattress business was well known across Canada. She had worked in the current-affairs department at CBC Television in Toronto and wanted to try her skills as a reporter back in her hometown. Sheila Knowles was the office manager, receptionist and secretary. A recent Miss Manitoba, she was very attractive, but unlike most of the attractive women who worked in various off-camera clerical jobs at the station, she had no desire to be on TV. A few years later, she would become a TV director. And then there was me, the former copy boy at the *Winnipeg Tribune*.

There were two newscasts a day, Monday through Friday—one seen at 7 p.m., the other at ten-thirty. On Saturday, there was one newscast at seven, and one at ten-thirty on Sunday. Those hours were chosen so they did not directly clash with the local news on the CBC at six and the network news at eleven.

There were three established "beats" for three reporters. As the most experienced, Don Hoskins wanted and was assigned to cover the Manitoba legislature. Jim Farrell had covered Winnipeg City Council as a radio reporter and wanted to still cover it. That left me to cover the Winnipeg Metropolitan government, a newly created level of super-municipal government to handle all of the overlapping responsibilities of the City of Winnipeg and the growing suburbs that surrounded it. Metro and its ten-member council were as new as CJAY-TV, and as new as I was to full-time journalism. But it was a great opportunity for me. The only full-time reporter in the small Metro press room was Warner Troyer of the *Free Press*. Later, he would go on to be a major reporter on *the fifth estate* on the CBC, but then he was a hard-working reporter covering a new level of government that he clearly thought was a good idea. He had terrific access to all of the councillors, the chairman and Metro's executive director, Elswood Bole, and worked closely with the Metro public relations man Art Fletcher, a former editorial writer at the *Free Press*.

Covering Metro Council was where I got my first taste of beat reporting, and it was very important. Learning how to follow stories, looking ahead to what is likely to happen next, anticipating developments and thinking about who can give you the inside information on a confidential basis are all the essentials of a good beat reporter. So, I learned, is luck, and also the courage to resist pressure. That is what I had when I reported my first scoop.

Under attack from the Mayor of Winnipeg and some of its better-known councillors, Metro wanted to have a big announcement that would prove its value. I had heard talk that twinning the St. James Bridge across the Assiniboine River was one of the projects being considered. I probably remember it because I crossed that bridge twice a day, to and from work at CJAY. One morning a couple of months after I started covering Metro, I noticed a work crew down on the river ice as I crossed on my way to work. I wondered if they might be sampling the river bottom, just east of the existing span, with the idea of putting a second span there.

Less than a month later, there was a notice in the Metro press room. Later that afternoon, there would be the release of details of a major announcement embargoed for publication until the next morning. This, remember was 1961, when newspapers were king. The embargo was tied so that the Metro announcement would be made the following morning, but all the details would be pre-written and appear in that afternoon's editions of the *Free Press* and the *Tribune*. That schedule of course worked against television, where the first broadcasts after the announcement would come hours later, at dinnertime.

"I am not going to take the embargoed handout." I told Warner Troyer. "I know what the announcement is."

"How do you know that?" he asked querulously, although through his sources he undoubtedly also knew what was going to be announced, but because of his insider status had agreed to go along and keep it quiet.

" It is the twinning of the St. James Bridge. I have seen them working around the present bridge each day as I go to work."

Then I went down the hall to the office of Art Fletcher.

"I am not taking the handout," I said. "I already know it is the twinning of the St. James Bridge."

He was furious. His first big announcement was about to leak.

"Who told you? I want to know," he almost yelled at me, at the same time confirming that my guess was correct.

"Nobody. I've seen them working at the site."

"Well, I hope you won't use it tonight," was all he could say.

I went back to the press room. Troyer was sitting there.

"What did Art say?" he inquired.

"He asked me not to use it."

"Are you?"

"What would you do?"

He sat there for about twenty seconds, time enough to review that the big day of the organization he believed in would in part be compromised, but also that he, as the most experienced and knowledgeable reporter covering Metro, was about be scooped by a neophyte. Then, in what had to be one of the most generous moves to help a beginner in journalism, he said, "If I were you, I would use it."

And that evening, fifteen hours before the announcement, CJAY-TV had its first scoop. It didn't really change the world all that much, but it gave me a great deal of confidence that I had made the right choice in jumping into journalism.

At the beginning of the 1960s, television news was very much in its infancy. We had two types of cameras to use in our coverage—hand-held silent film Arriflexes that shot about one minute of 16-mm black-and-white film, and Auricon sound cameras that shot three minutes of interviews or actual events. Because of those limitations, almost all film coverage consisted of clips from interviews done after new conferences or live events. A big appearance on the newscast, for a reporter, meant the back of your head and shoulders got into the shot while you interviewed someone connected with the story you were reporting on. Although your voice could be heard asking one or more questions, it was an anonymous way to appear on television—often at least five times a week. One of my friends joked that if I wanted to be recognized for my TV work, I would have to walk down the street backwards.

However, working at CJAY did provide "face time" on camera. As part of their application for the broadcast licence, the ownership group had promised to air a half-hour weekly program was local issues, just as the CBC did. After a couple of months, the program was launched, with Don Hoskins, Jim Farrell and me dividing up the half-hour to interview personalities from the provincial, city and metro governments. It was the first time I was on TV, talking to the camera—nerve-racking at first, but also intoxicating and addictive.

Television was still very much derivative of radio. There was much talking about "voice" and "reading" in terms of TV presentation—two things that are, of course, very important in radio but which on TV can actually seem artificial and even comical. However, that was only figured out later by Marshall McLuhan and others. In 1961 at Channel 7 in Winnipeg, it was still very much a consideration, and never having worked in radio, I didn't have much of a background in either voice presentation or reading skill. Still, holiday vacancies on an August weekend created the opportunity for me to actually "read" the news. It turned out to be very nearly a disaster.

On Saturdays, there was only the evening news, which ran from seven to seven-twenty. Because rules at that time did not allow for commercials to be aired in the body of newscasts, it was actually two programs: a ten-minute local newscast, followed by a commercial break and then a five-minute newscast covering national and international affairs. Although I was judged to look very young for someone presenting national and international news, it was decided that I would read the shorter newscast because of my lack of on-air experience.

Each newscast began with a recorded opening of visuals and music signalling that the news was on the air. Then there would be a break for commercials before the newscaster came on camera and read the news right through until a sign-off, followed by a recorded closing, and then more commercials.

I was well aware of the newscast formats. Two and sometimes three days a week, I took my turn writing and producing the newscast for others to read. Now, for the first time, I was writing the national and international news to read myself.

In later years, when in a new studio in Canada, the United States or Great Britain, the floor directors and camera crews would often remark on how cool and unflappable I seemed to be when settling in front of a camera. But that first night in Winnipeg was a far different story. As the commercials ran after the local news, I slipped into the anchor chair and put on my microphone. My heart was pounding. I looked off camera at the monitor to see that the commercials were ending and the opening of the newscast had begun. I looked down at my script, confident that there was a minute of commercials before I would have to look at the camera and speak. Suddenly, standing just off camera, the floor director—who cues the announcer—was waving his arm at me, pointing at the camera.

I was just about to speak to him and say, "Don't screw around, I'm nervous enough as it is!" when my eye caught the monitor and I saw, to my horror, *me!*

In a split-second flash, I remembered: there was no first commercial on Saturdays. The news began right after the opening.

"G-g-ood evening," I managed, as I began what was undoubtedly the worst newscast ever read to that point in time. Still, by the blink of an eye, I had avoided a career-ending mistake by swearing on the air.

In the more than forty years that have followed, I have read, reported, ad-libbed and interviewed hours and hours of television programming. But I have never forgotten my first time, in Winnipeg, in August 1961.

5

Saskatchewan—CKCK

I DIDN'T REALIZE I was learning some of life's lessons in the summer of 1961, ten months after I had been lucky enough to join CJAY-TV. Now it all seems so simple that they are not really lessons at all: when organizations begin to shrink for economic reasons, they almost never recover and expand again; and make your own decision based on your own objectives, not conventional wisdom or the preconceived ideas of others. Both of those lessons would serve me well when I would draw on them years later.

By late spring of 1961, after being on the air about five months, it became clear to the owners of CJAY that they had been wildly optimistic about the revenues the new station would generate, so they did what owners always do: they cut back and laid people off. Suddenly, CJAY went from a television operation resembling a privately owned CBC with a weekly variety program, locally produced programs for children and women, and a significant news operation to a much smaller, leaner and meaner operation the advertising revenues could sustain. That meant a lot of layoffs, including a number of people who had come from Toronto to take relatively senior programming jobs. In the newsroom, half the reporting staff was let go. Three of the six reporters were gone, and so was one of the three film cameramen. I survived the cut, not because of any great talent but because I was the lowest paid. In fact, my pay was so low that I actually received a raise as the others were being let go to help compensate for the extra work I was taking on.

When the dust settled, in addition to news director Bud Sherman, there were five of us left in the news department: deputy news director Al Vickery, Don Hoskins, Jim Farrell, Sheila Knowles and me. Monday through Friday, Vickery produced and wrote much of the dinner-hour news, and the three of us produced reports for the program. Then, every third day, Hoskins, Farrell or I stayed on and wrote and produced the newscast at ten-thirty, recycling the reports from the earlier broadcast. We took turns writing and producing the one newscast on Saturday, and Sundays Sherman had a news review program that he wrote, produced and hosted.

Beyond the layoffs, and despite my raise, budgets were tight. This meant more work in the newsroom and fewer opportunities for reporting. I quickly learned a lot about television and producing news programs, which later would serve me well, but although I wanted to do and learn more about that side of the business, I really wanted to be a reporter, and politics was my main interest.

What to do? Again I consulted my brother, Roger. Again, he had a suggestion that turned into a good answer. A few years earlier, while developing his own career, Roger had worked on the *Brandon Sun*, the daily newspaper in Manitoba's second city, 120 miles west of Winnipeg. Brandon wasn't large, but it was big enough to have, in addition to the newspaper, a radio and a television station. While there, Roger had become friends with a man named Jim Struthers, who was news director of both. Struthers had moved on to a similar job at CKCK in Regina. Regina is small compared to Winnipeg, and it was even smaller then, but CKCK was one of the biggest radio and TV stations on the Prairies, and Struthers was in charge of all its news operations.

Roger suggested I give Struthers a call and talk about job opportunities. I did, and a month later I was on my way to Regina, although I was going against the conventional wisdom that you didn't go from a larger city to a smaller one as a way of advancing your career.

I arrived in Regina on the Saturday of the Thanksgiving weekend in 1961, and went directly to CKCK Radio on Hamilton Street in the centre of the city, on the second floor of the Leader-Post Building, the home of the dominant newspaper in the province, the Regina *Leader-Post*. Both the paper and the radio station were owned by the Clifford Sifton family, as was CKCK-TV. The television operation was located in the middle of wheat fields east of the city, so far east it was beyond the bypass that diverted traffic on the Trans-Canada Highway around downtown Regina.

Radio stations are pretty quiet on weekend afternoons. But at CKCK that Saturday there was a very good-looking woman sitting behind the reception desk. She was also well dressed, particularly for a radio station on a Saturday afternoon. At the time, I thought if all the women in Regina were this attractive and well turned out, I was going to enjoy myself. I asked for Jim Struthers, and was told rather dismissively he wasn't there, and to come back on Tuesday morning after the long weekend. As I turned to leave, another woman came out of an office, apparently hearing voices and thinking I must be someone else. As I overheard the conversation, I learned that CKCK was sponsoring a concert that evening at which Gordon Lightfoot was the headliner. The second woman thought I might be Lightfoot. The first attractive woman had no such illusions.

When I began work the next week, I soon learned that the attractive woman was not a receptionist but a station executive. Her name was Audrey-Ann Taylor and she was the manager of station promotions, which meant she was in charge of all of the on-air and outside advertisements promoting the station and all of the contests for sponsors' products. It was a big job, certainly bigger than being a reporter in the newsroom.

When I first saw her in the fall of 1961, she was dating a football player on the Saskatchewan Roughriders. Regina was a small town then and the football players were like Hollywood stars. But when the football season ended most of them left town, giving us mere mortals an opportunity. Early in January, I asked her out.

As it turned out, our schedules worked for us, but wouldn't have for many others. After I had finished my regular hours at either the radio or TV station, I would usually go on to report on some evening event. This worked particularly well if I was covering a dinner event and I got a free hot meal. I would then go back to the radio station, edit some tape and leave a story for the morning newscasts. CKCK was a very profitable radio station, and Audrey-Ann and her assistant, Irene Deck, seemed to have enough work for four people. Often they would work into the evening, and I quickly noticed that Audrey-Ann would be finishing up about the time I had finished my story for the next morning. That made going for a drink or a late supper easy. Soon it became a routine and quickly we were seeing each other exclusively.

Reporters need good stories to report, and I had arrived in Saskatchewan at just the right time. A year earlier, the Co-operative Commonwealth Federation (CCF) had won its fourth consecutive provincial election under the leadership of Premier T.C. "Tommy" Douglas. But now Douglas was moving on. Earlier, in August 1961, two months before I got to Regina, Douglas had won the leadership of a new federal political party called the New Democratic Party. The NDP, as the party was commonly known, was an amalgam of the Canadian Labour Congress and the remnants of the federal CCF, which had been reduced to eight seats in the House of Commons in the sweep of John Diefenbaker's Progressive Conservatives in 1958.

Douglas defeated another man from Saskatchewan, Hazen Argue, one of the CCF's surviving members of Parliament and the party's leader as it awaited its merger convention. Argue was the only federal CCFer representing Saskatchewan, but the party's hierarchy and the Ontario-based labour movement wanted the NDP's first leader to be Douglas. The president of the CCF in its last year was David Lewis, who one day would succeed Douglas, as NDP leader. Before the 1961 convention, Lewis tried to talk Argue out of running against Douglas, but Argue refused to withdraw, a move that would later come back to hurt him. When the leadership ballots were counted, Douglas won almost four times as many votes, defeating Argue by 1,391 votes to 380. To further punish him, the party hierarchy left Argue off the slate it nominated for the party executive. Argue ran for the executive anyway, but didn't get elected.

None of that seemed all that important in late October 1961, when Saskatchewan CCFers met at the Trianon Ballroom in Regina to affiliate their party with the NDP and pick a successor to Douglas as party leader and premier of the province. But in a few months it would start to become very important, at least in Saskatchewan—and to me.

The CCF had been elected to a fourth majority government in 1960 on the promise of introducing medicare—public health insurance for everyone in the province. And people believed it would. After all, the party had introduced province-wide public hospital insurance in the 1950s, and this seemed like a logical next step—to everyone, that is, but the province's doctors. They were opposed to "socialized medicine" and had the backing of medical groups across the country and the American Medical Association—plus the Saskatchewan Liberal Party, which was the Official Opposition in the legislature, and later the federal Progressive Conservatives representing Saskatchewan.

But the delegates who gathered that fall in Regina to select Douglas's successor as party leader and premier didn't seem worried. They had a majority government and a deadline of July 1, 1962, to have medicare, as the health insurance plan was known, in place. They would no longer have Tommy Douglas in charge, but that was fine. He was going to lead the fledgling New Democratic Party in the next federal election, and a national medicare program was going to be a centrepiece of the federal party platform. Not only that, but the date of the next federal election and the deadline for the Saskatchewan medicare plan were almost certain to be in the same calendar year.

Douglas's successor was a foregone conclusion. Woodrow S. Lloyd, the provincial finance minister, easily defeated another cabinet minister named Ollie Turnbull. Most of my reporting from the convention was on radio, something new to me, but something I enjoyed. Unlike television, which required a camera and cameraman and short interview clips on film, on radio you could broadcast by picking up the phone, dialling the newsroom and having them put you through right on air.

By 1961, television had been in Regina for seven years. But it was still in many ways unchanged from the day the Siftons opened their TV station, CKCK-TV. And the dynamic was similar to the arrival of television in the United States at the beginning of the 1950s. Established people on radio generally wanted to stay there. Since a lot of the television programming came from the CBC network, the local TV announcers were not as well known as the ones on radio. And the two major personalities on TV also had radio jobs: Jim McLeod, who read the news in the morning on radio and the six-thirty suppertime news on TV, and Don Slade, a disc jockey who was the TV weatherman.

That it was still the age of radio and newspapers was evident in the selection of the new premier as well. Woodrow Lloyd had held a number of cabinet jobs, including two of the most important, education and finance. Many people said he was the match for Douglas when it came to brains. But Lloyd was by nature quiet, rather shy, almost withdrawn. In addition, he had an unfortunate facial tic that he couldn't control. On television, with the camera right in his face, the tic was very pronounced and distracting. A few years later, as television took over as the major way of communicating information, Woodrow Lloyd would not have been considered as a party leader and premier. Or he would have worked on his presentation limitations so he could be. In 1961, nobody seemed to think it mattered, and Lloyd took over as premier in early November to finish leading the government in a fall session of the legislature that had started a month earlier.

When the legislature was in session, I went in the morning to cover the committee sessions and then after lunch to the television station to write and produce the suppertime news. The regular television editor was a man named Harvey Gay, an Australian who, like me, had received some schooling in England and who covered the legislature in the afternoons when the House was sitting.

Covering those committee meetings taught me an important lesson that was true at every legislative body I subsequently covered: committees are where you get to know the members. You can mingle with them around the coffeepot, or you can approach them easily in the hallway with a question or request for a full interview. None of those things can you do as a reporter, when you are sitting in the press gallery, looking down on the chamber while the members are at their desks on the floor.

Getting to know the members quickly paid off with a scoop, although it had nothing to do with legislative business. In addition to meeting members at the committee-room coffeepot, I would often run into some of the Liberals late on weekday evenings in the coffee shop of the hotel where they stayed during the week when the House was in session. One evening, one of those members told me over coffee something I could hardly believe. He said that Hazen Argue, defeated for the federal NDP leadership a few months earlier, was now negotiating with the Liberal Party to cross the floor, sit as a Liberal and then run for the party in his riding of Assiniboia in the next federal election.

The next morning, I told my boss, Jim Struthers, who agreed it would be a big scoop. But we needed other confirmation before we could put it on the air. That evening, I was back in the coffee shop. I deliberately took a table with different Liberal members, and then casually asked if they were part of the group negotiating with Argue to cross the floor. Not them, they said; it was members of the federal Liberal Party who were talking with Argue.

Struthers agreed we had the confirmation we needed. I reported the story on radio and on TV. It set off a small stir in Saskatchewan, but in Ottawa Argue denied it to the Canadian Press. I wondered whether revealing the negotiations before they had been completed had effectively killed the talks, or whether, before the next election, what I had predicted would come true. Either way, I put the story to the back of my mind and didn't think about it for over a month, until it dramatically resurfaced in a threatening way.

When Douglas stepped down as premier, he also gave up the Weyburn seat in the Saskatchewan legislature that he had won when he became premier in 1944. December 13, 1961, was picked as the date for a by-election to elect a new MLA. That evening, I was in Weyburn as the votes were counted in a two-man race between former Weyburn mayor Junior Staveley, who as the Liberal candidate had run against and been defeated by Douglas eighteen months earlier, and Oran Reiman, a schoolteacher who was trying to hold the seat for the CCF/NDP. That night was Staveley's night. He won 54 percent of the vote. I phoned in the results from the returning office, then went over to Staveley's head-quarters to tape an interview with the winning candidate. When I had finished, I headed to the campaign office of the loser. No sooner was I through the door than I was hit by a hurricane. Hazen Argue grabbed me by the arm and dragged me outside, shoving me roughly through the door.

Argue was furious. Once outside, he grabbed my coat and threatened to kill me for reporting he was planning to switch parties. The fact that I told him I had it from good sources didn't placate him. Again he said he should kill me, something he could have easily done since he was a big man with a thick neck and enormous hands, and I weighed all of about 160 pounds. Instead, he shoved me away and stormed back into the campaign office. I waited a minute, then followed him back in. I still wanted to interview the losing candidate. However, inside, the rye bottles were already open. The loser was in no shape for an interview and declined to talk about his defeat. I didn't press the issue. Instead, I put my tape recorder in its case, and without looking at Argue, walked out, leaving the people inside to deal with the reality that they had just lost a riding they had held for twenty-one years.

I DIDN'T THINK about Hazen Argue again for the next three months. Instead, I began working seven days a week in 1962 to develop my on-air skills while I continued reporting the biggest stories Monday to Friday. I told Jim Struthers that I wanted more airtime, and he arranged for me to read the news on television on Saturday at twelve-thirty in the afternoon, and what was known as the afternoon news "run" on Sunday afternoons between one and six. I guess he figured there would not be too many people watching and listening at those hours.

I was glad for the chance, although working after Friday night and Saturday night wasn't always the easiest thing to do. On Saturday, I had to show up at the TV station at around 11:45 a.m. A feisty woman named Betty Neisner wrote and edited the news. I had to read it over, go into the studio and read the news, weather and sports at half past twelve. The newscast followed a show called *Kids Bids*, sponsored by the Old Dutch potato chip company. Children would save empty chip bags and bring them to the studio to use as "money" to bid on toys, games and sports equipment. The big prize, which never seemed to be won, was a bicycle. I came in and sat at the news anchor desk during the last few minutes of the program. When it ended, the kids filed past me, wondering what I was doing there as the cameras were swung around and pointed at me. As the studio door closed behind them, the news theme rolled and I was on. The same studio crew from *Kids Bids* worked on the news, but since there was just me and a couple of different camera angles, some of the crew were underemployed. One of them, a young man about my age named Boyd Dobson, would jump on the bicycle left in the studio and ride around on it—no hands—just out of camera range, trying to distract me as I tried to sound serious. He never made me laugh, but he came close.

Sunday afternoon on the radio was more work, but it was not all that hard. I was in the newsroom alone, ripping the news wire, phoning the police for accident reports and reading the newscast every hour from one to six, and a weather and sports update every half-hour. Nothing much happened on Sunday afternoon. Most of the traffic accidents had happened Saturday night. But one Sunday afternoon in March contained a big surprise.

Since I was alone in the station, I answered every telephone call. One Sunday, I picked up the phone to hear the familiar voice of Hazen Argue. No threat to kill me this time; instead, he told me he was in Regina on his way to his riding of Assiniboia to announce the next day that he was changing parties and joining the Liberals, and that he would be their candidate in a federal election expected as early as June. Since he was calling me, I told Argue I planned to report the news right away. That, he said, was fine with him. It was why he was calling.

As soon as I hung up, I called Jim Struthers at home. Jim was excited. He told me to call Argue back and ask if he wanted to be on CKCK-TV for half an hour that night. Argue, of course, was delighted. Struthers worked quickly. He persuaded the CKCK-TV managers to call in a crew and a director to put on a program that would run from nine to nine-thirty that evening in place of a regular CBC network news show. Then, at nine, with Argue sitting alone in a chair under a spotlight, Struthers, Harvey Gay and I made up a panel of three that grilled him on his decision to abandon the party he had tried to lead less than a year earlier for one he had fought all of his political life.

Argue loved it. He claimed the NDP was the tool of organized labour and that farmers' concerns were no longer paramount, as they had been in the CCF. Used to the Parliamentary Press Gallery, Argue probably didn't find our questioning too tough. But what he really loved was his time slot, which allowed him to be seen all over southern Saskatchewan, including in his own riding, right after the *Ed Sullivan Show* and before *Bonanza*.

At no time during that day and evening did either Argue or I mention his threat to kill me. And it didn't come up a month later, when I was in Assiniboia, Saskatchewan, to see him acclaimed as the Liberal candidate. And it never came up a few years later, and then again throughout the 1980s, when I would run into him in the halls of the Centre Block in Ottawa after he had become a senator following his defeat in the 1963 election and I was a member of the Press Gallery. I guess he was glad it had worked all right for him, and I was glad my big scoop was confirmed.

Argue's party switch set off speculation about another showdown between him and Tommy Douglas. The provincial seat of Weyburn that Douglas held from the 1940s into the 1960s was at the eastern end of the federal riding of Assiniboia that Argue had held for just about as long. Would the two candidates who had tussled for the NDP leadership a year earlier now fight it out for the same seat in the House of Commons? It was not to be. And for good reason. As a national party leader, Douglas could not contest a sprawling rural seat against a formidable candidate who, even as a party switcher, was seeking re-election for the fifth time. Since most of his time would be spent leading the national campaign around Canada, Douglas had to run in the riding of Regina, where he could easily get around the city, and where he could be in and out of town quickly on his campaign plane.

Douglas didn't make that clear until more than a month after Argue's announcement. And when he did, it was in a way that would be unheard of now. Instead of holding a big, splashy event that would generate a lot of attention, the New Democrats were still operating in the pre-television age. Douglas put out a press release with a time embargo on it. He wasn't even going to be in Regina when the news broke. When I saw the release, I grabbed a radio tape recorder and went around to see him. No longer in the imposing premier's office, he was working out of election committee rooms in a strip mall about a mile from the legislature. I asked for an interview, promising to hold the tape and not play it on the radio until the embargo time on the press release. Douglas and his campaign manager looked incredulous. No one had ever suggested anything like this before, and they were worried I would break the embargo. I pointed out that if I wanted to do that, I could just read the press release on the air myself. They huddled, then decided to take a chance. I had the interview no one else had, and I kept my word and held it until the agreed-upon time. The next time I saw Douglas, a few days later, he seemed genuinely happy with me. He wouldn't feel that way a couple of months later, on election night.

When he selected Regina as the place to run, Douglas joined a contest against Ken More, an amiable man who had worked in a men's store until he was swept up by the Diefenbaker tide in 1958 and became the Progressive Conservative member of Parliament for the province's capital city. Now he was trying to hold the riding against the former premier of the province. A very able lawyer named Fred Johnson was the Liberal candidate.

At any other time but the spring of 1962, that race would have dominated the political headlines. But in April and May, the long-simmering struggle over the provincial government's medicare plan was coming to a boil. The legislation setting July 1 as the day the plan would come into force was in place. The province's doctors, through the Saskatchewan College of Physicians and Surgeons led by Dr. Harold Dalgleish, said they would go on strike rather than work under government insurance. It all became very political. The government was supported by the labour unions—not a huge force in agrarian Saskatchewan—and by the credit unions and social-activist groups. The principal source of support for the doctors was a group with the title KOD—Keep Our Doctors—organized by the Saskatchewan Liberal Party, the Official Opposition in the legislature. The Progressive Conservatives came late to the game with another group known by its initials, SOS—Save Our Saskatchewan.

Looking back on how medicare has grown into a defining national characteristic of Canada, it is hard to imagine how feelings were running in Saskatchewan more than fifty years ago. The KOD was able to organize large rallies on the steps of the legislature, protesting against the government for creating a situation in which the province's doctors would withdraw their services. Given a choice between doctors and no public health insurance versus public health insurance and no doctors, public opinion clearly leaned towards the former. Tommy Douglas—the man who had promised public health care for decades, set the plan in motion before he left as premier, and was now leading the NDP—was promising the same kind of plan all over Canada. Time has shown he was on the right side of history, but on June 8, 1962, he was on the wrong side of public opinion in Saskatchewan. He went down to defeat in Regina to Conservative More by over nine thousand votes.

I was in the CKCK television studio on election night with an announcer named Bruce Cowie. As a CBC affiliate, the station was carrying the network's national election coverage, but at twenty minutes after each hour and again at fifty minutes after each hour, local stations could break away for their own updates of ridings in the station's viewing region. On those breaks, Bruce would give the numbers in the ridings across southern Saskatchewan and I would comment on ridings of particular interest—in fact, there were only two: Regina, where Douglas was running, and Assiniboia, where Argue was. The results in urban Regina came in quickly. From early on, Douglas was in trouble. In rural Assiniboia, the totals were much slower and Argue was hanging on by a razor-slim margin.

The CBC had set up a desk and chair in our studio for Douglas to make a statement on national television as the results were known. This was way before the days of live remotes and cameras and lights at the campaign headquarters of party leaders and other prominent candidates. As the results became clear, Douglas suddenly showed up with one aide. He was ready to speak to the nation. He was sitting about twenty feet from me as he read a prepared statement, trying to put the best face on what was truly a disappointing evening. The NDP had won only nineteen seats, and the leader's was not one of them. That was particularly galling, but so was the fact that the NDP total was six less than the party it had replaced, the CCF, won in 1957. True, it was eleven more than the

CCF had won in the 1958 Diefenbaker landslide. But now, four years later, the Tories had dropped ninety-two seats and the new party had taken very few of them. Even worse, the NDP was the fourth party in the House of Commons behind the minority Conservative government, the Liberals who comprised the Official Opposition, and a reinvigorated Social Credit Party.

It was a tough night for Douglas, but he did a pretty good job. He made most of the right noises and then ended with the Andrew Barton line: "*I'll lay me down and bleed awhile, / and then I'll rise and fight again.*"

The CBC desk was not set up for an interview. Douglas finished, the red light went off, and he got up and was ready to leave the studio. I rose out of my chair and grabbed his handler, telling him I wanted to interview Douglas in about eight minutes, when our next local segment was to begin. Not on, I was told; that was all Douglas was doing tonight.

"If that is the case," I replied, "I will have to go on TV and say that Douglas refused to speak to the people of Regina and his home province after he had lost." His handler doubted I would do that. I assured him I would. A quick huddle ensued, and Douglas came over to my desk and sat down without looking at me. We went on the air, and through the interview he was smiling and chatty, again putting the best face on a terrible evening. When we were finished, he got up, barely nodding goodbye as he left.

I didn't see Douglas again until 1965, and after that I saw him quite a bit into the 1980s. He was always smiling and cordial. I questioned him one on one in interviews and often at news conferences. We never talked about election night 1962. In fact, I think Douglas had a great capacity for putting defeats and disappointments out of his mind. It was one of his strengths, as he bounced back more than once from adversity. I doubt he ever thought much about any part of the 1962 election after the ballots were counted.

The Douglas defeat and the poor showing of the NDP emboldened the doctors and their supporters. There were some last-ditch negotiations in Saskatoon on June 30, but on July 1 the Medicare plan came into effect and the province's doctors stopped seeing patients, performing operations or making hospital rounds. Then something odd happened: nothing much at all took place. The government brought in a few pro–public insurance doctors from Great Britain to provide some essential emergency services, but people remained remarkably healthy, and there was no panic or crisis. The strike ended after three weeks, when the government agreed to a minor change in its legislation. The doctors went back to work and, as predicted by the out-of-province medical opponents, over the next eight years public health insurance became the law of the land.

Medicare was in, but Douglas was out. During the summer, a New Democrat MP from the interior of British Columbia named Erhart Regier resigned his seat so Douglas could run in his place. The doctors' strike had ended without incident, and everything seemed terribly normal. Suddenly, the bubbling political cauldron that had consumed the province—and certainly my work—was on the boil no more. It was as if, as the old saying goes, the dogs had barked and the caravan had moved on. By Labour Day 1962, I knew it was time for me to move on as well.

6

CKRC and the *Winnipeg Free Press*

COVERING A BIG story is exciting. Long hours, anticipating what will happen next, keeping up with developments—or even, sometimes, with breaking news—creates a great adrenalin rush. But when the story ends—as all stories do—there is a withdrawal, sometimes even a post-partum feeling, as the thing that was demanding all of your time and attention is suddenly gone.

I would have the feeling many times over the next forty years and would come to recognize it whenever it recurred and ultimately learn how to deal with it. But it was confusing the first time, in the late summer of 1962. The doctors' strike had come and gone, and so had the federal election and the campaigns of Tommy Douglas and Hazen Argue.

During the doctors' strike, the CBC had set up camp in the studio and newsroom of CKCK-TV. I was impressed by all of their resources, by the producers and reporters—particularly by a reporter named Tim Ralfe who was only four years older than I was and who was already on the national television network.

So as I wondered what I should be doing next, the answer seemed clear: I should apply to the CBC. Which is what I did—not to the national network, but to the CBC newsroom in Winnipeg.

I sent some scripts, audio tapes and film to a man named Herb Nixon, who was running the newsroom, and waited to hear back. I was still working at CKCK, and while waiting to hear whether I had a new job, I observed something that later would be very important in my career. In September of 1962 the fledgling national private TV network, CTV, launched its first national network newscast. The network itself had begun a year earlier, but this was its first foray into network news. The program had two anchors—one a grisly veteran named Baden Langton, the other a fresh-faced, smooth-talking, good-looking broadcaster (again, not much older than I was) named Peter Jennings. Peter went on to ABC News and became a top anchor in the United States. I first met him in Washington in 1975 and through his sister, Sarah, in Ottawa we later became friends twenty years later.

In Regina, CKCK-TV, where I worked, was a CBC affiliate and so, until the fall of 1962, was CHAB-TV, forty miles west in Moose Jaw. With the advent of the private CTV network, the Board of Broadcast Governors, which had licensed the newcomer, decided that Regina and Moose Jaw were one television market and CHAB was allowed to switch its affiliation. Watching CHAB wasn't very easy. (Reception was poor, as there was no cable or satellite TV yet. You could only receive local television signals through a rabbit-ear antenna on top of the set.) But Jim Struthers lived in the south end of the city, and with the rabbit ears on the top of his TV turned just the right way, he could get a fuzzy image from Moose Jaw. And that is what he and I watched the evening CTV launched its network newscast. As I looked, I didn't imagine I was about to embark on a journey that, in just a short ten years, would have me not just working on that newscast, but heading to the United States to be CTV's first Washington correspondent. Nor could I imagine that, forty-three years later, I would be standing on the stage of the National Arts Centre in Ottawa, paying tribute to Peter Jennings, who had died the month before.

That journey started out with a terrible mistake. I was hired at the CBC, and one year to the day after arriving in Regina, I was heading back east along the Trans-Canada highway to Winnipeg. But when I got to the CBC, things were not as I expected. Instead of reporting on television, I was assigned to write local and regional radio newscasts that some barely interested announcer, having come in just before airtime, would read over once and then broadcast into the ether, where hopefully someone had a radio on and would hear them.

I thought I had been tricked. I couldn't stand the work. I had to get out, and I thought I knew an escape route. After a week, I telephoned a man named Bob MacDonald. He had been the program director at CKCK-Radio when I first arrived there, and now he had the same job at CKRC, the Siftons' radio station in Winnipeg. One evening after work, we went for a cup of coffee. He offered me a job at his station at almost as much money as the CBC paid. I took it, and the next morning gave my notice. After three weeks at the Mother Corp., I was back in private broadcasting. But I wasn't on television, and I wouldn't be on a regular basis for another nine years. I had solved my short-term problem, but it was temporary. Over the next twelve months I seemed to be going backward, not forward.

At CKRC, I spent my first six months reporting. Back at the Metro government, around the city on a variety of stories and, when the legislature was in session, covering the Manitoba government. That's what I liked best, and it confirmed, if any confirmation was needed, that I wanted to be a political journalist. At the legislature, I had my first experience covering Duff Roblin, the premier of Manitoba. He was a

Progressive Conservative, with the emphasis on progressive. He won power in 1958 and began modernizing the province—often even though some Manitobans weren't too keen on being modernized. The pace of change was the issue as he sought a second mandate in 1962.

I convinced the powers at CKRC that we could interview Roblin, Liberal leader Gil Molgat and NDP leader Buzz Paulley individually, asking each the same question on a range of topics, and them edit them together to create a debate. The management liked the idea, and off I went to do the interviews. The last one I had to do was with Roblin, and on the Friday afternoon before the election I did that. I was going to edit the tape on Saturday for a program on Sunday. I had the Molgat and Paulley tapes at the station, but Friday night I left my tape recorder, with the Roblin tape, outside in my car overnight. Manitoba in December is frosty. The next morning, when I tried to play the Roblin interview, the cold had destroyed the recording.

What could I do? There could be no program without the premier's answers. I remembered he was having a Saturday afternoon coffee party in his Wolseley riding in the city's near west end. I showed up, and with the premier standing in a receiving line, I explained what had happened. He looked at me like I was the idiot I felt I was. But between shaking hands with the dear old ladies who had come to have a cup of coffee or tea with the premier, he answered my questions again. As soon as we were finished, I rushed to the station, did the editing and put the finished tape in a safe place. Whew! Program, and perhaps my career, saved!

At Christmas 1962, Audrey-Ann and I decided to get married. She had lived in Regina most of her life and liked being there, and had a job she enjoyed. But she willingly gave up her hometown and moved to Winnipeg so we could be together and get on with our plans. She also got an apartment and a job at CKRC—not as good as the one she left behind in Regina, but things were going along swimmingly. Then, suddenly, as they had two years earlier at CJAY-TV, the economics of broadcasting flared up and hit us in the face.

At the beginning of 1963, there were three private radio stations in Winnipeg, and CKRC was number three. That called for drastic action. Formats were changed and staff was cut. No more time for real reporting and interviews with the premier. The new format was rock and roll and the news was "rip and read." Top 40 hits made up the list of music played and peppy, quick news, weather and sports was the way information was delivered. There were three news readers—one from six until noon, the next from one to six and the last from seven until midnight. That was me, ripping the news off the teletype and shouting it down a microphone, and telephoning the police every hour to see if there were any accidents or fires. There was one reporter who didn't read the news. During the day, he drove around in the news cruiser, reporting live from the fires and accidents.

As was the case in 1961, I was lucky I wasn't laid off. But short of that, it was the worst thing that could have happened. I didn't like what I was doing, knew I had no future at it, and besides, it was ruining Audrey-Ann's and my relationship. She had come to Winnipeg and taken an inferior job so we could be together and get married. Suddenly, she was working nine to five and I was working evenings. We would meet for coffee every day as I was coming to work and she was leaving. Then I would be on the radio and she would be home alone. To add to the challenge, I also worked on Saturday afternoon, so we really had only Saturday evening and Sunday together.

Soon I started talking about getting out of CKRC and she started talking about getting out of Winnipeg. Something had to be done. I realized the thing I did best and liked most was reporting, so one afternoon before going in to read the rock and roll news, I took the elevator two floors farther up in the *Winnipeg Free Press* building and asked to see the paper's managing editor. Shades of my cold call at the *Tribune* a few years earlier. I saw his assistant. But again I was lucky—despite my not having any newspaper reporting experience, he took a chance and offered me a job. The only problem was it paid twenty per cent less than the radio job I had. But these were desperate times, and I took it.

Audrey-Ann wasn't crazy about the pay cut, but she did like dinners and evenings together. I was back reporting on the Metro government and the Manitoba legislature when the House was sitting, and suddenly in our lives the sun started shining again. A few months later, Audrey-Ann and I were married in Regina.

Life at the *Free Press* turned out to be a lot of fun. There were a number of young, married couples with no kids and not much money but who were ready to enjoy life. Our social world centred on the Winnipeg Press Club, parties at people's homes, and movie and dinner dates. Once a year, the Press Club produced a satirical revue called *Beer and Skits*. It was a lavish production involving familiar tunes with rewritten words to make fun of current political figures, local, national and international. As was the custom of the day, it was men only and mildly risqué. In my first year, I was recruited to play John F. Kennedy—and the next year, in the all-male cast, the female role of Gerda Munsinger, a former German prostitute allegedly involved with cabinet ministers of the Diefenbaker government.

When I joined the *Free Press,* my brother, Roger, was the star reporter. In fact, on his reputation I probably got my job. He covered the Manitoba legislature and he pretty well owned the beat, regularly scooping his rival at the *Tribune.* After I had been at the paper about a year, Roger left. He had been hired by *The Globe and Mail* in Toronto. I hoped the legislative beat would stay in our family, but it didn't. It went instead to a very nice man, a senior reporter in his forties named Bill Morris. I was part of the team of three assigned to cover the House when it was in session, and although there was no formal arrangement, I seemed to get the chance to interview most federal politicians when they were visiting Winnipeg.

Federal politicians kept me really busy in the fall of 1965. Searching for the majority he narrowly missed in 1963, Liberal prime minister Lester Pearson called a snap election and the country was off to the polls. In September, I got a foretaste of my life to come. Former prime minister John Diefenbaker, the Progressive Conservative leader, had to be nominated as his party's candidate in his home riding of Prince Albert. He was going there from Ottawa on a weekend for a Monday evening nominating meeting. It wasn't a campaign trip as such, and the FP papers, of which the *Free Press* was one, decided they would not send a reporter from the Parliamentary Press Gallery. Instead, I was the money-saving alternative. I joined the regular Ottawa-to-Saskatoon flight carrying Diefenbaker, his wife, Olive, and five Ottawa-based reporters at its stop in Winnipeg, then flew on to Saskatoon for Saturday night.

The Ottawa reporters all knew each other well, but they included me in their dinner plans that evening and made sure the next morning that I was invited to an off-the-record coffee session with Diefenbaker at the Bessborough Hotel before we all drove off north to Prince Albert. I appreciated their friendship, but I realized there was some method in their kindness. The PC campaign was desperately trying to recruit Duff Roblin from the Manitoba premiership to run for them federally in Winnipeg. The riding of Winnipeg South, where Roblin lived, had been narrowly won by the Liberals in 1963, and Roblin could easily take it back for the Conservatives. Would he run? That was the question journalists everywhere wanted to know. So, of course, did Diefenbaker and the people around him. Because I'd covered Roblin, I was a small centre of attention. When we arrived in Prince Albert before the nomination meeting, Diefenbaker aide Greg Guthrie took me aside to find out what I knew of the premier's plans.

Actually, if Roblin had confided in anyone, it certainly wasn't me. In Manitoba, it was generally assumed that the premier had his eye on the national stage and would like to become prime minister, but I speculated to Guthrie that if the party wanted Roblin to run in this election, Diefenbaker would have to ask him personally. Diefenbaker never asked; Roblin didn't run. The Winnipeg South Progressive Conservative nomination was won by my former boss, Bud Sherman, who had been so helpful in getting my career going, and he won the riding for the PCs. That was one of two more ridings the Conservatives had after the votes were counted on November 8. The Liberals had two more as well. After seven weeks of campaigning, nothing had really changed. The Liberals were still in government, but it was still a minority government.

One thing was clear that night: the results meant big changes would be coming in both the major political parties. Now committed to a career as a political journalist, I wondered how I might be a part of the unfolding events.

7

Kennedy in Winnipeg

JOHN F. KENNEDY was part of my introduction to journalism and my awakening to the powers of television.

As I worked as a copy boy at the *Winnipeg Tribune* in the summer of 1960, Kennedy dominated the news, winning the Democratic Party's nomination to run for president that fall. Then, in the campaign that followed, as I started my first job in television, he was taking part opposite Richard Nixon in the first televised debates of an American presidential campaign. The drama of his narrow election victory, the inspiring oratory of his inaugural address and the tense excitement that followed through his presidency; the Bay of Pigs, the Berlin Wall, the space race, the Cuban Missile Crisis and the civil rights struggle; all were acted out almost daily both in print and on the screen. His made-for-television looks and those of his wife and children, plus his cool style that seemed tailored to the medium, made him the most admired and inspiring president, certainly for the generation to which I belong, which was coming of age at the start of his presidency.

While I was getting immersed in both federal and provincial politics in Regina and then Winnipeg and had as my career goal a reporting job in the Parliamentary Press Gallery in Ottawa, I also had a larger vision: reporting from Washington. And since the news I observed from Washington was almost exclusively on television, I wanted to be a television reporter in the American capital, like Knowlton Nash of the CBC. But that was far in the future. I didn't think I would have anything to do with Washington or Kennedy as long as I was in Winnipeg.

I didn't think so, but I was wrong.

One day, while still at CKRC, I noticed that President Kennedy was going to be in Grand Forks, North Dakota, to receive an honorary degree from the state university there. I wanted to see him, and so did Audrey-Ann. In a move that would be unthinkable now—in fact, unthinkable only a few months later—I called the University of North Dakota's press office and said CKRC wanted to send two reporters to cover the president's event. Certainly, the answer came. I gave my name and Audrey-Ann's over the phone and was told to pick up our press passes when we arrived.

So, very early on the morning of September 22, 1963, we got in my car and drove south, across the Canada–U.S. border, 180 miles south to Grand Forks, onto the university campus and up to the field house, where the president was expected. We showed our CKRC IDs to a nice student handing out press credentials. He gave us each a tag to tie onto a shirt button, with our names already typed on them and CKRC next to our names. Then we were shown into the field house and down to the press area behind a temporary snow fence at the left end of the stage with a good view of the podium.

There were just a few North Dakota media there until, suddenly, a door flew open at the back of the arena and the White House press corps travelling with the president poured in. They quickly set up cameras as the presidential press secretary, Pierre Salinger, and an aide walked among the reporters, handing out copies of the president's remarks. For us, it was almost like watching a movie, particularly when the university band suddenly struck up "Hail to the Chief" and, from the back of the stage, John F. Kennedy walked into the spotlight.

He looked just like he did on TV, except better and brighter. In those days, all TV was black and white; here he was, in colour—reddish-brown, slightly dishevelled hair, tanned, flashing a gleaming smile.

The president of the university put a gown around the president's shoulders and gave him an honorary degree. Kennedy made a ten-minute speech and Salinger told the travelling press they had to pack up quickly and get to the bus that would take them back to their plane. Kennedy waved from the stage for a couple of minutes and then turned and disappeared out the door at the back of the stage from which he had entered.

Audrey-Ann and I were left standing by ourselves in the press area. We decided to go out the back door the White House press had used to see if we could see what was going on. And did we ever see. Outside was a narrow, paved driveway about the width of a back lane. Kennedy's convertible limousine was about thirty feet up the road to our right. The president was on the other side of the road, down a small hill, shaking hands along a temporary snow-fence barrier, behind which more than a thousand people were straining to see and touch him.

He worked the fence for a few minutes, then turned, came back up the hill and got into his car. As it started to move, he stood standing in the back, looking to his right and waving to the people along the snow fence. The car was slowly coming towards us. Audrey-Ann groaned; he was looking the wrong way—at the crowd, not at us. Immediately, I started waving both of my arms wildly above my head and told her to do the same. We were both standing there, waving like two people stranded on a desert island trying to attract a passing plane.

Then, with the slowly moving car about ten feet from us, it worked. We caught Kennedy's eye. He turned, his glance quickly passing over me and landed on Audrey-Ann. He stared directly at her. She stopped waving wildly and instead gave a rather shy, one-handed wave. As his car came directly up to us, with the president still looking directly into her eyes, his right hand came up to his forehead and he saluted. The car rolled by. I thought Audrey-Ann would faint, and to tell the truth, I too was impressed.

Kennedy had a car of Secret Service men trailing his convertible as he left the campus, but there was no security where we were standing and no one to keep us from coming out of the door. I think we were about six feet from him as he passed. I didn't think anything about the lack of security on that September morning. But I certainly did two months later to the day, when John F. Kennedy was in another open car in Dallas.

During those two months, I had moved from working in radio to my first job as a newspaper reporter. On November 22, I was still settling in at the *Free Press*. It was twelve-thirty—lunch hour. I was sitting at my place in the front row of reporters' desks, eating a sandwich I'd brought from home. The bells alerting a big, breaking story on the teletype started clanging, so loudly they could be heard out in the newsroom. Marion Lepkin, a copy editor sitting on the rim of the news desk, got up and went into the wire room. She came out white-faced, announcing to the room at large that President Kennedy had been shot.

At that moment, nobody knew how badly he had been hit. But the news desk swung into action. The press run about to start four floors down was halted. The forms holding the front page were taken off the presses and opened up. Editors huddled around the teletypes as the updates reporting the increasing seriousness of Kennedy's wounds and then, ultimately, his death came clanging in.

I sat there rather stunned. I had nothing to do. But the deskmen and editors swung into action in a cool, quick remake of much of the first section of the paper, getting the frames back on the presses and the paper out the door. As the papers rolled off the presses, people were standing in front of the *Free Press,* waiting to buy copies.

Reporters like me who had nothing to do just stayed out of the way. After about an hour, four of us went across the street to a restaurant that had a television. We could follow the story there over coffee instead of getting in the way around the teletypes in the office. After our recent experience in Grand Forks, Audrey-Ann and I took Kennedy's death more personally. We were in mourning.

For the rest of my first year at the *Free Press,* I was on what is known as "general assignment." That meant that each day I hoped either the city editor or his assistant would hand me a good assignment—or, even better, I would come across a good story myself. At the end of April 1964, that is what happened. It was a story about Kennedy and the investigation into his assassination, and it had been going on right in Winnipeg.

One evening, I was sitting at home after dinner when the phone rang. The call was from Don Slade, one of Winnipeg's top radio personalities and a friend of ours from both CKCK in Regina and now CKRC in Winnipeg. Don was the station's morning man, the top disc jockey job in any radio station. But he also did sales "remotes." He would go to a sponsor's location and broadcast what would now seem like infomercials on the deals available that day. Don had a regular and well-paying "remote" with a car dealer on Main Street in the north end of the city. And on this evening, Don also had an amazing story. He wanted me to meet with a salesman at the dealership who had approached him for help finding out what had happened to information he had given an FBI agent about a conversation he had overheard at the Winnipeg International Airport. He said the conversation was about the Kennedy assassination, and he had to flee for his life from the airport after he was noticed listening in.

I wondered if the "informant" was legitimate. Don said he thought he was, and that the FBI had come to Winnipeg to interview him. That was good enough for me. If an FBI agent had come to Winnipeg as part of the Kennedy assassination investigation, it was a story, no matter what else may have transpired.

Don arranged for me to meet the source. His name was Richard Giesbrecht and he sold cars for a living. On February 13, he said he had taken a new car to the Winnipeg airport to show a potential client who worked there. While waiting for the prospective buyer to get free from work, he had gone to the airport coffee shop. There, he sat with his back towards two men at the next table and could hear them talking. What he heard grabbed his attention. One man spoke with some kind of an accent, but it was clear to Giesbrecht that what both were discussing was the assassination of the president—and with an insider's knowledge. The gist of their conversation was how much the shooter Lee Harvey Oswald knew about the wider plot to kill Kennedy, and how much of whatever he knew he had passed on to his Russian wife, Marina, before the assassination and his own murder the next day at the Dallas police station. Marina Oswald was scheduled to testify before the Warren Commission investigating the assassination.

The more he heard, the more closely Giesbrecht listened, until he realized that two tables over, looking at him, was a big, tough-looking man trying to signal to the conversationalists that they were being overheard. Giesbrecht got up, took a look at the two men who were talking, and left the coffee shop to go to the RCMP office on the main floor of the terminal to report what he had heard. But halfway there, he stopped. The big man from the coffee shop was standing down the corridor in front of him. Giesbrecht doubled back, found a pay phone and called the RCMP office downtown. He was just into describing what he had heard when the big man approached him from another direction. Giesbrecht hung up and ran back up to the departures level. Not only were there no cellphones in 1964, but there was no airport security, either. Giesbrecht quickly made his way through two departure lounges, doubled back, got outside to the car he had brought and drove quickly away.

That evening, he told his brother and made notes of what he had heard. The next day, the brothers went to their lawyer, Harry Backlin, who in turn took Giesbrecht to the U.S. Consulate in Winnipeg. The consul-general told the FBI in Minneapolis, and on February 27 the resident FBI agent in Grand Forks came to Winnipeg to interview Giesbrecht. The agent—whose name, Giesbrecht told me, was Merle Nelson—had stayed at the Marlborough Hotel, where the two met. Giesbrecht repeated his story, and then went to the airport with Nelson and an RCMP officer.

Giesbrecht told me Nelson had said the Winnipeg information was very interesting and could be important. Remember, this was before the Warren Report decided that Oswald acted alone. But after Nelson left for the United States, Giesbrecht was unable to find out what, if anything, had happened to his testimony. Despite being afraid that what he had overheard had put him in danger, he wanted to know what was happening. At Don Slade's suggestion, he thought a newspaper headline might pry some information loose.

I agreed with Slade and with Giesbrecht's lawyer, who believed every word he said. Whether he had misunderstood or had a clear take on what he overheard was another matter. From my point of view, what was important—and a news story—was whether or not the FBI had been in Winnipeg as part of the Kennedy investigation. If I could prove that, I had a page one story. I called Agent Nelson in Grand Forks. I wasn't surprised when he wouldn't comment. Neither would regional FBI headquarters in Minneapolis. But there was one way to confirm the story that didn't need their help. I went to see the manager of the Marlborough

Hotel. The Winnipeg Press Club was in the basement of the hotel, and while I didn't know the manager personally, he was used to having reporters and editors around his hotel. I explained that I needed to confirm whether a Merle Nelson had stayed at the Marlborough on the evening of February 27. I wouldn't quote anyone, but I needed to see any confirmation that he had.

The manager called the front desk and had the clerk bring the hotel register to his office. In retrospect, these seem like primitive days, but in 1964 at the Marlborough, at least, guests still signed a hotel register when they checked in. The page was turned to February 27, and together we looked as the manager ran his finger down the names that had signed in that day. Then he stopped. There it was: Merle Nelson, Grand Forks, N.D., USA. I had my scoop.

My story ran on the front page of the Saturday paper. The headline read: PROBE KENNEDY DEATH HERE: FBI man visits Winnipeg to check assassination clue.

I did not identify Richard Giesbrecht by name in the story. He was afraid and wanted anonymity. But three years later, *Maclean's* magazine revisited the story and revealed his identity. From then on, he would surface from time to time in stories about the Kennedy assassination, particularly when Jim Garrison, the district attorney in New Orleans, tried but failed to convict a man named Clay Shaw for being an assassination plotter. Giesbrecht died in the late 1980s. He never varied his story about what happened that February day in 1964 at Winnipeg International Airport.

When the Warren Commission subsequently reported that Oswald acted alone, its report was greeted with great skepticism, by me included. Over the years, there has been endless speculation about who was behind the death of John F. Kennedy and how many people were firing at him that day in Dallas. The suspicion continues, although the longer time passes with no one coming forward with a deathbed confession about a more complicated plan than the Oswald-as-lone-shooter theory, the better that theory is starting to look.

After my Giesbrecht story ran, there were no follow-ups to do. Essentially, there was nothing left to write about the FBI visit. Soon, I was back covering Metro Council and then the provincial legislature. Politics, municipal and provincial, was my steady reporting diet.

8

Roblin Leadership Campaign:
Winnipeg Tribune

A s the Manitoba legislature started its winter session in February of 1966, election fever was in the air. The Roblin government was coming to the end of its second term and the premier was gearing up for another run. At stake could be more than just who would run the province. If the Conservatives won another healthy majority, it could set the stage for Roblin to run for the national leadership of the Progressive Conservatives.

In April, I was surprised by a phone call from Alan Rogers. He was now the managing editor of the *Tribune* and he invited me for coffee at a restaurant on Portage Avenue. Five years and eleven months after I'd asked him for a copy boy's job, he invited me to rejoin the *Tribune*—this time for the top reporting job on the paper. In fact, I would not only cover the provincial legislature, I would write a twice-weekly column that would appear with the national and international columns on the page opposite the editorial page. A column with my picture at the top. All that and more money, too. The *Tribune* job was also attractive because it would reconnect me with the Southam News Service. Top reporters at the various Southam papers usually got promoted to the news service, starting with the Ottawa bureau. In fact, the legislature job had opened up because the person who had it was now on his way to the bureau in Ottawa.

Two weeks later, I was back at the *Tribune*. It was, for me, at twenty-five years old, a dream job. I already knew the *Tribune* and how it worked because I had toiled there in the lowliest of jobs. I knew how the Manitoba government and legislature worked because I had been covering it off and on since 1963. Most mornings, I would make my rounds, calling on the premier, cabinet ministers and Opposition leaders. Almost always, they would invite me in, sometimes for a cup of coffee. I had a continuous stream of information flowing from them to me and from me into the pages of the *Tribune*.

Life away from work improved as well. When we married and I worked at the *Free Press*, we lived in a one-bedroom apartment on the top floor of a two-storey walk-up building in downtown Winnipeg. It was comfortable enough in the winter but ferociously hot in the summer with its flat, black tar-paper roof right above our heads. Still, it was close enough to walk to the *Free Press*, the Legislative Building and the headquarters of the Metro government, and we left our seven-year-old used car parked behind the building in an outdoor spot. We furnished it with a three-room deal we bought for about nine hundred dollars at a bargain furniture store named Genser's. God love them, we paid off the deal at forty dollars a month, cash that I would take over to the accounting office after I got paid.

A month after I started at the *Tribune*, we found a new apartment—a two-bedroom in a building with four floors and an elevator. Not that we needed the elevator. We lived on the main floor, overlooking the swimming pool. And yes, it was air-conditioned. To add to the feeling of economic freedom we got a new car. Still used, but only a year old. We thought we were living the dream! And for us, we were.

At work, the news gods were also smiling. In June, there was a provincial election. It turned out to be more tightly fought than at first people imagined it would be, but in the end Roblin prevailed and his government was re-elected with a majority only three seats smaller than he had before. Certainly, his victory and a third mandate were convincing proof that he was a political winner. It set him up nicely for whatever came next on the federal scene and the leadership of the Progressive Conservative Party.

The federal Tories had gone from a record majority government to a minority that collapsed on itself from within and two successive defeats at the hands of the Liberals. Many Conservatives wanted a change at the top. But John Diefenbaker didn't see it that way. In the most recent election, he had kept the Liberals in a minority and shown he was still a formidable campaigner, and although he was over seventy, he saw no reason why he should step down.

But Dalton Camp, the president of the party, was sure that the 1965 election results showed the Tories would never regain office with "The Chief," as his friends called him, still leading the party, and a lot of people agreed with Camp. But there was no mechanism to force a vote on Diefenbaker's leadership; a leader either had to resign or die before a contest could be held to replace him, and Diefenbaker wasn't inclined to do either. So Camp devised a strategy. He made his re-election as party president in 1966 a referendum on whether a leadership convention should be held. In a stormy party conference at the Château Laurier Hotel in Ottawa, he held off a challenge from Diefenbaker loyalist Arthur Maloney, and the party voted to hold a leadership convention in Toronto the following September.

Then the question quickly became: Who is going to run? Former cabinet ministers from the Diefenbaker government jumped into the race: George Hees, Michael Starr, Wallace McCutcheon, Alvin Hamilton. So did Donald Fleming and Davie Fulton, who had run against and lost to Diefenbaker the last time the party chose a leader in 1956. Camp himself considered running, but realized he was too polarizing a figure to win after triggering the leadership race. Instead, he turned to trying to recruit one of two provincial premiers he had helped in their recent election campaigns: Robert Stanfield of Nova Scotia or Duff Roblin from Manitoba. Roblin was rumoured to be his first choice.

Diefenbaker had tried to avoid a leadership race. Now he wouldn't say whether he would run to try and keep his job. This created a huge dilemma for Roblin. He wanted to run, but Diefenbaker was popular in western Canada, where a Roblin candidacy would have to draw strong support, and Dalton Camp wasn't. As the former cabinet ministers were mounting their campaigns and starting to visit Winnipeg looking for support, the word was out for Manitoba Tories to remain uncommitted. As I interviewed the various candidates, they all had one question for me: "What's Roblin going to do?"

In May, I received a tip from Stan Menzies, one of Air Canada's public relations people in Winnipeg, that Diefenbaker and his wife, Olive, would be passing through Winnipeg, changing planes as they went from Saskatoon to Ottawa. Menzies arranged for me to slip into the Maple Leaf Lounge at the Winnipeg airport and I approached the Diefenbakers, with whom I had travelled to Prince Albert a year and half earlier. I asked the usual question about whether he was planning to run, and Diefenbaker gave me the usual well-rehearsed answer he had been using for five months to fend off the question and keep his options open. Then he told me to put away my notebook—he wanted to talk privately.

"What's Roblin going to do?" he asked, low key and apparently in a good mood.

"He wants to know what you are going to do before he decides," I replied. "I don't think he will run if you do."

Olive Diefenbaker had been sitting quietly, smiling benignly as she usually did, and taking in the conversation. But my answered triggered something. She shot forward in her chair and almost yelled: "He's going to run! He's Camp's man! He's going to run! He's Camp's man!"

Like a spark, her words hit Diefenbaker and ignited his indignation. "That's right," he almost shouted. "He's Camp's man. He's Camp's man."

There wasn't anything left for me to say. I thanked them for their time, excused myself and left. Outside, I shook my head. The public impression of Olive Diefenbaker was that she was a gentle, calming influence on her mercurial husband. I had just witnessed the opposite. She was the one that got him riled up. A few years later, the story spread that the wife of a young Tory MP from Prince Edward Island had surmised that, contrary to her public persona, "Olive is a bitch." That seemed harsh. Still, when I heard what had been said, I knew where it came from.

A month later, I heard from a source that Dalton Camp was in Winnipeg to meet with Roblin. When I called Wally Fox-Decent, the premier's executive assistant, to ask about the meeting, he wouldn't confirm that any meeting was taking place. That made me certain that what I had heard was true. But where was the meeting being held? It would not be at the legislature, where Camp would certainly attract attention coming and going.

Again, I went to the airport—this time late in the afternoon, before the evening flight to Toronto. I checked the departure time, realized I was two hours early, and there was no sign of Camp. I decided to go over to the International Inn at the edge of the airport to see if Camp might be there. The hotel was owned by Sidney Spivak, who had become a member of the Roblin cabinet after being elected the year before. I went into the bar, looked around, and there, sitting by himself, was Dalton Camp.

I went over, introduced myself and offered to buy him a drink. I quickly found out he had come to Winnipeg to press Roblin to run, and to offer him his party organization if he would. The meeting, he told me, had taken place at the home of Sterling Lyon, another provincial cabinet minister, who lived along the Red River in the suburb of Fort Garry. Camp was disappointed that Roblin wouldn't commit.

Camp might have been disappointed, but I wasn't. I had a great story. The *Tribune,* like its rival the *Free Press,* was an afternoon paper, but each had a morning edition, with a new front page and new overnight sports pages, that was sold and distributed in downtown Winnipeg every morning.

The Camp—Roblin story was too good to leave to the afternoon paper. Besides, what if some other reporter found out? I went back to the office, wrote in detail everything Camp had told me, and went home knowing that I had a great scoop for the morning. Obviously, the premier and his people wanted the whole Camp visit to remain a secret, and I had that reinforced the following morning when I arrived for work at the Legislative Building. Walking through the front door, under the balcony that ran around the large rotunda with the two huge, polished buffalo flanking the foot of the staircase that leads up to the legislative chamber, I heard a booming voice from above.

"Newman, you son of a bitch!"

I turned and looked up, there was Wally Fox-Decent—who, the day before, had refused to confirm that any Camp—Roblin meeting was taking place—glaring down at me and shaking his fist. I smiled, turned and walked to the press room.

Spurning Camp turned out to be the first of two mistakes that Roblin made around the Conservative leadership, costing him his chance to make a bid to become prime minister of Canada. The second, he made six weeks later.

After Camp left Winnipeg without Roblin's commitment, he redoubled his efforts to get Nova Scotia Premier Stanfield to run. Apparently believing that Roblin was out, Stanfield agreed and made his announcement as a candidate on July 19. When I heard Stanfield's announcement, I felt a sense of disappointment. I, too, thought Roblin wasn't running, and I had looked forward to covering a leadership campaign. I wasn't the only one in Manitoba who thought that way. Vaughan Baird, the president of the Manitoba Progressive Conservative Party, gave me a quote virtually endorsing Stanfield, then quickly called me back, asking to withdraw his words. The Roblin campaign wasn't dead after all.

In fact, the campaign officially sprang to life on August 3, a month before the leadership convention was to begin. The *Tribune* had decided to give full coverage to the campaign, and I was assigned to travel with the candidate and his closest staff as they raced around the country on a private jet, trying to corral delegate votes on the way to the balloting at Maple Leaf Gardens in Toronto in early September. But before we left to begin the delegate search in Calgary, Roblin held a news conference to formally announce his candidacy.

"Why," I asked him on the record, "did you wait until now to become a candidate?"

I knew the answer was the arrival of Stanfield in the race took away the allegation Roblin was Dalton Camp's candidate. But he couldn't say that directly, so instead he replied by referring to Stanfield's candidacy obliquely: "Recently, the race became more respectable."

In a later era of modern media management and rehearsed answers to every possible question, that answer would never be said. A smoother, probably meaningless reply to an obvious question would have been rehearsed over and over. But it did happen that day. A month later in Toronto, it would turn out to have been the second big mistake of the Roblin leadership campaign, and along with spurning Camp's support, it would be fatal.

From the news conference to the airport. The Roblin campaign was off and I was travelling with it, one of four regular passengers on a six-seat private jet rented for a month from a charter company in Calgary. On board that first flight, as there was for virtually every flight of the campaign, were the premier; Joe Martin, his former executive assistant, who had recently gone to work as a management consultant; and Harry Mardon, a cheery Englishman who until recently had been the assistant city editor at the *Winnipeg Tribune* and was now the head of public relations at Investors Syndicate—now the Investors Group. Bud Sherman, my former boss and now the Progressive Conservative MP from Winnipeg South, was also on the first trip. He had grown up in Calgary and still knew a lot of people there.

With the two-hour time difference, we went straight to a hotel, where Roblin spoke with delegates from Calgary and southern Alberta. For me, it was not a very auspicious beginning. The meeting was behind closed doors, and, having to file for the next day's paper, I knew nothing of what was going on. When the meeting broke up, I complained. Mardon, who was the press secretary on the new campaign, wasn't very sympathetic. So I spoke to Sherman. He understood and told me the news from the meeting. Roblin was asked if he would stay in the race if Diefenbaker finally got off the fence and said he was running. Roblin answered that he would stay in.

The next day, that story was in the *Tribune*. Calling back to Winnipeg, Roblin, Mardon and Martin all realized that the story was good for them. I also pointed out that if I was going to travel with them, I would have to have access. After that, I did, sometimes almost uncomfortably so. I was privy to all their conversations on the plane and almost all of the meetings they went to. Often, I talked to delegates at meetings who would not speak directly to the candidate or his people. Since I was going to report what the delegates said in the next day's paper, I had no trouble passing on the information to Martin or Mardon, and sometimes Roblin himself, in advance.

The campaign was an eye-opener. Travelling in the private jet, Roblin raced around the country, meeting every possible delegate he could. Some were already committed to other candidates, like Hees, Fleming and even Fulton, who had been in the race earlier, but as delegates supporting candidates eliminated on earlier ballots would have the chance to make a second and even third choice, meeting everyone was important. In the five weeks leading up to the convention, we travelled from Victoria, on Vancouver Island on the west coast, to St. John's on the east coast of Newfoundland. From Lac St. Jean in Quebec to the interior of British Columbia and just about everywhere in between. I had lived in Montreal, Toronto and Regina, but the rest of the country was a mystery to me. It was a beautiful, warm August all over Canada while we raced around in our private plane as Roblin courted delegates and I discovered my country.

In the final days of the campaign, starting late became a virtue. The race was narrowing down to a contest between the two provincial premiers who joined up last. As we came to Toronto for the September 4 start of the convention, polls of delegates published in the *Toronto Telegram* and the Montreal *Gazette* both had Roblin ahead in delegate support and Stanfield not far behind.

However, once in Toronto, the Roblin campaign was suddenly uneasy. In Dalton Camp's base and with his Big Blue Machine controlling just about everything going on in the run-up to the voting, a glaring gap in the Roblin campaign became apparent. The operation to race around on the hunt for delegates had been brilliantly planned and executed, but convention week in Toronto had been left mainly to two young Progressive Conservatives who were dedicated and hard-working, but completely outclassed and outnumbered by the operation supporting Stanfield on the ground. Suddenly, spurning Camp's support seemed like a mistake. A big mistake, but perhaps not a fatal one. However, it could have made Roblin nervous. Whatever the reason, he made an unusually frenetic and not very effective speech at his first all-candidates' appearance at the Royal York Hotel, while at the same event Stanfield made an unusually good one. Then, to make matters worse, John Diefenbaker filed to be a candidate just at the deadline. Suddenly, a lot of delegates who could have mostly been Roblin's would be staying with Diefenbaker, at least on the early ballots, although Diefenbaker had no chance of winning.

On Saturday, Maple Leaf Gardens was packed. The tension was high, the atmosphere resembling the electricity accompanying the seventh game of the Stanley Cup finals. As the first-ballot results were announced, it was clear it would be a long afternoon. But from the first count, it appeared the die was cast. Stanfield had 519 votes, Roblin 347, just four more than Fulton. George Hees was next, with 295, and John Diefenbaker fifth, with 271. Alvin Hamilton, Donald Fleming, Wallace McCutcheon and Michael Starr all trailed in that order. If Diefenbaker had not been on the ballot, many of his votes probably would have gone to Roblin, putting him closer to or even ahead of Stanfield. Instead, the Nova Scotian had 172 more votes and the momentum going ahead.

After each ballot, the candidate with the fewest votes was dropped from consideration. But now the race was almost certain to come down to the two premiers. The second ballot didn't change much between the two top contenders, but they were starting to pull away from the field. Stanfield had 613 votes, Roblin 430. Now Stanfield was ahead by 183. Fulton was still in third place, but he gained only three additional votes from the first ballot. That showed that he would not be challenging for the leadership, but his supporters were staying loyal and ultimately their second choices could decide the winner.

After the third ballot, Stanfield's lead had slipped seven votes—717 to Roblin's 541. Still in third, Fulton's total had climbed marginally to 361. It was clear even to the other candidates that either Stanfield or Roblin was going to be the next leader of the Progressive Conservatives. George Hees withdrew and said he was supporting Stanfield. Diefenbaker walked out of Maple Leaf Gardens but sent his loyal colleague Gordon Churchill to show his support for Roblin. Fulton stayed on the ballot and so, for some reason, did Alvin Hamilton, whose vote total was melting away to just over 100.

As the fourth-ballot totals were announced, the Roblin team cheered. More of Hees's and Diefenbaker's votes had gone to the Manitoba premier than to his Nova Scotia rival. Stanfield was still ahead with 865 votes, but Roblin had cut his lead to under one hundred ballots with 771. Hamilton had 167 votes and, as the bottom man on the ballot, was eliminated from the race. Fulton's supporters stayed remarkably loyal in the face of his being unable to grow his numbers as other candidates were eliminated or dropped off. His fourth-ballot total was 357. But now, more than four hundred votes behind Roblin, Fulton knew his race was over and he took his name off the ballot, setting up a final showdown between Roblin and Stanfield. Each of the candidates and their teams had been assigned an ice-level box ringing the convention floor. Reporters and television crews were packed in tight in front of them. I was standing just below Roblin in his box, and as the race narrowed and other reporters moved from the candidates they were covering who had been eliminated, the area in front was becoming jammed. With word that Fulton had taken his name off the ballot, Joe Martin suddenly leaped out of his seat behind Roblin and started climbing over the reporters, where I was standing. I let him by me, then turned and followed him as he ran down a nearby tunnel under the stands, around a corner, into another tunnel and stopped before what appeared to be a closed dressing-room door. I was right with him as Joe banged on the door. It opened, and there was a young man Joe had known in the Young Progressive Conservatives. I didn't know then who it was, but later learned it was Lowell Murray, Davie Fulton's top aide and campaign manager.

"Lowell," Martin begged, "Fulton has to endorse Roblin. You know he's the best man for the job. He's the only one who can speak French. You know he likes Davie and will owe him."

Murray's face was covered with the disappointment of his candidate's defeat. He slowly shook his head.

"We're not endorsing anyone," he said in a rather soft voice.

"If you don't endorse Duff, Stanfield will win!" Martin insisted.

"We're not endorsing anyone."

Martin turned and passed me, walked back to the Roblin box, pushed his way through the reporters and started up the steps. The look on his face said everything, but when Roblin looked at him expectantly anyway, Martin just shook his head.

Having just witnessed what I had, the results of the final ballot were almost anticlimactic. Stanfield received 1,150 votes, Roblin 964.

Suddenly, it was all over. Roblin went home to Manitoba and, as he had promised when he ran for the federal leadership, resigned as premier. After a month of travelling the country and the big time of the Toronto convention, I realized that everything I could do in Winnipeg had now been done. I applied for and got a job at *The Globe and Mail* in Toronto. Before I left town, Harry Mardon and his wife gave a dinner for me and Audrey-Ann at the Winnipeg Squash Club. Duff and Mary Roblin and Joe and Sally Martin were the other guests.

Two years later, that *Globe* job took me to the paper's Ottawa bureau, and one day I was having lunch with Lowell Murray, who by this time was working for Stanfield, who was leader of the Opposition. Stanfield seemed universally liked by everyone who met him, but he was being roundly criticized for being a poor communicator, lacking any élan and speaking no French, all things Roblin was clearly better at. I asked Murray why, given the obvious differences between Roblin and Stanfield that were just as apparent two years ago at the Toronto convention, Fulton had declined to back Roblin and let events unfold so that Stanfield would win.

Murray paused for a moment, then explained. Fulton considered himself the epitome of respectability. When Roblin entered the race and said it had taken Stanfield running to make the Conservative leadership contest "respectable," Fulton was deeply offended. After that, there was no way he would endorse Roblin.

Ah, the second mistake.

9

The Globe and Mail: Moving to Toronto

GOING TO WORK at *The Globe and Mail* in October 1967 seemed like achieving a milestone at a reasonably young age. After all, the *Globe* was generally assumed to be the best newspaper in Canada, and not just by the people who worked for it. But within a few weeks of arriving in mid-October, I wasn't entirely sure I had made the right choice.

In Winnipeg, I had been the top reporter on the *Tribune,* author of a column on politics, invited to do commentaries on the CBC. In Toronto, I started, as new reporters did then at the *Globe,* working the evening shift from 5:30 p.m. until 1:00 a.m. My initial consolation came when I realized that I usually got the best story of the evening to cover, and after two weeks I went out to do a story about housing allowances for families living in poverty that was the top front-page story on Saturday morning with my byline on it.

But there were downsides too. Every fourth week, on a rotation basis, it was the fate of newcomers like me to be in the newsroom on Saturday during the day and cover whatever was going on. On a Saturday in November, I found myself standing on Yonge Street, not far from Eaton's department store, covering the Santa Claus Parade. I was standing not too far from the corner of Carlton Street, the home of Maple Leaf Gardens, where about two months earlier I had been at the centre of one of the biggest political stories of the decade. As I went home that evening, I thought, "Leadership to Santa Claus—is that really making progress?"

But there were also signs that things were going to go well. Also in November, I was sent to Winnipeg to cover the Manitoba Progressive Conservative convention where Duff Roblin's successor was picked. As a set-up to the convention coverage, I was asked to write a piece for the op-ed page, the page across from the editorial page, on the main contenders. Not many new reporters at the paper got to do that. While in Winnipeg, I had another interesting experience. When the news director at CJAY, where I had worked six years earlier, found out I was in town for the convention, he asked me to be part of the station's live coverage. I had only been gone a month or so, and still knew all the candidates and behind-the-scenes players, so I did that too.

Then, in early December, I had another lucky development. Prime Minister Lester Pearson announced that he was retiring, and the Liberal Party scheduled a convention for early April 1968 to pick his replacement. Each riding would send delegates to the convention in Ottawa, and those delegates had to be picked at meetings held by the riding associations. Since most of those meetings were going to be held in the evening, my assignment was to cover each of them, and since almost all had guest speakers who were also candidates for the leadership, I was able to get a firsthand look at all the contenders and get to know the Liberal Party power brokers in the Toronto area.

Pierre Trudeau entered the race and became one of the front-runners. But in Toronto in particular, it was difficult at first to gauge his impact.

The city was already represented by two strong candidates in the race in Finance Minister Mitchell Sharp and Transport Minister Paul Hellyer. A third strong Toronto candidate, Trade and Commerce Minister Robert Winters, at first said he wouldn't run—but then jumped into the contest.

Winters's off-again, on-again campaign turned out to be great news for me. As the various contenders announced they were running, the members of the *Globe*'s Ottawa bureau, the main political reporters on the paper, were assigned to the various candidates and their campaigns. By the time Winters changed his mind and announced, all the front-line political reporters had been assigned. However, I was writing about the Liberal leadership and Toronto-area Liberals almost every day. So when a reporter was needed to follow the Winters campaign, I was it. I followed the late-blooming candidate around for a couple of weeks. He seemed to get a good response wherever we went, but by the time the leadership convention began in Ottawa on April 3, I still wondered how someone who had started so late had any hope of doing well.

Trudeau was something new in Canadian politics. He was the first politician as rock star, and his leadership campaign reflected that. But like a lot of rock stars, you either loved him or hated him. The more conservative wing of the Liberal Party thought him a bit of a freak and something of a sideshow. The convention was coming down to a fight between the new and the old, the right and the left of the Liberal Party. Then, just before the convention, one of the candidates most firmly in the establishment camp, dropped out. Mitchell Sharp's campaign was mortally wounded when part of the budget was defeated by the Opposition in a poorly attended late-night session of the House of Commons. It looked as though the Liberals might be driven into an election campaign in the middle of their leadership race. A parliamentary manoeuvre and a second confidence vote meant an election was avoided, but Sharp's leadership campaign was effectively over. The day before the convention, he withdrew as a candidate and threw his support behind Trudeau. The backing of such a respected figure gave Trudeau, who was otherwise anathema to the party's right wing, some of the credibility he had hitherto lacked.

At the time, Sharp said he saw Trudeau as the way of the future, which in fact he was. Years later, Sharp told me he personally couldn't stand Winters, who he said had bad-mouthed him to people they both knew on Bay Street, while Sharp was finance minister. If Sharp was indeed trying to get back at Winters, as the votes in the 1968 convention unfolded, he certainly was successful.

It took four ballots and seven hours to elect Trudeau as the Liberal leader. He led from the beginning, but the most dramatic moment came after the second ballot, when Winters, who had finished third on the first ballot, narrowly passed Hellyer into second place. Their vote totals were close, but Winters had the momentum and there was tremendous pressure on Hellyer to drop out and endorse the man now narrowly ahead of him.

I was on the convention floor, standing right in front of the Winters box, when the results of the second ballot were announced. Suddenly, it was clear to almost everyone that if anyone was to stop Trudeau, it would be the late-entering Winters. And a crowd gathered in front of Hellyer to see what he would do. Winters's executive assistant, Tony Abbott, pushed through the crowd to speak to Hellyer. I pushed through too, just in time to hear former Liberal cabinet minister Judy LaMarsh make her now famous and impassioned plea: "You've got to go to Winters. Don't let that bastard win it, Paul!"

That was the best strategy to stop Trudeau, and the only person in the Ottawa Civic Centre who couldn't see it was Paul Hellyer. He stayed on for the third ballot, where his support dropped to 60 per cent that of Winters. Still he had almost 380 votes. If Hellyer had not been on the third ballot, and all his support had gone to Winters, Trudeau and

Winters would have been almost even as they went into the final show-down on the fourth ballot.

For some reason that was probably a mixture of vanity and long-term strategy, John Turner also stayed on the fourth ballot. With three candidates, it wasn't clear that anyone would get a majority. A fifth might be necessary. But when the tally was announced after the fourth ballot, Trudeau was 250 votes ahead of Winters and had 50.9 per cent of the vote.

"Ah, he's got it," said Winters in his booth, a smile hiding his disappointment.

His assistant, Tony Abbott, spoke more to the way the people supporting Winters felt: "I wonder which hippie will get to be minister of finance," he said.

It is interesting to speculate what would have happened if the final vote at the convention had gone the other way. Winters, of course, would have become prime minister. But about a year and a half later, in 1969, he dropped dead playing tennis in California. If he had died around the same time as prime minister, the Liberals would have held another leadership contest. Most likely, the runner-up from the year before would have won that time, and we would have had Prime Minister Trudeau anyway.

Still, as I walked out of the Ottawa Civic Centre on that April evening in 1968, I thought about the past seven months. I had covered two national leadership conventions with two different papers, and each time I had been with a candidate who went to the final ballot. I hadn't covered a winner yet, but I'd had some pretty good stories, and it left me wanting more.

...

No sooner was I back in the *Globe* newsroom in Toronto, again working the evening shift, than Pierre Trudeau called a general election. I was assigned as the main election reporter for the Metro Toronto area. I was still usually working nights, but I was going to nominating meetings, covering rallies and generally taking the political temperature of the ridings in and around the city. The experience was extremely useful, and something that I would build on later. I had met most of the important Liberals in Toronto during the recent leadership race. Now I was meeting the important Progressive Conservatives and New Democrats too.

Trudeau had called the election because the polls told him he would win a majority government, and the polls were right. Trudeau and the Liberal brand were particularly strong in Toronto and the surrounding suburbs. Even a star PC candidate like party president Dalton Camp went down to defeat to a political neophyte, Robert Kaplan. Kaplan would spend more than twenty-three years as a member of Parliament (including a decade in Opposition) and serve as solicitor general from 1980 to 1984, but in June of 1968 he was a Liberal nobody riding a tide of Trudeaumania to beat a Conservative somebody.

Election day was on a Tuesday, June 25, because the traditional Monday fell on the 24th, which is St. Jean Baptiste Day in Quebec and a holiday in that province. The main story in the next morning's *Globe* was by Ottawa bureau chief Anthony Westell reporting on the return of majority government in Canada after three minorities in a row. A smaller front-page story with my byline reported on a virtual Liberal sweep in Toronto.

We returned to Winnipeg and Regina that summer on our holidays uncertain as to what would be happening next. Our first year in Toronto had been professionally exciting because of the Liberal leadership race and the election, but neither of those was going to happen again anytime soon. And working so many nights had made it tough to get to know many people or enjoy all the city had to offer. On holiday, I dropped in at the *Winnipeg Tribune* to say hello and was surprised a few days after returning to work in Toronto to receive a letter from the editor, Tom Green, inviting me back to the paper to write a column at almost double the salary I was being paid when I left for *The Globe and Mail*. It was nice to be wanted, but I politely declined. We were going forward, not back.

Almost on cue, a couple of weeks later I showed up for work at my usual time of five-thirty to find a note in my mailbox directing me to see managing editor Clark Davey. What relationship I'd had thus far with the managing editor had been an easy one, and I wondered what he wanted. He asked if I would like to join the *Globe* bureau at Queen's Park and begin covering the Ontario legislature. Yes, of course I would. I was going back on a regular political beat and would be working more regular hours to boot. Then Audrey-Ann did me one better. Tired of staying home, and with me now keeping more conventional hours, she applied for a job at CFRB, the biggest radio station in Canada, and was hired to work in an arm of the company called Standard Broadcast Sales. Then, for each of us, a series of remarkable coincidences started to fall into place.

I had not followed Ontario provincial politics closely—in fact, at all. The Progressive Conservatives had taken office in 1944 and were still there twenty-four years later. John Robarts was the third premier in the Tory dynasty, and he was in the second year of his second mandate with a majority government. The Ontario government was the second-biggest in the country, with the second-biggest budget and governed the biggest and richest province in the country. *The Globe and Mail* had three reporters assigned full time to Queen's Park, as the legislature is known.

I arrived at the bureau in late September. By the end of November, I was there by myself. One of my colleagues had been reassigned as the paper's Washington correspondent, and the other became ill and never returned to work. There was a plan at the *Globe* to have Geoffrey Stevens, a former star reporter in the *Globe's* Ottawa bureau, become the Queen's Park bureau chief in the spring of 1969, after he had completed French studies during a sabbatical year in France, but in the fall of 1968 he was out of the country and unavailable to take up the slack. That left me. I was suddenly the acting bureau chief, with a variety of reporters assigned on a temporary basis to fill in.

Some of them were pretty good reporters. Michael Enright, who was later to have an iconic radio career at CBC, spent time in the bureau. We had been friends in the newsroom, and at Queen's Park we probably spent as much time laughing as we did reporting. Keith Spicer was a university professor by training, had been a member of the *Globe's* editorial board and was now trying his hand at reporting. He certainly raised the intellectual quotient of the bureau, although his main interest was in being a politician, not reporting on them. He of course went on to become Canada's first Official Languages Commissioner and then gained fame for his report on national unity after the failure of the Meech Lake Accord at the beginning of the nineties.

The other person who made a big impression on me in the bureau was Frances Russell. I had first met her when I started high school in Winnipeg; our mothers had been at university together. I next saw her at the *Winnipeg Tribune,* where she too was interested in politics, and we worked together covering the Manitoba legislature. Suddenly, two and a half years later, she was at *The Globe and Mail,* and this time we covered the Ontario legislature together. She did so well that when Geoffrey Stevens showed up to take over as bureau chief, she stayed on as the third person in the bureau. The three of us were a harmonious crew as we covered a government that had then been in office twenty-five years, and we tried to make it interesting.

While all of this was happening at the *Globe,* Audrey-Ann was having an even more spectacular experience. Shortly after taking up her job at Standard Broadcast Sales, the manager of promotions and station advertising at CFRB resigned. This was the job Audrey-Ann had done in both Regina and Winnipeg, and rather than go outside for a replacement, CFRB gave her the job. She suddenly had not only her own office, but her own secretary as well. The job meant she was in charge of all the contests and promotions CFRB ran on the air or at events like the Canadian National Exhibition and the Royal Winter Fair, plus the advertising it ran on billboards, in newspapers, and on buses or in subway stations. She was also on the station's executive committee, which meant she would be driven in the company car during the day whenever she was on business outside of the station, and—in my mind, most important of all—every few weeks got the opportunity to use the station's tickets to the Maple Leafs' games.

I was toiling away with two other people in the small *Globe* office in the press gallery at Queen's Park. But life there was pretty good, too. Press gallery members got special licence plates that permitted them to park for free near the front door of the Legislative Building. The press gallery lounge had a well-stocked bar, and the clerks would pour a drink or get you lunch pretty well anytime the House was in session. Free downtown parking, free tickets to hockey games, time for friends like my second cousin Jim Arnett and his wife, Alix—life in Toronto was very good indeed.

And this is why Audrey-Ann was so upset when I told her it was ending.

...

I HADN'T SAID more than a few words to Clark Davey after he sent me to the Queen's Park bureau because I didn't often see him. I went directly to the legislature in the morning and we filed our copy in the late afternoon by teletype to the newsroom on King Street, the same way correspondents did from Ottawa, Washington or anywhere outside of Toronto. So I was mildly surprised when, one afternoon in early September 1969, I received a call from his secretary asking me to come to the managing editor's office for a meeting.

He got straight to the point.

"Goldblatt wants you to go and Stevens wants you to stay," Clark said, referring to the Ottawa and Queen's Park bureau chiefs respectively. "I think it is a great idea so I am sending you to the Ottawa bureau."

Just two years at the *Globe,* one at Queen's Park and a month short of my twenty-ninth birthday, and I was joining the Ottawa bureau of the paper. The ambition I had hatched on the prairies covering Hazen Argue and Tommy Douglas was about to pay off. But as I thanked Clark for the opportunity, I knew that there was a problem. After coming to Toronto, reluctant to give up her good life in Winnipeg, Audrey-Ann had now managed, on her own, to recreate a life even more interesting and fulfilling in Toronto. But it was a Toronto life. The possibility of doing the same in Ottawa was nonexistent. I would be staying with the national newspaper in an important job on Parliament Hill. She would have to look around and see what was available at local radio stations smaller than the one she had worked at in Winnipeg and nothing at all like CFRB. I had to admit that if the roles were reversed, I wouldn't want to move, and I wasn't surprised that she didn't want to, either.

We talked about it long and hard. One fact seemed clear to me, and then to her, too: if we didn't go to Ottawa, my future at *The Globe and Mail* would probably be limited. Audrey-Ann didn't see that as the problem I did. A year or so before, I had been offered a job at the nickel mining giant Inco as executive assistant to the vice-president of advertising and public relations. Moneywise, and with the trappings of executive life, it was a very attractive offer, and I had a hard time resisting it. Why couldn't I pursue that type of career now, stay in Toronto, make even more money while she continued at CFRB and together we enjoyed the good life? I had turned down the Inco job because, in my heart, I wanted to continue to be a journalist, and now going to Ottawa was a big part of that dream.

The more we talked it through, the more her resistance faded. She loved working at CFRB but didn't see it as her life's work. We had been married for over five years, and if we wanted a family, we should start thinking about it. Ottawa, they said, was a great place to raise kids.

And so we moved. I went first, at the beginning of October, and Audrey-Ann arrived for good when we took possession of a stylish townhouse not far from Carleton University along the Rideau River. Until she arrived, I lived in an apartment hotel, where she would join me when she visited from Toronto on weekends until she wound up her CFRB job.

SHORTLY AFTER I joined the bureau, a new session of Parliament opened with a Speech from the Throne. As prime minister, Trudeau was dressed traditionally in what is known as a morning suit: long, dark tailcoat over striped trousers. A few weeks earlier, his sister had said he was two years older than he claimed. A few days earlier, the still-unmarried prime minister with the reputation for being a swinger had just turned fifty, something he was apparently reluctant to admit.

At a reception following the throne speech, I saw Trudeau standing alone. I had met him during the leadership campaign in 1968, but I knew he didn't know me so I went over, introduced myself and told him

I had just joined the *Globe and Mail* bureau. He was very noncommittal, almost drowsy, but that changed suddenly when Sidney Margolis from CJAD in Montreal approached.

"How does it feel to be fifty?" Margolis asked, laughing.

"Fuck off," Trudeau replied.

Trudeau's majority government had been in office a little more than a year and he was in high gear with his plan to make Quebecers feel more Canadian by making Canada a little more like Quebec. Primarily, that meant his official-language policy of turning the federal public service into a bilingual one. One particular critic was former prime minister John Diefenbaker. Ironically, it was the Diefenbaker government, when it had fifty members from Quebec, that introduced simultaneous translation into the House of Commons so that MPs could speak in either English or French and be understood by everyone. But beyond that, Diefenbaker was a defender of everything British. He had cried in 1966 when the Maple Leaf flag was raised on Parliament Hill, replacing the Red Ensign as the national flag, and he tried to make a big issue out of the Royal Mail being renamed Canada Post, although only with the Monarchist League did that have much resonance.

During the seventies, Diefenbaker was a big problem for new PC leader Robert Stanfield and most of his parliamentary colleagues when it came to Quebec. Conservative strength in Quebec was already weak with favourite son Trudeau and the Liberals in charge. The Quebec media in the press gallery reported every attack on the extension of French or reduction of British symbols as if it were the most important news happening, and by doing so, the image of the PCs in Quebec as the party of the United Empire Loyalists was being reinforced.

The other news was the wide variety of new spending programs the Trudeau government was developing. Regional development schemes for low-growth areas of the country, and redesigned unemployment insurance so it was more generous. What the government would not do was target urban areas for special spending, even though by the early seventies the trend towards urbanization and the movement of Canadians to the big cities were well underway. From a constitutional perspective, Trudeau viewed cities as the responsibility of the provinces, even as he lavished federal largesse over various other parts of the country, particularly the Atlantic provinces and Quebec.

I reported these developments straight up without comment as economic development stories. Only occasionally in a background piece would I also point out it was really pure politics. Under the constitution, no province could have fewer MPs than senators; the Atlantic provinces collectively have thirty senators, versus thirty-two MPs. Thus, the Atlantic provinces are far more represented in the House of Commons than straight numbers warrant. That was even truer in the 1970s, when there were only 264 seats in the Commons (compared with the 311 in the House after the 2011 general election). And because they are areas of slow economic growth, voters in Atlantic Canada are susceptible to government spending programs creating jobs and generous unemployment payments when they are not working.

The same is true for Quebec, where, beyond the Montreal area and the provincial government jobs in and around Quebec City, all the economic indicators show low growth. A lot of Quebec's seventy-five seats in the House of Commons are in areas that fit that definition, and at that time Quebec was the base of the Liberal Party. True, Atlantic Canada was not. Regional loyalty had trumped all, and the Atlantic provinces had given the bulk of their seats to Conservative leader Stanfield, the former premier of Nova Scotia. Still, I thought, there would be future elections to consider, and besides, spending money in Atlantic Canada deflected criticism the Trudeau government might have received from pouring money into Quebec.

While *The Globe and Mail* strove to be the "paper of record," there was fierce competition between it, the *Toronto Star,* the *Toronto Telegram,* the *Montreal Star* and the Southam News Service. As well, television was playing a bigger and soon to be dominant role in political coverage on the Hill. Cameras were crammed into the foyer of the House in front of the chamber. Cabinet ministers and opposition politicians alike scrambled to get in front of them after Question Period to take reporters' questions and try to add their spin to the news. By the spring of 1970, there were so many cameras and the situation was so chaotic that the politicians decided they could no longer navigate the traffic. They insisted the foyer be cleared of cameras, but they didn't want them to go far. They sent them fifty feet down the hall to an oval-shaped reception area known as the Commonwealth Room. All the cameras moved there, and so did most of the reporters. Print reporters as well as television. MPs wanted to be on television, and they followed the cameras down to the Commonwealth Room, hoping to be scrummed on camera. Even Trudeau would come down if he had something to say.

While television was a magnet for politicians, and in that way a help to print reporters, it also created a problem. Politicians now played to the cameras instead of to the note-takers standing beside them. That meant that instead of pausing when answering questions to let reporters scribble their remarks down in notebooks, they now looked right into the cameras and answered questions in complete sentences, one after the other, without stopping until they reached the next question. It was very difficult to keep up, writing down nonstop answers while at the same time thinking of follow-up questions you might want to add into the scrum yourself. After about six months of getting writer's cramp, I decided to turn to technology for help.

At Queen's Park, I had been selected by the *Globe* to take twice-weekly French lessons. One of the requirements for the course was to have a tape recorder so you could practise reading and speaking French into the machine and then play yourself back to see how you were doing. Audrey-Ann had found me a tape recorder through CFRB, and it came with us in the move to Ottawa. Because it came from a radio station, it looked like the bulky recorders radio reporters in the gallery used. I decided to try it out, to see if I could get more accurate quotes, on a trip I was assigned to take with the prime minister to southwestern Ontario. The first time Trudeau stopped to talk, I took out my mike and tape recorder and stood in with the radio and TV reporters to record his remarks. Other members of the press gallery were amazed. What was going on? Had I left a front-page byline in the *Globe* to become a radio journalist? Of course I told them no and explained what I was doing. Most newspaper reporters on the trip thought what I was doing was pretty silly. But as we boarded the bus to travel to Trudeau's next stop, Ken Mason from CBC Radio News sidled up to me.

"Could I borrow your tape for a few minutes?" he asked. "I missed the bit of Trudeau talking about marijuana. I can't ask my competitors, but I would appreciate it if you could help me out."

I lent Ken my tape. He seemed to think what I was doing made sense, but when I showed up the next Monday in the *Globe* bureau, and then on Parliament Hill, I was kidded, even ridiculed. A decade later, when I returned to Ottawa in 1981, what did I see the first time I went up to the scrums after Question Period? Every print reporter was carrying a tape recorder and holding it in as politicians were scrummed in front of the TV cameras. In fact, they were also doing something I never did—they were holding the tape recorders in front of politicians they were interviewing one on one, instead of writing down the answers in notebooks. The tape recorders were smaller than the one I had used in 1970, but the principle was the same, and so was the reason for using them. Although some of the print reporters were the same ones who had laughed at me ten years earlier, none seemed to remember that I had been the first to use a tape recorder.

10

Trudeau and the October Crisis

IT WAS REALLY a Quebec story, and it lasted in that province for over two months. But in Ottawa, what quickly became known as the October Crisis riveted everyone and dominated everything that happened in the national capital.

I was actually feeling rather mellow when it started. I had been in the *Globe* bureau for a year, had had at least my share of good stories and probably more, and had just received a raise, bought a new car and was feeling everything was in control.

When the news broke in Montreal on Monday, October 5, 1970, that the British trade commissioner, James Cross, had been kidnapped in that city by a gang of armed separatists, no one was quite sure what to make of it. For the better part of the 1960s, the separatists had been getting bolder and more violent, starting by blowing up mail boxes in the affluent English enclave of Westmount, moving on to robbing munitions and rifles from Canadian Forces armouries and planting a bomb that injured more than twenty people at the Montreal Stock Exchange. But this was the first time someone claimed responsibility.

They called themselves the Front de libération du Québec and went by the acronym FLQ. They had tricked their way into the Montreal home of Cross, grabbed him and spirited him away in a taxi. Once he was secure in their control and out of sight, the FLQ issued its demands for his release. They wanted half a million dollars in gold, a plane to take them to either Cuba or Algeria, and the release from jail or detention of twenty-three people previously arrested for breaking the law in the name of the FLQ. According to the ransom note, the twenty-three lawbreakers were "political prisoners." The kidnappers also wanted their "manifesto"—their demands and a screed about the need for an independent Quebec—published throughout the French-speaking media in the province.

As a crime, the kidnapping was the responsibility of the Montreal police and the Quebec Provincial Police. But Cross was a foreign diplomat accredited to Canada, and his seizure was both a matter for the federal government and an international incident. In the House of Commons in the first days following the grabbing of Cross, his foreign status meant that it was External Affairs Minister Mitchell Sharp who answered the Opposition's questions and whose press secretary gave the media briefings.

The day after the kidnapping, October 6, the FLQ manifesto—or at least parts of it—were published in some Quebec newspapers. French-language radio station CKAC in Montreal received a message from the kidnappers threatening that Cross would be killed if the FLQ's demands were not met. At this point, the federal government was resisting the publication of the kidnappers' screed. But the next day, the manifesto was read on CKAC, and the evening after that on Radio-Canada (the CBC's French-language arm) throughout the province.

In 1970, the House of Commons sat three nights a week. During these evening sessions, reporters could go into the lobbies behind the seats in the Commons to send messages in to the MPs in the chamber and meet with them in the lobbies when they came out. On the evening of October 8, the House was in session while the manifesto was read over Radio-Canada. I was in the press gallery with my *Globe* colleague John Burns. As Prime Minister Trudeau was getting ready to leave, we dashed out of the gallery, down the back stairs and into the members' lobby, where we were met by the prime minister's press secretary, Roméo LeBlanc.

"The prime minister isn't stopping. He's not saying anything," LeBlanc told us sternly. Just then, Trudeau emerged through the curtains from the House and started moving through the lobby, shaking hands and receiving pats on the back from Liberal MPs. Burns was filing the *Globe* story that night and would not be deterred. He started pushing his way through the MPs towards the prime minister. I felt a rush as suddenly LeBlanc charged past me, raced towards Burns, jumped on his back, put his arm around his neck and pulled him away just as he was about to reach Trudeau. There were no hard feelings; each was just doing his job. (The image of the two of them that evening flashed to mind more than once in the 1990s—Burns, working for the *New York Times,* won Pulitzer Prizes in 1993, for his coverage of the war in Bosnia, and 1997, for his coverage of the Taliban in Afghanistan, while LeBlanc served as Canada's Governor General from 1995 to 1999.)

As the federal government had feared, giving in to some of the FLQ demands only emboldened others. That weekend, on Saturday, October 10, Quebec's minister of labour was also kidnapped. Pierre Laporte was throwing a football with his nephew in front of his home when another group of three rolled up—again in a taxi—grabbed him and rushed away.

Monday, October 12 was Thanksgiving. In Ottawa, soldiers were deployed to guard government buildings and the homes of people believed to be at risk. As people arrived for work the next day, they were shocked to see armoured vehicles on the lawn of the Parliament Buildings and combat-ready soldiers standing on sentry duty. As I got off the bus and started up from Wellington Street to the Centre Block, I saw Trudeau's car arriving at the west door of the building. There were two camera crews and two reporters waiting for him, but as Burns and I had experienced a few days before, the prime minister was avoiding the media. I watched his arrival, assuming he would brush past the waiting media again. But he didn't. He stopped. I was still near the bottom of the Hill, but I began running up as fast as I could to try and get in on what was turning into a small scrum.

When I was about fifty feet away, Trudeau turned and went into the building. I reached the door, puffing, to find both Tim Ralfe of the CBC and Peter Reilly of CTV pleased and smiling about the exchange they had caught on camera.

"What did Trudeau say?" I asked them both.

Ralfe said that he had told Trudeau that soldiers in the streets made some Canadians nervous and asked the prime minister, "How far would you go with that?" Trudeau's reply? I asked.

"Just watch me."

The army was standing guard in Ottawa, but things were starting to spin out of control in Montreal. On Wednesday, October 14, sixteen prominent Quebecers—including future separatist leader and Quebec premier René Lévesque and Claude Ryan, who later became Lévesque's political opponent but was then editor of *Le Devoir*—publicly called for the exchange of so-called "political prisoners" for Cross and Laporte. Separatist groups demonstrated and rallied in Montreal, and Quebec premier Robert Bourassa asked Ottawa to send in the army to help police the province. A day later, he asked for "emergency powers" and, along with Montreal mayor Jean Drapeau, sent a letter asking the federal government for help. Ottawa invoked the War Measures Act, the statute dating back to the First World War, which allowed the authorities to hold people without trial, suspending the right of habeas corpus, the fundamental tenet of the legal system we acquired from Britain.

The War Measures Act went into effect on Friday, October 16. Its imposition was controversial as the Quebec police struck quickly to sweep up all sorts of people they had had their eye on for a variety of reasons. In the House of Commons, the New Democrats were opposed and the Conservatives weren't sure what to do. Leader Robert Stanfield at first embraced a civil-libertarian view and opposed the Act in his questions to the government on Friday morning in Question Period. But after a flood of phone calls and telegrams from Tory supporters across the country, damning his position, the Conservatives pivoted and got onside with the governing Liberals and public opinion in general.

Within the *Globe*'s Ottawa bureau, there was a split—although, this being the *Globe*, it was a civilized one. The split occurred along generational lines, but not in the way you would likely think. The older members—bureau chief Murray Goldblatt, columnist George Bain and senior reporter Clyde Sanger—all opposed the proclamation of the War Measures Act. The younger members—me, Burns and economics writer David Crane—approved. We thought that it was unclear how serious the threat was, but that events were escalating out of control and it was better to put on the brakes sooner rather than later.

The War Measures Act triggered an emergency debate in the Commons that rolled on into the weekend. On Saturday evening, Burns and I were assigned to cover it, as one MP after another put their feelings and thoughts on the record. In the early hours of Sunday morning, I was sitting in the press gallery above the chamber, when suddenly, a government minister rushed from behind the lobby curtains, interrupted the proceedings to ask for the floor and told the stunned, mostly empty chamber that Pierre Laporte had been found, following a tip to police, dead in the trunk of a car near St. Hubert Airport on the south shore of the St. Lawrence River near Montreal. In shock, the debate was adjourned. Burns and I regrouped by the *Globe* desks in the "hot room," the work area of the gallery. The room was starting to fill up. Word came that the prime minister was coming from his residence on Sussex Drive and would have a statement to make before the cameras in the Commonwealth Room. By now, the gallery was crammed with reporters and we pushed down to the Commonwealth Room to await Trudeau.

"Just a statement, no questions," Jim Davey, a deputy press secretary, announced just before the prime minister strode in. Trudeau's face was a mask of fury. First in French and then in English, he briefly extended condolences to the Laporte family but also expressed his contempt for the killers and a sense of shame.

"It was with a sense of shock and consternation that I believe all Canadians have learnt about the death of Mr. Pierre Laporte—who was so cowardly assassinated by a band of murderers. And I can't help feeling as a Canadian a deep sense of shame that this cruel and senseless act should have been conceived in cold blood and executed in like manner. And I want to express to Mrs. Laporte and to Mr. Laporte's family the very deep regret of the Canadian people and the Canadian government and our desire as Canadians to stick together through this very sorry moment in our history."

Ron Collister, the chief television correspondent for the CBC in Ottawa, was standing right in front of Trudeau with a live microphone. He ignored the "no questions" edict.

"What does this tell you about the kind of people you are dealing with?" he asked Trudeau. Stepping around Collister and starting to leave the room, the prime minister replied, "I can't tell you any more."

It was the middle of the night. There was not then, and nor is there now, a Sunday edition of the *Globe*, so Burns and I realized that there was a lot more to the Ottawa angle of this story than we would be able to tell by the time we would have to have our copy filed at seven-thirty on Sunday evening. It was too early to start phoning other politicians for their reactions or call sources in the RCMP and other security agencies to find out anything we could about the federal police role in ongoing events. So we decided to divide up what we already had: the scene in the House of Commons when the death was announced; the stunned reaction of MPs huddling around television sets in the lobbies, watching the news being broadcast from Montreal; and Trudeau's arrival and statement.

Sitting across from each other at the hot-room desk of the *Globe*, we typed out everything we had without thinking about how it might later fit into an overall story when, suddenly, it turned out we didn't have to think about that. We looked up and there was our bureau chief, Murray Goldblatt, up with the sun and downtown to take charge of the coverage. We worked away, using the phones on the wall of the hot room, John and I dividing up who to call. After each interview over the phone, we would return to a desk and write what we had learned. Then we handed over our copy to Murray, who was to weave it all together into one complete story.

And without Murray, it is not clear even now how that story might have turned out. Like all newspaper people, Murray had started as a reporter, but his real talent was as an editor and his career had been carried forward on that ability. He had been the national editor of the *Globe*, in charge of all stories from across Canada, when he was asked to take over the Ottawa bureau and bring leadership and organization to a group of young, keen reporters who had lots of energy, some experience, but no seniority one from another, nor the maturity to lead the most important bureau of the "Paper of Record."

On that October Sunday morning in 1970, Burns and I were certainly keen, and knew how to work a story and gather information, and although we'd been up overnight, we were still eager to cover every possible angle. By late afternoon, we had finished our reporting and left the gallery with Murray still combining our work into a finished article. The next morning, the front page of the *Globe* was all from Montreal and the discovery of Laporte's body. The front page of the second section had a big headline, too. It was over the story of what had happened in Ottawa, Trudeau's reaction, the scene in the House of Commons, and all the other reactions. It was a beautifully written story and it had a double byline—my name and John Burns. There was no mention of Murray Goldblatt. Burns and I were happy to have the credit, but in the office we each reproached Murray for leaving his own name off.

"No," he said, "it was you guys that stayed up all night."

After the Laporte murder, the story went quiet in Ottawa. Cross was still in FLQ hands somewhere in Quebec, most likely in Montreal, and the police raided the headquarters of the group that had kidnapped and killed Laporte, but they found only one of the gang there, Bernard Lortie. He was arrested and charged with the kidnapping and murder of Laporte. In Ottawa, the *Globe* bureau went back to covering stories about the things that are always the stock and trade of reporters on Parliament Hill—the economy, politics, foreign affairs, federal—provincial relations—and watched from a distance the search for Cross. Any new information from the FLQ came either from their lawyer or from communiqués that occasionally were sent to CKAC Radio and then broadcast all over Quebec.

The army was still on guard, as the War Measures Act was still in effect. At the *Globe*, George Bain was writing columns on a regular basis against its imposition. Shortly after the Laporte murder, and while he was writing his columns against the Act, we started having trouble with the phones in the bureau. We heard loud clicks when we picked up to dial out, or sometimes a click and then the phone would be cut off right in the middle of a conversation. Maybe we were paranoid, but to a person we believed someone was listening in on our conversations. Whether we supported the imposition of the War Measures Act or were opposed, everyone in the bureau assumed the listeners were members of the RCMP.

In Montreal, what news there was from the FLQ members holding Cross usually came through communiqués they sent to French-language radio station CKAC, which then broadcast and reported on the information received. Perhaps that is why news outlets like the *Globe* might also have been monitored. I became more convinced of that about a week after the Laporte murder. I was walking up Parliament Hill when I saw, approaching me from the other direction, Labour Minister Bryce Mackasey. It was unusual for a cabinet minister to be walking alone, but when we met, he stopped and we started talking about the still-ongoing crisis. Suddenly, he volunteered some information.

"You know why we didn't include press censorship in the things covered under the War Measures Act?" he suddenly asked.

"No, why?"

"Because it is mainly through the media in Montreal that we are finding out what is going on," he said, referring to the CKAC broadcasts.

It quickly led me to believe there would be no early resolution of the crisis and that Cross was likely to be held for a while yet, his life in danger every day.

And it turned out that was correct. Almost two months after he was seized, and after hours of painstaking investigation, the police found he was being held in a modest home in the north end of Montreal. After they negotiated with the hostage takers, he was released on December 3. For his freedom, the five kidnappers were given safe passage to Cuba on a special flight arranged for them.

Three of the four terrorists who murdered Pierre Laporte remained at large until December 28. Paul Rose, his brother Jacques and a man named Francis Simard were found hiding underground in a tunnel at a remote country farm. With them in captivity, the October Crisis had effectively passed.

Looking back, it is easier to put the October Crisis of 1970 in perspective. Critics claim the Trudeau government overreacted, but I disagree. The mayor of Montreal and the premier of Quebec were the ones who asked for the imposition of the War Measures Act, and the Act was the only piece of legislation then on the books that could be used. Complaints that the Quebec police overreacted when the Act was in effect were probably true, but that was the Quebec police, not the federal government. And a few years later, a new piece of legislation was brought in, less draconian than the War Measures Act, to deal with any similar situations in the future.

At the time of the kidnappings, it was not known just how large or widespread the FLQ really was. If you complain that the police should have known more but decry the infringement on civil liberties with the use of the War Measures Act, you are living the contradiction of a free society: how much the police should look into people's activities on a regular basis and how far they must go to preserve and protect when trouble breaks out.

Perhaps the most positive outcome of the events of October 1970 is that, while support for an independent Quebec remains relatively constant in the province. The brutal death of Laporte turned people away from violence and made separatism purely a political issue. Some people think it ridiculous to have political parties advocating the breakup of the country elected to the federal Parliament and sometimes in charge of the government in the province that they want to be independent. But I think the arrangement is brilliant. Now people seeking independence have to be politicians, not terrorists. They have to deal with the fickleness of public opinion, and when the separatists win there is no revolution.

And when they lose, there isn't a revolution either. Instead, when they lose either provincial elections or independence referenda, the separatists just accept the results and vow to try harder and do better next time. When you think of it that way, it is all very Canadian.

As I watched the October Crisis in Quebec unfold, I wondered about the role of the province's premier, Robert Bourassa. In the second week, as the situation in the province started to slip out of control, his government first asked for the army to be sent in to help the police, and then almost immediately asked for the special powers of the War Measures Act to be invoked. One of his cabinet ministers then became the second kidnap victim. Pierre Laporte wrote a letter to Bourassa pleading for his life; the letter was read on the radio. But the police were unable to find where he was being held, and less than a week later Laporte was murdered.

Through all of this, the premier had no public profile. There was no heroic attempt to take charge, to show grace under pressure. Later, it was learned that Bourassa was involved on a daily basis, but for safety reasons he was living underground in a bunker in Quebec City across from the National Assembly. His reputation was not enhanced by his lack of performance during the crisis. In fact, it gave rise to the feeling that Robert Bourassa was too young to be premier and was "weak."

Bourassa had been premier less than six months when the FLQ launched its kidnapping attacks. He'd led the Liberal Party back to power in the province in May of 1970, and a couple of months later I met him at the annual premiers' conference.

The conference was held in Manitoba, on the elegant passenger cruise ship *Lord Selkirk II*, a vessel with enough cabins for the premiers, their retinues and the accompanying media. A year earlier, while a member of the *Globe*'s Queen's Park bureau, I had been sent to Quebec City to cover the first of these conferences, which still continue as an annual event. Based on that scant expertise, and perhaps because I had come to the paper from Winnipeg, I was sent to Manitoba to report on the premiers' meeting.

The ship was tied up at Selkirk, at the southern end of Lake Winnipeg. After all were on board, it was to cruise up the lake to Norway House, and then turn around and come back. The trip would take two days. I was standing by the rail near the gangplank with three other reporters, watching as the premiers arrived. Bourassa was driven up, and then strode up the gangplank with a big smile and immediately asked: "Who is from *The Globe and Mail*?"

I identified myself. We shook hands and chatted, little knowing then that our meeting was the first of a number over the next twenty-five years that would deal with some of the biggest events in contemporary Canadian history.

11

Switching to CTV

IN THE FALL of 1970, Bourassa's opening question about who represented *The Globe and Mail* was on my mind a lot, and not just because
of the October Crisis. In September, shortly after Parliament had
resumed, I was in the fifth-floor cafeteria in the Centre Block for a morning cup of coffee. The cafeteria was crowded, and as I looked around for
someone I knew at a table with an empty chair, I saw a place next to Peter
Stursberg. He was an imposing-looking man with a deep voice who was
in the gallery representing the local CTV station, CJOH. He was older
than most of the gallery reporters, but had sleek good looks and a mildly
English air about him.

"Sturs," as people who knew him better called him, not only represented CJOH in the gallery, he also owned a small piece of the station.
In addition to his reporting duties, which he shared with a couple of
other CJOH staffers, he was also the producer of the interview program
Question Period, which was taped at the local station on Friday afternoon and shown across the CTV network on Sunday. As producer, he

got to choose the guests for the program, which gave him clout with all the politicians, at least the English-speaking ones. The panel of reporters who questioned the guest consisted of Bruce Phillips, the CTV network's bureau chief; George Bain, the *Globe and Mail* columnist; and Stursberg, which also gave him a national profile.

As I sat down beside him, he didn't seem particularly interested that I was joining him. We hadn't spoken before, but I had been in the gallery almost a year, had had many front-page bylines and just assumed he knew my name. I was aware of his early career. My mother remembered him in London after the war when we lived there, and he had stayed on in Britain after—as he liked to tell everyone—he was the "youngest war correspondent for the CBC." Looking for some casual conversation, I told him we had a mutual friend: Stewart MacPherson, a Winnipegger who ended up in London during the war, reported for the BBC and then became a popular host of entertainment programs like *Twenty Questions* before returning to North America. In 1961 he was the program director at CJAY-TV in Winnipeg as I was launching my career there.

"You know Stewie?" he said with some incredulity. "How do you know him?"

I told him of my time at CJAY, about the same time that CJOH was coming on the air in Ottawa. I also told him that I had been in England as a boy and that my family remembered him from there. That warmed up the conversation, and we chatted back and forth, and then returned to the press gallery to go about our respective business. I thought no more about our conversation until two days later, when my phone rang in the *Globe* bureau. It was Peter Stursberg. It turned out that George Bain would be away for the taping of *Question Period* that week. He asked if I would like to take his place.

You would think I would remember who the politician was on that program, but I don't. I do remember feeling my participation had gone quite well, a feeling underlined the next week when Bruce Phillips told me he thought so too, and so did CTV network executives in Toronto.

"If you are ever interested in a career in TV, let me know," Phillips told me. He had made the switch from print in the Southam News Service a few years earlier.

"Well, I am interested," I told him.

"Really? I am going to have an opening in a few months. Michael Nolan is leaving to go and teach at Western. Let's talk then."

We agreed that would happen, although I wasn't at all sure that I wanted to move in the next few months, or to move to CTV if I did. Working in the *Globe*'s Ottawa bureau had been one of my career goals, and while I had reached it, I had only been a year in the job. Still, being a TV journalist, particularly one reporting from Washington, was the other active goal I had, and as my experience with the tape recorder had shown, television journalism was in its ascendency. But CTV News was still very much a work in progress. It was dwarfed by the CBC. Certainly, everyone at the *Globe,* including me, was watching the CBC. Beyond the Parliamentary bureau of Phillips, Nolan and Max Keeping, I was not very familiar with the other journalists on the CTV newscast.

Still, no one at CBC was asking me if I was interested in a job. And after my brief experience with the Corporation in Winnipeg, I wasn't champing at the bit to work there again. I started watching the CTV newscast to get a feel for it, see what I thought about it, measure how good it was.

And what I saw was a pleasant surprise. It did not have the range of reporters and stories that the CBC did, but it had a competent and credible program that, at the end of the broadcast, left you with a sense that you knew what had happened that day. What it didn't have was any foreign coverage reported by its own people. The American NBC network supplied all of the foreign news, including news from Washington.

While I was doing this research, I was still working full out at the *Globe,* filing both for the main paper and sometimes for the Report on Business, and trying to have at least one "think" piece a month on the op-ed page. Ironically, the more I began thinking about a move to television, the more in demand my work for the *Globe* was, and the better the play it was getting.

In early March, I received a call from Bruce Philips. He said that if I was still interested, I would have to do a piece to camera that would be reviewed by the network news executives in Toronto to see if I had at least the promise of being a TV reporter. The next day, we met in the press gallery.

"Just write some story or commentary, just a couple of minutes, and then go outside with Rollie over there and tell it to the camera while he films you."

I had first met Bruce at the 1967 Conservative leadership convention, when I worked for the *Winnipeg Tribune* and he was with the Southam News Service. By the time I reached the press gallery, he was obviously aware that I was working at the *Globe.* But we didn't know each other, had never travelled on a story together or shared a beer in the Press Club. I knew nothing of his background, and he knew nothing of mine, including the fact that I had worked in television for one year in Winnipeg and one year in Regina. Neither was anything like network television, but both had given me the confidence to look a camera directly in the lens and know how to look up and speak directly to it when reaching the end of a sentence.

Script in hand, I went with Rollie out to the Senate side of the Centre Block. Checking the sun, he picked a spot near the statute of Sir John A. Macdonald.

"Are you ready?" he asked

"Yup."

"Okay. I'm rolling."

Rollie lived up to his name. He was short and roly-poly. Since he was obviously strong and this was to be a relatively short piece, he had not bothered to bring a tripod for the camera. Instead, he just held it on his shoulder.

I had written a piece about the race for the leadership of the federal New Democratic Party, which I was covering on a regular basis. I breezed through the report without a flub, looking into the camera at the appropriate moments. When I signed off my one take of the audition without any difficulty, I had a sense I had impressed.

"Jeez. For a newspaper guy, that was pretty damn good."

Bruce Phillips did not have the film processed in Ottawa. He shipped it directly to CTV headquarters in Toronto for processing and review by the people who would make the hiring decision, so he had not seen my one-take audition. That is probably why he sounded bewildered the following evening, when he phoned me at home.

"You blew them away. They think you are the next Walter Cronkite and they want to hire you right away," he said, sounding a little incredulous.

"Really. How much do they want to pay?" I asked.

"Well, they don't want to pay you like the next Walter Cronkite," he said. And when he told me the figure, I knew he was right. I told him I would think about it and be back in a couple of days. Still, as I hung up, I knew that I had a network television reporting job if I wanted it, and I figured the salary was just a first offer I could negotiate up at least a bit.

And negotiating it up was going to be necessary if I was to convince Audrey-Ann I should move. To be blunt, she didn't want me to move. Right after the Cross kidnapping, she had found out she was pregnant, and the last thing she wanted was a husband with a new job to worry about as we welcomed our first child after seven years of marriage. I didn't blame her, but I pointed out that this new job didn't involve a move to another city, as others had, that we would stay in our same home, I would still work on Parliament Hill and we would keep all of our friends and her support group for the new baby.

At first, she wasn't convinced. But as we both thought about and discussed it, it became clear that staying at the *Globe* would mean standing still while moving to TV was the path to the future. A trip I took to Toronto, to meet Tom Gould, then director of the news, and Don MacPherson, the vice-president of information programming at the network, produced a higher salary offer and we decided to accept.

Telling *The Globe and Mail* was difficult. I had enjoyed a rapid rise through the ranks, and now I was leaving after three and a half years. Managing editor Clark Davey was away when I made my decision, so I called the editor, Richard Doyle, and he couldn't have been kinder.

"Well, we've had your brother and we've had you. Any more at home like you two?" he said before wishing me luck.

The next week, I called Davey when he returned to the office.

"If you are just going for the money, come down here and I'll rub your back," he said, holding out the possibility of a raise if I stayed. No, I told him, television was something I just had to try.

"Well," he said, "if I were your age, I would probably do the same thing."

I went to work at CTV on April 19, 1971. The experience was almost nothing like those I'd had in Winnipeg and Regina a decade earlier. Television had come a long way in ten years, but luckily so had I, and although I was on a steep learning curve, the first assignment I took on was the NDP leadership convention. I had been covering the race for the *Globe*, knew all the candidates and other players well, and on voting day on Saturday, April 24 was standing on a raised platform in front of David Lewis as he captured a fourth-ballot victory to claim the leadership. It was an auspicious beginning.

The next few months were tougher, but I worked hard and learned a few tricks of the trade. As the warm weather came and golf season moved into high gear, Bruce Phillips was often quite willing to stay at the Royal Ottawa Golf Club and let me do the "feed" of our Ottawa stories into the *CTV National News,* which meant going into the studio and recording reports and commentaries that then played live into the news at 11 p.m. It was great experience, and I sometimes thought it might speed up by a few years my next career goal of becoming a television reporter in Washington.

In mid-June, I returned from covering a constitutional conference in Victoria. Audrey-Ann's predicted due date was still a couple of weeks away, but shortly after midnight in the early hours of Sunday, June 20, she announced that delivery was imminent and it was time to go to the Riverside Hospital, not far from where we lived. For almost twelve hours, she was in labour. We had decided to be surprised and did not try to find out if we would be welcoming a boy or a girl. But as we discussed names, we became convinced we were having a daughter. Believing that, we settled on two names, the choice to be decided upon at birth. If our new daughter looked like a Stephanie, that would be her name. If she didn't, we would call her Jennifer. So it was that, shortly after 1 p.m. on Sunday, June 20, 1971, we were caught completely off guard when Audrey-Ann gave birth to a healthy boy.

What to call him? We hadn't found any boys' names we particularly liked. Maybe that is why we decided we were having a girl. At a time like this, it seemed only proper to turn to the family tree. We chose the names of his grandfathers, whom he would never know, but who we were sure would have been crazy about him. My father's name was Lincoln Newman. Audrey-Ann's father's name was William Taylor. A few days later, we took our son home and set off on a life with Lincoln Taylor Newman.

12

Moving to Washington

M Y FIRST EXPOSURE to American politics was unplanned. In early November 1952, I went to bed in Montreal and turned out the light, but put on my radio. In the fall and winter, I would dial in WMGM in New York and often, through the static, hear the play-by-play of a Rangers hockey broadcast from Madison Square Garden. But this was a Tuesday night, and there was no hockey game to hear. Instead, I found myself listening to the results of the U.S. presidential election. The Republican candidate, Dwight D. Eisenhower, was defeating the Democrat Adlai Stevenson. The Second World War hero was trouncing the former governor of Illinois. After twenty years, the Republicans were reclaiming the White House.

As he always did, my father came in to tell me it was time to turn off the radio. For a few minutes, he waited, listening to the election results. I remember asking him his opinion. He had met Eisenhower in London after the war, when he had gone there with the Royal Bank. That didn't make any difference, because I remember his answer:

"Things usually go better for Canada when the Democrats are in."

I didn't pay much attention to things political in the United States after that. I did get hooked on Canadian politics in the elections of 1957 and '58. Then, in the spring of 1960, with my job as copy boy at the *Winnipeg Tribune,* I suddenly woke up to American politics. The election of John F. Kennedy as president, the Bay of Pigs, the space program, civil rights—suddenly, the news all seemed to be coming from Washington, and the U.S. was the place to be. Watching Knowlton Nash report for the CBC each night from the U.S. capital made me feel I was watching someone with a charmed life and a window on history. He had the job I wanted.

As I worked my way up the ladder in Winnipeg, Regina, Toronto and Ottawa, the political scene soured in the United States. Vietnam and civil rights riots, as well as the assassination of not one but two Kennedys and of Martin Luther King all cast a pall on our southern neighbour. But Washington was the centre of the news universe, and being a correspondent there remained among my top ambitions.

I joined CTV's Ottawa bureau in April of 1971. Four months later, on August 15, President Richard Nixon announced that the United States dollar would no longer be convertible to gold at thirty-five dollars an ounce. More importantly to the rest of the world, he announced a ten-per-cent surcharge would be applied to all imports entering the United States. And unlike times previous, Canada would not be exempt from the surcharge.

The Canadian government immediately cried foul. Our economies were heavily intertwined, particularly since the signing of the Auto Pact in 1965—almost seventy per cent of our exports went to the United States. With the dollar recently unpegged from its set value of 92.5 cents U.S., and now at par or slightly higher, the import surcharge would price Canadian goods out of the U.S. market.

Nixon announced his dramatic steps on a Sunday. At work on Monday morning, I phoned the Finance Department to see what the government of Canada might be planning. A trip to Washington to appeal directly to Treasury Secretary John Connally was likely in the cards. A government plane would probably be laid on, and there would be room for some reporters. Since CTV had no Washington correspondent, without checking with either bureau chief Bruce Phillips or headquarters in Toronto, I put CTV on the list.

Three days later, I was on a Canadian government plane with cameraman Bert Plimer, five other reporters, Finance Minister Edgar Benson and his deputy, Simon Reisman. The flight from Ottawa to Washington was just under two hours. The plan was for Benson and Reisman to meet with Connally in the early afternoon, and then hold a press conference at the Canadian Embassy in Washington before flying back around dinnertime to Ottawa. That would leave me time to get from the Ottawa airport to CTV's Ottawa station, CJOH, process and edit our film and feed my Washington story from Ottawa into the *CTV National News.*

I filmed my closing on the steps of the Treasury Building, went to the press conference at the embassy, and got back on the plane to fly to Ottawa. And then we sat. Traffic was very heavy that day at National Airport in Washington, and thunderstorms were delaying takeoffs and landings. As we sat on the ground, it occurred to me that I would not get back to Ottawa in time to have my film edited and a voice track recorded and mixed with my standup at the Treasury Department to play at the end. I began writing, in longhand, a script I feared might have to be read from a studio desk—a poor substitute for a report filmed in Washington, but a report on a big story none the less.

As luck would have, it we were airborne in time, arrived in Ottawa and, after rushing to CJOH, I had my Washington-filmed story ready for air as the newscast was signing on. When Harvey Kirck read the introduction, everything ran smooth as silk. I sat in the editing suite, watching the story go out across the country. Up I popped, the Treasury Building behind me as I signed off: "Don Newman, CTV News, Washington."

I was hooked.

I DON'T KNOW if it was because I was from a banking family, or I just thought money was important, but I had taken an interest in economic stories from the beginning of my career. In fact, I had followed the example of my brother, who, when trying to get the attention of editors at *The Globe and Mail* while working in Winnipeg, had freelanced stories to the Report on Business section of the paper. That interest was paying off now. Neither of my colleagues in the CTV Ottawa bureau had the interest in or the background for business and economic reporting, so I had the surcharge story all to myself. Nixon's economic measures were due to receive a big international airing in Washington in the fall of 1971, at the annual meeting of the International Monetary Fund. CTV had never covered an IMF meeting before. I convinced them that this time was different, and that I should be the reporter.

The meetings were held the second week in October. The weather in Washington was perfect—still warm, but the oppressive heat of the summer had departed and the first leaves were just beginning to show a bit of colour. Audrey-Ann came with me and we stayed at the Washington Hilton on Connecticut Avenue, a couple of miles from the IMF meetings. We arrived on Saturday, two days before the meetings were to begin. As we were walking back to our hotel from dinner, we noticed a small crowd around the side door of the hotel. Two black limousines were parked at the curb. As we reached the door, we realized that the crowd was being held back by Secret Service agents and that the limousines were there for President Nixon and his security guard.

All this was pretty exciting for a young couple from Ottawa. We joined the crowd to wait for the president, and while we waited we learned that Mamie Eisenhower, the widow of former president Dwight Eisenhower, was celebrating her birthday at the hotel. Nixon was at the party and the comedian Red Skelton was the entertainment. It appeared that the president would leave the hotel by the door right next to where we were standing. But suddenly the limousines moved up about twenty feet, a small door in the hotel wall opened, and a Secret Service man stepped out. The crowd, which by now had grown to about fifty people, groaned. Nixon would not be right in front of us.

The Secret Service men kept the line of spectators where it had originally formed. They obviously knew the cars were going to move. I thought they seemed pleased at their little trick—that is, until the president emerged.

"Mr. President! Mr. President!" we all yelled from our places. Nixon looked over, smiled, and then, to rising cheers from the crowd, walked towards where we all were waiting. The Secret Service men were not amused.

"Shit," said one of them, looking over his shoulder as he saw the president approach.

Nixon worked his way down the line, shaking hands. I was surprised at how soft his hand seemed, particularly for a politician who must have shaken a million hands or more.

"We are from Canada," I told him as he shook hands with me and Audrey-Ann.

"Great country," he said. And then he was in the limousine and gone.

We went into the hotel and waited for the elevator, figuring there was nothing more that could happen that evening. But we were wrong.

The elevator stopped, the door opened and we got in to find, among our fellow passengers already on board, Mamie Eisenhower and Red Skelton. Wow! we thought. Just your average night out in Washington.

Ten years later, I was in Edmonton, sitting in front of a TV, watching the coverage of the attempted assassination of Ronald Reagan by John Hinckley. As the tape rolled, the camera was focused on a small door that suddenly opened and Reagan stepped out. I know that door, I said to myself; that's the door where Richard Nixon walked out in 1971.

The IMF meeting, and a second one I covered in early December at the Smithsonian Institution in Washington, eased the import surcharge crisis, and trade between Canada and the United States returned to its normal flows. But having successfully reported from Washington on three different occasions had whetted the appetite of CTV News for more firsthand Washington coverage. I came to realize that the story was not necessarily all that important. CTV's vice-president of news, Tom Gould, and other network executives liked the idea of having their own correspondent popping up in the American capital with the White House, the Capitol or some other iconic American symbol as the backdrop to a report.

In May, I was in the press gallery in Ottawa when I received a call from Gould. He wanted me to come to Toronto to see him. The next day, in his office, he told me that he wanted me to be CTV's first Washington correspondent, and that while the job would come with a decent raise for me, I would have to find a way to do the job on the cheap. The CTV network was then owned by its member stations, and it had not been a unanimous decision to set up a Washington bureau.

That was all right. I was ready to do it. The start date coincided with the beginning of the new television season in September. But then Pierre Trudeau decided the fall was a good time for an election campaign, and I was held back in Canada until the end of October. Still, I had time to find a nice house and hire a good cameraman to bring from Ottawa with me. At the beginning of November, Audrey-Ann, Linc and I arrived in Washington to begin what would be one of the most exciting and interesting times of our lives together.

13

CTV and Watergate

M Y MANDATE FROM CTV News was to cover Washington on the
cheap. With that in mind, I planned to rent a one-room office
in the National Press Building a few blocks from the White House,
like other Canadian correspondents in the city—other Canadian correspondents, that is, except the CBC, which had a suite of offices and
a radio studio on the fifth floor of the building. However, Tom Gould
took care of the office issue for me. Either because he wanted to keep
costs as low as possible, or he thought I needed an experienced mentor,
CTV's vice-president of news arranged for me to share an office with the
Washington correspondent for the *Montreal Star*.

Ray Heard at that time had been in Washington longer than any
other Canadian reporter. He turned out to be extremely nice about the
arrangement, probably more than I would have been if the circumstances
were reversed. The *Star* had a typical one-room office with two desks.
Heard was using only one and didn't seemed to mind that I moved into
the other. Rightly, he did object to camera equipment being scattered

around the room. So Ray Gravelle, the cameraman who came with me from Ottawa, kept his gear in his car, parked in a lot next to the Press Building. When we went out on a story, we either took the car or went to the car park, retrieved the camera and whatever else we needed from the trunk and took it with us.

I arrived in Washington just as Richard Nixon was scoring his mammoth re-election victory, carrying forty-nine of the fifty states against the Democratic candidate, Senator George McGovern. Part of Nixon's margin of victory owed itself to last-minute manoeuvring when he announced that American troops would be leaving Vietnam after a decade of being pinned down in that debilitating war in which more than 58,000 Americans gave their lives. What surprised me then was how little attention was paid during the election campaign to a break-in committed on June 17, 1972, five months before the election, at the headquarters of the Democratic Party in an office and hotel complex in Washington called Watergate. All five of the burglars arrested at the scene of the break-in had direct connections to the Republican campaign to re-elect Nixon. Somehow, the importance of what had happened seemed lost on most of the media and the public in general. People seemed to accept at face value the characterization of the break-in by White House press secretary Ron Ziegler that it was a "third-rate burglary."

However, shortly after Nixon was inaugurated for his second term on January 20, 1973, the wheels started coming off his presidency. The chief judge of the U.S. District Court for the District of Columbia, John Sirica, tried the five men arrested at the Watergate, and noting their connection to the White House and the president's re-election campaign, he suspected a conspiracy involving others. He imposed conditional sentences of up to forty years on each of the convicted five. The conditional sentences worked: in March 1973, one of the five burglars, a man named James McCord, wrote to Judge Sirica, admitting to the conspiracy.

The first cracks were appearing, and a house-of-cards defence by the president and his aides was starting to collapse. Suddenly, Jeb Stuart Magruder, who had worked in the White House and then been deputy director of the president's re-election campaign, was implicated and admitted that he had committed perjury. John Dean, the young lawyer who was White House counsel to the president, was also implicated and started co-operating with authorities. By the end of April, just three months into his second term, Nixon had lost his two top White House aides, Bob Haldeman and John Ehrlichman, to the scandal. Much of the story was uncovered by two reporters at the *Washington Post*, Bob Woodward and Carl Bernstein. Woodward had a high-level source he nicknamed Deep Throat who gave him leads on Watergate as well as other illegal activities and break-ins in which the Nixon administration had been involved. At the time, there was a lot of speculation as to identity of the source. Thirty-two years later, Deep Throat was revealed to be a man named Mark Felt, associate director of the FBI at the time of Watergate.

As the number of people implicated grew, the United States Senate voted to set up a special committee to investigate Watergate and all its implications. Nixon was a Republican and the Democratic Party controlled the Senate, but the vote to establish the investigating committee was unanimous. Chaired by a courtly Southern Democrat named Sam Ervin, the committee began televised hearings in May and continued until the end of the first week in August.

Before the Senate committee was up and running, Nixon had appointed a new attorney-general, Elliot Richardson, and given him the authority to appoint a lawyer outside of the Justice Department to investigate Watergate. Richardson named Harvard law professor Archibald Cox to the role of special prosecutor. Cox was working independently of the Senate committee, but within a few months their paths would intersect in a dramatic way.

When the Watergate hearings began in May, it was clear they were going to be a big, running story that would dominate the news from Washington. The system I had worked out with the CTV newsroom in Toronto was not going to be adequate for our continuing coverage.

Before the hearings began, I often filmed a report to camera about a story I was covering, talking for a minute and a half, or sometimes a little longer, with either the White House, the Capitol or a notable Washington building or monument behind me. Sometimes I would not record a full report, but just a closing to a story. We called that a "tail." Either way, Ray Gravelle, my cameraman, would put the film in a dark bag, put the bag in a film can, and then put the can into an onion bag clearly marked TV NEWS. We would then drive to National Airport, making sure to arrive no later than three-forty-five, take the bag containing the film to the Allegheny Airlines freight shed, and ship it on the five-thirty flight from Washington—via Erie, Pennsylvania—to Toronto. In Toronto, a messenger would clear the film through customs—we had already filled out the form in Washington—and take the film to CFTO, the CTV station just off Highway 401 in the east end of the city, where the *CTV National News* was prepared and broadcast.

If I had recorded a full standup report, my work for that day was usually over. But more often, I had just recorded a tail, which left me with more work to do. I would take the bus home, arriving in time to watch the *NBC Nightly News* with John Chancellor. CTV had a contract with NBC and used a lot of its foreign coverage. Once, that had included stories from Washington, but with me now there to provide the Canadian angle on what was happening in the American capital, most of those reports were not needed anymore. On the other hand, the pictures from the reports were. So I would watch the NBC newscast, paying special attention to the Washington stories, while in Toronto, the editors at CTV would be doing the same. When the *Nightly News* ended at 7 p.m., I would have a telephone conversation with the editor keeping tabs on Washington stories. We would agree on the pictures and sound clips from NBC that I wanted to use. I would then eat my dinner while the editor worked to put the pictures and sound bites together. Between eight and nine, he would call me at my home, giving me the amount of time between each sound clip and what the pictures between the audio were showing.

I would then write a few lines of script to go under the pictures and lead into the sound bites. In a glassed-in porch on the side of my house, I had installed a "broadband" telephone, a phone that made conversations clearer and louder. When my script was complete, I would call the Toronto newsroom on the broadband phone and they would record my voice reading my script. Then the pictures, my voice and the sound clips were all edited together, and the tail I had filmed and shipped earlier in the day was added to the end for a complete report that would play when the *CTV National News* went to air at 11 p.m.

This system worked so well that I was often on the air at least five nights a week. If it wasn't Watergate, it could very well be the fallout from the Yom Kippur War and the energy embargo of the United States by the OPEC cartel of oil-producing nations. As well as the news, I did interviews for *Canada AM.* That program was launched in the fall of 1972, just as I was leaving for Washington, and it had an independent budget and appetite for interviews and longer reports. As the news heated up and the budget grew, from time to time I would rent a studio at WTTG, an independent station in Washington, and videotape two or three interviews that I would later ship to Toronto for *Canada AM.*

All of that worked fine until the Senate Watergate hearings began. Without facilities and staff, the day-long hearings carried live over the U.S. networks on a rotating basis could not be managed and produced properly for CTV. Instead, as the hearings continued, I went to Toronto during the week, watched the hearings on a feed from Washington, and then edited the tape with a producer (Craig Oliver, who became a major on-air figure at CTV), and wrote a script for the news that evening. I did my reports live into the news from a desk in the same studio as the anchor, Harvey Kirck. I had never before been involved in the sort of complicated videotape editing the Watergate committee reports required or worked in a television studio next to the anchor of a newscast. It was both a great experience and a great story to be reporting.

The news signed off at 11:25. I was in a cab and back to my hotel so I could get some sleep before my wake-up call at five-thirty. That was so I could jump out of bed, shower and get back in a cab to return to CFTO. There, each morning from Tuesday through Friday, I did a Watergate segment on *Canada AM*. The first year CTV had a Washington correspondent they certainly got their money's worth, even if a lot of the work was done in Toronto.

The first two months of the Watergate committee were fascinating. Various witness told different stories of what had transpired. Clearly, not all could be telling the truth, but there was no definite answer to the questions that had been posed early on by Senator Howard Baker, a key member of the committee and, like Nixon, a Republican.

"What did the president know," Baker asked, referring to the break-in, "and when did he know it?"

Since Nixon was not going to be a witness at the hearings, it appeared there would never be a final answer—until, that is, one afternoon in mid-July when a heretofore-unknown assistant in the White House was called to testify.

His name was Alexander Butterfield. He was a lowly White House staffer. But on July 16, 1973, he blew the Watergate scandal wide open when he told the Senate committee there was an audio-taping system at the White House that automatically recorded everything said in the president's Oval Office, the Cabinet Room and Nixon's private office in the Old Executive Office Building next to the White House. With that revelation, it became clear that conversations previously referred to and sometimes denied were now all available on audio tape, and everyone wanted to hear them.

The Watergate scandal started because the burglars had used some electrical tape to hold open the locks on stairwell doors leading to the Democrats' offices. Now it was going to end because of audio tape that recorded Richard Nixon's conversations.

THE WATERGATE COMMITTEE adjourned in August, and I took a family holiday on Cape Cod. But when I returned after Labour Day, an even busier year was about to begin. Nixon had refused to release the White House recordings of his conversations. They were protected, he said, by executive privilege, which meant things said to the president and by the president were to remain confidential. Not everyone agreed that was the case if there was the possibility of criminal behaviour. One person who took that view was Special Watergate Prosecutor Archibald Cox. When Nixon refused to hand over the tapes, Cox issued a subpoena for them, and when he defied the president, Nixon ordered Attorney General Elliot Richardson to fire him. Rather than obey the president's order, Richardson resigned. When the order passed to his deputy, William Ruckelshaus resigned too rather than dismiss the special prosecutor. Finally, Solicitor General Robert Bork—who, because of the resignations, was now acting head of the Justice Department—fired Cox.

I had just arrived with Audrey-Ann at a Saturday night dinner party when our babysitter called our hosts to say that CTV in Toronto was trying to get in touch with me. When I called the newsroom, I heard the story of what was to be called the "Saturday Night Massacre" and raced home to see what I could pull together for the newscast that night.

In Toronto, they assembled file pictures of Cox, Richardson and Ruckelshaus, along with some relevant tape. I wrote out a script, and, using my broadband phone, we had a story from the Washington correspondent on that evening's newscast. I made it back to the dinner party thinking I would be a bit of an outcast. I was wrong. The hosts had saved my dinner and everyone sat around the table while I ate, listening as I also described the evening's events. To that point, it was my most successful Washington social event. It was the end of our first year in Washington, and while we had made some friends, we didn't go out all that much. But as luck would have it that third weekend in October 1973, we had dinner invitations both Saturday and Sunday evenings. On Sunday evening I again had work to do. Don Cameron, the director of CTV News, decided that a good portion of the airtime for the network's current-affairs magazine show, *W5*, would be turned over to the big Washington story. Working with the program's production team, we hired a studio at the NBC-owned station in Washington and booked conservative-leaning syndicated columnist Robert Novak and Congressman Jerome Waldie, a Democrat from California, to be my guests.

For fifteen minutes, I interviewed them live into the program in Toronto. It was powerful material. Nixon's firing of Cox had completely backfired, and people were angry. Waldie, who didn't like Nixon anyway, made some big news when he said in the interview that he was going to introduce a motion in the House of Representatives to impeach Nixon. It was the first time around Watergate that anyone had talked of doing this, it was told to a Canadian audience first, and of course, it turned out to be prophetic. All in all, the interview was a great success, and when I showed up late for the dinner party, it was a repeat of the evening before.

Americans sat around me while I, like a messenger from a faraway place, told them the latest about what was going on in their own country.

Canadians had already heard about it and Americans were to hear a lot about it later. Two days later, Waldie introduced his motion in the House of Representatives to impeach Nixon. Novak went on to relentlessly pursue Bob Haldeman, Nixon's chief of staff, for his involvement in Watergate.

Don Cameron had been a Washington producer for the CBC in the 1960s and had done a lot of programming from the U.S. capital. It was his idea to do the Sunday night segment with Waldie and Novak. On Monday, he told me it was the best coverage he had ever seen from Washington. He didn't clarify whether it was the best idea—which he thought up—or the best interviews, which I did. I imagine he probably thought the former. But we did it together on Canadian television.

A new special prosecutor was appointed on November 1. His name was Leon Jaworski and he too wanted to listen to the Nixon tapes. The president continued to fight their disclosure, but in April of 1974 he released heavily redacted transcripts of what he said was on the recordings. The most redacted parts were Nixon's cursing in his office conversations. "Expletive deleted" was the euphemism used in the transcripts, and that phrase appeared many times.

As this was unfolding, some of the people who had testified before the Senate committee were now charged with offences around Watergate and the re-election campaign. Jaworski argued before the Supreme Court for the release of the tapes.

It was clear that things were building to a head and that the summer of 1974 was going to be even busier than the year before. Audrey-Ann and I decided to rent a cottage on Cape Cod for the entire summer. I drove Linc and her there at the beginning of July, and then most weeks was either in Toronto or Washington, depending on the latest news and how we were getting it on the air. Weekends I would fly first to Boston, then board an old DC-3 with seascapes hung on the walls and fly to Hyannis Airport on Cape Cod, where Audrey-Ann would pick me up and drive us back to our cottage in Dennis Port.

Things reached a critical point in the last week of July of 1974. The House Judiciary Committee was holding impeachment hearings to remove Nixon from office when the Supreme Court ruled that the president would have to give up his White House tapes. Almost simultaneously with the committee voting to send the case for impeachment to the Senate for trial, Nixon gave up the tapes to Special Prosecutor Jaworski. Initially, the tapes confirmed that Nixon was aware of the break-in and the attempts, almost immediately after it happened, to cover up connections to the White House and Nixon's re-election campaign. But it was a tape that the White House reluctantly released six days later that sealed his fate. It was a recording of a conversation between Nixon and his chief of staff, Bob Haldeman, in which Nixon agreed the Central Intelligence Agency should be instructed to tell the FBI to stop investigating the Watergate break-in on grounds of national security. Even Nixon's diehard supporters and his lawyers had to agree it was a case of the president breaking the law and obstructing justice.

After that, it seemed almost inevitable that Nixon would resign or face certain impeachment and removal from office. Not entirely clear about was what was going to happen or when, I went to Toronto on the theory that whatever came next would be big news and we would have to organize it from our national newsroom.

Around midday on Thursday, August 8 came the word: President Nixon would go on TV that evening to announce his resignation effective the next day. That announcement set off the most unusual and interesting thirty-six hours of my life.

In the newsroom, Don Cameron decided we would do a full-scale production around the Nixon resignation speech, and I would be the only anchor. Beyond that, *Canada AM* would originate in Washington the next morning—only six and a half hours after we had signed off the *CTV National News*—and I would anchor that too. The network would charter a private plane to fly me from Toronto to Washington and then back to Toronto after *Canada AM* so that I would be available for follow-up stories the next day.

And that is what we did. Amazingly, it all worked. I had never anchored by myself a broadcast as complicated or important as the Nixon resignation, but I was concentrating too much to be nervous and the production team around me were flawless. I then did a recap with Harvey Kirck on the *CTV National News* and jumped in a car that took me to the airport, where a twin-engine, two-pilot aircraft was waiting to take me to Washington. I tried to close my eyes and get a little sleep, but I was too pumped up to drop off.

Arriving at Dulles Airport outside Washington around 3 a.m., I was met by cameraman Ray Gravelle, who drove me to his home not too far from the airport, where we had a couple of drinks. Then his wife got out of bed and made us both a huge breakfast of bacon and eggs and a big pot of strong, black coffee. Ray and I then left for WTTG-TV on Wisconsin Avenue, not too far from where I lived.

A crew of producers from *Canada AM* had come down to Washington the day before to line up the guests. I did the interviews, throwing back to the hosts in Toronto from time to time for weather and other news. The two hours flew by, and before I knew it we had signed off and I was back in Ray's car, heading for Dulles Airport and the flight back to Toronto. Once airborne, I tried to nap, but again the adrenalin was pounding and sleep would not come. Back on the ground at CFTO, the network was live on the air with Nixon's farewell to his White House staff.

Wally Macht had taken the program to air, but there was no camera crew on duty and he was sitting in a small announcer's booth usually reserved for station breaks but sometimes used for voice-over coverage when no cameras were available. Wally opened the door to the booth and hurriedly waved me in. We squeezed in together, watching Nixon's lament about Theodore Roosevelt and his last wave from the helicopter Marine One as he flew out of the White House as president for the last time.

Then it was time to prepare for that night's *CTV National*. I was starting to get punchy from lack of sleep, but as the hours approached the adrenalin picked up again. I decided against trying to recut all the day's tape and instead slightly adapted the story as edited for the CFTO supper-hour news. That gave me time to think of what I wanted to say in my script about what certainly was a day for the history books.

It was a Friday night in August. Harvey Kirck was on vacation. A young up-and-comer who would go on to have a big career, Keith Morrison, was reading the news for the first time. He didn't seem nervous, nor did the floor director, whose job it is to cue the on-air people to whichever camera they are supposed to speak to and to count down backwards with their fingers as time runs out on video items.

I had worked with the floor director before, but I noticed as he came into the studio that he was carrying a *Playboy* magazine. He sat on a stool between two cameras, one pointed at Morrison, the other at me. He cued Keith into the introduction of the news and Keith quickly came to me with the big resignation story. I introduced my long tape package on Nixon leaving the White House. After a couple of minutes, I looked at the floor director. He was sitting on his stool, *Playboy* magazine open, turned sideways so he could better study the centrefold.

Well, I thought, I might have been back and forth to Washington on a private plane and reported on history being made, but clearly not everyone was impressed.

14

Ford, McGovern and Ted Kennedy

W ITH RICHARD NIXON gone and Watergate for all intents and purposes over with, I had the same feeling I had first felt at the end
of the doctors' strike and the arrival of medicare in Saskatchewan—but
not for long. Unlike in Regina, in Washington there is always major news
and good stories to report, even if nothing is likely to top the first—and
only—resignation of a president.

There was a brief Watergate echo on Sunday, September 8, 1974,
when President Gerald Ford, who had succeeded Nixon from the
vice-presidency, suddenly and without warning appeared on television
to announce he had pardoned Nixon. At that point, Nixon was not
charged with anything, so the pardon had the double effect of both surprise and being pre-emptive. If Nixon was to have been charged with a
criminal offence—and there would have been pressure to charge him
with at least obstruction of justice—there was now no point. Ford had
made Nixon immune from prosecution.

The Ford pardon created a brief flap, but attention soon shifted to the November midterm elections for the House of Representatives and a third of the seats in the U.S. Senate. Presidents are elected every four years, and in succeeding Nixon in August, Ford would serve out the remainder of the term until the beginning of 1977. Members of the House of Representatives serve two-year terms, and all 435 seats in the House are up for election in years when the presidency is contested and again two years later. There are 100 senators, and their six-year terms are staggered; every two years, a third of the seats are up for election. The November 1974 midterms were to be held two years after Nixon's stunning forty-nine-state landslide victory and three months after his resignation in disgrace, and the fallout from Watergate could have a big impact.

I did a few stories about the likelihood of Democratic Party gains in the elections, but there was one race in particular that I found interesting. In the 1972 presidential election, the ultra-liberal, Vietnam War opponent George McGovern had managed to carry just one state against Nixon—not his home state of South Dakota, but the Kennedy stronghold of Massachusetts. In 1974, McGovern was running for re-election to the Senate from the state he had lost when contesting the presidency. To make things tougher, his Republican opponent in South Dakota was a former Vietnam prisoner of war named Leo Thorsness. It seemed to me that one way to tell the story of the midterm elections and the Watergate effect would be to cover McGovern's re-election bid. I convinced the producers at *W5*, CTV's current-affairs and documentary program, that I should do a longer piece on McGovern and I set off to shoot the story in October 1974.

McGovern was an affable and relaxed campaigner, partially because things had turned his way and he knew it. One reason Nixon had done so well two years before was because he announced just before election day that a drawdown of American troops in Vietnam would begin soon and American prisoners of war would be released. This was what McGovern had been campaigning on, and by 1974, it had happened. In fact, his opponent, Thorsness, was one of the released POWs. On top of that, of course, the man who had vanquished him in the presidential election was now disgraced and gone from office.

My crew and I travelled with McGovern for two days and Thorsness for one. Only once did I think something I was doing might affect the outcome of the election. At one small-town stop, a football was produced and the reporters and cameramen started tossing it around. It came to me, and McGovern clapped his hands, wanting me to throw it to him. It was just a couple of months after the Canadian general election campaign in which Robert Stanfield had dropped a football under similar circumstances while hanging around with reporters, and the pictures of him fumbling the ball were somehow seen as a metaphor for his campaign as he lost the election. Suddenly here I was, a Canadian, throwing the football to a high-profile U.S. politician while the news cameras from CTV as well as the American networks CBS and NBC were taping the toss.

I didn't want to be an influence on an American election, so I lobbed an underarm pitch to McGovern that any sixth-grader could catch. The watching crowd went "ooh" and laughed. McGovern laughed too, and then drilled the ball back at me as though he were the quarterback for the Chicago Bears. Okay, I thought, you started it, and fired it back at him. Back and forth it went for about six tosses until the campaign bus honked and we put the football away.

McGovern didn't drop the ball, and he didn't drop the election. In fact, in the wake of Watergate the Democrats won an additional forty-eight seats in the House of Representatives and four additional Senate seats.

...

It took two resignations to make Gerald Ford the president of the United States. Ford was the leader of the minority Republican Party in the House of Representatives in the fall of 1973, a role similar to but not as important as the leader of the Opposition in the House of Commons. But in the fall of 1973, Richard Nixon's vice-president, Spiro Agnew, found himself in deep trouble. He was accused of accepting bribes from construction companies for state highway contracts when he was the governor of Maryland before Nixon picked him as his running mate in 1968. To escape a jail term, Agnew agreed to resign as vice-president and plead no contest to the charges against him.

That meant Nixon had to find a new vice-president. Already the clouds of Watergate were beginning to gather, and he wanted someone who would not be controversial, but also someone who would not automatically seem to be presidential material and a good replacement if pressure mounted for Nixon to resign. Ford fit both those criteria. As leader of what was then the perpetual minority party in the House, Ford realized he had to go along to get along, something that fit naturally with his friendly personality. Beyond that, no one accused him of being too smart. In fact, a rather cruel joke about Ford among the few people who didn't like him was that, as a football player at the University of Michigan, he had played too many games without wearing a helmet.

Ford was easily confirmed by the Senate as Agnew's replacement. As is the case with most vice-presidents, he didn't attract much attention until suddenly, in the summer of 1974, Nixon resigned, putting the unlikely Ford into the Oval Office. When he was being questioned in the Senate before being confirmed as Agnew's replacement, Ford had said he would not run to be the Republican candidate for president in 1976, at the end of Nixon's term. Democrats and Republicans alike sought that pledge. A sitting vice-president seeking the presidency has a built-in advantage, particularly in seeking his own party's nomination. However, now that he was in fact president, Ford said that promise was no longer in effect, since he was no longer vice-president. In fact, Gerald Ford wanted to run for president in 1976, and he was making plans to do so.

Part of those plans included getting out and around the country, particularly to populous states like California. But in September of 1975, going to California almost cost Ford his life—not once, but twice. The first time was on September 5, when Ford was in the state capital of Sacramento, and a crazed woman follower of the mass murderer Charles Manson named Lynette "Squeaky" Fromme pulled a gun on the president as he walked past. The gun did not fire and the woman was apprehended. Less than three weeks later, on September 22, in San Francisco, a woman named Sarah Jane Moore pulled out a gun. She got a shot off, but someone in the crowd saw her draw the gun and hit her arm as she fired, causing her to miss.

Assassination attempts on the president are big news. I was in Washington when Fromme made her abortive attempt and was unable to report upon it—I didn't usually travel with the president. But as luck would have it, I was in San Francisco when Moore took her shot, and was the only Canadian reporter in the vicinity, which gave me a huge advantage.

I had gone to San Francisco almost a week earlier to cover the arrest of Patty Hearst, the newspaper heiress who had been kidnapped a year and a half before by a radical group of revolutionaries called the Symbionese Liberation Army. After a few months in captivity, she turned into one of its most fervent members, taking part in a bank robbery, another holdup and car thefts. It was a pretty captivating story—rich girl turned revolutionary—and her supporters and detractors were milling around each day outside the San Francisco courthouse and city hall after her arrest.

On the afternoon of the twenty-second, my crew and I left our hotel on Union Square to drive some film on the Hearst story to the airport for shipment to Canada. We were diverted around the square because of a crowd outside the St. Francis Hotel, across from where we were staying, that was waiting to see President Ford come out after speaking to a group of his supporters at lunch. We drove onto the freeway and started heading south towards the airport, listening to music on the car radio. Suddenly, the music was interrupted by a news bulletin. A shot had been fired at Ford as he emerged from the hotel. Secret Service agents had pushed him into his car and he was driven quickly away. His condition was unknown. I hit my turn signal and barely looked as I crossed four lanes of traffic to get to the next off-ramp. Leaving the freeway, I was in a part of San Francisco I had never seen before, with small homes and a few corner stores. I pulled up in front of a small corner store, went in, handed the person behind the counter a twenty-dollar bill and asked to use the phone for a long-distance call I would put on my credit card.

I called Toronto and, speaking to the editor on duty, told them I was in San Francisco and that a shot had been taken at President Ford. He didn't believe me, as nothing had yet moved on the news wires. I started to get annoyed, when suddenly the bells on the wire-service teletypes started ringing.

That evening, CTV was the only Canadian news service with first-hand reporting on the assassination attempt, and again the next morning on *Canada AM* when I got up at 4 a.m., because of the time difference, to talk about the experience with one of the program hosts. I received a lot of kudos from network colleagues, including both of my main bosses, Tom Gould and Don Cameron. Who says you don't have to be lucky to be good?

...

WHEN I WENT to Washington, national medicare in Canada was still in its infancy. It was so new that hardly anyone in the United States knew it existed. One person who didn't was Senator Edward Kennedy, which was unusual because, even in the mid-1970s, Kennedy was pushing for a public health insurance program to cover all Americans. Kennedy was using the National Health Service in the United Kingdom as an example of the kind of health care he wanted. All of the usual opponents, like the American Medical Association and the big insurance companies, were in full fight against him, and there were many parts of the British NHS that made it easy to oppose him.

One evening at a dinner party, I sat across from a man who worked in Senator Kennedy's office on the heath care file. I asked him why Kennedy and his team weren't using Canadian medicare as a better model for public health insurance in the United States, since it was run by the provinces but basically functioned like a private health plan that covered everyone. He said they weren't doing that because he didn't know what I was talking about and neither did the senator, and he wanted me to tell him more. I told him I would get back to him, but in the next few days a great opportunity arose that I couldn't have planned for.

When I first went to Washington, a nice red-haired woman named Mary McLaughlin was a producer at *Canada AM,* and we had worked together a number of times on interviews I had done for the program. After the 1974 Canadian election, she left the network and went to work for Marc Lalonde, the Liberal cabinet minister whom Prime Minister Trudeau had recently made minister of health. On the phone Mary told me Lalonde was coming to speak at a conference in Washington, but would have some extra time. Was there anyone interesting he might have a meeting with?

"Well," I said, "if I can get him a meeting with Senator Edward Kennedy to talk about Canadian medicare, would that be interesting enough?"

"Wow! You bet," Mary said.

I didn't know how this was going to work. Lalonde had only so much time on a certain day and Kennedy was a very busy senator. Still, I called my new contact in the senator's office and said I could get him an exclusive briefing on Canadian health care from the federal minister of health, but it would have to be at a very specific time. Furthermore, I said, there was another condition: after the meeting, Kennedy would have to give me an exclusive interview without the Canadian minister present.

With those conditions, I wasn't sure how things would work out. However, within hours, I got a call back. The senator had agreed and would be available. Then I called Mary. She was excited and said she had told Lalonde what I was trying to do and he was excited too.

On the appointed day and time, I had my camera crew set up outside Senator Kennedy's office. Down the hall, escorted by a security guard, came Lalonde and Mary. They were met by my contact in the senator's office and disappeared inside for the meeting. After about forty minutes, the office door opened and out stepped both the minister and the senator. I was the only reporter around and Lalonde greeted me warmly. As he and Kennedy stood together, I asked each of them questions about their meeting, and not surprisingly, each was very complimentary to the other. Then they shook hands. Marc Lalonde and Mary McLaughlin said goodbye and walked away down the hall, and Kennedy disappeared into his office.

With that, I wondered if the deal for the exclusive interview with Kennedy might fall through. I needn't have worried. Before I could go and knock on his office door, Kennedy came back out.

"I hear we are to have our own interview," he said.

Ray Gravelle rolled the camera and gave me the cue.

"Senator Kennedy," I said, "a lot of Canadians wonder how a rich,

Welcome to the Broadcast

powerful and important country like the United States does not have a public health insurance plan for all of its citizens."

As Kennedy heard the question, he started to smile. "Well, Mr. Newman," he responded in the accent he and his brothers had made famous, "a lot of Americans wonder about that too."

That evening, the *CTV National News* ran clips of Marc Lalonde and Ted Kennedy after their meeting on Canadian health care. The next morning, *Canada AM* played the film of my interview with Kennedy saying he would now use the Canadian health-care model to try and convince Americans to adopt a public health-care plan.

Dinner parties and old friends can be a good way to cover the news.

15

Carter and Reagan

WHILE I WAS busy covering the unfolding Watergate scandal in the spring and summer of 1974, two events occurred that would play a big part in the next chapter of American history—and of my career. The results of the 1972 presidential election had been so devastating to the Democratic Party that it decided it couldn't wait four years to try and rally supporters. Two years after its crushing defeat, the party held what is called a midterm convention in Kansas City. All of the party luminaries showed up—big names like former vice-president Hubert Humphrey, the presidential candidate who narrowly lost to Richard Nixon in 1968; Ed Muskie, senator from Maine, Humphrey's vice-presidential running mate and unsuccessful candidate against George McGovern for the Democratic presidential nomination in 1972; and a host of others from the Senate who hoped to be the party's candidate for president in 1976.

In Kansas City, there was a large built-up platform for television cameras in the centre of the convention floor. The main American networks had full-time fixed positions for their cameras, but the other news organizations, like CTV, were allotted spaces for fixed periods of time and then had to vacate the platform and give way to others. One evening during the weekend meeting, we had just finished filming and taking our gear from the platform when, on the convention floor, I was approached by a pleasant-looking man I had never seen before.

"Hello," he said, "would you like to meet Governor Jimmy Carter of Georgia?"

I had never heard of Governor Carter, but I said sure, why not. Carter's press secretary, Jody Powell, took me around the camera platform and introduced me to a rather short man wearing a grey suit, with a shaggy head of grey hair and a big grin that made him resemble a cross between Howdy Doody (the puppet) and Alfred E. Neuman (the *MAD Magazine* figure).

"Hello," he said holding out his hand, "I'm Jimmy Carter and I'm running for president."

It all seemed rather incongruous. Here was this man, standing by himself in the middle of about 1,400 members of the Democratic Party, claiming he would be their candidate for president in about two years' time.

"What do you think your chances are?" I asked.

"Pretty good," was his reply.

Luckily, at that moment Powell arrived with another unsuspecting person to meet the governor. I wished Carter good luck and beat my retreat. The next time I saw Carter was about a year and a half later. He and Powell would still be trying to meet people, but they would be a lot further down the campaign trail than I could have guessed was possible, with a lot further still to go.

...

WHEN SENATOR BARRY GOLDWATER was running as the Republican candidate for president against Lyndon Johnson in 1964, late in his flagging campaign his party bought national television time for a speech in support of him by a movie and television actor named Ronald Reagan.

Reagan had begun his political life as a New Deal Democrat supporting President Franklin Roosevelt. But in the 1950s, after marrying his second wife, an aspiring actress named Nancy Davis, he adopted the conservative views of her father, a doctor, and emerged as a prominent spokesman warning of a Communist menace in the United States. He was embraced by the right wing of the Republican Party, and trailing badly in the 1964 election, they summoned him to try and give Goldwater a boost.

His speech attracted a lot of attention. It didn't do anything for Goldwater, who went down to humiliating defeat, but it did a lot for Reagan. Two years later, he ran as the Republican candidate for governor of California and won. He flirted with running for president in 1968, but Richard Nixon had a lock on the nomination, so he ran for re-election in California in 1970 and won easily. Now, in 1973, his second term was coming to an end and re-election seemed likely. But Reagan said two terms were enough and he would not try for the governorship again. Everyone who followed politics knew why: with Nixon unable to run again, the Republican presidential nomination for president would be open in 1976 and Ronald Reagan meant to win it.

There is a smart-alecky saying in Washington that politics is show business for ugly people. Since the arrival of television and Jack Kennedy, that had been less true, but the arrival of former actor Ronald Reagan stood the saying on its head. A movie actor in the 1940s and '50s, and on television in the '50s and '60s, he was a combination of show business and politics, with the looks for the former and the glib responses and ability to simplify complicated topics for the latter. Still, his detractors were many, even in the Republican Party.

"With Ronald Reagan, if you strip away the glossy sheen, what do you get?" went one put-down. "Glossy sheen."

Nixon's resignation and Ford's elevation to the presidency didn't change anything for Reagan. Although Ford now wanted the Republican nomination in 1976—and as the incumbent president would seem to have a big advantage—until the double resignations that took him to the Oval Office, nobody, including Ford himself, had ever thought of him as a presidential candidate and he was unknown as a national campaigner. Reagan still had to combat charges he was "just an actor," but he had twice been elected governor of the largest state in the country and was a formidable campaigner. Besides, now in his mid-sixties, time was running out on Reagan's presidential ambitions.

The first time I saw Ronald Reagan in person, he was on a stage at the National Press Club in Washington. He had come to the capital to declare that he was running for president. He looked just as he did on television. He appeared younger than his age, partly because he had thick hair with little apparent grey in it. His performance was smooth, and he said his campaign would follow "the eleventh commandment": Speak no evil of any fellow Republican. I wasn't the only reporter at his news conference who wondered how he would manage to do that when he was challenging a president from his own party to win the presidential nomination.

16

U.S. Election '76

Tʜᴇ ɴᴇxᴛ ᴛɪᴍᴇ I saw Jimmy Carter after that first meeting in Kansas City, he was standing beside a large van in snowy New Hampshire in January of 1976. His aide, Jody Powell, was standing with him. They were waiting for me, my cameraman, Ray Gravelle, and Joanna Tsoukatos, an American I'd hired in mid-1975 to be our sound person as we set out to cover the presidential election.

Powell knew we were joining the governor's campaign. I had laid out a careful four days in New Hampshire, covering not only Carter but also Congressman Morris Udall from Arizona, Senator Birch Bayh from Indiana, former senator Fred Harris from Oklahoma, and a Kennedy relative and former vice-presidential candidate, Sargent Shriver. New Hampshire is a small state that holds the first presidential primary, and with only one city and two other urban areas, covering that number of candidates wasn't all that difficult.

Carter and Powell didn't remember our brief meeting in Kansas

City, but they were hoping for more than just a Canadian television crew to cover the governor that day.

"Where did you say you are from?" Powell asked.

"Canada," I said. "CTV."

"Too bad you're not CBS," was his reply.

Still, Powell was amiable and Carter approachable as we drove through the snow and woods to small towns and villages where people supporting him would host groups of neighbours in their homes while Carter gave them his pitch. After two days of following him and the other Democratic candidates around the state, I thought he had made as good an impression on me as anyone else, and that also seemed to be the case with the Democratic Party members he was wooing to vote for him in the primary.

The person who was the biggest disappointment was Sargent Shriver. He was a Kennedy brother-in-law, married to Eunice, sister of John, Robert and Edward. President Kennedy had made him the first head of the Peace Corps, and he had been George McGovern's replacement running mate in 1972, after first choice Thomas Eagleton was dropped from the ticket after admitting to health problems.

Shriver didn't seem to have his heart in this campaign. Perhaps he was just too patrician to do retail politics in a state where most Democrats are blue-collar union members. A joke that ran through the press corps seemed to sum up his problem.

"Shriver goes into a blue-collar bar in the east end of Manchester, the only city in New Hampshire. 'Beer for everyone,' he calls out as the patrons look up. 'Oh, and I'll have a Courvoisier.'"

Carter was a born-again Christian who didn't drink or go to bars. But he worked hard and campaigned cheerfully, portraying himself as the Washington outsider he was and just the person the country needed after the Watergate scandal. His problem was that, as a native Georgian and former governor of the state, he was clearly a politician from the Deep South, something he had to combat in New Hampshire and elsewhere.

One day, travelling on the campaign, I commented to a correspondent from the *Detroit Free Press,* "Some people don't seem to trust Southerners."

"Yes," he replied. "They are called Northerners."

But in a crowded New Hampshire field, it turned out that enough Northerners did trust Carter. On primary night, February 24, he won just over 28 percent of the Democratic Party's votes, enough to give him victory in a field where six other candidates also collected varying degrees of support. It wasn't by much, but it was a win, and the man from Georgia was on his way.

If THE FIELD of Democratic presidential hopefuls was crowded, the Republican Party race was just the opposite. Early on in the Democratic race, candidates like Carter moved around with one or two aides and a small group of reporters trailing them. If you wanted to cover them, you made your own arrangements and kept up as best as you could.

As the unexpected, unelected president, Gerald Ford decided the best way he could keep his job was to be seen doing it. In the first half of 1976, Ford rarely left the White House, and when he did, it was on presidential business where he could be seen being president. When he did travel, it was on Air Force One, the presidential jet. The White House press corps travelled with him en masse.

However, any hope that he would be unchallenged for the Republican nomination had been dashed by Ronald Reagan's announcement he was running. And as the campaign began, the Reagan strategy was the opposite of Ford's. Reagan was everywhere, showing off his good looks, camera-ready style and campaign skills he had honed serving two terms as California governor. And because there were just two Republican candidates, and one of them was in the White House with the reporters there, the Reagan campaign attracted a big media following from the beginning.

This was obvious to me when the crew and I joined the former California governor's campaign for the first time in Florida, which held its primary two weeks after New Hampshire. We arrived in Fort Lauderdale and were told to report the next morning to a hotel where the candidate, his campaign staff and the press were staying, and to bring our bags with us. Doing as we were told, when we showed up and identified ourselves we were given press badges, our names were checked off a list and we were told to board the bus, which was almost full with other journalists. The bus followed Reagan around to a couple of stops in the Fort Lauderdale area before heading for the airport, where we boarded Reagan's chartered plane and flew from sunny Florida back to the snows of New Hampshire and the airport at Manchester. There, two more buses were waiting: one for the candidate and his top aides, the other for the travelling press. It was all very much like a party leader's tour on a Canadian federal election campaign.

Right from the start, Ronald Reagan was a big deal. As we travelled between some of the campaign stops, a couple of reporters and a camera crew would be permitted on Reagan's bus. You could not interview him on tape, but you could get pictures of him travelling and the reporters could talk with him on an off-the-record basis. Although I had just joined the campaign, I asked for access to the candidate's bus, and perhaps because most of the other reporters travelling with Reagan had already had their chat or didn't want to talk off the record, on the second day I was told the crew and I could ride with him for one stop. So as the crew shot from a comfortable distance, I chatted with Reagan.

I asked him how he could campaign against Ford and maintain his eleventh commandment of not saying anything critical about another Republican. He wasn't criticizing Ford personally, he said, he was just describing different policy choices he would make if he were president.

There was no doubt those policy choices were more right wing than Ford's, or any others suggested in much of America. Still, our brief chat left me with the idea that Reagan was certainly as sharp as the Democrats, including Carter, whom I had been travelling with, and in his campaign appearances at places like Dartmouth University and scrums with his large travelling press contingent, he was certainly getting a tougher workout that any of the Democrats campaigning in New Hampshire.

Reagan fought Ford for the Republican nomination before losing on the floor of the party convention in Kansas City. Ford chose Senator Bob Dole as his running mate. Carter clinched the Democratic nomination in the primaries. At the party's convention in New York he chose Senator Walter Mondale as his candidate for vice-president. I was pleased; we had mutual friends in Washington. Mondale and I are godfathers to twin brothers. And I had predicted he would be Carter's running mate.

17

Time for a Change

THE DEMOCRATS AND Republicans had their plans ready for the fall election campaign in the summer of 1976. I didn't. And my uncertainty went back to a telephone call I had received three years earlier.

In the summer of 1973, a man named Denny Harvey phoned me. I did not know him, but I knew of him. He had been at the Montreal *Gazette* and the editor of *Weekend* magazine, and in early 1973 he had been named the new chief news editor of the CBC. That meant he was in charge of all television news on the network. He had been recruited from outside to bring order out of the apparent internal chaos that had somehow afflicted CBC television news at that time.

Harvey told me he liked my reporting from Washington on CTV. But what he really had liked was my reporting from Ottawa when I was with *The Globe and Mail*. As a newspaper person himself, he was clearly partial to people with the same background. Now, though, we were both in broadcasting and he wanted me to leave the CTV bureau I had opened ten months before and join the CBC bureau instead. He had a plan for me and the current CBC television correspondent, Don McNeill. Together we would share the radio and television reporting duties for the CBC in Washington. The current radio correspondent, a pleasant fellow named Colin Godbold, was scheduled for reassignment and would be leaving soon.

I told Harvey it was nice to be considered, but there were two great obstacles. The first was that, having been selected CTV's first Washington correspondent, I would consider it inappropriate to leave after one year and join the main competitor I had been sent to take on. I said I would not consider any new jobs until I had been in Washington for one complete election cycle unless something went wrong with my relationship with CTV. That meant I wasn't moving until after the 1976 presidential election. Then, thinking ahead to some future possibility, I said I would likely consider only television positions at some future date. I didn't want to do radio. I was polite to Harvey and privately pleased by the offer. If the CBC was trying to hire me away, it must mean my reporting was having some impact on them.

The following March, I had another opportunity to move, although this time within the CTV network. I can't remember the story I was working on, but it must have been a big deal, because I was at the NBC station in Washington, preparing to feed a story to Toronto for that evening's newscast. The event was important enough that the network was spending money to actually send a complete story instead of the usual NBC pictures with my commentary over my broadband telephone. I remember it, too, because of the odd timing of the call, at about 9 p.m.

I was working on the story and the call came from Don Cameron, who was the number-two man behind Tom Gould in the CTV News operation. He told me the job of London correspondent had come open, and before everyone else in the news service descended on him the next day asking for the job, he wanted me to know that if I would like it, the job was mine. In the middle of Watergate, just a year and a half in Washington and having already lived in London, I thanked him and said no. Ironically, five years later, at CBC, I would give the same response to a London move.

After talking with Denny Harvey in 1973 and setting my sights on waiting until after the 1976 presidential election before I would consider a move, I found a strange psychology developing. I was certainly staying put until the presidential election, but what was I going to do after that? CTV was happy with the way the United States was being covered, and I could continue to do that indefinitely. But nothing lasts forever, and it is better to have a plan as to what you want to do next than to have the fates one day decide. Besides, from sharing an office with the *Montreal Star* to having a two-room office in the National Press Building, with a full-time sound person and office manager and a much better travel budget, I realized that I had probably taken CTV's Washington presence as far as I could.

To help keep it fresh for me, Cameron had also offered me a part-time position as host of *W5,* the network's newsmagazine program, and I would from time to time go to Toronto for a week as one of the hosts on *Canada AM.* But my sense of the limits of how far CTV could go was underlined as we planned our coverage of the Democratic and Republican nominating conventions. As before, starting with Watergate, for big, expensive events I would go to Toronto and either report or host the network coverage from the studios at CFTO. I wouldn't be on the floor, mingling with the delegates, scrumming the candidates with my crew, enjoying all of the different pleasures that come with covering a political convention.

My situation was underlined one afternoon as I was having a beer in the National Press Club with John Picton, the correspondent for *The Globe and Mail.*

"Where are you staying in New York?" he asked me, referring to the site of the Democratic National Convention.

"Actually, I am staying in Toronto, where I'm covering it from to save CTV money," I told him.

"Oh," Picton said with a twinkle in his eye, "and when the Republicans are in Kansas City, will you be going to Winnipeg?"

The remark was amusing, but it wasn't that funny to me. And it underlined a problem that was probably going to continue as long as I was at CTV. Still, I liked the network, liked the people I worked with, was well treated and it felt like home. But as most young people come to realize, there comes a time when you have to leave home if you are going to grow, and in the summer of 1976 I was wondering if that time might have come.

Before the conventions began, Queen Elizabeth and Prince Philip came to the United States on their way to the Summer Olympics in Montreal. I covered part of their tour, and the CBC had sent down the anchor of *The National*, Lloyd Robertson, to do live broadcasts. I had not met Lloyd before, but of course I knew him from TV, as he did me. One evening in Philadelphia, we sat at the same table in a restaurant, along with Larry Stout of the CBC, enjoying dinner and a glass of wine. To me, Lloyd seemed the epitome of the CBC and the big-money special coverage the Corporation was able to produce.

A week later, I was in my office, gathering files to take with me to Toronto for the Democratic convention, when the phone rang. It was a man named Mike Daigneault. Denny Harvey had moved up the CBC ladder and was now the head of English broadcasting, and Daigneault, who had come from the *Gazette* with Harvey, had succeeded his patron as the chief news editor.

"Denny told me to call you. He says you may be interested in making a move."

I was flattered that Harvey had remembered our conversation three years earlier. I had thought that, with his climb up the ladder to a top job at the CBC, he would have forgotten. In fact, I had assumed that he would.

"We had that conversation three years ago," I told Daigneault, "and the three years are almost up."

Since I was coming to Toronto the next week, he agreed we would meet privately—away from both the CBC and CTV—to see if we had things we wished to explore. And when we did—the following week, in the lounge at the Westbury Hotel—I was surprised at Daigneault's suggestion.

"I am beefing up our Ottawa bureau. I am going to appoint a chief political correspondent, which we haven't had for a couple of years, and Denny and I agree that with your *Globe and Mail* experience in Ottawa and now your television experience, you would be great for that job."

I was surprised. Three years before, the conversation had been about staying in Washington, and I had assumed that would be the topic of this meeting. So I made it the topic.

"That would be a great offer if I wanted to return to Ottawa, but I think I have Washington figured out pretty well for a Canadian reporter and I want to stay there for a few more years," I told him.

I wasn't sure if my answer meant the end of my possibly working for the CBC. We talked for a few minutes about the American election and what it took to cover Washington well, and then the conversation drifted off to other topics, including how much we enjoyed playing tennis. I had my right foot in a cast at the time, having broken it a couple a weeks earlier when I slipped and went right over on my foot while playing a game on a damp court early in the morning at Georgetown University. For many of my friends, like my tennis partner Val Sears from the *Toronto Star*, breaking a foot in a non-contact game like tennis was pretty funny. It wasn't funny to me. I had heard it snap as I went over. If Daignault thought it funny, he was kind enough not to let on. After about half an hour, he wound up the meeting.

"Give me a couple of weeks," he said. "I will put together an offer for you to be our Washington correspondent."

"Fine," I said, without committing to anything. "I'll be looking for it."

I had mentioned my meeting with Daigneault to Audrey-Ann, but to nobody else. Certainly to no one at CTV. Because of the two political conventions, I ended up staying in Toronto a lot of the summer, hosting *Canada AM*. Audrey-Ann and Linc came up to be with me. Linc stayed with Audrey-Ann's sister Barbara and her husband a lot of the time, but CTV had put us up in a small suite at the Plaza II Hotel on Bloor Street and we made good use of the pool and the room service. Our coverage of the political conventions in New York and Kansas City was adequate, given that I was reporting from Toronto.

What really was working that summer was *Canada AM*. During the time I was on the program, it was gathering some of its biggest ratings ever, even though we were in the depth of summer. Around the network, people were in a very happy mood. I was, too, although I was also wondering when I would hear from Mike Daigneault.

I was back in Washington when I received a letter from him spelling out an offer—salary, benefits and everything else I needed to know. It was a good offer, not a blockbuster, and probably something I could have had CTV match if I tried. But the real attraction was going to a bigger network, with more opportunities and other possibilities for different jobs and responsibilities down the road, as well as in the short term with more facilities for covering Washington. I told Audrey-Ann about the offer, and we thought about it for a few days before I called Daigneault and told him I accepted on one condition: I still felt honour bound to stay with CTV through the presidential election campaign and could not join the CBC until after that, and wanted there to be no announcement of my move until the election as over. Daigneault had hoped that I would be covering the election for the CBC, but he agreed to my condition. Then came the tougher part. I called Don Cameron and told him that I would cover Washington through to election night, but after that I was leaving CTV.

"Where are you going?" he asked. "CBS, NBC?"

"You won't like this," I said. "I'm going to the CBC."

"I don't like it," Cameron said, "but neither will you."

Two weeks later came the blockbuster news that Lloyd Robertson was leaving the CBC to go to CTV. He said his reporting aspirations were being thwarted by the journalists' union at the CBC and management there was unwilling to fight for him to do reports from the field. Suddenly, I was getting calls from CTV. Andrew Cochrane, the producer of *Canada AM* and a man I liked, suggested that with Robertson coming to CTV, I might like to stay. I couldn't see what that had to do with me, although it certainly had a lot to do with Harvey Kirck, who had been reading the news alone and would now have to share the job with Lloyd. Come to Toronto and talk to Don Cameron, Cochrane said. He wants to see you.

So I did. Having given my word on taking a job with the CBC, I was uncomfortable with the idea of going back on it without any good personal reason. I met with Cameron, who predicted that with Robertson at CTV, the network would forge ahead and the CBC would be crippled, so I should stay and be a part of the brave new day. While I liked Lloyd and knew he had a following, it was obvious that at a network the size of the CBC there were a lot of people who could read the news. I didn't see how Cameron's prediction was going to come to pass. And neither, apparently, did the CTV board of directors.

When Tom Gould announced that Robertson was moving networks, he claimed a great coup for CTV. In addition to the new anchor, he said that CTV would expand its twenty-minute newscast to half an hour so that its two-man anchor desk of Robertson and Kirck would have more airtime and viewers would have more news. When the proposal for an expanded newscast went to the CTV board two months after Lloyd joined the company, the board turned the proposal down. Tom Gould, the man who had brought Lloyd Robertson to CTV, resigned. Lloyd stayed on for another thirty-one years.

I worked directly with Lloyd after his arrival. It was my last broadcast for CTV—American election night, November 2, 1976. The program originated at the CFTO studio in Toronto. The network had flown in Frank Mankiewicz, who had been Bobby Kennedy's press secretary, as a Democratic Party commentator, and Pat Buchanan, who had written speeches for Richard Nixon, to do the same for the Republicans. Lloyd and I worked well together. The returns were late coming in, and the race was close. We were on the air until 4 a.m., when Carter was elected president. After the sign-off, I got up from my chair and walked around the set and the newsroom, shaking hands. Then I put on my coat, waved a last goodbye and walked out the door.

18

Moving to CBC Washington

I HAD BEEN WARNED, and it was true: nothing was simple at the CBC.

I joined the "Corp," as it is known to its employees, on November 8, 1976, the Monday after the U.S. election that made Jimmy Carter president. I joined the network at the national newsroom in Toronto rather than the Washington bureau. I had briefly worked for the CBC in Winnipeg, but hadn't liked it. Now I was back and about to have one of the top jobs in the television news organization. Spending some time at the centre of the system, learning at least a few of the ropes, made sense. But what didn't make sense was that although I had already been given the job as television correspondent in Washington, I was now coming to Toronto to apply for the job.

That's right: apply for a job I had already been given and had a letter of confirmation setting out the terms and conditions of my employment. I had to apply from within the CBC because that was the way the union rules worked. To make sure the union couldn't grieve my appointment, I had to join the CBC at a lower level, become a union member and then apply for the Washington assignment. So I came into the CBC at the lowest end of the pay scale, as a writer on the desk at *The National.*

I also had a contract called an "ad rem" (short for additional remuneration) that boosted my monthly income up to the level for the Washington job. It was perhaps the largest ad rem contract ever given out at CBC News, and probably the only one ever given to someone at the bottom of the pay scale. Beyond that, the CBC had agreed to fly me back to Washington on my days off, so hiring me was costing a fair bit of upfront money. This was necessary to make sure the job was given to a union member already working at the CBC. If I had just gone to work in the Washington bureau, the union would have grieved that its members had not been given a chance to apply for the job. And since that was true, it was very likely that the grievance would have been upheld. So a month in Toronto, living at the Four Seasons—then a motel across the street from the CBC on Jarvis Street—was a relatively small price to pay for the chance to be the CBC's Washington correspondent.

It also gave me the chance to meet the people in Toronto I would be working with—mainly over the phone—from Washington. Two in particular stand out to this day: Tony Burman, who was the lineup editor on *The National* in 1976 and went on to become the chief news editor and then head of all news and current affairs at the Corporation; and John Owen, who joined the CBC the same day I did as a writer on *The National.* John came from the United States, where he had been working at a public broadcasting station in Milwaukee. He had come to Canada to work for a "real" public broadcaster like the CBC. John became the foreign editor, the producer of *The National,* the chief news editor and finally the London bureau chief before leaving the CBC to do other journalism in London. Like Tony, he is as smart and as funny as he was in 1976, and both of them remain friends. Tony also left the CBC, moved to the Middle East with Al Jazeera, and is now living in Toronto, so it is not difficult to keep up. Every time I'm in London, I make sure to look John up.

The executive producer of *The National* was Trina McQueen, the first woman to have that job. It turned out to be just one step up the ladder. Trina went on to become a CBC vice-president before leaving the Corporation to embark on an equally successful career at CTV. And the new anchor of *The National* was Peter Kent, with whom I had worked at CTV. Right after he took over in the anchor chair, the Parti Québécois scored its first surprising victory in the provincial election in Quebec, and René Lévesque was about to be premier. Everyone was caught flat-footed. The CBC decided it would have to air a special program the next evening, and part of that broadcast would include reaction from Washington, where the CBC had no correspondent—the correspondent in waiting was a Group Five writer in the national newsroom who had yet to be formally appointed to the job. Suddenly, that Group Five writer was on a plane to Washington and into the CBC bureau.

I pulled together a report on Washington reaction as best I could. But it wasn't easy. I had never worked with the CBC's Washington people, and some of them still saw me as a competitor and rival. Beyond that, there wasn't much Washington reaction—mainly surprise. And finally, we had to feed the story out of CBS's Washington bureau. Over the next few years, I would get to know that bureau and the people there very well. But that evening, I didn't know them and they didn't know me. It was a baptism by fire, but we got a report together and made our deadline and the program.

After that excitement, it was back to the national newsroom, where I took my turn writing copy and editing tape. It was good practice; I had done it before, particularly during my reporting on Watergate, but it wasn't something correspondents in the field usually did. After two weeks, rotating five days in Toronto and two in Washington, the job of

Washington correspondent was posted according to the union rules. I applied for it. I don't know if anyone else did, but a few days after applications closed two weeks later, I was duly appointed. By then, it was almost Christmas. Full-scale reporting from Washington didn't resume until January of 1977.

But once it did, there was a lot to report. Jimmy Carter was inaugurated as president on January 20, with Walter Mondale as his vice-president. Shortly after that, Lévesque came to New York as premier of Quebec and made a speech touting separatism at the Economic Club. The speech was sponsored by the First Boston Group, which was selling Quebec government bonds for the PQ in the New York market. I covered Lévesque's speech and did an interview with a managing director at First Boston. An American who knew nothing about Canada, he talked airily of an independent Quebec in a few years. As we were leaving his office, I pointed out that he was in the same position as someone selling Confederate Bonds during the American Civil War. He suddenly got very rude and arrogant. Then I laughed.

The federal government wanted to counter Lévesque's American foray. Prime Minister Trudeau's director of communications was a man named Richard O'Hagan. I had first met Dick when I worked in Regina and he worked for Lester Pearson, who was then the federal Opposition leader. We had been in touch when he was with still with Pearson in the Prime Minister's Office, but really got to know each other when I moved to Washington and he was the minister counsellor for information in the Canadian embassy. He knew everyone in Washington, and was generous with introductions. He and his wife, Wanda, were two of the most popular people in official Washington—not easy for a Canadian, particularly one who was not an ambassador. To make the circle even smaller, one of the O'Hagans' daughters went to Beauvoir School in the same grade as our son, Linc. The O'Hagans went back to Ottawa and back into the

Prime Minister's Office to help Trudeau win his majority in 1974, but they'd kept up their Washington contacts.

One of the people that O'Hagan knew well—better than me, certainly—was Mondale. Now that "Fritz" was vice-president, he was also the president of the U.S. Senate. Through him, O'Hagan and the embassy arranged for Trudeau to come to Washington and address a joint session of Congress. He also had a breakfast meeting the next day with President Carter. The CBC went all-out on the coverage. Peter Kent came down as the anchor, and together we broadcast Trudeau's speech live from Capitol Hill. The next day, we had live coverage of Trudeau's press conference, and to do his full duty for Canadians, Vice-President Mondale gave me an interview in his White House office about the visit.

When I asked Mondale for the interview, I wasn't entirely sure how he would react. I had known him for about three years, and Audrey-Ann shared mutual friends with his wife, Joan. He had given me an interview in his Senate office when I was at CTV. Now, as vice-president, he had a different kind of schedule that was less of his own making, and he might not be able to find the time. Beyond that, I hoped he hadn't discussed the interview with his wife, Joan.

When the Carter-Mondale ticket won on November 2, the Mondales got to move. The vice-president has an official residence called Admiralty House, on Massachusetts Avenue in northwest Washington along a stretch of the street known as Embassy Row. That meant the Mondales had a house to rent. As Canadians in Washington for a limited time, Audrey-Ann and I were renting a home a little further north, two blocks outside of the District of Columbia boundary in Maryland. "Why not move and rent our house instead?" Joan Mondale proposed.

We knew the house and we did go with the real estate agent to do a walk-through. It was a month before the swearing-in of Carter and Mondale, but Secret Service agents were on each of the three floors in the house and in the basement. It was a bit creepy having them watch us as we looked at the house. The house was big, old, and not as well appointed as the one where we were living. There would have been a certain cachet in living in the house of the vice-president, but to Joan Mondale's disappointment, we decided to stay put.

Luckily, either Fritz Mondale didn't care who lived in his house or he didn't tell Joan he was seeing me, because the interview went off without a hitch. Trudeau would visit Washington twice more while I was the CBC correspondent there—once to visit President Carter when it appeared that the Mackenzie Valley natural gas pipeline was going to go ahead, and the other for a meeting of the North Atlantic Treaty Organization heads of government. From time to time, other cabinet ministers would be in Washington, but most of the reporting covered American domestic issues that had some other far-reaching impact.

Shortly after taking up the post as CBC correspondent, I realized I would have to deal with a problem I had seen on the horizon at CTV but not seriously considered. In 1976, American television network news organizations were switching from capturing footage on film to recording it on new, portable television cameras using three-quarter-inch videotape. The new arrangement was known as ENG, for electronic news gathering, and stations in Washington were quickly acquiring the new technology and getting rid of their film processing and editing facilities. The Washington bureau of CBS News was one of the first to make this change, and since CBS and the CBC had an agreement to use each other's facilities, I was now unable to operate with film in the CBS bureau.

In Canada, the CBC was also making the change, although only in Toronto, Ottawa and Montreal at first. At English network headquarters in Toronto, there was a realization that we had a problem in Washington, but dealing with it posed a further complication. Our camera crew was made up of freelancers hired on annual contracts. The cameraman, Mike Carnell, came from Canada and provided his own camera gear. The sound man, Richard Ayo, was a Cajun from Louisiana who used gear also provided by Carnell. In Canada, when the switch from film to ENG happened, the freelance film cameramen were hired into the CBC as employees and given training to use the new technology. That was more complicated for staff outside of Canada, and whatever happened to the Washington camera crew would have implications for CBC operations all over the world.

After thinking about it, I realized that the only way to make the changeover work would be for Carnell to buy the ENG equipment and continue to operate with Ayo as though they were still using film. Obviously, the CBC would have to give him a much bigger contract to make this feasible. After convincing Carnell to make the investment if he had the extra money, I went to Toronto to convince Cliff Lonsdale and the others running CBC television news that if they wanted to maintain coverage standards from Washington, they would have to spend more. Luckily, they agreed. Soon, Washington was the only CBC location outside of Canada covering the news on portable videotape equipment.

Carnell and Ayo were on a steep learning curve with the new gear, but so was I. I had never been in an ENG editing suite trying to pull together a coherent television story while working against a tight deadline. At CTV during Watergate we used one-inch videotape that employed a different process. Once again, luck rode to the rescue. When I started at the CBC, a new assistant had been hired to work with me. She was very nice and a good researcher, but she didn't know much about television. About the time we were getting the new technology, she decided to leave and go to law school. This is where the luck came in. The office manager put an ad in the *Washington Post* for someone to work in the CBC bureau—television experience a plus. Luckily, a woman named Linda Blazer saw the ad. She had been a field producer at the NBC News bureau in Atlanta. She had just come to Washington with her boyfriend, an NBC correspondent named Tom Pettit, who had been transferred to cover Capitol Hill. However, there was no job for Linda at NBC in Washington, so she was keen to work with us. She already had ENG videotape experience in Atlanta, and was quick, clever and fun to work with. She soon became not just our colleague but our teacher and a friend.

Besides her experience, Linda had another important attribute. Coming from Atlanta, she knew many of the people working at the White House with President Carter. Linda knew Jody Powell, his press secretary, and some of Carter's other people who had come to Washington with him. Together, we had a formidable bureau. Our camera crew had been together in Washington for almost a decade. I had been in Washington for five years and had developed contacts at the State Department and on Capitol Hill, and knew the vice-president, and our producer knew people at the White House. To cast the web even wider, soon we were sending stories to Toronto from the CBS bureau at least three times a week, and that was giving us an in there. And we knew everything going on at the NBC bureau too—our producer was keeping house with one of that network's top correspondents. If it was happening in Washington, we felt we had it covered.

Most of my reporting centred on American politics or international events, although sometimes domestic Canadian politics would play into the coverage. That happened in the fall of 1977, when I was covering the annual meeting of the International Monetary Fund. It was the first visit to the IMF meeting in Washington for Jean Chrétien, the first francophone Quebecer to be federal minister of finance. The IMF meeting is a huge event. Finance ministers and central bankers from around the world give their views on current economic conditions and their prescriptions for making things better. The IMF meeting operated like the United Nations, with simultaneous translation covering a number of languages. But since it was based in Washington, a lot of IMF business was done in English. At a previous IMF meeting, I had covered John Turner when he was finance minister, and although he could speak French, he gave Canada's presentation in English.

After Turner's resignation, Chrétien's appointment was meant to signal more than just a competent minister with experience in other departments now being in charge at Finance. At a time when the separatists, led by René Lévesque, were in power in Quebec, it was meant to signal that a French-speaking Quebecer could handle the top cabinet portfolio.

At the IMF meeting that fall, Chrétien decided to make the point internationally as well—particularly in the U.S., where Lévesque had spoken in New York and the Quebec government was aggressively promoting its view of Canada. When he was called to the podium to speak for Canada, Chrétien began his remarks in French, and kept speaking French right through to the conclusion of his speech. Delegates, expecting to hear an English presentation from the Canadian finance minister, were suddenly putting in their earpieces and twisting their dials for the translation. More than one American standing near me asked, "What is he doing?"

Whatever Chrétien had to say about world economic conditions wasn't very different from any of the other speeches that day. What I thought was significant was that the speech was all in French. But when I told the producers in Toronto that that was the story, alarm bells went off. If the story was reported the way I suggested, would both I and the CBC seem anti-French? Would we be playing into the hands of bigots and racists? Would we be exacerbating a problem that was a lot bigger issue in Canada then than it is considered today? Unfortunately, I had not been able to get hold of Chrétien after the speech, but I was sure I knew why he had spoken as he had. And I was convincing. The producers of *The National* agreed to take the report I was filing and run it as I proposed, pointing out that it was unusual but there was a reason. I was right. He was making a point about a bilingual Canada and the important role that French-speaking Canadians increasingly played in it.

Apparently, after the program that evening, the telephone lines lit up at CBC stations across the country. And the reaction was as predicted. Some people blasted me and the Corporation as racists, other people blasted Chrétien for being a French Canadian. There was even a newspaper editorial on the speech and my report. As I went back to the IMF meeting the next morning, I wondered if maybe I had misunderstood the reason for the all-French speech, but I couldn't think of any other reason why Chrétien would have done what he had done. I was walking into the hall when, without first seeing him, I walked right in front of where Chrétien was sitting. Obviously, he had received a report on news coverage from the day before, because he yelled across at me: "Hey, Newman, I hear you had a good story last night."

ABOUT A MONTH after covering the IMF, I was sitting in my office at the CBC bureau when another piece of Canada arrived at the end of the phone.

"Hello, Dun, it's Bub," said a familiar voice I was struggling to place.

"Who?" I asked.

"Bub, Bub Bourassa," came the reply.

And yes, it was the former premier of Quebec, about a year on from his surprise defeat at the hands of René Lévesque, apparently calling one of the few people he knew in Washington, looking to have lunch.

I took him to Chez Jacqueline, a fancy French restaurant on Pennsylvania Avenue west of the White House, near the World Bank and the IMF. He was impressed, not just because of the quality of the restaurant but because Secret Service agents were standing by the door and next to a private room where Vice-President Mondale was having lunch. I was hoping that Mondale might come out while we were in the hall, see me and say hello—that would have impressed Bourassa—but it didn't happen.

Instead, we talked about Quebec politics and the former premier's plans. He told me the Liberals had lost the election because not enough people in Quebec still went to church on Sunday. He said that, before election day, priests were told to instruct their parishioners to vote against the separatists and for the Liberals, but church attendance was in such decline that not enough people had received the message.

Bourassa was in Washington to speak at the School of International Relations at John Hopkins University. Since his defeat, he had been speaking at universities in the U.S. and Europe. I asked him about longer-term plans.

"I am going to go back to Quebec, become leader of the Liberal Party again, and then return as premier," he told me.

I wondered if he had become delusional after his defeat. There was no great record of people thrown out of office managing to step out of politics and then return to their former glory. And he had all of this planned even before the first Quebec referendum—the outcome of which no one had any idea—had been announced. Without being asked, I offered him my counsel.

"Look," I said, "I don't think that is a very good plan. You have had your time as premier, that has ended, you are still young, have a lot of talent and many possibilities. You will just waste your life running after a dream of what used to be. It is time to move on."

"No, no," he said, "it is very doable. Just watch, I'll be there."

And he was. Not right away, but within eight years. In 1980, the first referendum on "sovereignty-association" was defeated. A year later, René Lévesque won a second majority government, and in 1982 the Constitution was patriated without the support or signature of the PQ government. In 1984, Bourassa was back as leader of the Quebec Liberal party, and in 1985 he was again premier. Since then, I have been reticent to offer blunt advice about Quebec politics, especially to Quebecers!

DURING MY FOUR YEARS at CTV, I'd been to New York only occasionally. After my arrival at the CBC, two events made me a regular visitor to the Big Apple. René Lévesque and the Parti Québécois took office in Quebec, and immediately the Canadian dollar started its downward drift against the U.S. dollar. Suddenly, the financial markets in New York were of greater interest to Canadians, and both the federal and Quebec governments were active around Wall Street. At one point as finance minister, Jean Chrétien came to Citibank headquarters in New York to secure a multibillion-dollar line of credit that Ottawa could draw upon should it need to defend the Canadian dollar against a rapid decline. I was in New York for the ceremony when the agreement was signed. Few Americans in the room had met Chrétien, and he was at his vintage best at the ceremony.

"I am glad my father can't see me now," he said, surrounded by the rather stiff, buttoned-down Wall Street bankers. "He tell me, 'Never borrow money.'"

In New York in the fall of 1977, I witnessed something that only became clearer with passing years. Menachem Begin and his Likud party had just won power in the elections in Israel. Since the founding of the country in 1948, Israel had been governed by the Labour party, and Labour was widely supported by the Jewish community in both the United States and Canada. That was true in the 1977 election, but Begin and his more right-wing party had won anyway. Now he was coming to New York to meet the people who had backed his opponents and kept him out of power for years.

For the occasion, a who's who of the Jewish community in both the United States and Canada was packed into an elegant ballroom at the Waldorf-Astoria wearing black tie and long dresses. But Begin wasn't so formal. When introduced, he stepped out onto a stage at one end of the room wearing a grey business suit, white shirt and tie. Looking down at the assembled in all their finery, he shrugged and said, "So, I'm sorry. I won."

To a person, the crowd rose and cheered him with a standing ovation. Since that time, some commentators have tracked a growing tendency towards militancy among both North American Jews and other strong supporters of Israel, including evangelical Christians. In fact, on that same trip to New York, Begin made mention of Christians in the Middle East, who until then had not been much discussed or thought about.

The day after his triumph at the Waldorf-Astoria, Begin visited the United Nations. Meeting with reporters after making the usual courtesy calls, Begin was dealing with the familiar questions about the West Bank, Gaza and other issues when he suddenly, on his own, introduced the topic of Christians in Lebanon. Begin said that he wanted to assure American Christians that Israel would protect the Coptic Christians in the neighbouring country to its north.

At the time, there were no follow-up questions because until then no one had considered the issue. But as events would unfold over the next few years a war developed in Lebanon between Muslims and Christians in the country, with the Christians and the Israelis fighting together. In the even longer term some of Israel's most active supporters in Canada and the United States have been evangelical Christians.

In 1978, a new reason for frequent New York trips arose: Canada was elected to a two-year term on the United Nations Security Council. That meant that there was not only a Canadian position on whatever happened to be going on in the world, but that position got full exposure before the Security Council, and our country had a vote on the issues of the Middle East and other important topics.

The Middle East was a perennial issue at the United Nations, but the biggest story about it in 1978 didn't happen at the UN in New York. It happened on top of a small mountain in Maryland, ninety miles northwest of Washington. At the Camp David presidential retreat in the Cacoctin Mountains on September 5, 1978, President Carter welcomed both Prime Minister Begin and Egyptian president Anwar Sadat for open-ended negotiations aimed at securing a peace treaty between their two countries and advancing the peace process throughout the entire Middle East.

The Camp David peace talks were perhaps the most unusual story I covered. In some ways, they would be replicated in the Constitutional negotiations around the Meech Lake Accord in Canada a decade and more later. But at Meech Lake, there was access to the principals— the prime minister and the premiers—on an ongoing basis. At Camp David, there was effectively a cone of silence. With the exception of a trip President Carter arranged to the Gettysburg battlefield, from the time they saw Begin and Sadat each arrive at Andrews Air Force Base and board helicopters bound for the presidential retreat, no reporter saw either leader—or Carter—until the talks concluded.

Camp David is a presidential residence in a wooded, mountainous park. The security around the camp is the equal of that at the White House. Carter, Begin, Sadat and their advisers all stayed on site. Reporters were kept well away in an American Legion hall in the small town of Thurmont, at the foot of the mountain. And there were a lot of reporters. Not just the American press and the usual foreign reporters from Washington, but significant contingents of journalists from both Egypt and Israel. Each day, a brief statement would be released that usually didn't say much more than the talks were continuing. Sometimes, reporters from either Jerusalem or Cairo would seem to have a better idea of what was going on and were useful to speak with. But it seemed to me, more often than not, that they were either just speculating or dealing with each others' gossip.

Each day, I would be in Thurmont with the camera crew. We would walk around all day, trying to figure out what to report and, after pulling a story together, drive up the mountain to the barred gate of the retreat, with the big Camp David sign, to tape a closing to the report. Then we would go back to Thurmont and feed the bits of the story we had taped down a line set up by CBS to their bureau in downtown Washington. Linda would be there as the feed came in; then, with an ENG editor, she would take our tape, along with any she could use from CBS, and package our story and feed it to Toronto for *The National.* This system worked well because the *CBS Evening News* aired at six-thirty and our first deadline was 10 p.m.

Thurmont was so small, there was no place to stay. The international press were in motels in either Frederick or Hagerstown, two small cities within driving distance. I spent one night in a motel in Frederick, but that convinced me to make the ninety-minute drive back to Washington each evening, sleep at home and then drive back the next morning. But that plan changed on Saturday, September 16, when, instead of the usual brief statement, the assembled reporters were told that the next day would be the final day of the conference. One way or another, there would be news. I decided that the crew and I would stay overnight and that Linda would come up from Washington. We spoke with our CBS colleagues, who agreed that we could use their editing facilities and line in Thurmont after they had used them. On Sunday morning, we were all in place, waiting for something to happen. The tension was rising. The big American network news anchors, including David Brinkley and Barbara Walters, were coming in from New York and Washington, hanging around the American Legion hall like the rest of us. Then, at four in the afternoon, came the announcement: there would be news today, but it would be released in the early evening at the White House.

The scene at the Legion was like something out of a movie: cars screeching out of the parking lot, racing for the highway and heading south to Washington. The crew and I were right there in the race. We relied on facilities at CBS to get live on the air from Washington, and obviously those resources were going to be used by CBS. Finally, a deal was worked out allowing us to have one camera set up in what was actually a rather large broom closet. I sat in front of it but had no audio feed from the news conference, so I couldn't tell what was going on. Most of the program came from Toronto, with the CBS pictures of what was happening at the White House added in. It was a frustrating and disappointing end to twelve days' reporting on what turned out to be a major breakthrough in the Middle East.

This wasn't the final Camp David event. One of the accords agreed to was a peace treaty between Israel and Egypt, and in the following months there were details to be worked out. I had the opportunity to meet Israel's top negotiator, Foreign Minister Moshe Dayan, and his Egyptian counterpart, Vice-President Hosni Mubarak, during talks at the Madison Hotel, just up from the White House on Sixteenth Street. Dayan, of course, was the hero of the Six-Day War in Israel, and less than three years later Mubarak would be president of Egypt, following the assassination of Anwar Sadat.

When all the *I*s were dotted and the *T*s crossed, Begin and Sadat signed a formal peace treaty, with President Carter as witness, in front of the White House on March 26, 1979. This time, I was better placed. Like other television networks, the CBC had a platform on the White House lawn, with the signing ceremony going on behind us. And this time, I could hear what was going on.

WHILE I COULD hear the Peace Treaty signing at the White House, I couldn't hear the control room in Toronto while I was on the air. Kneeling in front of me on the platform at the White House, Linda Blazer had a telephone connection to Toronto, and when it was time to send it back to Knowlton Nash, who was anchoring the broadcast, she held up a sign she had printed in large black letters on a piece of cardboard: BACK TO CANADA.

That sign symbolized more than the program, because "back to Canada" was where Audrey-Ann and I had decided we were going with our family. At the end of 1978, the CBC foreign correspondents had met for their annual meetings in Toronto, and at those meetings new assignments were announced for some of us. The CBC was finally filling the chief political correspondent's job that I had been offered in 1976, and David Halton was moving from London to fill it. My new assignment was to go to London to replace him, and Joe Schlesinger would come from Paris to Washington. Halton seemed happy with his move, and Schlesinger was delighted with his. Me, I wasn't so sure.

Audrey-Ann and I had already discussed what we would do when the Washington assignment came to an end. We expected that would be after the 1980 election rather than before it, but either way the calculations were the same. We had been out of Canada for seven years, and although getting from Washington to see family and for them to come and see us was easy, Linc in particular had no idea what being a Canadian was all about and no interest in his native land. We, too, had lost the thread of daily life in Canada. Staying on as a foreign correspondent in a new posting would only exacerbate that problem, as well as adding more distance and more problems than the easy life in Washington. From meeting colleagues at the foreign correspondents' meetings, it seemed to me you could be away from Canada too long, lose your friends and contacts and find that your children would rather live abroad even though they were Canadian citizens.

All of these things were on our minds when a move to London was offered. I had one other thought: reporting is not something you should do forever, even if you can. The better reporters are often in their mid-thirties to mid-forties, with the right balance between energy and enthusiasm and the experience they have acquired through whatever they are covering. But even then, they need a change of pace. I would never have imagined it in the excitement of first being in Washington, but by the late seventies I was beginning to have trouble maintaining enthusiasm for covering a close Senate vote on a test ban treaty with the Soviet Union when the story was essentially the same one involving the same senators on a close vote to turn over the Panama Canal to Panamanian control.

And there was one other, more immediate consideration: money. CBC foreign correspondents were paid in Canadian dollars, with an adjustment for the cost of living in the cities where they were posted and the exchange rate between the Canadian dollar and the local currency. No sooner was I at the CBC than the Parti Québécois took office and the Canadian dollar began to slide in value against the American dollar. The formula that was meant to calculate the adjustment in the correspondent's allowance was not flexible enough to catch the continuing slide. As 1977 turned into 1978, Canadian employees in the United States were taking first a fifteen-, then a twenty- and finally a twenty-five-per-cent pay cut because of the Canadian dollar's drop. Because of the bureaucratic organization of the CBC, the heads of the news departments at both radio and TV could do nothing about it. Some drones in the administrative section at head office were in control of the pay calculations, and either out of ignorance or spite at the amount of money correspondents were being paid, they ignored instructions to make the appropriate adjustments. The dollar had dropped against other currencies as well, but the gap in the U.S. was the most egregious. It was a very uncomfortable situation, and not one that I was happy to prolong.

So when the correspondents' rotation was announced, on one level I was certainly open to a move. And London was a plum assignment. No doubt more CBC noses would be out of joint. First Washington and then London, the top two correspondent jobs, and the first two jobs offered to me at the CBC. But despite the prestige of the appointment, I still felt about the assignment the same way I had in 1974, when it had been offered while I was at CTV. I liked London, and had grown up there for five years as a boy, but it held no romance or mystery for me. I knew it would probably be my last reporting job, that by my mid-forties I should either be a program producer or a program host or get a job outside of journalism. Staying out of Canada for another four years wasn't going to help those prospects, particularly when I would have worked for almost eight years at the CBC without ever being in Canada and would have few connections with anyone in the country.

Audrey-Ann agreed, so I told Cliff Lonsdale, "Thanks but no thanks." He seemed surprised, particularly since he had no other job in mind for me. To be truthful, neither did I, but I felt certain something would turn up in Canada that would be a good step to take, and I turned out to be right. In April, Lonsdale called and told me he had an offer he wanted me to think about. A reporter's job on *The National* was opening up in Alberta, which had become the big story on the energy front and a big problem for the CBC. Would I consider going there to try and make inroads with the premier, Peter Lougheed, and the Calgary business community, which seemed to have a very low opinion of the CBC? Lonsdale thought having a former Washington correspondent cover the Alberta end of the fight with the federal government might improve the CBC's chances for better access, which at that moment was next to nil. To sweeten the pot, he offered to pay me the same as I was earning in Washington, which was a lot more than the Alberta national reporter would normally make.

I talked it over with Audrey-Ann and took some advice from John Owen at *The National.* The PR people in Toronto said they would get me some publicity when I arrived in the province. I was just about to agree to the move when I got a telephone call from someone I hadn't spoken to in three years: Don Cameron at CTV. He told me his network was opening a bureau in Beijing and the current Washington correspondent, Dennis McIntosh, was going to be its first reporter in China. Since it was known I was leaving the CBC bureau, he wondered why and whether I would like my old job back. I told him about the currency-exchange problem and de facto pay cut.

"Well, you know we pay in U.S. dollars," he said.

I told him I would call him back in a few days, but as I thought briefly about it, I realized that it was back to the future—before back to the future was in vogue. I called him back and thanked him but said I was sticking with my plans. Then I got ready to move to Edmonton and meet up again with Peter Lougheed.

My mother, my elder brother, Roger, and me in Winnipeg, about to leave for England in 1946, a year after the end of World War II.

My parents in London, England.

With Dad and Roger in our English
garden in Mill Hill, London, in 1947.

A family seaside holiday on the Cornish coast.

My first publicity photo, with
Don Hoskins at CJAY-TV
Winnipeg in 1961.

My photo at the CKRC
radio station in Winnipeg,1963.

President John F. Kennedy
when I covered him at the
University of North Dakota
on September 22, 1963,
two months before he was
assassinated in Texas.

Clowning with the comedy team of Wayne and Shuster at the Winnipeg Press Club in 1965. (*Left to right: Bob Noble,* Winnipeg Free Press, *Johnny Wayne, Frank Shuster, me,* Winnipeg Free Press, *and Don Slade, CKRC*)

Interviewing Manitoba premier Duff Roblin in August 1967 as he announces his leadership bid for the federal Progressive Conservatives.

My wife, Audrey-Ann, after we moved to Toronto in 1968.

Visiting Washington for CTV in October 1971 to cover my first IMF meeting. (Audrey Ann and I encountered President Nixon at the exact location where President Reagan would be shot and wounded a decade later.)

With cameraman Bert Plimer in Hamilton, Ontario, covering Pierre Trudeau in the 1972 federal election campaign. That's Trudeau behind us.

Our son, Lincoln Taylor Newman, in the spring of 1973, shortly after we moved to Washington.

My *Canada AM* interview with U.S. senator Daniel Inouye, a member of the Senate Watergate Committee, in August 1973.

Interviewing hockey legend Gordie Howe for CTV in Houston, Texas, September 1973, about his comeback in the World Hockey Association.

A family vacation on Cape Cod, right after I covered the resignation of President Nixon in August 1974.

The 1974 Democratic National Convention in Kansas City, where I first met future president Jimmy Carter.

In New York in 1976 on a story about President Ford's gaffes, with *Saturday Night Live* producer Lorne Michaels (*left*), a Canadian, and comedian Chevy Chase (*centre*).

Interviewing presidential candidate Jimmy Carter during the New Hampshire primary in February 1976.

Reporting for CBC on the Iran hostage crisis at the White House with cameraman Mike Carnell and sound man Richard Ayo, spring 1979.

Audrey-Ann and I talk with U.S. Secretary of State Cyrus Vance at a party in New York in 1979.

19

Alberta Bound

GOING TO ALBERTA in September of 1979 was like a trip back in time. Back to Canadian politics I had not covered in seven years, and to looking at the country from a western perspective, which I had not done in twelve years. Back to reporting on network television with just a cameraman and a film camera instead of videotape, and back to reporting on an important national figure I had first reported on eight years earlier. Strangely, both that earlier meeting and the television experience I had at that time helped prepare me for what was coming next.

I had first met Peter Lougheed on August 29, 1971, at a barbecue in the backyard of a Calgary organizer. The following day, Lougheed would lead his Progressive Conservative party out of the political wilderness and into power. Forty-two years and four premiers later, they're still there. I was in Alberta with CTV to cover the provincial election, but was only there because of a mistake.

I had originally left Ottawa with cameraman Bert Plimer and flown to Saskatoon to report on the summer meeting of western MPs in the federal Progressive Conservative caucus. At the previous year's meeting, western Conservatives were grumbling about the leadership of Robert Stanfield, with former leader John Diefenbaker using some of his lieutenants to stir the pot against his successor. Then still at *The Globe and Mail,* I had not gone to Saskatoon, nor had any other Ottawa reporters. But I had an inside source at the meeting I had telephoned just to check if anything had happened, and he provided the details of a strong story I reported in the paper.

Now, a year later, I was working to make a name in television. Saskatchewan seemed like a good place to find out what was going on in an important but disruptive part of the caucus of the Official Opposition. However, the prospect of more complaints and bad coverage had convinced Stanfield and his people to get the meeting cancelled. The party didn't want any publicity about either the prospective meeting or the fact that it had been shut down, so I flew into Saskatoon, having invested CTV money to get me and Plimer there, to find out there was no story to report.

I didn't want to call Geoff Fry in Toronto and tell him I had wasted network money, so I tried to think of an alternative. The Alberta general election was the following Monday. It had generated little coverage outside the province. Lougheed and the Progressive Conservatives seemed likely to improve upon the six seats they had won five years earlier. Long-time Social Credit premier Ernest Manning had stepped down after serving for twenty-five years and left the party in the hands of the pleasant but lacklustre Harry Strom to face the Tories and the energetic young Lougheed.

The CTV affiliate stations in Calgary and Edmonton were the most powerful television stations in the province, but *CTV National News* had no reporters stationed in Alberta and had carried nothing about the election campaign. After all, Social Credit always won in Alberta, didn't it?

But, trying to justify my pointless spending to Saskatoon, I decided to propose that I spend even more money. I told the Toronto headquarters I wanted to charter a plane to get Plimer and me from Saskatoon to Edmonton in time to cover a Lougheed rally that night, and then to Calgary the next day for a similar rally to end the PC campaign that evening. I was a bit surprised when Fry agreed. Perhaps he didn't want to explain to his boss about two tickets to Saskatoon that led to no story.

I hired a small charter and we flew to Edmonton. We covered the two rallies and filed a setup for the weekend that reported only on the Lougheed campaign. Both rallies had been held in the identical Jubilee Auditoriums in each city. Both houses were packed and had an energy and enthusiasm that forecast that—in the urban centres, at least—the PCs were on the move. The reporting was very one-sided, but given the circumstances, it turned out to be very prophetic.

I was to report on Monday, election night, from CFRN, the CTV affiliate in Edmonton. But I decided to stay for the weekend in Calgary, where reporters from the rest of Canada were staying. Lougheed was running in Calgary West, and organizers also wanted him to be at party headquarters on election night. It was fortuitous that I decided to stay.

Sunday afternoon, I received a call from Joe Hutton, Lougheed's press secretary on the campaign, inviting me and the other out-of-town journalists to a barbecue that evening. It was a convivial affair. Since none of us would be covering Lougheed the day after the election, since he was providing us with a pretty good story win or lose, and since he was particularly likeable, the atmosphere was relaxed as we drank beer and downed juicy hamburgers. At one point, I sat down in a lawn chair to concentrate on eating, when Lougheed came over with his hamburger and sat down next to me.

"Just between us," I said between mouthfuls, "how do you really think you are going to do?"

"Well, there are seventy-five seats in the legislature. We are going to win twenty-five of them for sure. The Socreds have twenty-five sure seats. Whoever wins the most of the other twenty-five will form the government. I hope it is us, but I don't know."

The next night, I was in Edmonton, in the newsroom at CFRN. The *CTV National News* with Harvey Kirck was broadcast from Toronto at 11 p.m. Eastern time and seen live throughout Ontario, Quebec and Atlantic Canada. At the same time, it was recorded and played back at eleven o'clock local time over stations west of Ontario. Earlier in the day, I had filed a story to Toronto with early pictures of people voting and film from the campaign rallies I had attended at the end of the previous week. Then I filmed a stand-up to end the report, which basically said of the outcome, "Who knows? Who really knows?" That report ran on the *National News* from Atlantic Canada all the way to the Saskatchewan–Alberta border, even though in Saskatchewan it was already out of date because that province is on the same time as Alberta in the summer. But when 11 p.m. hit in Alberta, the *CTV National News* had to report what had happened in the election, even though viewers in the province would have been watching live results on their TVs all evening.

In the CFRN newsroom, I sat at a desk, watching the results come in and crafting a report that I would deliver live to a camera from the election set. While I was talking, my live report would be cut into the *CTV National News* and seen immediately in Alberta, while it was recorded along with the rest of the news for replay an hour later in British Columbia. While I was on screen, the tape of the newscast would keep rolling, my out-of-date filmed report seen only by the technicians making the switch, and the minute that filmed report ended, they would switch back to the still-running feed of Kirck and the rest of news. That meant I had to be precisely on time. I had to be finished and signed off a second before the switch was made. Being too short would leave me sitting forlornly on camera with nothing to say. Too long and I would be cut off in mid-sentence.

Covering an election two times zones behind network headquarters in Toronto, into a newscast that had originally aired two hours earlier but now had to be updated for viewers in Alberta and British Columbia, was a challenge CTV hadn't tried before, and now it was up to me, with all of five months of network TV experience, to make it work. To say I was nervous would be an understatement. I hadn't done very much live TV, and certainly never into a gap in a rolling tape of a newscast. What's more, this was a huge story: the government in Alberta was changing after thirty-six years.

About five minutes before airtime, I went into the studio, where people were milling around, wrapping up the coverage of their election-night broadcast and its historic result. A floor director pointed to my little desk and gave me a microphone. There was a monitor beside it, and while I couldn't hear, I could see Harvey Kirck's craggy face come up after the opening, and the news was on the air.

"I have no camera," I pointed out to the floor director, trying not to sound too shaky.

"Don't worry, it's coming," he said as a camera suddenly wheeled around from the election-night set and pointed right into my face.

"Get ready, I'll cue you."

One more glance at the monitor as the news rolled by, and then I stared at the camera. The floor director stood just off to the side from the camera lens.

"Five seconds," he said, his fingers counting down as he cued me. I read my script, remembering to look up into the camera whenever I could. I had timed my report with my wristwatch a number of times in the newsroom and I knew I was in the ballpark, but didn't know if I was going to be under, over, or right on time. I was nervous, but didn't flub a word. As I approached the end of my script, the floor director put up both his hands, fingers extended, to signal I had ten seconds to finish. Then, counting silently backwards, he put down one finger as each second ticked away. With four fingers still in the air, I was finished. All I had to say was, "Don Newman, CTV News, Edmonton."

I stole a glance at the monitor. For a split second I was there, and then up popped Harvey with the rest of the news. It had worked. I had gotten away with it.

As I went back into the newsroom to collect my things, I thought about the result. The Social Credit party had kept twenty-five seats. The NDP had captured just one. The Progressive Conservatives had forty-nine. Lougheed was right. Not only had he won the most of the other twenty-five seats he said were in play, he had taken all but one. Pretty impressive forecasting, I thought.

I left for Ottawa the next morning and didn't see Lougheed again for more than two months. And when I did, it was not where I expected him to be.

Around noon one day, I was walking down Wellington Street across from the Parliament Buildings when I saw, approaching me from the other direction, someone who looked familiar. If this wasn't Ottawa, I thought, I would think that was Peter Lougheed. A little closer, and the approaching figure waved. It *was* Lougheed.

"What," I inquired, "is the newly elected premier of Alberta doing walking down the street in Ottawa by himself in the middle of the week?"

'Well," he replied, "there is a first ministers' meeting at the Conference Centre next week that I will be attending. It is my first one. I have never been in the Conference Centre and I have never been at a meeting with simultaneous translation. The finance ministers are meeting at the Conference Centre this week, so I have come down to sit in the background and see how everything works."

Note to self, I thought. Lougheed works hard, tries to leave nothing to chance and is always well prepared. We shook hands and said our goodbyes, agreeing that we would be seeing each other the next week when the premiers met with Prime Minister Trudeau.

But the next day, I received a phone call from Dave Davidson, one of the top reporters at Canadian Press and the president of the National Press Club. Lougheed had agreed to speak at lunch at the club. Would I like to introduce him? Of course, I said.

The next week, the first ministers' conference was a coming-out party for Lougheed. He was part of the story each evening, and I had him in my report three nights in a row. But after that, I didn't see him again before I left for Washington, although I did see him once while I was there.

In the spring of 1977, I had been at the CBC for about six months when the Canadian embassy sent out a release that the Alberta premier would be in Washington and would meet informally with the Canadian journalists in town. It was after the first OPEC embargo and oil price shock, in 1973, and before the second, in 1979, but Alberta and the federal government were already squaring off over the price of domestic energy and exports to the U.S., and Lougheed was down to take the temperature of Americans on the future of energy prices.

I looked forward to seeing the premier. But he was remarkably cool as I went up to say hello.

"Why did you go to the CBC?" he asked rather curtly.

"That is where reporting can have the most influence. That's where the opinion leaders are watching."

"Hmmn," he replied, before turning away. I wasn't aware then that he was already in a fight with the CBC. Two and a half years later, I would find out just how serious that dispute was when I showed up in Edmonton as the next representative of CBC National Television News.

...

ONE PERSON I DIDN'T expect to encounter in Alberta was Pierre Trudeau. But in October of 1979, about a month and a half after arriving there, I did. On the eve of his sixtieth birthday—after his defeat in May by Joe Clark and the Progressive Conservatives and at a time when he was struggling as leader of the Opposition—I encountered Trudeau on a short flight between Edmonton and Calgary.

He was in Alberta to speak at Liberal Party meetings in the two biggest cities. He had spoken the evening before in Edmonton, and was now travelling to Calgary for a speech that night. His travelling companions were Jim Coutts, a native Albertan who was his chief adviser both in office and now with the Liberals in Opposition, and former Alberta MP Jack Horner, who had been an unlikely convert to Liberalism, jumping from the PCs to a job in Trudeau's cabinet a year after Joe Clark became Tory leader in 1976.

Ever the performer, Trudeau was dressed like a cowboy in jeans, boots and a rather stylish cowboy hat. At Coutts's suggestion, he sat down beside me for the thirty-minute flight.

"I got the clothes last year when I was marshal of the Calgary Stampede parade," he explained. "I thought I would wear them again."

"You certainly stand out," I agreed.

But it turned out the clothes were not the only connection to the previous year's Stampede. The plane was no sooner airborne than one of the flight attendants came by. Young, blonde and attractive, she leaned over and introduced herself to Trudeau.

"Remember me?" she asked. "I met you last summer at the Stampede parade. I was one of the runners-up to Miss Stampede."

Trudeau faked it. "Ah, yes—I didn't know you were in aviation," he said, instantly inflating the role of flight attendant. "Tell me your name again."

Having learnt her name, Trudeau went on to ask if she would be in Calgary that evening. When she said she would be, he continued, "I am speaking tonight at the Four Seasons Hotel. Why don't you come down this evening? When I am finished, we can talk."

She quickly agreed. Nine-thirty was set as the time for the rendez-vous. While the conversation was going on, I had my head buried in a copy of the *Edmonton Journal,* but it was impossible not to hear every word. As she moved away, Trudeau turned to me and said, "I met her at the Calgary Stampede."

For the rest of the short flight, we gossiped about politics. Trudeau was a couple of weeks away from announcing his resignation, but he gave no hint of his plans. Instead, when I mentioned my friend from United College, Lloyd Axworthy, who had just joined the federal Liberal caucus (after years of experience in Opposition in the Manitoba legislature), Trudeau said he was planning to ask Axworthy for some lessons on asking questions in the House.

Arriving in Calgary, Trudeau, Coutts and Horner got off the plane ahead of me. I was staying for just a few hours in Calgary and had no bag. When I descended to the baggage carousel, Trudeau and his travelling companions were waiting for their luggage. Walking past, I waved at Trudeau. He looked back at me with a smile, and winked.

20

Lougheed: Energy and the Constitution

O N SEPTEMBER 12, 1977, I was in Washington, getting ready to go to New York to cover the opening of the annual session of the United Nations General Assembly. On that evening, people across Canada who were tuned in to CBC Television saw a program called *Tar Sands*. It was a relatively new form of program called a "docudrama," a dramatic re-creation of a recent public event with actors playing the main characters. The names were changed and the circumstances marginally altered, but to anyone the slightest bit knowledgeable, it was clear who the actors were intended to be.

The docudrama format allows those making the program to put a spin on the events being portrayed. Lougheed felt *Tar Sands* depicted him as a bumbling young incompetent who had been taken to the cleaners by wily operators in the oil industry when he signed the agreement with Syncrude to create the first massive commercial development to extract oil from the tar sands around Fort McMurray, northeast of Edmonton.

Even before the program aired, Lougheed's lawyers had warned the CBC that the program was apparently defamatory. After it aired, he sued, alleging damage to his character and reputation. He also stopped any direct dealings with the CBC. Reporters from the Corporation would still attend government press conferences and briefings, and when ministers scrummed in the halls of the Legislative Building, CBC microphones and cameras would be part of the scrum. But there were no one-on-one interviews with Lougheed, either at the CBC or in his office. And, following his lead, there were not many ministers willing to co-operate either.

I became aware of just how serious this was after I had agreed to go to Edmonton. Since I was arriving to cover a story that was heating up, having no access to the premier of Alberta and little to his cabinet was going to be a huge problem. Beyond that, in Alberta, dominated by one party with an "us against them" mindset, if the premier didn't like you, it tended to percolate beyond the halls of government into the community at large.

Still, as I arrived in September of 1979, I had some cockeyed confidence that I would overcome this problem. But how to go about it?

I decided to try and use my meeting with Lougheed at the barbecue in 1971. After almost a decade on television, he certainly knew who I was, so I called Ron Liepert, his press secretary, and asked for a private meeting.

"He doesn't do CBC interviews," Liepert answered. "You know that."

"Indeed," I replied, "but this is just a private courtesy call."

Liepert said he would tell the premier I had called. He called back a day later with a time for a meeting.

From the corridor, the premier's office in the Alberta legislature is deceptive. You go through a simple doorway and arrive at the receptionist's desk. But to get to where the premier actually works, you walk down past a row of offices occupied by the premier's staff. It reminded me of the hallway down to the chief news editor's office at the CBC in Toronto, only bigger and grander.

Lougheed was sitting at his desk as I entered. He didn't stand up or offer to shake hands. He did offer me a seat, though, and asked a question. A question he had asked before.

"Why did you go to the CBC?"

Fortunately, it was just the opening I needed. I didn't remind him he had asked me before.

"Because," I said, "that is where the decision makers and the opinion leaders get their news. That is where what you report resonates and has an influence."

And then I went on: "That's why I am here in Alberta. There is recognition that you and the province are important players, and I am here to give the kind of coverage to Alberta that I gave to Washington."

Lougheed didn't seem too impressed.

"I have heard that before, and nothing happened. Why would it be any different now?"

"Because I'm here. I didn't come from Washington just to sit around."

Lougheed appeared not to be buying it.

"Well, I'm suing the CBC. My lawyers have told me if I go to the CBC and appear on television with them, it will damage the credibility of my case."

"Well," I said, playing my last card, "I am going to be on TV from here two or three times a week. If you're not going to be available to come on when I ask you, don't complain if you don't like what I say."

That got his attention. He thought for a second, and then made a proposal.

"I'm going to Vancouver next week to speak to the board of trade. It is an important speech for me. If you come and cover it, I will take what you are saying seriously."

I knew I would have to get Toronto's approval to go, and fight the protestations of Colin Hoath, the national correspondent on the west coast. But I realized it was all or nothing.

"Okay," I said. "I'll be there. I hope the story is worth it."

Because of the time difference, I had to wait until the next morning to call Toronto. When I did, the suggestion that I follow Lougheed to Vancouver was greeted with skepticism. But luckily, my arguments prevailed, or my useful time in Alberta might have come to a quick end.

Ten days later, I was in the ballroom of the Hotel Vancouver, which had been set up for the board of trade lunch. The TV cameras were set up near the back of the room, right in front of the head table. At an event like this one, reporters stood behind their camera operators and behind the cameras. From the head table at this event, the reporters would be invisible.

So I waited until just after Lougheed and the rest of the head table had taken their places. Then, before the meal and the speech to follow, I stepped around in front of the camera in plain view of the head table. I could see Lougheed scanning the room. Suddenly, I caught his eye. His face broke into a big smile and he waved to me. Rather like a long-lost brother, I waved back.

The speech was a good one and gave me a story worthy to lead *The National.* Alberta was in the midst of negotiating a new energy-pricing agreement with the recently elected Progressive Conservative government of Joe Clark. Clark was also from Alberta, but with a national mandate, his government was finding the negotiations tough going.

Alberta wanted the world price for the oil it produced. Ontario, in particular, demanded that oil produced in Canada be made available at less than the world price as a competitive advantage for its manufacturing industries. In his Vancouver speech, Lougheed said if the negotiations didn't arrive at a price acceptable to his province, then his government would stop selling oil and natural gas from Alberta to the rest of the country. It was a huge escalation of the pricing disagreement, rife with regional, constitutional and political ramifications.

It was also a terrific story, one that I had to mount from a Vancouver newsroom where I didn't know anybody, and working in a time zone three hours behind Toronto. But when I called the national newsroom, I was surprised at the lack of excitement. Everyone in Toronto, it turned out, was fixated by the announcement that Joe Clark was fudging on his election promise to move the Canadian embassy in Israel from Tel Aviv to Jerusalem. He was appointing former PC leader Robert Stanfield to conduct a study of the planned move and make recommendations on whether it should go ahead.

Everyone knew this was a fudge to get Clark out of an election mistake. And while it was interesting, it didn't seem it was half as important as the premier of Alberta threatening to leave the rest of the country without any oil from his province. As I argued strenuously about the importance of my story, I was losing valuable time to prepare the report for air. Still, I got it done and fed it to Toronto. I had to wait several hours to see *The National* play in Vancouver. My report was the second story in the lineup. The Jerusalem climb-down led the news.

But the story was high enough in the lineup to convince Lougheed. A few days later, I got a call from the premier's secretary, inviting me to have coffee with Lougheed. This time, he got up from his chair, came around from behind his desk and shook hands. He offered coffee, and an idea.

"While I can't go against my lawyer's advice and prejudice my case, it seems to me that if I am stopped in the hall by a reporter as I go about my business, it is my duty as premier of Alberta to answer the reporter's questions.

"So if you need me, just call Ron and ask him if the premier will be going down the hall at the time you want to talk. You can have your camera there and we'll talk. I'll tell Ron, but we will keep this amongst ourselves."

Of course, I quickly agreed. His press secretary didn't much like my direct access, but it worked. I didn't tell anyone at the CBC in either Edmonton or Toronto, and on *The National,* at least, people seemed to think it was a natural evolution of reporting. But it worked, and not only was Lougheed good on his end of the deal, as he started appearing as part of my reports, but other cabinet ministers became more accessible as well.

The arrangement became even more important after February 18, 1980, when Pierre Trudeau and the Liberals returned to office. Just before the Clark minority government's defeat in December, Ottawa and Alberta had worked out and agreed to a new four-year energy-pricing deal. But the Liberals weren't interested in inheriting that agreement. It was back to square one on energy negotiations, and those talks were going to be much tougher than with the PCs.

Soon Lougheed, and more often his energy minister, Merv Leitch, were appearing regularly in my reports on *The National.* I wasn't promoting what they were saying, just giving it fair reporting. That was all right with them, because as I had argued with the premier, they were getting access to the most-watched newscast in the country, the one watched by the decision makers across the country, particularly in Ottawa and Toronto.

And the Alberta–Ottawa story was getting larger with each passing month. Alberta had negotiated a replacement for the now elapsed four-year deal after tough bargaining with the Clark government, but that agreement evaporated with the defeat of the Progressive Conservatives on the budget that would have helped implement it. Alberta was eager to have a new arrangement in place, but after resuming office in February, the first priority of the Trudeau government was, not surprisingly, to fight and win the Quebec referendum on sovereignty-association to be held three months later, in May.

And even after that referendum was won by Ottawa and federalists in Quebec, the energy issue sat in the shadows. As part of his winning campaign, Trudeau had promised "real" constitutional change to Quebecers. That included "patriating" the British North America Act, which was approved by the British Parliament at Westminster in 1867 to create the original four-province Dominion of Canada. That act remained the fundamental Constitution of Canada, and to change it took an amendment passed in London. A patriated act would mean that Canadians would be fully in charge of their own constitutional destiny.

Efforts to make the Constitution Canadian had been tried for many years, particularly through the 1970s in the face of the rising threat of Quebec separation. But all efforts had foundered on whether there should be a change in the division of powers between the federal and provincial governments, and on the even more difficult question of how amendments to a fully Canadian Constitution would be accomplished.

In June 1980, the federal–provincial energy agreement expired and Alberta raised the wellhead price of natural gas by two dollars. Federal energy minister Marc Lalonde objected, but did nothing about it. By then, the federal government was concentrating on a first ministers' meeting to be held on the Constitution in Ottawa in September.

That summer, my focus suddenly shifted. I briefly entered a world of déjà vu. I was part of the CBC Television team that covered the Republican convention in Detroit in July, where Ronald Reagan was nominated as the party's presidential candidate, and the Democratic nominating convention in New York in August, at which President Jimmy Carter fought off a challenge from Senator Edward Kennedy to run again for his party. But I was quickly back to my present reality when

I returned to follow Lougheed to the premiers' conference in Winnipeg. All the talk there was of the upcoming constitutional talks the following month in Ottawa. Lougheed saw the constitutional talks and the looming energy showdown as one and the same. He wanted provincial control of natural resources strengthened in any agreement; he believed that would stop what he saw as an attempt by the Trudeau government to commandeer Alberta's energy resources and arbitrarily set artificially low prices for them in other parts of Canada, as well as claim for Ottawa the lion's share of the tax revenues those resources produced.

Away from Alberta, I still had to maintain the fiction that I had just run into Lougheed, so that he would talk to me. And that summer in Winnipeg I had to be a lot more energetic. The premiers were meeting at the Manitoba Legislative Building and staying at the Fort Garry Hotel, eight blocks away. I had arranged to "run into" Lougheed at the back door of the hotel, and had my cameraman set up there. But I had to cover the final press conference at the legislature before I could go to the hotel for the premier's arrival. Lougheed had a car and driver; I didn't. So I ran the eight blocks down the back alley behind Broadway Avenue to be at the back door and, slightly out of breath, greet Lougheed at the hotel when he drove up.

Three weeks later, I was in Ottawa as one of the floor reporters for CBC's live coverage of the first ministers' conference. There was no all-news channel in 1980, and each day the full CBC network was pre-empted for this important national coverage. I was equipped with a portable microphone and battery pack. There were two mobile, portable cameras assigned to the meeting floor and there were fixed camera positions around the conference room. All the benefits of being a known media player that I had missed in Washington were present in Ottawa, and it made life a lot easier. In addition to Lougheed, there were three other premiers I had known and reported on when they were ministers in the governments they now led—William Davis from Ontario, Sterling Lyon from Manitoba and Allan Blakeney from Saskatchewan. Trudeau and most of his ministers I had known from my pre-Washington time in the Parliamentary Press Gallery, and Lloyd Axworthy I had known since university.

The other reporter equipped to roam the floor was Mike Duffy, a member of the CBC's Parliamentary bureau. Together we commanded the floor for four days, from the opening of the conference on September 8 through September 11. With no agreements in sight, on Friday, September 12, the first ministers went behind closed doors for a day of private bargaining. That gave everyone a night off. That evening, a wild party ensued at an Irish bar in the Byward Market, with many of the reporters, premiers' staff and others in Ottawa for the conference dancing late into the night. Only one premier showed up to take part. Richard Hatfield of New Brunswick was the life of the party.

On Saturday, September 13, we were at our places, ready to broadcast live when the conference resumed its final session. Strangely, nothing had leaked overnight about what agreements had been reached in the closed-door bargaining the day before. Still, our producers assumed that something must have been agreed upon, and as we went to air they instructed anchor Knowlton Nash and chief political correspondent David Halton to speculate about just how large the agreement might be. I was standing on the floor of the conference, listening in my earpiece to Nash and Halton doing their speculating, when suddenly one of those contacts from earlier years paid off. Tugging on my arm, screaming at me, was the executive assistant of Manitoba premier Sterling Lyon.

"They're wrong!" he almost shouted at me. "The CBC has it wrong. There is no agreement. Nothing has been agreed to. The CBC has it wrong!"

I immediately pressed down on my intercom button to speak to the control room, shouting to Arnold Amber, the producer in charge of the broadcast, "I have just heard directly from Lyon's office there is not any agreement at all. You have got to tell Knowlton and David to get off talking about one."

Amber was stunned. But when I repeated the message, he agreed a change would have to be made. Usually, a reporter uses the intercom button to tell the control room he or she wants to get on the air with an interview or to relay some information to a camera. I had called Amber without any thought of going on air myself, but suddenly there was a portable camera before me, and I heard Nash say in his smooth voice: "Don Newman has something to tell us from the floor."

Since I hadn't planned on going on camera, I hadn't thought about how I was going to tell the chief correspondent and anchorman of *The National*, as well as the network's chief political reporter, they had been misinforming Canadians. But now I was on air coast to coast to do just that. Luckily, the words came out all right.

"Knowlton, I think we may all have been too optimistic. I have just heard from a very strong source in the Manitoba delegation that in fact the first ministers had no more success in reaching any agreements behind closed doors than they did in the four days we reported on them here in public. Apparently, when they take their places in a few moments, the prime minister will report just that. Of course, having failed to reach any agreements, I guess we will see what comes next, and whether the prime minister plans to go it alone on patriating the Constitution without any provincial support."

And, like a real pro, that's what Knowlton picked up on. He and David began discussing whether, without any agreements, Trudeau would try to go it alone on patriation, completely ignoring the fact that just two minutes earlier they had been speculating on what agreements had been reached.

The failure of the constitutional conference further convinced

Lougheed and the Alberta government that Trudeau and Ottawa were ready to move in on the province's natural resources. Back in Edmonton, the premier moved to give his government some legislative authority to prepare for what he was sure was a coming fight. First, he introduced legislation to give Alberta the power he had said eleven months earlier in Vancouver that he was ready to use in a resources pricing fight. The new law would give the Alberta government the ability to decide which refineries across Canada could receive Alberta crude for refining. The law would also apply to natural gas and to tar sands production.

That wasn't very controversial in Alberta, but the next piece of legislation to be introduced was. It was a bill to allow the provincial government to hold a referendum on any topic of its choosing. Lougheed said the intention wasn't to enable a referendum to try and take Alberta out of Confederation, but not everyone was sure he meant that. With western separatism already nascent, his referendum legislation set off some alarm bells.

The federal budget was set to be brought down on October 28. Everyone knew it was to deal with energy pricing and supplies, just as the Clark government's budget of ten months before, which had led to its defeat, had been.

In 1979, I had been in Calgary, doing an insert into the *National*'s budget program with people from the energy industry and other businesspeople. Now, with a Liberal budget that was to be even more controversial, I was to be in Edmonton to cover Alberta's political reaction. I called Ron Leipert in the press office to ask for the premier to take part in the program, even though I knew he was unlikely to come to the CBC. Leipert said Energy Minister Leitch would be the only person to speak for the Alberta government on budget night, and what time would I like him at the CBC?

The arrangement made and Toronto informed, I was starting to think of other budget reaction I should gather when the phone rang. It was my competitor, Robert Hurst, CTV's national correspondent in Alberta, and he was distraught.

"What am I going to do?" Hurst asked. "Leitch is the only person speaking for the government on budget night and you have him. My network wants reaction from Alberta and now I'm screwed."

Hurst had been the assignment editor at CFTO in Toronto when I was the CTV Washington correspondent and I had seen him around the newsroom from time to time, particularly during the Watergate coverage I originated in Toronto. I didn't know him very well, didn't have any strong feelings about him one way or another, and was glad it was him with the problem and not me.

Still I decided to help him, sort of. It was the kind of help that could only be offered in western Canada, where outdoor parking lots are divided by low fences with electrical outlets in them. Electrical cords are used to connect the outlets with block heaters under the hoods of parked cars in the cold winter months so the cars will start after sitting outside for a period of time.

"If you want to try it, I will let you set up your camera and lights in the CBC parking lot next to the building. Then, when Leitch comes out after being on TV with me, you can grab him for an interview and rush the tape back to feed it into your program." Hurst offered profuse thanks and said he would follow my idea the night of the twenty-eighth.

The federal budget was presented as promised, all about energy and energy pricing. And as the Alberta government feared, the National Energy Program unveiled by Finance Minister Allan MacEachen was even more draconian than expected, with a scale of price increases below what Alberta wanted and with Ottawa taking bigger share of the revenue pie.

Also as promised, Merv Leitch was with me for some time, denouncing the National Energy Program on the network budget special being broadcast across Canada.

"It is even more disagreeable than we thought it could be," he said, adding that Alberta and the federal government were "clearly in a confrontation."

The next day, I phoned Hurst to see how things had worked out for him. He was disconsolate. Leitch had stopped in the CBC parking lot to do an interview with him, and he had rushed back to feed it into the CTV budget program. The CTV affiliate was CFRN, the same station where I had done my Alberta election night report nine years earlier. But it was across town from the CBC, and by the time Hurst got there with the tape of Leitch, CTV had signed off its budget special. He had failed to get the Alberta reaction to the story of the night.

A few months later, Hurst was replaced as the CTV Alberta correspondent, but it had no lasting effect on his career. He went on to be based in the Parliamentary Press Gallery and work for the network as a foreign correspondent. He stepped down in 2010 as president of CTV News.

In political terms, in Alberta, the National Energy Program was the equivalent of the Japanese attack on Pearl Harbor. Two days later, Lougheed went on provincewide TV to spell out Alberta's retaliation. He would have legislation passed to allow his government to cut the million barrels of oil produced in Alberta each day by sixty thousand barrels. And the cuts could go on indefinitely. The provincial government would give three months' warning before an impending cut. Virtually the entire province came together behind Lougheed and his government as Ottawa's intrusion into the province's stewardship of its natural resources and main source of income was condemned and resistance promised.

So heavy was the outburst and the flow of news that my departure for Washington to be part of the CBC's live coverage of the U.S. presidential election was delayed for three days. I finally made it and played a fairly significant part in the program. But the next day, I was back on the plane for Edmonton. Ronald Reagan's election as president was big news, but in Canada the energy fight was the big story of the moment and, together with the impending showdown over the patriation of the Constitution and the role Peter Lougheed was determined to play in those events, it meant I would be right in the middle of two stories that would help shape the future of Canada. Not only that, but as the only CBC network correspondent in Alberta, I had half of each of those great national stories virtually to myself.

The decision to come to Edmonton was certainly paying off.

21

Alberta '81

THE WINTER IN Alberta in 1981 was mild. The temperature had gone above freezing on Boxing Day, and while it would dip below zero in the evening, it would climb slightly above again the following day. That was good news for me and my new cameraman, Tom Sharina. We spent the early months of 1981 mostly outside of Edmonton, in the countryside and the small communities that dot the landscape between Red Deer and the provincial capital.

We were reporting on the impact of the National Energy Program, and there was a real impact. Oil companies were shutting down drilling operations, taking their drills out of the ground, packing them onto fleets of flatbed trucks and moving them across the border into the United States, where they believed they would earn greater profits. Machine shops in towns like Drayton Valley were losing more than half their business when the drills moved out, and in Red Deer a company lost more than half its work converting mobile homes for oil-rig workers living near drilling sites. At the beginning of March, the first reduction by Alberta of sixty thousand barrels a day to eastern Canadian refineries went into effect. The standoff was in place, and there was no sign of a break.

Things were heating up on the constitutional front, and doing so more dramatically. Following the failure of the first ministers' constitutional conference the previous September, Prime Minister Trudeau had introduced legislation in the House of Commons to permit the federal government to act on its own and take control of the Constitution from Great Britain. Now Premier Lougheed was playing a leadership role in creating a united front amongst the provinces that were opposing the federal plan. The opposing provinces challenged the go-it-alone scheme in three different provincial courts, with disappointing results. Both Manitoba and Quebec judges said Ottawa had the authority to proceed alone. Only Newfoundland said that what Ottawa was doing was wrong.

In April, the eight premiers opposing Trudeau pulled an audacious stunt, holding a one-day conference in Ottawa, in the shadow of Parliament Hill, to unveil their own version of a constitutional agreement. They used the Government Conference Centre, where the prime minister usually hosted first ministers' meetings, and the television networks gave live coverage to the conference.

Shortly after, whether it was the publicity, the split rulings in the provincial courts, or both, Trudeau decided to ask the Supreme Court for a ruling on whether Ottawa had the right, without provincial support, to go to the government of the United Kingdom to bring the Constitution and the ability to amend it in future it back to Canada. The Supreme Court justices heard the arguments and then retired to deliberate. For the moment, that put the constitutional file on hold.

The spotlight switched to the energy file, where things were beginning to stir. In the second week of June, federal energy minister Marc

Lalonde and Alberta energy minister Merv Leitch met for four hours in Banff to see if there was reason to get negotiations going on a new energy agreement. The location was symbolic. Lalonde had travelled to Alberta, but the meeting was held in a federal national park. I went to Banff to cover the meeting, even though it was private and behind closed doors. Their conference lasted four hours, which seemed like a good omen, and they announced their agreement to get together again in about three weeks.

A few days later, I found out just how much had been agreed to. As in Washington, where I would meet people and find out information at my son Linc's school and sports events, the same held true in Edmonton. I was at a little league baseball game one evening. On the same team as Linc was a boy named David Johnston. His father often came to the games, and because we had things in common, we usually talked. David father's name was Dick, and he was the intergovernmental affairs minister in the Lougheed government. At a game shortly after the Lalonde–Leitch meeting in Banff I asked him how the talks were progressing.

"It will all be done by Labour Day," he said. "We have to get a deal to stop the cutbacks and get a higher price, and Ottawa has to know the price of oil to bring down its budget in November. Leitch is going to meet with Lalonde in Toronto at the end of the month, and it should all be done by the end of August."

"That's very interesting," I said.

"Don't quote me," he replied.

And I didn't. I said sources were telling me that the new Ottawa–Alberta energy deal would be done by the beginning of September, and laid out the reasons why that would happen when I reported the story on *The National* the next night.

...

AFTER REPORTING THAT there would be an energy agreement by the beginning of September, I realized that the time I wanted to spend in Edmonton was coming to an end. Luckily, the television season and the school year both start in September, so a summer move is often feasible. I had raised the possibility of a move with Vince Carlin, who had succeeded Cliff Lonsdale as chief news editor. He had agreed in principle that, as the big story in Edmonton wound up, I should move on.

The question was where. At the CBC, most of the action is in Toronto, but for political journalists the Parliamentary bureau is the place to be. I had been to Ottawa numerous times from Edmonton and felt right at home returning there, although I also liked Toronto and the feeling of action there, both at CBC headquarters and in the city generally.

In Toronto, there were some specialist reporting jobs for *The National*. The business and economics reporter might be something I would be interested in. The job of chief political correspondent, which I had been offered in 1976, was now filled by David Halton, and I didn't want go to the Ottawa bureau to be just a reporter. Besides, I still had it as an objective that, in my forties, I would work on a specific program, either as the host or producer, rather than reporting on *The National*. Here I was, forty, soon to turn forty-one.

To further complicate things, in the spring of 1981, the technicians at the Corporation were on strike. Managers who normally would be thinking about changes for the coming season were instead trying to do technical jobs they didn't know much about to keep the network on the air.

But just when it appeared that I might have nothing new to do, it suddenly appeared that I might have *three* choices. First, I received a call from Mark Starowicz. I didn't know him personally, but I knew him by reputation. He was credited with reinventing the CBC radio program *Sunday Morning* and turning the daily *As It Happens* interview program, along with its host, Barbara Frum, into must-listen radio in the age of television. Now he was moving to TV, putting together a five-day-a-week current-affairs program to run directly after *The National.* The newscast would move to a time slot one hour earlier, at 10 p.m., and together the two shows would fill up an hour of information programming in the last hour of prime time.

Starowicz wanted to know if I was interested in auditioning for a job on *The Journal,* as the new program was to be called. I didn't really know enough about the program or the job to know if I was interested, but with the ongoing technicians' strike making it difficult to get on the air, not to mention the possibility of two days in Toronto, I said sure.

The audition took place in a ground-floor studio in the main CBC television building on Jarvis Street. I was met by a producer I did not know, who told me what to expect: I would do an interview, which would be interrupted by a series of breaking news alerts on an ongoing story. The interview would be a "double-ender," with only an audio connection between me and the person being interviewed. I would be looking at a blank green screen while asking the questions and listening to the answers, and then turning to speak to the camera with the breaking news updates.

Starowicz planned to build *The Journal* around double-enders. The person asking the questions would be taped in Toronto, while the interviewee would be recorded wherever they were. The tape of the person answering the questions would then be fed to Toronto and edited together with the questions, and a seamless interview would appear on the screen that evening. It was not only cheaper, it made many more interviews possible than would be the case if it were necessary to bring cameras to the interview subjects or get them into a studio and do the interviews live, even if "live" meant recording them for broadcast at a later time.

I don't remember who I was interviewing, but shortly after it began, I was told to report that a passenger plane approaching Paris was in trouble. As the interview went on, I was interrupted a couple of more times with news of the plane, until finally I had to report that it had crashed and there were no survivors.

The audition finished, I stood up to leave the studio when I ran into Starowicz himself.

"That was pretty good," he said, "but I have to be honest with you."

He then told me, as everyone suspected, that he was negotiating with Barbara Frum to be the main host. However, Frum was playing hard to get. With the technicians' strike likely to end soon and the launch of the program approaching, he had to be ready with alternatives.

"If I don't end up with her, I may give you a call."

"Okay," I said, not sure I was all that interested even if an offer did come.

I then stopped by the office of chief news editor Vince Carlin, and when I told him why I was in Toronto, he was mildly upset—not, it turned out at me, but at Starowicz, who apparently had promised not to raid *The National* to staff his new show. Obviously, that promise had been made when Starowicz thought he had Barbara ready to go. Eventually, she did agree, and when *The Journal* went to air there were no people from *The National* on its staff.

That day, it turned out Vince Carlin had his own idea about what I should be doing next. He proposed that I move to Ottawa to become the host and editor of a program called *This Week in Parliament*. At first blush, that didn't sound very interesting. The program had no fixed time slot, and instead appeared between sporting events on Sunday afternoons, sometimes for thirty minutes, sometimes for forty or forty-five. Beyond that, the program had very low production values.

The program had made its debut in 1977, when sessions of the

House of Commons were first televised. The cameras were installed and controlled by MPs, who didn't want shots of empty seats—of which there were usually many during debates—or of members asleep at their desks, which actually was rare. But the cameras greatly increased the ability of TV reporters to convey most of what was going on in the Commons. They edited exchanges in Question Period to make them snappy and give them punch, making their nightly news reports more compelling. In contrast, *This Week in Parliament* ran long, unedited chunks of tape. Watching it was like watching a feed direct from the House, and often a bit like watching paint dry.

Carlin said all that had to change. The program would also be moving to a regular half-hour time slot on Saturday evening, right before *Hockey Night in Canada* in the east and right after it in the west.

"It has to be a lot better than it is. You could improve it as your own show and you would be in Ottawa for the news specials the producers want to have you on."

The idea was intriguing. I would have my own show and I would be in Ottawa. But I realized that the writer and producer I would inherit with the program had shown no interest in making it better, so virtually all of the improvements would be the direct result of my own efforts. It really would be "my own show."

Vince agreed I could think about it and get back to him, and I began mulling it over on the flight back to Edmonton. But no sooner was I home than I had something else to think about: a phone call from the executive producer of the hard-hitting newsmagazine program, *the fifth estate.*

I had first met Robin Taylor when we were both general assignment reporters at the *Winnipeg Free Press.* He then followed me to the *Winnipeg Tribune,* and we had often reported at the Manitoba legislature together when it was in session. When Robin married, he took several months off in the Bahamas. When he returned, he was in need of a job. By then, I was at *The Globe and Mail,* and when he called me I was glad to put in a good word of recommendation to managing editor Clark Davey. Soon, Robin was at the *Globe.*

I then went to Ottawa, television and Washington. He went to the CBC. Extremely able, Robin rose quickly, and by the summer of 1981 was the executive producer of *the fifth estate.*

On his call, he told me that one of the three hosts on his show was leaving. He was coming to Calgary to talk with someone who wanted the job, and he would like to come to Edmonton to say hello. I knew there was an opening coming up on the *fifth,* but having discussed the possibility of joining the program when it launched in 1975 while I was still at CTV, I had not considered applying for the opening now. Still, a chance to see Robin for an evening was always a good idea, and I invited him home to dinner.

We spent the evening reminiscing and catching up. Finally, Robin came to the point.

"You have heard that Ian Parker is leaving the program? I would like you to replace him."

Frankly, I wasn't surprised, but I wasn't ready to respond, either. To this day, *the fifth estate* remains a great program, but it is primarily a producers' program. There are four times as many producers as hosts, and the hosts get briefed by the producers as they cycle through the various stories they front on the air. Ultimately, it is the producers who own the stories and decide what is reported. What's more, *the fifth estate* is based in and broadcast from Toronto, but most of the stories don't happen there. There is a lot of travelling for hosts, producers and crews. If I really wanted that, I would have stayed a foreign correspondent.

Still, I was very flattered and pleased that Robin wanted me as a host on one of the CBC's signature programs. The technicians' strike was still on, and there was no immediate rush, but we agreed we would talk in a couple of weeks and that I would telephone him.

Over the next two weeks, I went back and forth in my head, looking for reasons to go to *This Week in Parliament* or *the fifth estate*. Clearly, the *fifth* was more prestigious; few at the CBC or anywhere else in Canadian television would not want that job. Moving to *This Week in Parliament* would seem to some people like moving from Washington to Edmonton. But politics and Parliament were my main interest, and *This Week in Parliament* would be an opportunity to build something myself, rather like opening the CTV bureau in Washington or getting Lougheed onside in Alberta.

Usually, answers come to me with a certain clarity, but it was still not clear to me what I should do when the time came to call Robin Taylor. I placed the call, and suddenly my mind was made up for me.

"Don," Robin said, "I'm really embarrassed. Bill Morgan is the head of current affairs, and when I told him I wanted you as my new host, he told me I couldn't have you or anybody else from *The National*. I'm really sorry; I have to withdraw the offer."

I was stunned. Shot down by the petty internal politics of the CBC. I didn't know what to say.

"Well, I guess that's it. Thanks for thinking of me."

I hung up—annoyed, but with a sense of clarity I had been lacking for the last few weeks. I picked up the phone again and dialled. A familiar voice answered.

"I have thought it over," I said. "I really want to make something of *This Week in Parliament*."

"That's great," Vince Carlin replied. "Get ready to sell your Edmonton house and we will announce the move as soon as the strike is over."

Within a couple of weeks, the strike ended, four months after it had begun. At almost the same time, so did the impasse between the federal and Alberta governments over energy pricing and taxation. I was still in Edmonton, watching on television, when Premier Lougheed and Prime Minister Trudeau signed the agreement in Ottawa. The deal was signed the day the third sixty-thousand-barrel cut to Alberta oil shipments was to have gone into effect.

Three weeks later, I was in Ottawa, looking for a house, when the Supreme Court handed down its decision on the question of whether the federal government could unilaterally ask the British Parliament to send the Constitution home to Canada. The court decided that while Ottawa had the right, it was convention to have at least significant provincial support before making such an important request. That was interpreted in both Ottawa and the provincial capitals to mean that there had to be at least one more attempt to get provincial support for patriation. That meant another, probably final, showdown between Ottawa and the provinces over patriation. It was a showdown that would be held at the Government Conference Centre in Ottawa, where all the other constitutional meetings had been held, and when it happened, I would be in Ottawa with my new program and a part to play on the news specials that would cover the conference.

Returning to Ottawa was like going home, and the timing could not have been better.

22

Special Coverage and Live TV

DOING LIVE, BREAKING-NEWS television is like being a trapeze artist without a net. I know, because when I started in network television with CTV in 1971, I had been in the Ottawa bureau for a week when I was thrown into a live special covering the NDP convention that saw David Lewis succeed Tommy Douglas as the party leader.

History has a way of repeating itself. A decade later, I had been in the Ottawa bureau of the CBC for four weeks when I was thrown into a live special. This time, it wasn't a party leadership, but the last-ditch attempt by the federal government and the provinces to come to an agreement on patriating the Constitution from Great Britain and agreeing on a formula for amending it once it was a Canadian law.

There were other differences as well. In the intervening ten years, I had done a lot of live television, both at CTV on *Canada AM* and on a variety of specials at CBC. In fact, part of my new assignment in Ottawa was to be available for specials.

There was also a big difference between a party leadership convention and a conference that, whatever its result, would have historic implications and affect Canada's future. Prime Minister Trudeau had agreed to the conference after the Supreme Court ruled it would be legal but unconventional to bring the Constitution home, and then amend it, without significant provincial support. He already had Ontario and New Brunswick onside, but so far that was not enough. If no others would agree, could he then go ahead? Or, without additional provincial support, would Ontario and New Brunswick withdraw their backing?

Although I had been in Washington for most of the 1970s, I had covered the 1971 Victoria Conference and the failed 1980 constitutional conference that led to Trudeau's threat to go it alone on patriation. In 1980, my floor assignment at the conference was to follow all of the action, but to concentrate on interviews with Peter Lougheed of Alberta and the other western premiers. And it was the same at the conference just over a year later. The week before the conference was to begin, that assignment was made infinitely easier when I received a call on November 2 from Judy Wish, the Alberta government representative in Ottawa. She invited me to meet with Lougheed for a drink at a hotel across the Ottawa River in what was then Hull, Quebec.

As he usually did, Lougheed was in Ottawa to take the temperature privately before a big federal–provincial meeting. And so he wouldn't attract attention, he was staying in Quebec rather than at the Château Laurier, where he would be during the conference.

"What do you think?" he asked me.

Reporters are used to asking the questions, but if truth be known, they often love being asked their opinion. This was one of those times for me.

"I think there'd better be a deal or there could be serious trouble," I said.

"How so?" he asked, for the moment neither agreeing nor disagreeing.

"If there is no deal and Trudeau decides to go ahead on his own, Lévesque will scream bloody murder and perhaps use it as a reason for another referendum. Then you seven other premiers in the 'Gang of Eight' will be in a bind. Do you agree with Lévesque and oppose Trudeau, particularly when the patriation idea will have support in the rest of the country with Lévesque in opposition?"

"That's right," Lougheed agreed. "Where do you think a deal lies?"

Stating the obvious, I said, "It has to be around the Charter of Rights and the amending formula. The provinces will have to accept the Charter of Rights, and Ottawa will have to accept the amending formula proposed by the provinces."

"I see that too," he said.

Then, discussion of the conference was dropped. Lougheed changed the subject. He wanted to know the relative merits of opening an Alberta government office in either Washington or New York.

The conference opened on a Monday. By and large, it followed the same pattern as the one the year before, and other ones going farther back. Ottawa, Ontario and New Brunswick were on one side and the other eight provinces on the other. Although there was occasionally an undertow of subtle change going on, the form that change might take was not clear.

But near the end of the second day, there was a break. Trudeau proposed immediate patriation of the Constitution with no changes, followed by a two-year negotiating period, followed by a national referendum on what had been negotiated. Surprise: Quebec premier René Lévesque said he saw merit in the idea. The other seven premiers, who had been his allies in the "Gang of Eight," said they didn't. Suddenly, there was a split in the opposition. Trudeau mocked at a press conference that there was now a "Gang of Two": Ottawa and Quebec.

When the conference began, Lougheed moved into the Château Laurier, where all the other premiers were staying. All, that is, except Lévesque. He was staying across the Ottawa River in Quebec, at the very hotel where, the week before, I had met Lougheed for a drink. And that turned out to be important. With Quebec now isolated from the other dissenting provinces, negotiations began on an upper floor of the Government Conference Centre—a Beaux Arts–style building that was once Ottawa's railway station, located across the street from the Château—where the daytime sessions were held. In the talks, federal justice minister Jean Chrétien, Ontario attorney general Roy McMurtry and Saskatchewan attorney general Roy Romanow were trying to hammer out a deal.

What finally emerged was an agreement to include a Charter of Rights that the provinces had rejected, although it would contain a "notwithstanding" clause that would allow any government to opt out, for up to five years, of any court-based decision on the Charter ruling it did not like. The opt-out could then be renewed. The constitutional amending formula was the one the provinces supported; most changes could be made with the approval of the federal Parliament and the legislatures of seven of the provinces which together had at least fifty per cent of the national population.

Trudeau at his residence and the premiers at the Château knew what was going on, but Lévesque and the Quebec delegation were asleep across the Ottawa River with no idea. When Lévesque found out the next morning, he was livid and refused to agree. Most reporters, me included, were like Lévesque. I had to be at the Conference Centre at least an hour and a half before the nine o'clock conference start time, and like the Quebec premier, I was at home sleeping. But when I got to the Conference Centre the next morning, there was a rumour circulating that a deal had been reached. The conference was late in starting, and when we went on the air it was clear that something was going to be announced.

As was the case a year earlier, we were filling the air by talking about a deal we really knew nothing about. This time, that job fell to Peter Mansbridge who had replaced Knowlton Nash as anchor of news specials. Next to him sat David Halton. It wasn't clear how I'd get on, and unlike in 1980, no one was rushing up to me to say the CBC was wrong and tell me what was really happening.

I decided, since I had a wireless microphone and headset and could listen to the broadcast and be in contact with the producer, I would move over to a central door through which some of the premiers might enter. Eureka! No sooner had I arrived than Saskatchewan premier Allan Blakeney came through the door. I had first met him twenty years earlier, covering the medicare story, and again over a variety of first ministers' conference in the past few years.

"Allan, is there a deal?" I asked him as I took hold of his arm.

Seeing we weren't on the air, he said, "Yes, but it doesn't include Quebec."

"Can you say it on the air?" I asked.

"Pierre won't like it. But okay. But you will have to ask me."

I yelled into my intercom to the control room that I had the Saskatchewan premier and he would talk about the deal. Anchoring a program is like steering a ship, but Mansbridge steered seamlessly into introducing me, not entirely sure what I was going to talk about.

The room was filling up, and the conference might start at any moment, forcing Blakeney to leave me high and dry. Quickly, I introduced him and ran through, probably a little too fast, the information he was willing to share. Yes, there was a deal. No, Quebec had not agreed. Yes, there was a deal on the Charter of Rights and the amending formula.

A couple of minutes later, Trudeau entered the room through a side door. I knew there were televisions on in the lounge where he had been waiting. It seemed a reasonable assumption he had been listening to Blakeney and me. In fact, he looked rather stone-faced as he went through, in much greater detail, what had been agreed to. When he was finished, he walked right towards me, heading for the door Blakeney had used to enter the room.

"Prime Minister, can I get a word?" I said with a friendly smile as he approached.

His face set as if in concrete, he walked right past me, saying nothing. But clearly, he had been watching on television, and I knew then how to identify a look that could kill.

23

This Week in Parliament

IN MANY WAYS, the Ottawa to which I returned in October 1981 was very similar to the one I had left nine years earlier. Once again the Liberals were in power and Pierre Trudeau was prime minister. Some of the big cabinet names, like John Turner and Donald Macdonald were gone, but others, like Allan MacEachen and Marc Lalonde, were even more important than when I left. Joe Clark, who served nine months as prime minister, was now under pressure as he led the Progressive Conservatives as the Official Opposition. Ed Broadbent had made good on his ambition to lead the NDP. To be sure, there were many new faces, but I knew Ian Deans of the NDP, whom I covered at Queen's Park, and Lloyd Axworthy, now a cabinet minister, whom I first met in Winnipeg.

But the people involved in *This Week in Parliament* I did not know well, except that the program known at the CBC by its acronym, *TWIP,* and the people working on it as Twippers. Originally, there were three people on the staff: a host, a writer and producer. The host's on-camera portion was taped Friday evening in the foyer of the House of Commons by a Parliamentary bureau news crew working on a weekly rotation, and the show was edited together, again on rotation, by an electronic news editor in the bureau.

All three of the original staff members have since died. Bill Casey was the gentleman host I replaced, and he went on to have a good career at the CBC. Ironically, he later proved to be very good at putting together intricate retrospective stories of big events—something *This Week in Parliament* had lacked. But Bill was new to the bureau when he began on the show and the writer and the producer were CBC time-servers, determined not to break a sweat, and Bill wasn't prepared to rock their boat.

I, on the other hand, was. Well, actually, I didn't rock their boat, I beached them. Improvements to the show would have to be my idea, and I would have to implement them myself. So I did, and with no objection from them as I did most of their work.

A lot of changes were badly needed. No longer was the show to be a Sunday afternoon vagabond. It was to have a fixed time slot every week on Saturday evening. (And great timing, before *Hockey Night in Canada* in eastern and central Canada and after the game in most of western Canada.) From the start, I wanted the show to be fast-paced, with stories and debates covered both with explanatory on-camera appearances as well as voice-overs between MPs speaking. No more would there be shots of the Speaker when not much was going on—that wasn't getting on air. No more would an Opposition MP ask a question with a long preamble. I had the preamble edited off and cut to the nut of the question. And no more would viewers see the camera pan over to the minister rising to answer. On my program, he was edited so that he was already on his feet and talking.

My first *TWIP* went to air Saturday, October 10, 1981. I hadn't discussed my plans with anyone in great detail, and my instructions were vague. Vince Carlin had told me to make the show better, but hadn't been specific. Allan Pressman was the manager of the Parliamentary bureau, and he—not the bureau chief, Elly Alboim—was executive producer of the program. However, there had previously been very little for Pressman to produce, and besides warning me about how little support I could receive from the writer and producer, he merely wished me luck. That lack of support could have been perceived as a limit to what I could do. I preferred to see it as an opportunity. With no one telling me what to do, I had editorial freedom so long as I kept to the general mandate of the program. And that's what I exercised on the first program and every program thereafter.

When my first *This Week in Parliament* aired, it caused a bit of a stir. No one had paid much attention to the program before, and when they saw all the changes, some expressed amazement. Carlin sent me a note saying it was just what he had hoped it would be. While Pressman was generally ecstatic, some reporters and producers were a bit nonplussed that there was something new and different to contend with in the bureau.

After that, the pressure was on to keep up the quality, but in truth it wasn't all that difficult. Mondays and Tuesdays of each week, I would follow what was happening on Parliament Hill. Sometimes I would go to a House committee meeting or sit in on Question Period, but I didn't usually have to do very much. On Wednesday I would have a good idea of the stories likely to be on the program, would check in with the tape library for comments by ministers and other MPs from scrums outside the House, and would set aside the tapes I would be using. Thursday, I would start writing the script, assembling the clips and copy for the stories from the first three days of the week. I would work late into Thursday evening completing that and adding new and relevant developments from that day's Question Period, scrums and debates. By the time I left Thursday night, I had a working script, the tape segments identified and a good idea of what the program was going to look like. Friday, I polished the script as I checked with the bureau researcher on what was coming up the next week and with the government House leader's office on the status of bills debated in the House that week.

During the time that Ray Hnatyshyn was government House leader, his assistant was a wonderfully helpful woman named Judith LaRocque. A former procedural officer in the House of Commons, she went beyond the call of duty—probably should have had a credit on *TWIP,* had that been appropriate. Later, in a small way, I tried to thank her. After Ray Hnatyshyn became Governor General, Judith went to Rideau Hall as secretary to the Governor General, a role she also held under his successor, Roméo LeBlanc. Each year when the Governor General laid a wreath at the National War Memorial on Remembrance Day, Judith would also appear on camera. While she was on the screen, I would identify her as "Judith LaRocque from Hawkesbury, Ontario." Although Judith was never able to watch the broadcasts, she told me her mother was thrilled when I mentioned her. Judith continues to have a very successful career, having been a deputy minister and an ambassador.

Friday evenings, I always went with the crew to the foyer of the House of Commons. While they set up the lights, I would commit to memory the script I had written. Sometimes I would deliver the on-camera pieces while walking slowly across part of the foyer, just to make it more visually interesting. Because there was a faint, echoing quality to the empty foyer, I would also read the voice-over pieces into the camera while I was there, so that the audio would sound the same on them as it did on the on-camera part of the show.

For variety, the crew would change the camera location from time to time. The cameramen loved this part; it gave them a chance to be creative. Because I could memorize faster than they could relight and move the camera, I would sing while they made the changes. The same echo we worried about on the voice-overs actually enhanced the sound of one's singing voice. Because most people had gone home, I didn't think anyone but the crew could hear, although sometimes, fairly early in the shoot, Prime Minister Trudeau would come down from his office on the floor above, sweep through one end of the foyer, down the steps and into his car. You always knew when he was coming; two security men would come down the stairs first and wait for him at the west door of the Centre Block, where he exited to his car.

I hadn't actually spoken to Trudeau since our plane flight in Alberta, but at first, when I would see his security men coming, I thought I might catch his eye and either say hello or at least wave. But it never happened. He would keep his eyes down, walk through the foyer and ignore me.

Finally, I thought, "Screw him." The next time I saw the security men come down, I was standing against the low, concrete wall at the end of the foyer above the steps he descended on his way to the door. I knew he would be right behind, but instead of looking for him, I stayed by the wall and turned the other way. I heard him start down the steps, and as he passed by, I heard his familiar voice say: "Singing again tonight, Don?"

I whirled around with a smile on my face, ready to speak, only to see his back going through the door. *Got me again.*

Most weeks, that is how the program unfolded. In March 1982, there was a particular challenge, when the Progressive Conservatives refused to come into the Commons for a vote and the division bells summoning members to the chamber rang nonstop, around the clock for fifteen days. I had to do two shows, taped in the foyer with those loud bells ringing.

The first few weeks in 1981, *TWIP* was getting about 400,000 viewers. Then the numbers started climbing, to 500,000 and then 600,000. On a really cold Saturday night in January, with a good hockey game to follow, we topped 700,000 viewers. Our highest-rated show ever took place on

Saturday, March 3, 1984, three days after Pierre Trudeau announced his resignation. The Liberal Party executive was meeting that afternoon at the Château Laurier Hotel to decide the rules for the leadership race and the date of the convention to pick Trudeau's successor.

As executive producer, bureau manager Allan Pressman was so excited, he proposed that we do a *TWIP* special, live in our Saturday time slot from the foyer of the House. Somewhere he had found the money to bring in a truck that usually did remote broadcasts of football games and conventions, and the crew to run it. I asked Liberal Party president Iona Campagnolo to hurry from the meeting at the Château the short distance to Parliament Hill to give us the scoop on the decision. I prepared a tape segment covering Trudeau's walk in the snow to reach his decision and reaction from around Parliament Hill, and a second, shorter one with reaction beyond Ottawa. I invited NDP leader Ed Broadbent to appear live, and my colleagues David Halton and Whit Fraser, who covered the NDP, to join me as a panel to interview Broadbent and Campagnolo.

It was a cold evening with a bit of blowing snow as we went to air at six-thirty. There was no sign of Iona Campagnolo. I introduced the first tape pack standing in front of a camera and then moved to the desk, where David and Whit were already seated facing Broadbent. There were no commercials on *TWIP*, so the second tape pack had to run between the end of the Broadbent interview and the beginning of the Campagnolo one so we could get him out of the chair and get her into it with a mike.

As the first tape pack ended and the Broadbent interview began, there was still no sign of Campagnolo. From where I was sitting, I could see the stairs up which she would come, and I was looking at them as much as I was following the interview. If she came too late, she would miss the show entirely, and if she came too close to the end of the program, there would not be time to make the switch from Broadbent to her. She was essential to the news being made here about what was coming next.

Suddenly, with about eleven minutes left, Campagnolo appeared at the top of the stairs. Quickly, I cut off the discussion with Broadbent, introduced the next short tape pack, and the technicians hustled Ed out of the chair and Iona into it. I came back on camera with eight minutes left. During that time, as we talked to her, she delivered the goods— telling us, and our viewers, the date of the convention, the candidates' spending limits and the plans for regional debates. We got it all in under the line and I signed off just in time for *Hockey Night in Canada.* It was all worth the effort and extra cost. CBC had the scoop, and when the ratings came out early the next week, a lot of people had seen us make news. Over 800,000 people had watched the program.

The Campagnolo program was part of a plan to expand the show beyond its original mandate of reporting just what happened in any given week in the House of Commons. Instead, I wanted to have a program that dealt with all relevant political events, with me as both the host and editor, and that's what I made *TWIP* into. Over the years, I made changes as I went along. In 1983 I added an interview segment, and while the interview with an MP was usually about a story from the House that week, I also used the time to keep alive stories that were long-running but not always in the parliamentary news. The free trade negotiations with the United States, the Meech Lake Accord manoeuvres during its three-year ratification period, the ins and outs of party politics, leadership races and conventions—all of this and more was grist for my mill.

A big and welcome change came in 1986, when Nancy Swetnam joined me to help produce the program. We added all sorts of production values, new theme music and a much higher-end look to the program. She became very adroit at packaging the House portion of the program, and after we got an autocue, I no longer had to memorize the scripts I wrote. Between Nancy and that teleprompter, my job became a lot easier.

There was a lot of satisfaction to be had from essentially starting a new program by myself and taking it forward, and it was not only easier to do *TWIP*, but also the other parts of the job I had come to Ottawa to do: news specials. Before 1986, I had to work on live specials and then complete *TWIP* by myself and get it to air. Luckily, the specials often seemed to be at the beginning of the week, but occasionally I would have to work overnight Friday and all day Saturday to get the show to air. I didn't complain, though, because those specials were covering our history live, as it unfolded, and the subject matter of the specials was also often relevant to my Saturday program.

By the mid-eighties, we had the program where I wanted it to be, and the news gods were smiling, with plenty of leadership races and conventions, major trade negotiations with the United States, and con- stitutional negotiations that started off promisingly but ended up almost tearing the country apart.

This Week in Parliament had become a lot more than what went on in the House of Commons.

24

Conservatives in the '80s

T HE FIRST TIME I had a real conversation with Joe Clark, he bought me a beer. It was on a Sunday at the end of January 1972, and we were in the dining room of the Château Lacombe Hotel in Edmonton.

I had met Clark in Ottawa, where he and his friend Lowell Murray were both working on the staff of Opposition leader Robert Stanfield. I knew Lowell better than Joe, but each of us knew who the other was when our paths crossed.

I had just arrived in Edmonton from Ottawa en route to covering a finance ministers' meeting at Jasper. The last leg of the trip was to be accomplished on the westbound transcontinental train, which was to leave Edmonton in a few hours for Vancouver. To pass the time, I decided to have a beer, but in Alberta in 1972 bars closed on Sundays, and to have a drink in a licensed restaurant, you had to buy food. I had eaten on the flight from Ottawa and wasn't hungry, but I looked into the hotel restaurant and who should be sitting alone at a table, eating, but Joe Clark. He waved, and I went over. After the hellos, I got down to the main point. Would he, I asked, order a beer on his lunch tab that I would then drink and pay for? He did even better. He ordered my beer, and he paid.

Clark told me he was in Edmonton on his way to a political nominating meeting the next evening in Edson, Alberta. Because of a fight in the PC ranks in 1968, the Yellowhead riding had gone to the Liberals. Now Clark was going to be one of a number of candidates vying for the Tory nomination to try and win the traditionally Conservative riding back. When I pressed him on his chances of winning the nomination, he said they were not all that good. Either he was being overly modest or didn't know his own strength. He won the nomination, and then the seat in the election that fall. One more election, two years later, and a leadership convention in 1976, and Clark was leader of the Progressive Conservatives. In the general election of May 1979, he did what no one else was able to do: he defeated Pierre Trudeau and took the Tories into office with a minority government.

But that was where his luck ran out. His government was defeated six months later on a confidence motion opposing the budget. Clark then lost the general election two months after that, and the Conservatives tumbled back into opposition. At a party convention in Ottawa in early 1981, only two-thirds of the delegates wanted him to continue as leader; the other third wanted a convention to replace him. After that disappointing result, Clark told members of his restive Parliamentary caucus that if he could not win more support when the party next voted on his leadership in two years, he would step down.

It was a cold January when the PC Party gathered in Winnipeg in 1983, and the tension and hype surrounding the meeting were second only to those of a leadership convention itself. Clark had been subjected to continual sniping from within the party since 1981, and more than one potential rival had been subtly—or not so subtly—organizing to try and dump him. The votes were being counted on the question of whether the party should hold a leadership convention; if Clark did not improve on his 1981 level of support, he would have to quit and trigger a leadership race for his job.

There was a lot of jostling for position going on. At one point, a large group of Quebec delegates were brought en masse by bus from their hotels, and an attempt was made to register them all at once, with one cheque covering their registration fees. That was not on, said the convention organizing committee. Each would have to show personal identification to pay their own fee. The Quebec delegates got in line while someone rushed off to find a bank that would cash a cheque for thousands of dollars. I came out to watch the scene, and it was then that I first saw Brian Mulroney in action.

I was in Washington in 1976 when Mulroney burst upon the public consciousness with his high-flying but unsuccessful run for the PC leadership that Clark ultimately won that year. I had not met him until the Ottawa convention in 1981, when we passed in a hallway at the Château Laurier Hotel and he introduced himself. Now I saw him again in the lobby of the Winnipeg Convention Centre, going up and down the line of waiting Quebec delegates, shaking their hands, joking in French, making sure they all stayed in place until they could be properly registered as delegates and then, two nights later, vote the way he wanted them to vote: for a leadership convention.

CBC Television News was in Winnipeg in leadership convention mode, with an anchor booth, floor reporters, fixed cameras on the convention floor and roving cameras as well. On the night of the voting, I was at my post as a floor reporter, interviewing people as they came out of the polling room and asking them how they voted. It was very unscientific and inane, but it did what one must always do on television: fill the time. Then the polls closed and the counting began.

Shortly after, a rumour began circulating that Clark was doing very well in the counting, that his support was over seventy per cent, maybe even seventy-five. Despite no announcement of the results, his supporters on the floor heard the rumours and became very excited. A band was on stage playing while the count went on, and extemporaneously Clark supporters started dancing with glee. Flora MacDonald, who had been minister of external affairs in the short-lived Clark government and was now supporting her former boss, caught the spirit. I stepped out of the way so my floor camera could get a good shot of Canada's former top diplomat joyously cutting a rug.

Upstairs in the booth and at other spots on the floor, people were speculating on the size of the Clark victory and what it could mean. I wasn't saying anything because I didn't know what the vote result was. As time was beginning to drag, a large man with a full shock of white hair whom I didn't know walked over to me. I had noticed him earlier, because he looked the way the Man from Glad would look if he were a nightclub bouncer.

"Has it occurred to you that if Clark had done all that well they would have come out and announced it right away?" he asked. "Why do you think it is taking so long? Maybe he hasn't done that well."

"Who are you?" I asked.

"Labelle. Richard Labelle, from Quebec."

"Do you want to make that point on TV?" I asked.

"No. But you think about it."

I decided I should put it on the air myself. I called into the control room and said I wanted to report something. I said on air, "Down here where I am standing on the floor, some people are beginning to wonder why it is taking so long to announce the results. They are saying that if the result is so good for Clark, it would have been announced quickly, and it hasn't been. I don't know if the people saying that know anything more than the rest of us, but it is something worth thinking about."

Those few words were about as welcome as my report at the constitutional conference in 1980 that we were mistaken and our speculation that there was an agreement was not accurate. That time, I was dead certain I was right, because I had an inside source. This time, I too was speculating, but against the flow of the rest of the program. But the more I thought about it, the surer I was that I was on the right track.

And minutes later, that was confirmed. The formal announcement of the results showed nothing had changed in the two years since the last vote on a leadership convention. One-third of the party wanted one, two-thirds didn't. The delay in announcing the result was to give Clark time to decide what he wanted to do. Twice as many people apparently wanted him to stay as to leave. But he had not been able to gain any more supporters, as he had told his fellow Conservative MPs he would. That, in the end, was the clincher. Clark announced he would resign as party leader and become a candidate to succeed himself at the ensuing leadership convention.

Suddenly, people who had been dancing in support of Clark stood silent in stunned disbelief. A small group, the third who wanted Clark out, cheered at the result. Then, something very odd happened: Clark's supporters, with him on the stage, suddenly picked him up and hoisted him on their shoulders, then down from the stage, carrying him through the crowd that now applauded him and out of the room. It was almost as though the fallen warrior had been placed on his shield and carried from the field of battle.

On the floor, people happy with the result were eager to be interviewed, although most of them had very little to say that was different. The interview that has stayed with me was with a Clark supporter. Nancy

Jamieson had worked with Clark when he was prime minister. To this day, her mind is sharp as a tack, and in 1983, although she was no longer working with him, Jamieson was still Clark's close and great supporter. She looked devastated, but after all the people who had come on to trash Clark, I thought I should try and get one of his supporters on. When the program came to me, we started to talk, but it was too much. Her voice broke, tears started to form, and I cut short the interview and sent the program back up to the booth. And then, although I didn't know her very well, I gave her a hug.

THE LEADERSHIP CAMPAIGN that followed was as rough and dirty as any I have observed. Clark, in his campaign to regain his job, and Brian Mulroney, in his effort to displace him, were the two main protagonists, and they weren't taking many prisoners. Each was signing up as PC Party members blocks of new Canadians, young people, senior citizens and any other group they could find, so that they could go to delegate selection meetings and vote for those running to become riding delegates supporting the candidate that had signed them up. Jason Moscovitz on CBC Television uncovered and reported with compelling videotape a group of residents from the Old Brewery Mission in downtown Montreal who had been signed to Conservative Party membership cards by the Mulroney campaign and bused to vote at a constituency meeting to select delegates.

As the leadership campaign rolled on through the winter and into the spring of 1983, Parliament rolled along in session, too. That meant I was in Ottawa every week, following the race through contacts and friends in the various campaign headquarters, and in the case of the Mulroney campaign, in the cafeteria of the West Block on Parliament Hill. The West Block houses MPs' offices and committee rooms, and it has the largest and best cafeteria among the Parliament Buildings—and the prices are reasonable. The high-end Parliamentary Restaurant is on the top floor of the Centre Block.

As fate would have it, in the fall of 1982, Linc changed schools. He left the elementary school at the end of our street for a private boys' school in Rockcliffe Park, a wealthier neighbourhood than our own. He'd been in three schools in four years, as we moved from Washington to Edmonton and then Ottawa, and we thought he needed the attention of smaller classes and a vigorous athletics program to get him on track. But Ashbury College was about a twenty-minute drive from our house, and it started at ten to eight each morning. I was his driver. Linc seemed to have time for breakfast, but I never did. So early on, I realized that after dropping him I could be on Parliament Hill in fifteen minutes and have breakfast in the West Block cafeteria.

I was soon invited to join a table of regulars that ate there each morning: two Conservative MPs, Otto Jelinek from Ontario and Gordon Towers from Alberta; a man named Rick Logan, who worked for Robert Coates, the president of the PC Party and an MP from Nova Scotia; and Tommy Van Dusen, a longtime veteran of the Hill who had worked for John Diefenbaker when he was prime minister. Sometimes, former MP Doug Fisher, who was now writing a column for the Sun newspapers, would also join us.

To a man, they all loathed Joe Clark and wanted Brian Mulroney to replace him. To some extent, all of them were willing to share information from the Mulroney campaign, but by far the best information came from Rick Logan. He had a wicked sense of humour and made terrible puns, but if you caught on to his drift and listened carefully, you could find out a lot about both Mulroney's campaign and how his opponents thought Joe Clark was doing.

On the other side, my best connection to the Clark campaign was

Senator Nate Nurgitz. He was, and still is, a wonderful man whom I first met in Winnipeg when he tried unsuccessfully to win a seat for the Conservatives in the 1966 provincial election. Nate was one of just a few people Clark had appointed to the Senate in his nine months as prime minister, and he was loyal to his patron, but also realistic about his chances and prescient about how undeclared MPs and senators were really planning to vote on the leadership.

The convention was to run from June 8 to 12, with the leadership vote to be held on Saturday, June 11. As the delegates flooded into the city at the beginning of that week, I ran into a familiar face in the bar of the Four Seasons Hotel near Parliament Hill: the "Man from Glad" I had met in Winnipeg, Richard Labelle. He was an important organizer for Mulroney in Quebec, and like the people from Ontario and Alberta that I had been having breakfast with for the past year, he too thought Clark would probably lead on the first ballot but that Mulroney would eventually take the prize.

I didn't disagree. Each leadership convention has its own dynamic, but generally speaking, if one person emerges as the front-runner and the candidate to beat, that person had better either win on the first ballot or have such a commanding lead that people not prepared to support the candidacy initially fall into line on a second ballot. While six months earlier Clark had had two-thirds of the party voting against a leadership convention in Winnipeg, he wasn't going to have at least half of the delegates at this convention voting on the first ballot for him to continue. What is more, by running against him, it was clear the other candidates thought Clark should be replaced as leader. It was unlikely that their failing to do well on early ballots would lead them to endorse him on subsequent votes.

However, the Clark campaign was doing a good job of spinning that their man was ahead and that subsequent ballots would take him over the top. And since his campaign was staffed by people who had worked on Parliament Hill and in the party for years, and who were known and generally liked by many reporters, that was an idea that took hold.

At the final meeting the day before our convention coverage began, Arnold Amber, then executive producer of CBC news specials and the person who would drive the program each day it was on the air, met with his five main anchors and reporters. At the end of the meeting, he went around the room, asking each of us who we thought would win. All of my colleagues said Clark. I said nothing.

Amber looked at me quizzically. "You don't agree?"

"No."

"Who do you think will win?" he asked.

"Mulroney."

THE CONVENTION WAS held in Ottawa at the Civic Centre, a hybrid piece of construction that has a nine-thousand-seat hockey arena built underground, beneath the north grandstand seats of the Lansdowne Park football stadium, which gives the rink its unique roof line. The action was all on the floor of the arena, with the candidates sitting in boxes just above ice level and their supporters ranged in the seats behind them.

At this convention, I was again to be a roving reporter, with a battery pack powering both my microphone and the audio system through which, in one ear, I could hear the program being broadcast and in the other, instructions either from the control room when broadcasting or editorial control when I wasn't on the air.

Each of the five major candidates had a reporter assigned to stand on a riser in front of them and catch their comments as the results unfolded. My job was to roam the floor, finding out what was really going on, who

was talking to whom between ballots, and where the supporters of eliminated candidates were going to cast their ballots once their favourite
was out of the race.

As part of my preparation for the coverage, I had created a system of
small file cards with the names of the three leading candidates—Clark,
Mulroney and John Crosbie, the only other candidate with a realistic
chance of winning—and the MPs and senators who were supporting
each of them. I didn't create cards for two other former cabinet ministers in the race, Michael Wilson and David Crombie. Each was well
thought of but had little caucus support and no hope of winning. The
only role either might play was to endorse one of the favourites when
they dropped off the ballot, although each seemed to have so little support that an endorsement might be more symbolic than effective.

Once I had created the three lists on the file cards, I put an elastic
band around the group for each candidate, and before going onto the
convention floor I put them in the back pockets of my suit pants. I did
refer to them from time to time, but the real value of those cards was the
research that went into creating them in the first place. I knew most of
the information on them by heart.

Convention voting day, Saturday June 11, dawned bright and hot.
As the voting began in the Civic Centre, it was already really warm
inside—just a harbinger of what was to come. Before long, it was like
a steam bath. Delegates cast their votes on the first ballot, and again,
after what seemed like a long delay, the results were announced. And
those results accurately predicted how the leadership would turn out
three more ballots later.

At the bottom of the ballot, three no-hopers who had run for vanity
or some other unclear reason had 124 votes between them and were all
off the ballot. One of the three was Peter Pocklington, then the owner of
the Edmonton Oilers. He and his other two compatriots all announced

their support for Mulroney. So too did Michael Wilson, who could have stayed on the ballot, but, with only 134 votes, decided it was time to move on. David Crombie had fewer votes than Wilson, just 116, but he was not automatically eliminated. Many wonder why he stayed when Wilson, with more votes, had chosen to go.

At the top end of the results, John Crosbie was in third place with 639 votes, Brian Mulroney in second with 874 and, leading on the first ballot, Joe Clark with 1,091.

Clark's supporters let out a big cheer when his number was announced. Clark waved, perhaps not quite as enthusiastically as he might. If you look at a videotape of the Clark box as the result is announced, you can see Clark flinch as he hears the numbers. A woman standing next to his wife, Maureen McTeer, offers her congratulations, but McTeer, knowing the way the arithmetic will ultimately develop after winning less than thirty-seven per cent of the first-ballot votes, says clearly enough for any novice lip reader to see: "It's not enough."

I was going around the floor, interviewing various delegates on the air, when I heard in my ear the voice of Elly Alboim, the Parliamentary bureau chief, who had editorial control of the broadcast.

"We have some interesting tape just shot outside in the stands in Lansdowne Park. It seems to be a meeting between some Clark people and people with Crosbie. One of the people in the meeting is Nate Nurgitz. See if you can find him and see what it all about."

Finding a person on a crowded convention floor is a bit like finding a needle in a haystack. But down in front of the Clark section, there was the good senator from Manitoba. The meeting, he explained, had been triggered by the first-ballot results. It was clear that if things just unfolded ballot by ballot, Mulroney was going to end up with the most votes at the end. The Crosbie people were arguing that the only way to stop that was for Clark to drop out, endorse Crosbie and deliver all or most of his delegates to his former finance minister and put the Newfoundlander over the top.

"Will you say all this on the air?" I asked.

"Well, a bit of it," he said. And he did, telling me a meeting had been held, summarizing what had been discussed and saying that it wasn't going to happen. While we were talking, pictures, shot from a distance, of the meeting in the football grandstand ran over our conversation.

The second ballot began with four candidates, and when the results were announced, it was clear why Crombie had stayed on despite his low vote total. On this ballot, he had just sixty-seven votes, and as the low man was eliminated. He immediately endorsed Crosbie and went to sit in his box. Crosbie's vote total had gone up on the second ballot, but he was still third, and had Crombie not stayed on the ballot, Crosbie would have been the low man and forced off the ballot. His friend had given him at least one more ballot to try his luck.

The focus of attention, though, was on the top of the ballot, where Mulroney was closing the gap, now just sixty-four votes behind Clark, each with about thirty-five per cent of the vote. Clark was stuck; Mulroney was gaining. The universe was unfolding as the first-ballot results had predicted.

The third ballot, though, showed little change from the second, with Clark narrowly in front but Mulroney now just twenty-two votes behind. Crosbie had almost thirty per cent of the vote, but he was third on the ballot and was eliminated from contention. On the fourth ballot, it was mano a mano. But it was really no contest. Clark got his biggest vote total of the day. But Mulroney got 259 more and won the Progressive Conservative Party leadership with fifty-five per cent of the convention vote to Clark's forty-five.

On his second try, Brian Mulroney had become leader of the Progressive Conservative Party. The PCs had a new leader, but little did we know at the time how much more was about to change.

25

Liberals in the '80s

THE LIBERALS WERE watching the Progressive Conservative leadership race almost as closely as the Tories. And as Brian Mulroney wrestled the Tory crown from Joe Clark in June 1983, it underlined what most people following politics had already assumed: the Liberals would also need a new leader before the country next went to the polls, most likely in 1984.

Pierre Trudeau had cancelled his retirement in 1979 to return triumphant and reverse his defeat to Joe Clark in May of that year with a victory and a government with a small majority in February of 1980. The unspoken assumption throughout that campaign was that, if re-elected, Trudeau would serve no more than a couple of years before retiring for good, leaving his successor with a majority government and at least two more years to govern and establish a reputation as prime minister. And after the successful patriation of the Constitution in April of 1982, which was viewed as Trudeau's legacy, people began looking for signs that that was about to happen. But they looked in vain.

By the fall of 1983, Mulroney had entered the House through a by-election in a Nova Scotia riding and was leading the Opposition in Question Period and beyond. For someone who had never done it before, he was surprisingly good as a questioner, although Trudeau and the other old pros in the Liberal cabinet like Marc Lalonde, Allan MacEachen and Lloyd Axworthy could verbally smack him around if his questions got too far under their skin. But what went on in the House didn't seem to matter much. The Liberals were lagging badly in the public opinion polls, and an economy slow to recover from the recession of 1981–82 wasn't helping.

In the late fall of 1983 and early winter of 1984, Trudeau began a "world peace tour" of foreign capitals, including Washington and Moscow. The tour didn't seem to affect world peace, nor did it do much for Trudeau's poll standing, even though he managed to be awarded the Einstein Peace Prize in Chicago. It was a prize unheard of in Canada, and it was unclear what Trudeau had specifically achieved to deserve it.

In February 1984, a newspaper reported that Trudeau's office was keeping a "secret" file on Mulroney. It turned out the file was a folder of newspaper clippings and not much else, but Mulroney feigned indignation. As I sat down to watch Question Period that day, I expected there would be quite a ruckus in the Commons. There was a lot more than I had expected, because in Question Period the day the story broke, every Tory question was about the file. Usually, the prime minister responds only to questions from the other party leaders, but on this day, Trudeau got to his feet to take every question about the Mulroney file. And with every response, he hit the ball out of the park. It was a bravura performance, unseen in the House of Commons in anyone's memory before or since. Liberal MPs' cheers for him grew louder and louder. After Question Period, in the lobby behind the government benches, the cheering continued as Trudeau walked through on his way to his office.

On *This Week in Parliament* that Saturday, Trudeau's performance was a big part of the program, and I concluded that the prime minister certainly appeared to be at the top of his game and showed no indication he was slowing down or thinking of resigning. What happened next shows what I actually knew about what was going on.

Trudeau resigned.

He claimed to have taken a walk in the snow on the evening of February 28, and seeing no sign in the sky that he should stay on, only the snow that was falling, he decided to quit. For a man who loved a show and being the centre of attention, his announcement that he was leaving was very low key. Just a scrum as he stood in his shirt-sleeves outside his office. It was a leap year. Trudeau took his leap on February 29.

THAT WEEKEND, THE Liberal Party executive decided that the convention to replace Trudeau would be held at the Civic Centre in Ottawa between June 14 to 17, in the same place and exactly a year and a week after the Tories had chosen Brian Mulroney to lead them. But unlike the Conservative race in 1983, where there were two strong contenders and one other who also had a chance of winning, from the start of the Liberal contest John Turner was far and away the front-runner. On the face of it, that would appear odd. Turner had been the up-and-coming bright young man in the Liberal party of the 1960s. After he was elected to Parliament from a Montreal riding in 1962, some saw him as the John F. Kennedy of Canadian politics. He probably saw himself that way too, but the picture changed in 1965 when Trudeau was recruited to run for the Liberals and dealing with Quebec nationalism became the paramount issue in the country. Turner had gathered a strong following among young Liberals when he ran for the leadership in 1968, but his support was no match for the party heavyweights. However, in a move that created the view he could be the next in line, Turner hung on until the final convention ballot, although he finished a weak third behind winner Trudeau and runner-up Robert Winters.

Turner served in the Trudeau cabinet, first as justice minister and then as minister of finance. He was an important minister, but not part of Trudeau's inner circle. Staying on the ballot and then keeping in close contact with his supporters from the last leadership cast him as a rival to the prime minister, and as the fortunes of the Trudeau government ebbed and flowed, whenever there were low Liberal poll numbers some people in the media and in the party would start talking about a leadership change, with Turner taking charge.

This became more prevalent after Turner abruptly quit the government in 1975 and moved to Toronto and a place at the Bay Street law firm McMillan Binch. There, he was a "rainmaker," attracting clients and dispensing advice on Canadian and international affairs. Sometimes that advice became public, either through loose-lipped clients or through newsletters the law firm sent its clients. On more than one occasion, Turner's views on public policy clashed with those of the Trudeau government. Within the party, two camps were growing: one that supported Trudeau and thought Turner disloyal, even a traitor; the other made up of loyal Turner supporters who thought Trudeau had pushed him from the cabinet to cut off a rival and who now wanted Turner to replace Trudeau and restore Liberal fortunes.

At the time, it appeared to be just a fight between two talented men with large ambitions, one of whom had the job the other wanted. In retrospect, it is clear that what really was happening was the beginning of a schism within the Liberal Party that would run its course over the next thirty years and culminate with the "natural governing party" collapsing into a third-place rump stuck in the back corner on the Opposition side of the House of Commons.

With the Liberals' defeat in the 1979 election and Trudeau's decision to step down, it appeared Turner had his chance to reach for the prize. Turner, however, let it pass, saying the timing was wrong for his family. Any time to run for a party leadership is usually a bad time for some, if not all, members of a politician's family. The fact that the Liberals were in Opposition in 1979 might also have been a contributing factor in Turner's decision. The front-runner to replace Trudeau became Donald Macdonald, another former finance minister who had also left the cabinet a couple of years after Turner and was also at a Toronto law firm.

Whatever Turner's reasons, it didn't matter. The Clark government was defeated on a budget vote and Trudeau rescinded his resignation and came back to lead the Liberals again to power. Now, four and a half years later, Trudeau had resigned again, and for Turner it was now or never. Approaching his fifty-fifth birthday, gone nine years from politics, if he didn't jump in now, when much of the Liberal Party, the media and the country were waiting for him, his status as leader-in-waiting would evaporate and he would become just another rich Bay Street lawyer who had once been a cabinet minister.

Beyond those rather obvious facts, whoever won the leadership this time would be prime minister. They were down in the polls, but the Liberals were the government and their mandate did not run out until February of 1985. Perhaps a new, popular leader could build the party back up, take the measure of Mulroney and keep the Liberals in power.

At least that was the conventional wisdom in the party and much of the media, and when Turner announced his candidacy in mid-March, the dual jobs of leader of the Liberal Party and prime minister of Canada were his to lose. Then, for the next month or so, it appeared he might lose it.

Turner was still a commanding figure in person—that is, until he opened his mouth. Then he seemed hesitant; it was clear his skills—public speaking, answering questions concisely, knowing when not to talk—were rusty, and more importantly, television had changed politics dramatically in the nearly ten years he had been away. Now the light ENG equipment and the videotapes they carried meant that camera crews and reporters could follow up close, asking questions in real time. Now newspaper reporters, who had originally scoffed when I was the first gallery person working in print to use a tape recorder, all carried tape recorders much smaller than the one I had used, catching virtually everything that happened and was said.

Turner was overwhelmed. Instead of looking like a commander riding to the rescue, he often looked rather like a respectable suburbanite who had mistakenly walked into a topless bar and was trying to maintain his composure as he looked for the way out.

Perhaps because of his shaky start, or maybe just fired by their own ambitions and career calculations, six other candidates soon joined the race. All were members of the Trudeau cabinet, although none of the big names—Marc Lalonde, Allan MacEachen or Lloyd Axworthy—jumped in. Axworthy had considered running; Trudeau had been encouraging, telling him he could handle being prime minister. Prime Minister Lester Pearson had told Trudeau the same thing at the beginning of 1968 before Trudeau entered the race and became Pearson's successor. However, Axworthy abandoned any hope of running after his fellow Winnipegger—and the man he hoped would be his financial angel—refused to support him. Izzy Asper was already well along building the Global Television empire, and Axworthy had supported Asper a decade earlier when he was leader of the Manitoba Liberals and Axworthy was its only member in the provincial legislature. But Asper wasn't about to support an Axworthy leadership bid now. He was backing everyone's favourite, John Turner.

Turner's path was also made easier when Donald Macdonald declined to run. Macdonald had been the favourite for a few days in 1979 after Turner decided not to run and before Trudeau came out of retirement, but in 1982 Trudeau appointed him chairman of a royal commission studying Canada's economic future. It was soon reported that he was being paid eight hundred dollars a day in that post. Not a lot of money for a Bay Street lawyer, perhaps, but a lot of money for most Canadians. Macdonald's everyman status was always questionable, but it wasn't helped when, at a press conference, I asked him if he thought he was being overpaid and he replied, "I think I am worth more." He probably was, and he was probably just having some fun, but television had changed the news while he wasn't paying attention and that comment stuck to him and would have hurt politically.

Two of the cabinet ministers who ran against Turner were seen as journeyman politicians seeking to enhance, if they could, their standing in the party and perhaps secure more prominent cabinet jobs in the future: John Munro and Eugene Whelan. Mark MacGuigan and John Roberts were both regarded as bright but lacking in the political charisma that takes a politician to the top tier. Donald Johnston was a relative newcomer. He had been Trudeau's personal lawyer and was elected in a by-election in 1978. Since the party returned to power in 1980, he had held a couple of significant cabinet portfolios, was recognized as smart and engaging and, compared to the others, was a fresh face.

No one would say that about Turner's main rival. He had been elected to the Commons just a year after Turner, in 1963 and had worked his way up through a series of cabinet jobs, including being the first French Canadian to serve as finance minister, and he had played a role

as justice minister in the last-ditch negotiations that lead to the patriation of the Constitution. Where Turner had split with Trudeau and left
politics, he had stayed the loyal soldier, even facing humiliation when
the prime minister once announced changes to economic policy without
bothering to consult with his finance minister.

Where Turner was a Bay Street smoothie, had been a Rhodes scholar
and once dated Princess Margaret, his rival presented himself as more
of a populist than he really was, a little guy from small-town Quebec.
But he had political instincts second to none, and he one day would be
a successful prime minister. In 1984, the time was not right for him.
Nevertheless, as Turner reached for the Liberal crown in June of that
year, he had a formidable opponent in Jean Chrétien.

26

Liberal Convention, Turner and Election '84

AFTER THAT SUCCESSFUL edition of *This Week in Parliament* in which Iona Campagnolo announced the date and rules of the Liberal leadership race, I wanted to make the contest a regular part of the program. After all, the winner was going to be prime minister, public interest was high, and since I was off to a strong start, I didn't want to lose momentum. So I created a special segment featuring the news of the campaign from the preceding week. Early on, the segment consisted predominantly of candidates' announcements, debates, policy announcements and gaffes. I also decided to do something I hadn't thought of a year earlier with the Conservatives: I would create my own profile of each of the candidates, focusing on some aspect of their campaign that made it stand out. I decided the last profile would run on Saturday, June 9, the weekend before the convention was to begin. And I decided the final profile would be on the campaign of John Turner, the most likely winner. The week before that, the spotlight would be on the campaign of his most formidable challenger, Jean Chrétien.

Sometimes, finding something unique about a campaign was difficult. John Munro was unusual because the campaign headquarters were
in his hometown of Hamilton, not Ottawa; Mark MacGuigan's was in
Toronto, where his best-known supporter was former Toronto Maple
Leaf and Detroit Red Wing hockey player Red Kelly, who had also sat for
three years in the House of Commons as a Liberal MP. Don Johnston's
campaign seemed to have the best computer system. Eugene Whelan
had a small office on Sparks Street in Ottawa, just down from Parliament
Hill, but no one working in it. He and his executive assistant seemed to
be running the campaign on their own. Chrétien had the most members
of Parliament amongst his supporters, and a big part of the campaign
fell to a northern Ontario MP named Keith Penner to ride herd on them
from his Parliament Hill office. Turner had the biggest campaign and
the biggest staff. He also had the largest organization ready to work the
convention floor on voting day. That was my focus on his campaign.

In retrospect, by far the campaign that had the longest-lasting
impact on Canadian politics and my reporting on it was that of John
Roberts. It was being run entirely by the executive of the national Young
Liberals, all in their early twenties or even younger. These members of
the youth wing of the party realized they were not going to have mean-
ingful roles in the other leadership campaigns, particularly that of John
Turner, who seemed to be the candidate most supported in their hearts.
So they went to Roberts with a proposition: they would work for him
if he would let them take over the campaign. Lacking a better offer and
strapped for cash, Roberts agreed they could run his campaign.

On an evening in May, I went with my crew to meet with Roberts
and his campaign team in a storage space above a store in central
Ottawa. There were about twenty Young Liberals sitting around, with
Roberts in the centre, and for the cameras they ran through a strategy
session. Basically, the campaign team was pitching ideas and Roberts

was commenting on them. He was good-natured and they all seemed to like him, even when he turned down the idea of saving money by getting into a Winnebago and driving across the country to meet with potential delegates. Roberts seemed to think it would take a lot of time for each delegate met and not be productive.

As I met and interviewed some of the Young Liberals working for Roberts, I was impressed by their knowledge of politics and commitment to the political process. Four particularly stuck in my mind: Brigitte Fortier, who would later work for Turner in the Opposition Leader's Office and for Jean Charest when he was premier of Quebec; Richard Mahoney from Ottawa, who could do a wicked impersonation of Turner; and two young men from Saskatchewan, David Herle from Regina and Bruce Ogilvie, the president of the Young Liberals, from Saskatoon.

Enjoying a beer with Herle and Ogilvie later, I was impressed by their commitment not to the Roberts campaign, but to the leadership bid of John Turner. As westerners, they said it was essential that Turner lead the Liberals, move the party to the right and undo what they said was the damage Trudeau had caused in their part of Canada. They knew Roberts had no chance of winning, but they planned to work as hard for him as they could, then try to get him and whatever delegates he had to go to Turner if their support was needed on later ballots. I made a mental note to myself to keep an eye on them after the results of the first ballot were announced if Turner had not won cleanly.

The convention opened with Turner in the lead and Chrétien the only one of the other candidates who might catch him. However, it seemed likely that Turner would fall short of a clear majority on the first ballot, giving the candidates lower down the field a chance to become the kingmaker.

The candidates were to address the convention on the Friday evening before the Saturday afternoon vote. Late in the afternoon, with nothing to do until the speeches began at 7 p.m., I was strolling behind the seats on the floor level of the Civic Centre when I came across the lounge set aside for party VIPs to relax and have a drink. It was off-limits to journalists, but I looked into what seemed to be an empty room to see who might be there. There was just one person, Liberal Party president Iona Campagnolo, who saw me, waved me in, offering a seat next to her and a drink. I took a seat and declined the drink, and we began chatting.

"You know we are going right into an election after this is over," she volunteered.

"Really? Why?" I asked.

"Don't you remember 1968? It worked then for Trudeau and we are going to do it again."

Yes, I assured her, I did remember the convention that Trudeau won in 1968 and the election shortly after in which he won a majority government.

"Actually," I said, "I was there. And the situation now is nothing like it was in 1968. There is no guarantee the outcome will be the same as it was then."

"You'll see," the Liberal Party president told me.

As I left, I filed away her information for any slow moment in the broadcast, either that night or while waiting for the results of the voting the next day.

At the Liberal convention, as at the Conservative one the year before, I was a roaming floor reporter with a remote microphone and audio system, with a variety of cameras, both portable and in fixed locations, available for me to do reports or interviews from the convention floor. As I went on the floor to get ready for the broadcast, I thought of the challenge facing the candidates. The farewell for Trudeau had taken place the evening before, and he was in top form, speaking without notes, standing without a podium, sometimes adopting his "gunslinger" pose with his thumbs in his belt loops. That got a cheer from the crowd each time he did it. He was going to be a tough act to follow.

Speaking order was drawn by lot, and that added to the drama. The other five candidates would speak before Turner came on in the sixth spot, and he would be followed by his main rival, Chrétien, who was to have the final word.

The other five candidates gave it their best shot. Their supporters tried to drum up enthusiasm, but in fact it was like watching the preliminary bouts leading up to a heavyweight title fight. Turner came on to a large, orchestrated demonstration and began his speech with some words about Trudeau that were surprisingly warm. However, neither Turner speaking them on the stage nor Trudeau listening in the stands looked as if they really believed them. Still, it was an effort at fence-mending and keeping the party together, and perfunctory or not, it was necessary.

There was nothing memorable about the rest of Turner's remarks, but he got off the stage without doing himself any damage, and as the front-runner, that was his strategy. That left only Chrétien, who, after going through the routine thank-yous and pleasantries, shifted into high gear. His most memorable line was designed to contrast his well-honed campaigning skills with the rustiness still hanging on to Turner.

"Give me Brian Mulroney on the campaign trail for seven weeks and you'll see what I will do to him!" he roared. And his delegates and his campaign workers roared back. When Chrétien finished on a high note, his supporters rose and gave him a standing ovation. A lot of other Liberals did too. It was a barn burner of a speech. But then something happened. As Chrétien walked off the stage, his supporters wouldn't sit down. Obviously, this was his only chance to try and build momentum and shake people loose before the vote the next day, and his campaign had decided to make it appear as though he had captured the convention with his speech. So as the ovation continued, out from backstage Chrétien came for a curtain call. As he walked around the stage waving, I pushed my way up to the front by the podium, where he would have to pass as he left, yelling to the control room over my intercom that I was going to try and talk to him. As he finished his walkabout and headed towards me, I was waving my microphone at him. It caught his eye. He bent down and we were on TV.

I said something about how he must be happy. Yes, he said, he was. A couple of more equally banal exchanges and he turned and walked off the stage. But the orchestrated cheering and the standing ovation didn't stop. And suddenly, there was Chrétien again, coming out for a second curtain call. This time, as he finished his walk around the stage, he came over directly to me. Watching from the control room, the director yelled in my ear, "You're on!"

"Mr. Chrétien," I shouted over the roaring crowd as other reporters were pressing in to hear our exchange, "is this it? Do you think you have the leadership?"

"Yes," Jean Chrétien replied, "I think I've got it."

The rest of the broadcast revolved around whether or not the Chrétien speech and demonstration would have a big impact on how the delegates would vote. My view was that it might bring him some support from people who had been planning to vote for one of the other five lesser candidates, but it wouldn't shake Turner's backers. Others, as I would see the next day, weren't so sure.

Before the broadcast ended for the evening, I was looking around the convention floor, trying to find Allan MacEachen. He was a true Liberal warhorse, having first been elected to the Commons in the general election of 1953, defeated in the Diefenbaker sweep in 1958, but re-elected in 1962. He had been an MP ever since. He first served in the cabinet of

Lester Pearson, was a leadership candidate in 1968 and then served in a number of important posts in the Trudeau government, among them finance minister, external affairs minister, government House leader and deputy prime minister. In 1968, when he ran for leader, John Munro supported his bid. This time, he had not declared his support for Munro or any of the candidates but had announced he would not be running in any subsequent election. That meant that, like Trudeau, he was leaving Parliament. I thought that deserved an interview on television, and I also thought it would be interesting to see whom he was going to back for leader.

MacEachen was from Cape Breton and on the left of the Liberal Party. That meant, based on policy, he would likely back Chrétien. But MacEachen was also of the Liberal establishment, and Turner was the establishment's man.

As far as I knew, MacEachen hadn't been interviewed anywhere else. But although I tried, I couldn't find him. I wondered why he was keeping a low profile.

Voting day, Saturday, was warm and sunny, just as it had been a year before for the Conservative convention. However, it was not as warm inside the Civic Centre as it had been the year before, and it wasn't likely to warm up as it did in 1983. Then, it had taken four ballots for Brian Mulroney to catch and defeat Joe Clark. The Liberal event should not run more than two ballots before Turner was crowned the new leader— unless, that is, Chrétien's speech the night before had really shaken a lot of delegates loose and Turner's big lead had dropped precipitously.

Then, before the voting began, two things happened. First, as I was lining up my first interview of the program, I was suddenly interrupted by the two co-managers of the Roberts campaign, David Herle and Bruce Ogilvie. They had already told me they were supporting Turner in their hearts, but now they wanted to do more.

"We want to go on TV right now and say we are endorsing Turner," Ogilvie said to me. "We think Chrétien's speech had an impact and we want to reverse the trend."

I looked at them standing there, perhaps twenty-two or twenty-three years old, intense, worried, proposing to do something that would make a bit of instant news, likely not have any impact on the outcome of the leadership, but could have a huge impact on them—an impact that could haunt them for years to come, perhaps all of their lives.

In a story before the convention, the *Ottawa Citizen* had described me as a "veteran" reporter. My first reaction reading it was that I was not a veteran—I hadn't served in the armed forces, and at forty-three I didn't think I was very old. But now, looking at Herle and Ogilvie, I felt aged indeed.

"Look," I told them, "we can go ahead now if you want, but you should understand that if you do, no one will ever trust you again in the Liberal Party. As Roberts campaign managers, bailing on him before the first results are known, you would be seen as committing an act of betrayal and your reputations will be ruined."

That stopped them short. They asked what they should do. I told them to come over to me quickly after the first-ballot results were known, and if it still made sense to endorse Turner—or anyone else they wanted—I would quickly put them on the air. A few seconds of thought, and that is what they decided to do.

While I was having this initial conversation with Herle and Ogilvie down on the convention floor, Turner was in his box with his campaign team. Suddenly, a roar went up from the people backing him. Into his box and over to Turner with a warm handshake was Allan MacEachen. That was a signal to any waverers on the more progressive side of the party. The former deputy prime minister and Trudeau ally was signalling that he was backing Turner and they could too.

Then the voting began, and the first-ballot results were about as predicted, with Turner about six hundred votes ahead of Chrétien and two
hundred short of the majority needed to win. All of the other candidates
were well up the track, each with less than 10 per cent of the vote. All
of them but one dropped out. Donald Johnston, who finished a distant
third, decided to do what Turner had done sixteen years earlier: stay on
the ballot with the two front-runners even though he had no chance of
winning. Roberts finished fourth and dropped off to endorse Chrétien,
even as his two campaign managers were on TV with me, throwing their
support to Turner. It was Herle and Ogilvie who backed the winner.

Turner went over the top on the second ballot, with 54 per cent of
the vote. As the candidates and Trudeau gathered on the stage for the
final formalities, party president Campagnolo did the first of two things
she would do over the next couple of months to help cripple any chances
Turner and the Liberals had of staying in power. Introducing runner-up
Chrétien to make the motion to have Turner's win declared unanimous,
she said that although Chrétien had finished second, he was "first in our
hearts," as if somehow the wrong man had won. For his part, Trudeau
came to the stage but didn't seem to be sharing in the excitement of the
outcome.

The long-lasting impact of the Roberts campaign derived from the
young Liberals who ran it. David Ogilvie was killed in a car crash that
summer but Herle and the others became key players in Paul Martin's
political career.

TURNER BECAME THE leader of the Liberals the day he won the convention on June 16. He did not become prime minister until Trudeau
resigned and he took office on June 30. Trudeau had promised patronage

appointments to a number of Liberal MPs, and if he made them before leaving office, the party would lose its majority in the House of Commons and Turner becoming prime minister could have then been complicated by the fact the Liberals were in a minority. So, instead of Trudeau making the appointments, Turner pledged in a letter to the outgoing prime minister that he would make the appointments before calling an election. As things turned out, that was a huge mistake. If Trudeau had made the appointments in June before leaving, he would have carried the stigma of doing the often necessary but publicly dirty work of handing out jobs. When Turner went to be sworn in as prime minister, the governor general, Jeanne Sauvé, might have questioned whether he could govern without a majority. Turner would have had to promise to call Parliament together in early September, and after losing a vote of confidence, call an election that he could have run in without defending the patronage appointments.

Instead, to keep his electoral options open for a late fall or even spring election in 1985, Turner agreed to make Trudeau's appointments for him. Then he decided to have a summer election anyway, which meant he had to name almost twenty Liberal MPs, bagmen and hangers-on to plum government and judicial jobs on the eve of calling an election, and then had to defend the appointments in the subsequent campaign.

The immensity of the mistake became apparent in the segment of the English television debate involving Turner and Mulroney. Neither man had a clear advantage until late in the debate, when Turner mistakenly veered into the patronage issue. Realizing his opportunity, Mulroney pounced, tackling Turner for the string of jobs he had handed out at Trudeau's behest just as the election was called. Startled, Turner stiffly replied that he had had no option, but Mulroney had him up against the ropes.

"You had an option, sir. You could have said that this is wrong for Canada . . . You had an option, sir, to say no and you chose to say yes."

Turner struggled to explain that he had to make the appointments to make sure there was a Liberal majority so he could become prime minister.

To me, the Mulroney attack was devastating. Peter Mansbridge and I were in the studio at CBOT, the CBC station in west Ottawa, covering the debate. We had a Liberal, Conservative and NDP spokesperson with us to add their comments. I was surprised when the enormity of what had just happened didn't seem to register. Each went through their pre-pared party lines, spinning the debate as though they hadn't been watching. When Peter came to me for my opinion, I was blunt. I said there was only one thing that had mattered that evening on television, and that was the hammering Turner took from Mulroney on the patronage issue. It was, I said, the only thing that would register and be the sole takeaway of the evening. It would be the headline in the next day's papers. All of which, of course, proved to be true.

The debate was on July 25; the election was not until September 5, but for all intents and purposes, the campaign was over after the first three weeks. The debate had been the final nail in the Liberals' coffin. The first mistake was to call an election when the party was completely unprepared, and when the people around Turner—as well as Turner himself—had been too busy fighting for the leadership to do any election planning. True, the departure of Trudeau and the leadership convention had brought the Liberals up in the polls, but much of that support was thin at best and maybe even illusory.

As I had told Iona Campagnolo, the situation in 1984 was a long way from the one in 1968 after Trudeau had won the Liberal leadership and rolled into a successful campaign. She hadn't believed me, but then, shortly after the election was called, she made a second gaffe even bigger than her "first in our hearts" remarks about Chrétien at the end of the convention. Turner was at a Liberal campaign event in Edmonton. Campagnolo was on the stage with him, and when she introduced him, he gave her a hug and patted her bottom. She immediately drew attention to the pat by patting him the same way. Regardless of your take on the incident, bad form or not, Campagnolo had made it an issue that the media, feminists and Conservatives picked up on. Women opposing the Liberals showed up at Turner rallies with cardboard shields over their rear end with "Don't pat my bum" written on them. It was the picture of Turner as one of the boys, out of touch with contemporary Canadian manners that did him damage.

I was never sure how Turner's wife, Geills, reacted to the bum-patting publicity. A few days after the story broke, I was standing next to her at a small event in Ottawa and we were chatting about nothing in particular. Turner was working the room, and as we talked, he moved right in front of us with his back to us. Suddenly, in our conversation, Geills raised her voice and said, loud enough for her husband to hear: "Don Newman! Stop patting my bum!"

Of course, I was doing nothing of the kind, but it was also clear that Turner had heard her. He ignored the comment and kept on moving, shaking hands. Geills Turner looked at me and laughed. For revenge, I thought about patting her bum. But I didn't.

My major assignment before election night was to do a story that would predict who would be in the Conservative cabinet. With it clear that Mulroney was going to win, speculation had shifted to whom he would pick as ministers. Looking for information, I called Bill Neville. He had been Joe Clark's chief of staff during the nine-month Tory government five years earlier. When the Conservatives went out of office, Brian Mulroney had recommended him for a top executive job with the Canadian Imperial Bank of Commerce. When

I called, he was back in Ottawa with his own consulting company and was one of the best-informed people in Ottawa on matters concerning the Conservative Party. He also knew how politics and the media interacted. After I assured him he would not be quoted as my source, he gave me the entire cabinet lists, including the surprising fact that Robert Coates, the former president of the party and a Nova Scotia MP, was going to be named minister of defence. When the cabinet was sworn in on September 17, my story—based on Neville's list—was accurate in every respect.

Election night was a new experience for me. I was in the studio at election central in Toronto. In my two previous television elections in Canada, I had been at the headquarters of the prime minister of the day— Pierre Trudeau in 1972 and Joe Clark in 1980. Now I had the responsibility of reporting the results of the ridings in Manitoba, Saskatchewan and Alberta, following the results as they appeared on the screen, talking a little bit about the winning candidates and explaining any upsets or other surprises. It was my inaugural experience on how election-night broadcasts work behind the scenes, and I was immediately impressed by how so many people are needed to keep a high-powered program clicking over like clockwork.

Elections are usually held on Mondays. But since Monday, September 4 was Labour Day, the election that year was held on Tuesday the fifth. There wasn't too much drama. Only Newfoundland and Labrador stayed relatively loyal to the Liberals. Everywhere else, the blue Conservative machine was on a roll, through Atlantic Canada, into Quebec, then rampaging through Ontario and across the Prairies before coming to rest in British Columbia. All across the country, the Tories were picking up seats from the Liberals. It was only in B.C. that the Liberals picked up a seat that had previously been held by the Conservatives. The upscale riding of Vancouver Quadra went against the national tide and defeated the

Conservative who had held it since 1972. When the votes were counted, Bill Clarke had lost the riding by about 3,200 votes to his Liberal challenger, John Turner.

Since the results were so decisive, there was a lot of airtime to fill as we waited for the different party leaders to come before the cameras to claim victory and accept defeat. At one point, Peter Mansbridge and David Halton began a discussion on how unusual it was to see such unanimity across the county. The huge Conservative majority, they said, was an indication all Canadians wanted change. Keeping to my usual role of looking at things through a different angle, I dissented. All Canadians wanted change except Quebecers, I said. They had voted for continuity. With Pierre Trudeau, Quebecers had a prime minister from their province and they liked it. Now they had voted for the same thing in Brian Mulroney—a Quebecer who was about to become prime minister.

Trudeau had been able to keep Quebecers satisfied during his time in office even as he lost support elsewhere in the country. It was their support that kept the Conservatives to a minority in 1979 and allowed Trudeau to return nine months later. For a period, Mulroney would be able to keep Quebecers happy too, increasing the number of seats he won in the province while losing them everywhere else in the next election. But like Trudeau, his efforts to keep Quebec onside led to disaffection with him in other parts of Canada, and ultimately he couldn't keep Quebec happy, either.

What happened was the most amazing change in Canadian political history. From a record majority government in 1984 to the almost total oblivion of the Progressive Conservative Party in 1993. A remarkable turn of events in just nine turbulent years.

27

The Mulroney Years Begins

THE MULRONEY YEARS started on September 17, 1984, with the swearing-in of his cabinet. Two weeks earlier, he had won the biggest Parliamentary majority in Canadian history, capturing 212 of the 282 seats in the House of Commons. Since John Turner had been prime minister only for the disastrous summer election campaign, Mulroney was effectively succeeding Pierre Trudeau when he came to office. And he was the antithesis of the man who had served as the Liberal prime minister for fifteen years.

Where Trudeau was cool and cerebral, Mulroney was warm and passionate. Where Trudeau often seemed reserved, Mulroney was gregarious. He came to office with complete control of his party and the House of Commons. He wanted to do big things, and he tried to do them.

Brian Mulroney was great for journalists. He took a big interest in what they were writing and saying about him and his government. He would get mad, but seldom held a grudge. After leaving his employ, Michel Gratton, one of Mulroney's former press secretaries, wrote a book about working for the prime minister entitled *"So, What Are the Boys Saying?"* after Mulroney's oft-asked question about the latest gossip.

My experience with Mulroney in the foyer of the House of Commons when I was taping *This Week in Parliament* was the direct opposite of my experience with Trudeau. While Trudeau hurried by without a glance, Mulroney stopped almost every week to joke. He would follow what was on the program, occasionally ribbing a member of the Opposition in the House of Commons for something they had said when I interviewed them. After a party in the fall of 1984 to mark the retirement of Southam News columnist Charles Lynch, Mulroney sent me a picture taken by his photographer of the two of us talking. Above his signature, he wrote, "Please use better clips of me next week!"

However, it was not all sunshine and roses. In September 1985, Fisheries Minister John Fraser came under scathing Opposition attack. The CBC program *the fifth estate* revealed that Fraser had overruled his department's inspectors and allowed cases of tainted tuna to go to market. Fraser tried to defend himself in Question Period. Then Mulroney came to his defence. For six days over two weeks, Fraser hung on to his job until finally bowing to the pressure to resign. For the moment, the story seemed to pass, until Mulroney gave an interview to the *New York Times* ahead of a meeting he was having with U.S. president Ronald Reagan.

The Prime Minister's Office distributed transcripts of the interview to the press gallery. The clerks in the gallery first made an announcement over the intercom that the transcripts were available. About half an hour later, the clerks made another announcement: the Prime Minister's Office wanted the transcripts back. Why, I wondered, would that be, and quickly grabbed a copy of the transcript that had been delivered to the CBC bureau. The reason for the recall jumped right out.

Asked about the tainted tuna affair by the *New York Times* reporter,

Mulroney said that as soon as he heard about Fraser overruling the food safety inspectors, he fired his minister.

"Bang, he was gone!" was the actual quote. That, of course, was at variance with what had really happened. Perhaps because it was a slow week; perhaps because I was offended that Mulroney would give an interview and try and spin an American reporter with untrue information that no Canadian reporter would accept; and certainly because the Opposition had jumped all over the discrepancy during subsequent Question Periods, I gave the incident big play on *This Week in Parliament*. I put the Mulroney quote up on the screen, and then used clips from each day as the defence of Fraser went on, superimposing the date and the day number of the defence. Clearly, there was no "Bang, he was gone!"

After that, the story passed as quickly as the transcript had sprung up. I had forgotten all about it, but apparently Mulroney hadn't. A couple of weeks later, he held a meeting with the premiers in Vancouver, and I was there as part of the live-coverage team. After one morning session, he scrummed on his way out of the room. I was standing in the group of reporters and shouted out a question. He looked at me, eyes flashing, and replied, "I don't have to answer that from the CBC—even from you, Mr. Newman."

I was amazed. The other reporters were, too, and looked around before shouting out more questions. When the scrum broke up and the prime minister left, I went over to one of his press secretaries to inquire what his attack had been all about.

"He is still pissed at you for hammering him on the transcript story," was his reply.

Not much I can do about that, I decided. In fact, if I had to do it again, I would do it the same way. However, taking a public shot at me apparently got it out of Mulroney's system. A couple of weeks later, I was on Parliament Hill, doing my on-cameras, when Mulroney came down from his office on his way home. He stopped, came over and joked as though nothing had happened.

MULRONEY'S ATTITUDE TOWARDS reporters had a positive effect on his staff. Even before the tuna incident, on the Conservatives' first day in office, at the cabinet swearing-in ceremony at Rideau Hall, Mulroney's press secretary, Bill Fox, and I got into an uncomfortable exchange. I was set up with a live camera and microphone in the room where the cabinet and the Governor General were to have their group picture taken. So was Pamela Wallin, then with CTV.

Peter Mansbridge and I had been flown from St. John's, Newfoundland, where we were covering the Canadian tour of Pope John Paul II, especially to cover the swearing-in, and we were flying out that evening to Vancouver to resume the coverage of the Pope. My assignment was to interview only the new ministers, and when Fox came over to tell me without explanation that no interviews would be allowed, I told him what he could do with that edict, also pointing out that the prime minister lived at 24 Sussex Drive across the street, not at Rideau Hall. When the door opened a minute later and the new ministers started strolling in, it was clear they had been given the no-interview edict as well. I waved to a couple of them. They declined to come over to where I was standing, behind a velvet rope. What to do? Suddenly, George Hees came into the room, delighted to be back in a federal cabinet after more than two decades and at the age of seventy-four not impressed by directions from a press secretary.

"George," I called out. "Come over here and talk to me." He did, in a bound, with a big grin on his face. With that, the ice was broken, ministers lined up to talk to me and Pamela, and the cone of silence had evaporated.

You might have thought that Bill Fox would be mad and hold a grudge. But he didn't. In fact, a few weeks later, I was standing with a group of reporters waiting for the prime minister. I didn't have any question on my mind to ask; I just wanted to hear what was said. A door opened, and in walked Fox with Mulroney.

"We don't have time for many questions," Fox warned the assembled group. "First question, Don Newman."

I liked Bill Fox before that and I have liked him (and his wife, Bonnie Brownlee) ever since.

28

Air India

A S THE MULRONEY years started to unfold, *This Week in Parliament* was the weekly chronicle of the government's political ups and downs. In the winter of 1985, I acquired another program to help document the week's developments. *Sunday Report* had been launched in 1982 with Peter Mansbridge as host. It ran across the network at 6 p.m. Sunday evening, and along with a newscast had interviews with four different CBC reporters on important stories of the past week. One story was always from Ottawa, at least one of the others was international and two were often on legal, medical, scientific or business news. In early 1985, Mansbridge wanted to give up the show. A search was on to find his replacement, and I asked John Owen, who by then was the chief news editor and in charge of all news programming, for a chance to do the program. The show producer was Desmond Smith, who was enjoying auditioning different aspirants by letting them each do one program while he assessed their talents. Owen said he would tell Smith to give me a try.

When my turn came, it was a bit like my tryout fourteen years earlier for a job in the Parliamentary bureau at CTV. I knew Smith slightly by reputation. He was a Canadian who had worked for at least one American network, and he knew me only from *TWIP.* What he didn't know was that I had been at CTV for five and a half years, had frequently hosted *Canada AM* and was no stranger to live or live-to-tape TV. Beyond that, I had been on most of the live news specials for the past five years, so live television held no terror for me.

To fit with the schedule of the technical crew, which also worked on a program the day before called *Saturday Report,* and to hold down their overtime, two of the four interviews for *Sunday Report* were recorded on Saturday afternoon. The other two interviews were taped Sunday afternoon. The host then sat in the studio at 5 p.m. in Toronto as the show went to air in Atlantic Canada at six o'clock local time, introducing the previously recorded interviews and weaving it all into a seamless web. If that program was fault-free, a tape of it was played again at 6 p.m. Eastern time, and then rolled out across the country to play at 6 p.m. in every time zone.

On a Saturday morning early in March of 1985, I flew down to Toronto to meet with Smith and the three other people who worked to put the program on the air. I did the two interviews scheduled for Saturday afternoon. One we did twice because Smith didn't think the reporter's answers were clear enough. The second day involved two more interviews and then a clean broadcast of the entire program. In truth, there was nothing in the program I hadn't done before, and I guess Smith figured that out watching. After we finished and I got ready to return to Ottawa, he took me aside.

"Listen," he said, "did you just want to do the program once to say that you have done it or are you interested in being the regular host?"

Actually, when I asked for the opportunity, I wasn't sure I wanted to do it every week. After all, I was already working full-time on one weekend show. Two on the weekend, including one that entailed a trip to Toronto every week, had not been my ambition. Still, I had enjoyed the experience and told Smith I was interested.

"Okay," he told me, "I have two more to audition in the next two weeks, and then it's yours." And that is how I got to be in the anchor chair for the coverage of the biggest terrorist attack in Canadian history.

On Saturday, June 22, I had flown to Toronto before lunch, gone to the CBC Television building on Jarvis Street just north of Carlton Street and done two interviews for the next day's *Sunday Report*. After speaking with Des about the two interviews planned for the following day, I walked over to the Sutton Place Hotel at the corner of Wellesley and Bay—my regular Saturday night home—checked in and then went out for dinner with friends. It was a birthday celebration, and it went a little longer than I was used to on what for me was a work night. I went back to the hotel and the next morning had breakfast in my room before checking out and walking back to the CBC.

I arrived at my usual time of noon to find more activity going on than usual. My inquiries as to what was happening were met with disbelief. Hadn't I heard? An Air India plane that had left Canada last night, bound for London en route to Bombay, had blown up over the Atlantic near Ireland. There were no survivors among the 329 people aboard. Most of those killed had been born in India but were now Canadian citizens.

Obviously, our plans for *Sunday Report* were out the window. All of the show was to be about Air India; some of it might be taped, but most of it was going to be live. The CBC News team in Toronto was mobilized. Extra producers, writers and technicians were brought in to work flat out. At one point, I was down in the studio, just completing a taping, when in walked Arnold Amber, the executive producer of news specials.

"We've just been cleared to do an hour-long special on the network tonight. Since you are here, you are the anchor."

But before the special, there was *Sunday Report*. We did the program live at 5 p.m., and then an updated version at six, followed by a third at seven. That had to be it. With the special going to air at eight for release in Atlantic Canada, there was no more studio time.

By the time I had done the third program, I went up to the newsroom, grabbed a sandwich from the food that had been brought in and marvelled at the scene that had unfolded. The top people from the news specials team—and all of them were top people—and the top people from the desk on *The National* were all working feverishly to pull a complete and complicated program together.

And what an amazing program it was. The production crew had assembled tape from all over Canada, as well as interviews for me to do with people in Toronto, Montreal, Washington, New York and, amazingly, in Cork, Ireland. Peter McCluskey, a producer at the CBC in Toronto, was on holiday in Cork. That beautiful seaside city on the south coast of Ireland had been turned into the headquarters for the search and recovery efforts for the Air India wreckage. He had called the desk in Toronto to let them know where he was. Somehow, the producers had convinced a TV station in Cork to open its doors in the middle of the night, point a camera at McCluskey and let him talk to me.

Complicated TV programs like the one that night need a script. Writing the script that night was Mark Bulgutch, then the top writer on *The National*. Writing for television news is a lot more difficult than it sounds, but if you knew how to read from a moving teleprompter, then Mark could put the right words on it the right way so that you could read his scripts cold without having seen them before. And that's what was happening that evening. Tape and reports were becoming available as we were on the air. Interviews lined up suddenly disappeared. Some of the tape items were as long as five minutes. That gave us a chance to regroup as we went along. Freddy Parker, director of *The National* and CBC News specials, was running the show from the control room, a reassuring voice in my ear directing me what to do next. At one point, with about a minute left in a report, he spoke into my ear telling me, "Read page eighteen next."

I looked at the script pages on my desk. There were two page eighteens, each different. I looked at the autocue on the front of the camera. The words there were different from either of the two pages on the desk. In confusion, with about thirty seconds left before I was back on the air, I swung around in my chair and shouted to Mark, who had his head down, producing more copy, "Mark, there are three page eighteens. Which one should I read?"

Without looking up or batting an eye, he kept typing and shouted back, "Read the one in the autocue."

But of course.

I signed off, but we weren't finished yet. Fred Parker was speaking to me again in my earpiece.

"Stand by, we have some new material. We are going to do it again."

And we did. Not all the material was new. Some parts of the first show were rolled into the second, and together it went off again as a seamless web. When the second program signed off, there was a great sign of relief. The events had been tragic, but with tight deadlines and with most of the people having to come in to work from all over the city, the CBC had managed to pull off a remarkable news special on Air India not once but twice in succession. Add to that the three different editions of *Sunday Report*. I felt I had done a full day's work.

You can often take for granted working with good people and an organization committed to excellence. That evening, I realized what it really meant. I was glad to work where I did and proud to be part of it.

I was also exhausted. I called a cab and went out to Pearson Airport to catch the last flight to Ottawa. In the boarding lounge, a fellow passenger recognized me.

"Hey," he said, "you are with the news. You must know something about the Air India thing."

Too tired to talk, but not wishing to be rude I replied, "Just a bit."

29

Turner and the '88 Campaign

WHILE THE MULRONEY government was bumping along in office with its record majority, John Turner and the Liberal Party moved along as the Official Opposition with the smallest number of seats the party had ever won.

Having been chosen to save the party and keep it in government, and instead having led it to its most humiliating result ever, Turner found his leadership in a constant state of siege. The fact that those targeting him were Liberals hoping to replace him with Jean Chrétien didn't help. Nor did his rusty political skills and his slow realization of how television had changed politics.

But despite the crushing results of the election in September 1984, by November of 1985 there had been enough missteps by the Conservatives that some polls had the Liberals back on top in public support. This was good news for Turner as he headed to a big Liberal policy conference in Halifax. He performed well there, but as would be the case over the next three years, some of the air came out of his balloon after Chrétien showed up at the conference, selling and autographing copies of his new autobiography, *Straight from the Heart*. Chrétien was mobbed as he sat, signing books. Turner supporters tried to suggest the enthusiasm for Chrétien was just a regular occurrence at a book launch. On television, I remarked that if that were true, Canadian novelist Margaret Atwood should get into politics.

In 1986, Turner faced a review vote at a party convention. If he lost, there would be a leadership convention, which would undoubtedly replace him. Going into the vote, the question was not one of winning or losing, it was how high the number would be in his support. In 1983, Joe Clark's Progressive Conservative Party leadership had ended when he decided sixty-six-per-cent support from his party was not enough to carry on.

Turner refused to discuss how much support he needed, but he launched a campaign that took him around the country, speaking to Liberal riding associations, trying to keep the party faithful behind him. As a centrepiece for his speech, he used his opposition to the Mulroney government's free trade agreement with the United States, which the prime minister had proposed and on which negotiations were soon to begin. It was prescient. The same issue two years later would bring Turner and the Liberals back from the brink of electoral disaster in the general election of 1988.

For a segment of *TWIP,* I decided to travel with Turner on a trip to Elliot Lake in northern Ontario to report on his campaign to save his job. We flew in a small plane with his campaign team, and he was in good form, both in the speech he gave and at a reception later.

I also did a fairly long interview with him in the Opposition leader's boardroom on Parliament Hill. I asked him how he had come through the previous two years, from briefly being prime minister, to humiliating defeat, to now a daily fight not just with the Conservative government but with his own party to remain relevant and ready to fight again in 1988.

"Mr. Newman," he replied, looking directly at me with a strong stare, "my mother told me that adversity builds character. Believe me, in the past two years I have built more character than I will ever need."

Jean Chrétien had resigned from Parliament in early 1986. No longer did he have to be part of caucus solidarity and give even an appearance that he was supporting his leader. Instead, he remained generally out of sight while his partisans carried forward the fight, often through the media. On a late November weekend, the Liberal Party gathered in a policy conference at the Ottawa Congress Centre, a conference that would culminate with a vote on whether the party should hold a leadership convention. No one thought Turner would lose outright, but everyone knew he needed a credible level of support to carry on, although there were differing views on what constituted a credible level.

I was standing with a live portable microphone and a portable live camera at the bottom of the steps where Turner would come off of the stage after the result was announced. I knew if the result was positive, Turner would want to talk. I asked one of his aides if he would stop if the result was a disappointment. No, I was told, Turner wouldn't stop if the result was a disappointment because he wouldn't be coming this way. He'd be going out the back door if fewer than seventy per cent of the delegates voted against a leadership convention.

But he did stop and talk. Seventy-six per cent of the delegates voted no to a leadership convention, giving their support for Turner to carry on, and for a while it looked as though Turner's major party problems were behind him. But by early 1987, rumblings had started again that his leadership was a liability to the party. Part of Turner's problems stemmed from the Meech Lake Accord, the deal Mulroney crafted with the provincial premiers to get Quebec's signature on the Constitution.

Among other things, Meech recognized Quebec as a "distinct society," without defining what the term meant. Mulroney felt he was a latter-day Father of Confederation, getting Quebec's federalist premier, Robert Bourassa, to sign on where separatist René Lévesque had refused Pierre Trudeau. Turner supported Meech Lake, and so did most Liberals from Quebec. But Pierre Trudeau and a lot of other Liberals didn't, nor did Jean Chrétien. The Liberal Party was split. Once again, the split was a threat to Turner.

In April, there were rumours that Turner's leadership was going to be publicly challenged. I was in Cornwall, making a speech, on the day the story broke. I received a phone call telling me to rush back—we were doing a live special. We did, although in the end, not much happened.

On Saturday night that week, the Parliamentary Press Gallery held its annual dinner. It is a highlight of the Parliamentary year, a black-tie, fancy-dress affair that still survives, although not with the fun and panache that it did when all that went on was off the record, the Governor General and the party leaders all made speeches poking fun at themselves and each other, and press gallery members put on skits lampooning the politicians and themselves. In 1987, I was president of the press gallery. At the dinner introducing John Turner, I got my words jumbled. I meant to call him the "leader of the Official Opposition." Somehow it came out differently, as "the official leader of the Opposition." The room roared. Fortunately, so did John Turner.

In fact, he could not have been upset at all, because the week after the dinner I received a telephone call I was not expecting. Doug Richardson, Turner's chief of staff, said the Liberal leader was going to call me and ask me to be his communications director. Doug said he hoped I would take the job, and that if I did I would have direct access to Turner and would not have to work through him.

A year before, I had told Turner I was not interested in running to be a member of Parliament for the Liberals or any other party. I didn't have strong partisan views, didn't vote (I never voted in elections I was covering—I felt it would be like a referee cheering for one of the teams in a game) and loved my job. I told Richardson that, but he said Turner wanted to talk, and I should expect a call.

"Donnie," Turner deeply drawled when I picked up his call about an hour later, "it's John. How are you?" Turner was interesting that way. In any kind of formal situation, press conference, interview or public meeting, he always called me Mr. Newman. In any informal setting, he seemed to roll back the clock to 1966, when Lloyd Axworthy introduced us while I was covering a Manitoba Young Liberal meeting and Turner was the guest speaker.

"I want you to be my communications director," he told me.

"That's flattering," I said, "but I don't know anything about being a communications director. Besides, you wanted me to be a candidate, and now this idea. Why the change?"

"Easy," he told me. "If you run as a candidate, that's one seat. Communications director, that's thirty-five!"

"John, that's really flattering, but I am afraid I can't be any help to you," I said, ending the conversation.

The end of that story turned out well for Turner and a friend of mine. His search for a communications director continued, and finally settled on a colleague from Washington days, Ray Heard. Ray wanted the job and Turner had a good communications director.

Turner also got a new chief of staff, Peter Connolly. And he crafted the issue for the coming election campaign. As part of his opposition to the Canada–U.S. Free Trade Agreement, Turner argued that Mulroney had not campaigned on the idea in the election of 1984, and in fact had spoken against free trade when he sought the Conservative leadership in 1983. That, Turner argued, meant Mulroney and the Conservatives had no mandate to use their majority to pass a free trade deal before Canadians gave them one in an election campaign. To make sure that couldn't happen without an election, Turner asked the Liberal majority in the Senate to hold up passage of the free trade bill until after an election. Effectively, he had determined the ballot question, whenever the election was called.

So, with a new chief of staff, a new communications director and the election issue he wanted, it would appear that John Turner was well positioned for the coming election campaign in 1988. It would appear that way, but in truth, he wasn't.

30

Election '88 and the Free Trade Debate

THERE ARE MANY reasons why the Liberals did not win the 1988 election. The biggest reason was that they didn't deserve to win. Any chance they might have had, they threw away with constant back-biting and attempts to undermine John Turner's leadership.

The role of Turner himself in this failure is significant but hard to define. Through errors of commission and omission, he often made himself an easy target. The party's dismal showing—winning only forty seats—in the election four years earlier meant that none of the Parliamentary caucus owed him any loyalty. They had elected themselves. They had won in spite of him, not because of him.

Turner had come to the party leadership and then crashed and burned in the 1984 election because he was ill-prepared to step into the faster pace of television-era politics that had transformed the electoral game in the nine years he had been away. In the ensuing four years, he had picked himself up, dusted himself off and set about adapting to the changes as best he could. At various times, he had employed three different TV coaches, learned to try and give short, pointed answers suitable for TV clips rather than long-winded responses. He also stopped complaining that complicated subjects were too difficult to deal with in short, punchy answers.

He had also tried to change his style. During the 1970s, as both justice minister and then minister of finance, Turner wore three-piece suits and often striped shirts and looked like the epitome of the Bay Street lawyer he would become in 1975. He toned the look down for the 1984 election, and did so even more after the crushing defeat. By 1986, he often appeared without a jacket at all. Instead, he wore a bright Liberal red cardigan sweater over his shirt and tie, a look he tried out for the first time on television with me during an interview following a caucus meeting in January of 1986.

But with all the changes, his performance remained spotty. He would burst with activity, followed by periods of somnolence. The activity bursts usually came after an internal uprising within the party, often prompted by supporters of Jean Chrétien or even Chrétien himself. After Turner supported the Meech Lake Accord, Pierre Trudeau joined the critics. Chrétien had no reason to want Turner to succeed; he wanted the leader's job himself. Trudeau didn't want Turner to succeed because he felt the new leader had been disloyal to him when he was prime minister. And after Turner supported the Meech Lake Accord, Trudeau felt his successor as Liberal leader was destroying the country.

Turner could never be sure when these drive-by attacks on his leadership would be launched. He had to be vigilant, while at the same time keeping the pressure up on the Mulroney government in the House of Commons and trying to hold the Liberal caucus together. That was never easy. There were Chrétien and Trudeau loyalists in the caucus who were always looking for cracks in his leadership, and there were others who were willing to follow but who found that, despite his bonhomie, he was in fact distant and aloof from many of them personally.

His seventy-six-per-cent party support at the leadership review in 1986 had been impressive. But less than six months later, in April 1987, there was an incipient caucus revolt he had to stare down, and an even more serious one a year later, when just over half of the forty Liberal MPs signed letters asking Turner to step aside. Turner refused to accept the letters and fought on, only to face an unprecedented revolt against his leadership right in the middle of the 1988 election campaign.

News of the earlier revolts against Turner's leadership had come either from the perpetrators or people loyal to the leader, trying to shame those plotting against him. The news of the election campaign revolt in 1988 came from CBC Television News.

The election had been called on October 1, to be held on November 22. In the weeks leading up to the call, public opinion surveys had shown the Progressive Conservative government rising in support, as were Prime Minister Mulroney's personal approval ratings. It looked like the PCs would have the wind at their backs on the run to Election Day. It also looked like Turner and the Liberals would have the wind in their faces. Turner still had the free trade issue, and while he mentioned it at the start of the campaign, he didn't feature it as he might. He then unveiled a traditional big-spending child care plan at a rally in Montreal, but neither he nor other party officials could explain how it would be funded. Still viewing Turner through the prism of his meltdown in 1984 and the subsequent problems that bedevilled his leadership, the travelling media with him gave him poor and critical coverage. His passionate opposition to free trade stirred crowds at campaign stops, but the reporters covering the campaign had heard it so often they didn't take his repeated attacks as news.

While Turner was running an old-style, take-it-to-the-people campaign and getting hammered for it, Mulroney was running the traditional front-runner "bubble" campaign designed to keep the press away and manage everything he said. Reporters complained about the "boy in the bubble," but the public didn't seem to care. The polling in the first weeks of the campaign showed the Conservatives going up and the Liberals going down, and amongst the three party leaders, Turner was getting the lowest ratings. Ed Broadbent and the NDP's campaign were not setting the world on fire, but it was Broadbent's fourth national campaign, he knew the ropes, and he wasn't getting the scrutiny Turner was.

As the campaign began, my assignment was to get ready for election night, when I would be giving the results from the then ninety-nine ridings in Ontario and the thirty-two ridings in British Columbia. I stayed in Ottawa in the Parliamentary bureau, not entirely alone, but many of my colleagues were travelling on the campaigns, and Elly Alboim, the bureau chief with whom I worked closely, had gone to Toronto to run the election coverage from the national newsroom on the fifth floor of CBC headquarters on Jarvis Street.

At the end of the second week, on a Friday evening, I was getting ready to leave the office when Elly called me from Toronto.

"Keep this to yourself, and you won't believe what I am going to tell you. Mansbridge and I have been picking up rumours of a plan to dump Turner in the middle of the campaign. Have you heard anything about that?"

No, I assured him, if I had heard anything like that, he would be the first to know.

"Well, call around and see what you can find out."

I didn't need that suggestion. I would have done it anyway.

I decided to go over to Liberal Party headquarters on Laurier Avenue, four blocks south of the National Press Building. It was after business hours, but when I arrived, the door was still open and a receptionist was at the desk. I told her who I was and asked for Senator Al Graham, the national campaign co-chair and a man I had known and liked for a number of years. The receptionist left her desk and walked down a hall into an office. A few minutes later, she emerged to tell me he was unavailable.

It was clear that Graham was, in fact, in the office. Sooner or later, he would have to come out and walk right past where I was standing. I told the receptionist I would wait. She then went down the hall again, entered the same office and returned, saying nothing to me. About twenty minutes later, Graham appeared with his coat on, accompanied by a younger man I had not met. Graham stopped, said hello and introduced me to John Webster, who I knew was the Turner campaign manager.

I got right to the point. "Al," I said, "I am hearing that you and other top strategists on the campaign are telling Turner that he has to quit. That he has to be replaced if there is any chance for the party in November."

Graham smiled. He was then and still is personally charming.

"Where did you ever get that?" he said. "That would be crazy. That's not true."

Webster said nothing through this exchange. But I noticed when I first raised the question of replacing Turner, his eyes seemed to bug out. The elevator came, and the three of us rode down to the ground floor together. I could sense the discomfort in both Graham and Webster, but the outright denial left no further room for questioning. I went back to the bureau, called Elly and told him what had happened and that I suspected something was indeed afoot. We agreed we would keep asking questions and talk again on Monday.

Elly called me Monday morning, and while I had nothing new to tell him, he had news for me. Over the weekend, he had heard that senior Liberal MPs running for re-election were also concerned about the state of the campaign and wanted Turner to step down. He told me to come to Toronto and work with him and Peter on developing the story. My job would be to focus on the MPs where I had the best contacts.

I quickly decamped for Toronto and set up at a desk in the elections unit. The MPs who now apparently wanted a change at the top were all Turner loyalists: Herb Gray in Windsor, André Ouellet in Montreal, Bob Kaplan in Toronto and Lloyd Axworthy in Winnipeg. All were out campaigning every day and every evening, in their own ridings but also in the ridings of other, lesser-known candidates where their name recognition and experience would be a plus.

I decided phoning Herb Gray would be a last resort. He was known as "the Gray Fog." His answers to questions were so vague and so narrow that it was impossible to learn anything. I tried the other three, none of whom I could reach immediately, but after a couple of tries I did reach Ouellet at his home in Ottawa. I went right to the point, asking him directly: was it true that he and other leading Liberal MPs were trying to get Turner to quit in mid-campaign? Ouellet denied it directly.

By the time I got to Toronto, Peter and Elly had virtually all of the details in place. A script telling the story had been written and rewritten, and graphics had been assembled to give a visual dimension to a story that had few pictures. Only five people knew exactly what we were working on. In addition to Peter, Elly and me, the chief news editor and head of CBC Television News, John Owen, and Arnold Amber, the executive producer of news specials, who would produce our election night show, were in on the story. As the chief executive of the news department, Owen had the final say on whether we would go to air with a story this explosive and this sensitive. Each evening at around seven, we would meet in Owen's office to review what we knew and whether we could broadcast it. The original information that Peter and Elly had gathered was one good source for the story. To put it on the air, we needed another one we could all trust, and for a couple of evenings we had to agree that source was missing.

On Tuesday evening, the script was ready and Peter was standing by to record the story for that night's *National*. But that elusive second source made Owen and the rest of us pull back and we didn't go to air. I was feeling the pressure, I had reached only one of the four MPs I was targeting and I had to speak to the others. Later that evening, I called Bob Kaplan's campaign office in Toronto. It was after eleven, but the woman who answered said he was there but on another call. Fine, I said, I'll hold, no matter how long it takes. It took thirty minutes. Finally, Kaplan came on the line.

I had first met Kaplan twenty years earlier, in the election campaign of 1968, when I was covering the local Toronto ridings for *The Globe and Mail* and he was running as an underdog against Progressive Conservative Party president and star candidate Dalton Camp in the riding of Don Valley West. That spring, he caught the Trudeau wave and found himself a giant-slayer and an MP. Shortly after I had gone to the Press Gallery in Ottawa, and even after eleven years away in Washington and Edmonton, we had maintained a cordial relationship.

I told him why I was calling. His answer gave me a chill.

"Oh no, not that again," he said. "I have just spent a half an hour on the phone with Graham Fraser talking about the same thing."

Alarm bells went off. Fraser was the Parliamentary bureau chief of *The Globe and Mail*, a reporter with a reputation for being meticulous. Obviously, he had been hearing what we had been hearing and was working the story as hard as he could. Being scooped by the *Globe* was a real possibility.

I took Kaplan through everything we knew, but particularly about him, Axworthy, Gray and Ouellet wanting a meeting with Turner to tell him he had to go. Kaplan was masterful; he didn't deny anything I told him, but he wouldn't confirm it either. On some stories, a non-denial is as good as a confirmation, but not on one this big. I wasn't able to get Robert Kaplan to be our second source.

My last hope was Lloyd Axworthy. I had met him thirty years before at university in Winnipeg. We had stayed in touch and after the Liberals went into Opposition and he was no longer a cabinet minister, we had time for lunch a couple of times a month. We also trusted each other implicitly and had the kind of relationship reporters sometimes get with politicians. They are not close friends, but they share confidences, knowing that their anonymity will be respected. When the Conservatives were in power, I had that kind of a relationship with Michael Wilson, Don Mazankowski, Ray Hnatyshyn and Tom Hockin. Near the end of his time in office, I was developing it with Brian Mulroney.

The next morning, I was relieved there was no Graham Fraser story in *The Globe and Mail* breaking the news we had been working on. When I told my CBC colleagues, we all realized that we would have to nail the story that day or we would probably be scooped. I tried Axworthy at his Winnipeg riding office and was told he was out campaigning and then would be going directly to the airport to fly to Toronto, where he would take part in a debate on free trade that was being taped to be shown on *The Journal,* the CBC's flagship public-affairs program that aired immediately after *The National*. I checked the Air Canada schedule, saw there was a flight from Winnipeg arriving around 5 p.m. and confirmed with Axworthy's office that it was the flight he was taking. Time was of the essence. I had to talk to Lloyd before he began taping the debate. By the time he was finished, it would be past the deadline for *The National* and the opportunity to run our fantastic scoop missed.

I decided I would go to Pearson Airport to meet him and share a taxi into the city while we talked. But when I got out on the street to hail a cab, I realized I didn't have enough cash to take one cab to the airport and the other back. What to do? There were no ATM machines on every corner in 1988. So I went over to the Royal York Hotel, jumped on the hotel shuttle bus and rode it out to Pearson for five dollars, arriving just before the Winnipeg flight landed.

I went down to the arrivals area, where Lloyd would pass through and perhaps pick up a bag. When I got there, I saw a man in a dark suit, obviously a limo driver, who came over to me and said, "Hello Mr. Newman. Are you here to meet Mr. Axworthy?"

I allowed that that was indeed why I was at the arrivals area of the airport.

"I wish I had known. I could have brought you out. I am here to pick him up and take him to the St. Lawrence Hall for the debate."

Great, I told him. I'll ride back with you. Lloyd arrived a few minutes later and seemed pleased I was his welcoming committee. Together we got into the limousine for the ride back to town.

Lloyd and I had a shared respect and I knew that he would not lie to me. He knew I wouldn't burn him. Years earlier, he had told me something that I thought he understood I would report. When I happened to mention to him that I was going with the information, he blanched and said it could be a big problem for him. Realizing that I had missed the signals, I went back and changed the story to leave out what he had told me. He knew I had made the change, and after that, he was even more open to telling me information and confirming other stories I had as long as I didn't use his name.

Now, in the limousine, I spelled out everything we had, including that he, Gray, Kaplan and Ouellet wanted a meeting with Turner to tell him he had to step aside for the good of the party, and that the election campaign team wanted to show the leader polling data that led to the same conclusion.

"That's all correct, but he won't see us, so nothing is going to happen," Axworthy said. "Our only hope now is the debate."

With Axworthy's confirmation, I could hardly wait to get to the newsroom. I dropped him in front of St. Lawrence Hall and had the limo, which was being paid for by *The Journal,* take me up Jarvis Street to the CBC. I ran into the building and took the elevator to the fourth floor and raced around the corner to Owens's office. The others were already there. They looked up, but not too expectantly.

"We can go with it. I have the second source."

Peter's face broke into a wide grin. The others weren't so sure. The evening before, when we had discussed whether we had enough information to report the story, I had been the most resistant to going to air. Now, twenty-four hours later, I was claiming it was all right. Patiently but quickly, I took them through what I had asked Axworthy and what he had said in reply, making sure to include his view that Turner had stared the rebels down and the moment had passed. That view was reflected in the story that went to air. First Arnold Amber and then Elly Alboim agreed we had the confirmation we needed. The final decision belonged to John Owen.

"Let's go," John said.

And go we did. To make the presentation work, Sheldon Turcotte was called in to read *The National.* Peter reported the story into the broadcast much as any reporter would, although he was introduced with all the appropriate bells and whistles. John Owen had alerted *The Journal* that we had this exclusive, explosive story. But *The Journal* had few details and no time to line up a panel or otherwise discuss the amazing revelations, so I was asked to go on with Barbara Frum and talk about what we had discovered. And this I did, but in a delayed fashion.

The night *The National* broke the story was also the first time that Wayne Gretzky was playing in Edmonton against the Oilers with his new team, the Los Angeles Kings. The game itself was not important, but the return of Gretzky after being traded the previous summer was a good story and the CBC decided to carry the game as though it were a Stanley Cup final. That meant *The National* played at 9 p.m. in central Canada, an hour earlier than it usually did. It was then followed by three hours of hockey, which was then followed by *The Journal.* Barbara Frum and I recorded a segment around 10 p.m., and each of us was home in bed and fast asleep by the time people had the opportunity to see what we had to say at 1 a.m.

The next morning, the Toronto edition of *The Globe and Mail,* which went to press after *The National* had been on the air, had a front-page story reporting most of the same details. The byline on the story: Graham Fraser.

But that was the only newspaper support the story received. Instead, print journalists seemed incensed that they had been scooped by television. The critics focused on the fact that there were unnamed sources quoted in the story, something that is a staple of print journalism. Apparently, on TV that was a no-no. What was good for the print goose wasn't acceptable for the television gander. The most hypocritical newspaper reaction I saw was in the *Ottawa Citizen.* Three days later, in its Saturday edition, it ran an editorial decrying the CBC story and its unnamed sources. On the front page, as its line story, it had an "exclusive" from reporter Greg Weston. How did he get his information? Weston didn't name any sources. They were all people close to the story or who had inside information. In other words, unnamed sources.

As big an explosion as the story made, its impact passed quickly. The following week, in the English televised debate, the whole campaign turned on a dime. In the last half-hour, debating one on one with

Mulroney, Turner suddenly unleashed a ripping attack on the prime minister and the free trade deal, accusing him of reversing more than a hundred years of building a Canadian nation that could resist the continental pull of the United States, and with "one stroke of a pen," signing a flawed free trade deal.

"And once the economic levers are gone," Turner intoned, "the political levers will follow."

It was a devastating attack, all the more effective because no one had thought Turner had it in him. It was a reprise of the "you had an option, sir" attack levelled against him by Mulroney four years earlier, only this time the shoe was on the other foot.

As we had four years earlier, Peter and I were broadcasting the debate. Unlike in 1984, when I said I thought Mulroney had probably won with his performance, this time I was a little more cautious. Turner, I said, had won the debate and had put the Liberals "back in the game."

For the week after the debate, the polls had the Liberals winning the election. But Mulroney burst out of his bubble to campaign full out, the Conservatives and their business allies flooded the airwaves and papers with pro-free trade and anti-Turner ads, and by the weekend before the election, they were comfortably back in the lead and widening the gap. On Election Day, Brian Mulroney was returned to office with a second majority government, the first Conservative prime minister to do that since Sir John A. Macdonald. But his seat total had fallen to 169. The NDP had gained 10 seats and now had 43. But Turner's Liberals had gained 43 seats. Their total now was 83. John Turner had restored his party and restored his reputation. Not bad for a man whose party had wanted to dump him two weeks into the election campaign.

After the vote, the furor over our story died down, but newspaper reporters were still sniping away about the sources and its presentation. In late winter, the CBC organized a two-day retreat at Queen's University to discuss the election and its coverage. CBC journalists, party workers and strategists and editors and reporters from some of the major newspapers were invited. One of those who attended was Turner's chief of staff, Peter Connolly, and in the last hour of the conference the discussion turned to the CBC story that Liberal Party strategists and frontbench MPs had tried to get Turner to resign in mid-campaign before the debates. What, Connolly was asked, was his view of the story? He looked around the room, pausing for dramatic effect.

"It's true. It's all true," he said.

31

Meech Lake

Wɪᴛʜ ᴛʜᴇ ᴘᴏᴡᴇʀ of hindsight, we can now see that a meeting on the evening of April 27, 1987, is responsible for much of what has since happened in Canada.

Prime Minister Brian Mulroney had invited the ten provincial premiers to meet with him at Willson House, once the stately summer home of a prominent industrialist and inventor and now a federal retreat and conference centre overlooking the shores of Meech Lake in the Gatineau Hills north of Ottawa.

All the premiers were there: Liberals Robert Bourassa from Quebec, Ontario's David Peterson and Joe Ghiz from Prince Edward Island; Conservatives Brian Peckford from Newfoundland, John Buchanan from Nova Scotia, Richard Hatfield from New Brunswick, Grant Devine from Saskatchewan and Don Getty from Alberta; Howard Pawley, the New Democrat from Manitoba; and Bill Vander Zalm, the Social Credit premier from British Columbia. They were there to talk about changes to the Constitution, changes that would get the signature of the Quebec government on the Canadian Constitution the other provinces had accepted in 1982, but that the separatist premier of Quebec, René Lévesque, had refused to sign. Federalist Robert Bourassa and his Quebec Liberal Party were back in power and wanted to sign on to the Constitution, but they would only do so if parts were changed to be more attractive to nationalistic Quebecers.

The process to get Quebec's signature began at the premiers' annual conference the previous summer in Edmonton. Enough agreement had been reached that by April it was time for federal involvement. What emerged from that Willson House meeting was a bombshell: an agreement to expand provincial powers in immigration and in appointments to the Senate and the Supreme Court; more control over fiscal compensation for provinces opting out of federal spending programs in areas of provincial jurisdiction; and a constitutional veto for every province. All of those powers would be available to every province of any size, all the way from giant Ontario to tiny Prince Edward Island.

But the most controversial clause of the agreement dealt only with Quebec. It said the Constitution would be amended so that Quebec would be recognized as a "distinct society." Arguably, the other changes would affect Canada more, and make it a more decentralized country with a less powerful federal government. But at least those changes were spelled out, and people could decide whether or not the changes were a good or bad idea. The distinct society clause was ambiguous. It certainly sounded like special status for Quebec, but what did it really mean? The phrase would be placed in the preamble of the Constitution, not in a specific section, and it would in effect be left to the courts to decide the impact of distinct society recognition case by case as it was invoked going forward.

However, the very fact that the distinct society concept was in the agreement immediately raised doubts as to whether the Meech

Lake Accord, as the deal was called, would go forward and be ratified. Technically, there should have been no problem; the federal government and all of the provinces held majorities in their respective Parliaments. Party discipline alone should have been enough to get positive votes in Ottawa and each provincial capital within the three-year time frame for approval.

But getting the legal language for the final version of the accord proved difficult, because already opposition to the proposed changes was growing. In the House of Commons, both Opposition leader John Turner and NDP leader Ed Broadbent made their political calculations and endorsed the accord. Almost immediately, it backfired on Turner. The accord flew directly in the face of many of the constitutional principles embraced by Pierre Trudeau and his Liberal governments, and, now out of office, Trudeau was leading the charge against Meech.

In newspaper articles, in English and in French, in Toronto and in Montreal, Trudeau accused Mulroney of being a "weakling" who had sold out Ottawa's interest in order to get a deal. For many in the Liberal Party, Trudeau became a catalyst against the agreement. Trudeau's articles appeared in late May. Their impact was felt shortly after, on the second and third of June. Mulroney had called the premiers to Ottawa to sign off on the final legal text of the agreement. But a meeting that started at dinnertime on June 2 did not wind up until the sun was rising and people were getting ready for breakfast on the morning of June 3. Only then did all the provinces sign off, and a hurriedly convened public signing ceremony was arranged to be televised that afternoon from the Government Conference Centre.

The prime minister and the premiers met at the Langevin Block, across the street from the East Block, just down from Parliament Hill. At the dinner hour, reporters began gathering with camera crews outside the main door of the building, at the corner of Elgin and Wellington Streets, across from the National War Memorial. It was a beautiful warm evening. An ice cream shop just down the street did a brisk business until around ten-thirty, when it shut down for the night. The clock on the Peace Tower struck midnight with no sign the meeting was about to end.

Around 6 a.m., the tired premiers suddenly emerged, but after all that waiting, they weren't saying anything. They would hold their comments until later, at the televised signing ceremony at the Conference Centre.

QUEBEC GOT THE ball rolling. On June 23, 1987, the National Assembly passed a resolution accepting the Meech Lake Accord. Robert Bourassa's Liberals used their majority to put the resolution through over the objections of the separatist Parti Québécois. More importantly, the Quebec approval started the three-year clock running for Ottawa and the other provinces to approve the deal so that the Constitution would be amended.

However, a few months later, trouble began for the Meech Lake Accord and its backers. In New Brunswick, Conservative premier Richard Hatfield was a strong supporter of the accord. But in October 1987, his government was swept from power, replaced by Liberal Frank McKenna, who won every seat in the provincial legislature. McKenna said he would not go ahead with Meech Lake as it stood. Six months later, another Meech-supporting provincial government fell. The accord was contentious in Manitoba. When a minority Progressive Conservative government led by Gary Filmon replaced the New Democrats of Howard Pawley, Filmon could only remain in office with the support of the Liberals. Sharon Carstairs, the Liberal leader, was opposed to Meech.

The biggest stumbling block for acceptance of the accord was the recognition of Quebec as a distinct society. It cut to the heart of two views of what Confederation had meant in 1867, how Canada was made up then and how it should operate now. Francophone Quebecers believed that in 1867, "two nations," an English-speaking one and a French-speaking one, had agreed to come together to form the country Canada. It didn't matter that there were three English-speaking provinces at the time and only one where French was the majority language; there were two linguistic nations, in their view. That should still be reflected even if there were nine provinces that Quebecers called "English" Canada and only one province where French is predominantly spoken.

That was at odds with what most people outside of Quebec thought in 1867 as well as today. In this narrative, Confederation came about when four former British colonies came together to become provinces in the new county of Canada. With minor adjustments around linguistic and religious guarantees, each of the provinces had the same powers and responsibilities vis-à-vis the federal government and each other. These conflicting visions of the country—"two nations" versus "one Canada"—have been at the centre of most constitutional arguments, particularly since the Quiet Revolution in Quebec in the 1960s and the Alberta oil-wealth boom of the 1970s.

The Meech Lake Accord was an attempt to square that circle. Not only did successive Quebec governments want recognition of their distinctiveness, they wanted additional powers from Ottawa to express just how Quebec was so. Even before Meech Lake, the federal government was transferring money and powers to Quebec. To preserve constitutional symmetry, the same opportunity was given to the other provinces to opt out of federal programs and take the money instead to introduce similar programs of their own. But while Quebec used this "opting out" provision, the other provinces didn't. In Meech, however, most of the powers were going to every province. If the accord were approved, the federal government would be even weaker as a consequence.

Although that seemed clear, not many people seemed too concerned. What was on everyone's mind was what the distinct society clause really meant. The truth was no one did know for certain. The problem facing the sponsors of the accord was never more apparent than when Senator Lowell Murray, the Mulroney government's minister of federal-provincial relations, appeared before the special Commons committee reviewing the agreement for any "egregious" errors. Murray had to skate—claiming on the one hand, for people watching in Quebec, that the clause was significant and would guarantee provincial rights, while in the next breath trying to reassure people from the other parts of Canada that the clause was mainly symbolic and would not change very much at all. Obviously, that was a contradiction, and the longer people outside of Quebec thought about it, the less convinced they became.

Having written about his views on Meech, Trudeau then solidified opposition to the accord with a virtuoso performance on live television before the Commons committee. Public opinion was turning against the deal. But the greatest threat to getting all the provinces to agree to the constitutional changes arose in April 1989. In Newfoundland, the Progressive Conservative government was defeated, having spent much of its seventeen years in office fighting Ottawa over control of its offshore resources. The Liberal Party, led by Clyde Wells, took power, with thirty-one of the fifty-two seats despite getting a slightly smaller share of the popular vote. Wells was strongly opposed to Meech. A year and a month before the deadline, three provinces had said they could not or would not ratify.

In November, another first ministers' conference was held in Ottawa to discuss the accord. By this time, CBC Newsworld, the 24-hour all-news channel, had come on the air, and coverage of Meech Lake, pro and con, helped to fill the airwaves. In my new role, I and other network anchors were invited to a lunch the day before with Norman Spector and other federal officials there to talk up Meech. It came down to me and Spector arguing the finer points, while others looked on in amazement.

As the calendar turned, and with only six months left until the ratification deadline, Ottawa began to fight back. In New Brunswick, on March 21, Premier McKenna introduced what he called a "companion accord" to Meech Lake. McKenna had not expressed flat-out opposition to Meech, but had said he wanted changes specific to his province. This companion accord was designed to address those changes. Like many other legislatures in the previous ten years, New Brunswick had had live television cameras installed in its legislative chamber. Suddenly, the world was made for Newsworld. As I prepared to televise McKenna introducing his companion document live in the legislature, I invited two senators with interests in the Constitution to join me and comment: Conservative Gerald Beaudoin and Ontario Liberal Lorna Marsden.

There was no suspense as to how the New Brunswick legislature was going to view the companion accord: McKenna's Liberals held every seat. Interestingly, Quebec Conservative Beaudoin didn't think the proposal would find much acceptance in Quebec, and Ontario Liberal Marsden though it was a good idea. I signed off our coverage with the thought that at least McKenna was trying to break the logjam around Meech. As I was saying goodbye to my guests, the light on the phone on the anchor desk started blinking. Phones don't ring in TV studios, as that could be heard on the air. They have blinking lights and, if possible, can be picked up without making any noise.

I picked up the blinking phone, thinking it was the control room, the newsroom or perhaps Toronto. I was wrong.

"Hello, Don," said the deep, mellifluous voice on the other end. "This is your secret source."

I was stunned. The prime minister had phoned me before, but never when I was in the studio. And when a call comes from a prime minister, first an operator comes on, asks if you are who she thinks you are, and then asks if you can take a call from the prime minister. When you say yes, you can sit as long as ten minutes before the prime minister comes on. This time, though, Brian Mulroney had clearly dialled it himself, from his office or from 24 Sussex Drive or from somewhere else.

"I was listening to what you had to say about Frank, and I just wanted to keep you in the loop," he said. "Frank's hand was on the pen, but my hand was on his."

"That means you will accept the companion accord?" I asked.

"We'll see. Stayed tuned," the prime minister replied.

Within a few days, Mulroney appointed a committee of MPs headed by Jean Charest to study the companion accord. Charest, of course, went on to become premier of Quebec, but at that moment he was between cabinet posts in the Mulroney government.

But while Mulroney was trying to build support for the companion accord, events were working the other way. Less than three weeks after it was introduced in the New Brunswick legislature, the Quebec National Assembly passed a resolution rejecting any additions or subtractions from Meech, including the McKenna accord. And when, on May 17, the Charest Committee reported its approval of the companion accord, the wheels really began to fall off.

Charest's report came just before the May long weekend. I was at home, enjoying a day off, when the phone rang. It was CBC colleague Debra Brown. She then lived with, and is now married to, Daniel Lessard, who was with Radio-Canada on Parliament Hill.

"I thought you should know. Lucien Bouchard is at 24 Sussex Drive, meeting with Mulroney. Daniel is scrambling to get tape."

Lucien Bouchard had been wooed by Brian Mulroney before the 1988 election. Bouchard had voted for sovereignty-association, whatever that was meant to be, in the Quebec referendum of 1980, and his arrival in the Mulroney government was seen as a signal to nationalist voters in that province that Mulroney was okay. In fact, in the election of 1988, Quebec was the only province where the Conservatives had won more seats than in their landslide 1984 victory. But through careful leaks, Bouchard, a Conservative MP and cabinet minister, had let it be known he was opposed to any companion resolution. He thought it was watering down the special recognition of Quebec, and a short while earlier he had gone to a reunion of the provincial Parti Québécois in his home area of Lac St. Jean, a clear signal that all was not well.

Thanks to Debra, we were well covered on the Bouchard–Mulroney visit, and the next day Bouchard made it official: he had quit the Mulroney cabinet and the Progressive Conservative Party. However, he kept his seat in the House of Commons and shortly after formed the Bloc Québécois, a party in the House of Commons working for Quebec independence. Unlikely though it may have seemed at the time, within less than four years the Bloc would be the Official Opposition, with Bouchard as its leader.

Bouchard left the Conservatives on May 22, 1990, one month and one day before the deadline for the approval of the Meech Lake Accord. For Brian Mulroney, these were desperate times. Time to roll the dice. And there would be a new way to report on what happened next.

32

Newsworld Launches

I T'S SAID THAT timing is everything, and even if it isn't everything, it is certainly a very great deal. For the launch of Newsworld, the CBC's all-news channel, since renamed the CBC News Network, the timing could not have been better.

The news gods were smiling that summer. Ottawa in particular and politics in general are often quiet in summer, but not in 1989. In addition to the Chantal Daigle abortion case at the Supreme Court, there was the race for the federal NDP leadership, the biennial conference of the Progressive Conservatives after their election victory the previous autumn, and in Quebec City the annual premiers' conference, with less than a year to go before the deadline to ratify the Meech Lake Accord and three provinces withholding their assent.

But despite there being all that news to report when Newsworld signed on, the channel was ill-equipped to report it. That is because, as I had been told three months earlier, all-news was not a priority for the CBC.

The channel came on the air on July 31, 1989, signing on from Halifax because, to secure the licence, the CBC had panicked and promised an unwieldy and ultimately unworkable network originating at different times of the day from CBC studios in Halifax, Ottawa, Winnipeg and Calgary. The application for the licence was crafted that way because the only other contender for an all-news licence was the owner of a television station in Edmonton who clearly had no existing capability to launch a national news service, but made much of the fact it would be based in the West. Sadly, the CBC did not rely on the obvious fact that it already had the resources, locally, nationally and internationally, to run an all-news channel. Instead, it also promised to originate programming from five cities across the country. The CBC won the licence it would have received anyway, but was stuck with an ungainly system that gradually unwound over the years, at great expense and a lot of adverse publicity.

The original plan called for afternoon programming from Ottawa, but not from the Parliamentary bureau. A lifestyles show was going to be recorded and played from CBOT, the CBC television station far from Parliament Hill. Political news was to be fed into programs originating from Calgary and Halifax and into a two-hour news program late each afternoon from Toronto. Political figures were to be interviewed by hosts far away from Parliament, with little firsthand knowledge of the players, the politics, and how the federal government worked. And to be aired live or live to tape, via costly satellite connections, involving numerous chase producers often calling the same people for interviews.

The great weakness of the system was that the network was designed by programmers and not by news people. The fact was, the all-news network initially had very little news. Within a day of signing on, that was apparent. I received a call from Joan Donaldson, the person who had set up the network and was now running it.

"You made good points about how Ottawa political news should be covered at our meeting in May," she said. "Would you now please come on and help us cover it?"

And so I did. Suddenly, in addition to running the day-to-day operations of the bureau I was jumping on and off Newsworld much of the day.

A few days after that routine started, I received a call from Trina McQueen.

"You are great on Newsworld," she said. "Could you help them out in the morning?"

"I thought you didn't want me wasting my time on Newsworld," I kidded her. Things had certainly changed. Now the vice-president of news wanted me to come in early to do breakfast television.

The planners of the network had not realized just how "wired" Parliament Hill had become. Our bureau's top technicians, Carlos Schoenfeld and Ken Furness, had cabled much of the foyer and some of the meeting rooms back to our bureau. In addition, the National Press Theatre, where most big news conferences were held on the main floor of the National Press Building, was seven floors below our bureau, and we could go live from there too. And we had access to a mobile unit that could go to remote locations and broadcast live back to the bureau.

All of that provided grist for the mill at Newsworld as well as better coverage for *The National* from the Ottawa bureau. Every day was a new adventure because, for the first time, we were doing things live on an ongoing basis as well as adding more value for *The National.* Two things in particular gave me a good idea of how the network would evolve.

In 1989, the annual premiers conference was held in Quebec City. It was not my idea to cover it for Newsworld, but when it was suggested, I wished I'd thought of it. The coverage was going to be rudimentary. I would go with a camera crew and a producer. Since none of the sessions of the conference were open, I would be limited to doing interviews with as many premiers as would agree to be interviewed.

But the story could be big. It was less than twelve months until the deadline for the ratification of the Meech Lake Accord and the recognition of Quebec as a distinct society. But since the premiers had signed off on the accord in June of 1987, elections in three of the provinces had produced new governments. Two of those governments were opposed to Meech, and the one in Manitoba was a minority where both Opposition parties were opposed. Quebec premier Robert Bourassa had the most riding on the outcome of Meech, and now he was hosting the conference where the new premiers opposed to Meech would be among his guests.

The cameraman I took was a genial fellow from the Parliamentary bureau named Larry Brown. The producer was Arnold Amber, the head of news specials for the CBC, the man who planned and ran election night coverage, the man who had organized and executed the widely successful coverage of the tour of Pope John Paul II in 1984. He was a big deal with not too much to do that summer. We enjoyed working together, and he had selected me to be the host of the Remembrance Day broadcast. He had a great sense of humour, was a tough perfectionist, and he and I spent a lot of time laughing. I was both surprised and pleased that a top producer like him was coming on the story.

The other person I worked with leading up to the conference would became a key player with Newsworld in the future. I was still doing a section into *Saturday Report* with Knowlton Nash, although with Parliament not in session, my part of the program was either an interview or a panel discussion. Since the key person at the Quebec City meeting would be the host, I decided to ask for an interview with Premier Bourassa. He didn't give many English interviews, so I considered it a coup when he agreed. This was an interview that would be shown primarily on the main

CBC network, not on Newsworld, so the job of organizing it fell to Dave Mathews, the network producer from the Ottawa bureau who was in charge of *The National's* coverage of the premiers' conference. Six years later, we would join forces, he as my senior producer, to take the *Politics* broadcast to air on Newsworld, beginning the most successful run of any program on the news network to this time.

On Friday, August 18, we met with Bourassa at the office the premier of Quebec keeps in the Hydro-Québec building on Boulevard René-Lévesque in Montreal. I had neither seen nor spoken to Bourassa since our Washington lunch in 1978, but he came out of his office with an effusive greeting.

"Ah, my old friend. How are you?"

The interview was a good one. The Supreme Court had ruled that parts of the Quebec language law limiting English on public and commercial signs were unconstitutional. Under some pressure, Bourassa was planning to use the "notwithstanding" clause of the Constitution to ignore the ruling. In English-speaking Canada, where support for the Meech Lake Accord recognizing Quebec as a distinct society was already fraying, such a move by the federalist Bourassa was seen by many as an ominous decision. When I raised this issue with him, I realized why the Quebec premier was so keen to be on English TV.

"People in English Canada should understand why I am doing this. If I don't, they will be very unhappy with what comes after me." In other words, if he didn't vigorously defend the French language, the separatists would come back to power, and referendums on leaving Canada and the breakup of the country could follow.

It was a strong interview, and it added heft to my *Saturday Report* program the next evening. But the real revelation of the premiers' conference was yet to come.

The conference started on Monday, August 21. I was up early with

Arnold Amber and Larry Brown in the rotunda of the Quebec National Assembly Building to interview premiers on their way in. I knew them all from federal-provincial conferences and had probably been on television with most of them before. Still, I was surprised at how keen they were to be on that morning. And their enthusiasm only grew. As the conference unfolded over the next two days, premiers were soon lining up, waiting to talk. I was surprised, yet not amazed, as I had already believed that politics and Newsworld would be made for each other. Arnold was more surprised. Being from Toronto, he had the more common CBC view, held there, that the all-news channel would be a minor player. After a few days in Quebec City, he wasn't so sure.

The premiers' conference was just one of the stories that helped lift Newsworld off the ground, at least in Ottawa. The rather amazing thing was that, although Parliament was not in session, Ottawa news seemed to be filling the channel. I was on so often that some people were making fun of it. At the time, the only all-news channel in the United States was CNN. In our country, it was joked that Newsworld was becoming DNN, "the Don Newman Network."

IN 1989, WITH ED BROADBENT stepping down, I decided to interview two of the candidates running for the leadership of the federal NDP for my slot on *Saturday Report*. Steven Langdon and Howard McCurdy represented adjoining ridings in Windsor, Ontario, in the House of Commons. Langdon, an economist who specialized in international development, and McCurdy, a civil rights activist and the party's first African-Canadian MP, had each made an impression in Parliament after getting elected for the first time in 1984. Re-elected in 1988, each had decided to run for the party's top job.

I decided to do the interview at the CBC station in Windsor and asked Anna Maria Tremonti to join me to help with the questioning. Tremonti was the bureau's main reporter following the NDP, and she was from Windsor, so a trip home to see her parents was also a bonus. Like my Bourassa interview the week before, we did the interview on Friday, to be shown the next day. It ran on Saturday, September 3. Audrey-Ann and I were at home alone that weekend. Linc was in Toronto with friends to see the Rolling Stones in concert at CNE Stadium. Both his parents had some trepidation about his going out of town to attend what was sure to be a pretty wild and exciting event, but he had just turned eighteen. With instructions to call if he got into any trouble, we had agreed he could go.

I was watching the Langdon–McCurdy interview on *Saturday Report,* and as it ended, the telephone rang. I picked it up to hear an operator say, "Would you take a call from the prime minister?"

"Of course," I said, and then was put on hold while the prime minister came on the line.

Hearing me say hello but then making no conversation made Audrey-Ann nervous.

"Who is it? Who is it?" she wanted to know. "Is it about Linc?"

At that moment, Brian Mulroney came on the line, and with a laugh in his baritone voice, asked, "Can't you get any better guests than those two?"

Before I could answer, Audrey-Ann was standing in front of me.

"What is it? Is it about Linc?" she said, this time her voice rising.

"I'm sorry, Prime Minister, I have my wife right in front of me. Our son is at the Rolling Stones concert in Toronto, and she thinks you are the police phoning about him. I have to tell her it is you on the phone."

"Oh, yeah, I heard about that concert. Caroline wanted to know if she could go," he replied. Caroline was his daughter, a few years younger than Linc. "I told her I didn't think that was a good idea." Rock 'n' roll out of the way, I engaged him on his comment about the quality of my guests.

"Obviously, if you'd come on, the quality would go way up," I said to him, since I suspected that was the real reason for his call.

His answer was quick: "Set it up with the office."

The next Friday, we taped an interview on the veranda at Willson House. The entire interview was about the constitutional accord originally negotiated at the house and named for the lake next to it. In the face of growing opposition in English-speaking Canada, Mulroney was cranking up the warning that the accord must be ratified or the consequences could be dangerous in Quebec. Suddenly, both of us seemed to realize that he might be going over the top.

"So, what exactly do you think will happen if Meech isn't ratified?" I pressed him.

He paused. "The sun will come up the next morning," he said, finally. That was the comment that made the headlines.

NEWSWORLD HAD BEEN on the air just over a month when I received another call from Joan Donaldson.

"You were right about Ottawa," she told me. "The thing is, I need you to do a daily show five nights a week on politics. Will you?"

I told her I would think about it, and I did. I was already devoting a lot of my time to getting political news onto the channel, but taking on a program with a fixed time slot, Monday through Friday, would mean giving up quite a bit else I was doing. However, I was the one who had argued that everyone else had missed the point and the potential of

Newsworld. I had already been able to make my point in the first month the channel was on the air, but now there was an offer to prove it completely. I called back and said, "Let's do it." A few weeks later, in October of 1989, *Capital Report* was born.

33

Constitutional Failures

BRIAN MULRONEY INVITED the premiers to Ottawa for a dinner on Sunday, June 3, 1990, to see if there was enough common ground to try one more time to get consensus and convince the governments of Manitoba, Newfoundland and New Brunswick to pass the Meech Lake Accord through their legislatures before the June 23 deadline.

Dinner was served Sunday evening at the new Museum of Civilization in Hull, Quebec, a building with a striking, symbolic design situated across the Ottawa River from the Parliament Buildings. It was a warm late-spring evening as the premiers gathered inside and reporters gathered outside to await news of what, if anything, would happen next. It was late, after dark on an evening approaching the longest day of the year, when the announcement was made that the first ministers would reconvene the next morning at the Government Conference Centre to continue their talks. Apparently, there was sufficient agreement to consider trying for a consensus.

What happened next was perhaps the most unusual week in Canadian politics. I don't think we will ever see anything like it again. Ever since, politicians have refused to put themselves out there in the same way, and it is doubtful they ever will. And even if, for some reason, the memory fades for politicians and they again trap themselves in a marathon week of closed-door negotiations—punctuated by public statements spinning the different points of view, speculation and rumour over what was really going on, and an emotional roller-coaster ride that first promised success but then collapsed in failure—Canadians will not be able to follow what is actually happening the way they did the first week in June 1990.

That is because politics, technology and economics have so decimated the ability of the media to operate on the scale they did then. The CBC in particular would not be able to come close to mounting the blanket coverage today that we did then. Some people thought the fate of the country hung in the balance; others weren't so sure about that, but thought it was still probably the best "Canadian" moment since Confederation. In the run-up to the dinner meeting that triggered the week of negotiations, it was clear that Mulroney wasn't going to let the premiers get out of town without one last massive try for an agreement. To plan for that, Ottawa bureau chief Elly Alboim had convinced the CBC to bring the reporter who covered each provincial legislature to Ottawa for the conference. Their job was not to get on air on the live specials, *The National* or Newsworld; it was to go to the briefings given by politicians and officials from their home provinces and then report back information to Alboim. He would then brief those of us who would be going on air. The result was that, as the week unfolded, the CBC's coverage had a running account of the negotiations from a variety of perspectives and was generally ahead of the curve, at least as much as that was possible in a story where all the action took place in private.

In terms of constitutional deal-making, the week turned out to be a failure. In terms of television network making, it was a huge success. Live coverage of the comings and goings of the premiers and the prime minister at the Conference Centre were covered live, both on the main CBC network and on Newsworld. But after that, only Newsworld would be on the air with more or less continuous coverage and speculation.

It turned out I had the best assignment of all. For the arrivals and departures, reporters had to stand behind a rope on the east side of the Wellington Street entrance. I was placed with a hand mike, behind the rope, next to the CBC camera. If the prime minister or a premier was speaking to the assembled reporters they looked directly at me.

Mulroney spoke from the centre. So did some premiers, although others, like Ontario Premier David Peterson, preferred to come over the rope and be directly interviewed in a scrum. Either way, my prime location, and the fact I was from the biggest news organization, going live across the country, usually gave me first access to whoever was speaking. The premiers would even come directly to me. On top of that was the system of intelligence gathering that I was briefed on daily, which more often than not gave me a head start on a lot of the issues that were being discussed.

On the first day, the first ministers fell into a routine that lasted through the week. Around 9 a.m. they would arrive at the Conference Centre, most of them stopping to be interviewed. The prime minister always stopped. Then, at lunch, they would emerge, say a few words, go across the street to the Château Laurier, where they were staying, and then return after lunch, usually with fewer interviews for an afternoon session. Sometime after six, they would again emerge, a round of interviews with shouted questions to the politician at the central mike or one-on-ones with different reporters would follow, and then the first ministers would go off to dinners and evening work for the next day while reporters filed their stories. The next day, the sequence would be repeated.

Because of Newsworld, my day was more complicated. Around seven in the morning, I would show up at the small studio in the Parliamentary bureau, which I used to get on the air to interview at least one and maybe two premiers for the morning show. The producers of the morning show had chased and booked the guests; all I had to do was show up and talk to them. Then I would hurry down to the Conference Centre and get into position. I would follow the ins and outs throughout the day, pausing in midafternoon to do an interview into Newsworld with someone also waiting around at the conference. Two Opposition politicians from Manitoba were particularly helpful in that regard. Conservative premier Gary Filmon had a minority government and needed Opposition support to get anything through his legislature, so he brought both the Liberal leader, Sharon Carstairs, and the NDP leader, Gary Doer, with him, to keep them in the loop and see if they would accept Manitoba being part of any agreement.

But the two of them were not inside the talks. They were outside, and like most politicians, they liked talking and they also liked appearing on TV. Carstairs was particularly opposed to Meech, so much so that she got special treatment from Quebec premier Robert Bourassa, who held a private half-hour meeting with her. Carstairs spoke no French, so the meeting was in English. Bourassa spoke English well, but not perfectly, as he revealed when reporting after the closed-door meeting to a scrum of reporters and live cameras. "I have just exposed myself to Mrs. Carstairs for thirty minutes," he said quite seriously, as listening journalists tried not to chuckle.

By Friday, time was starting to run out. The meeting that day went late into the evening, with a commitment to meet again on Saturday. Saturday dragged on, until suddenly there was an announcement that the premiers and prime minister would be meeting around the big table in the main conference hall. For the third time, they were going to announce agreement on the Meech Lake Accord.

Around the table, under the glare of the TV lights and cameras, Mulroney sounded a tone of triumph. The premiers agreed to accept Meech Lake because the meeting was committed to a new round of constitutional talks that would variously deal with Senate reform, extra powers for the territories and aboriginal and language issues. All the premiers except one sounded both relieved and pleased with the result of the week's work. The one who didn't was Newfoundland's Clyde Wells. He said he would have to meet with his province's legislature and submit the agreement to it. I had talked to Wells enough in the past year to sense his mood through his tone of voice. I knew he wasn't happy. And I knew he *really* wasn't happy when he brushed by me and refused an interview on his way out.

Suddenly, I felt something was wrong. As at the conference in 1980, when we had first reported there was an agreement but it turned out there wasn't, and again in 1983, when we reported Joe Clark was safe as Progressive Conservative leader when he wasn't, I felt the coverage going too far too fast. It wasn't just the CBC; everyone was reporting the same thing. I signalled that I wanted on the air, and then said that, based on my unsuccessful attempt to interview Wells, I didn't think this was a done deal yet. I was the first to report that. Again, I was a bit like the skunk at a party. No one else joined in to agree with me.

But it would turn out I was right, although the Meech Lake Accord failed to be ratified in a way that no one predicted. Wells took the agreement back to his legislature, the Newfoundland House of Assembly. Debate began, and first Brian Mulroney, then David Peterson went to St. John's to speak without precedent to the legislature and urge passage.

But while that debate was going on, in Manitoba the debate couldn't get started. The two Opposition leaders had come onside, albeit reluctantly in the case of Carstairs, but the aboriginal community had not. To get the agreement to a vote before June 23 took unanimous consent of the legislative chamber, and on the first day, and then the second that consent was requested, a First Nations member of the assembly named Elijah Harper refused to give his agreement. In Manitoba, the agreement to ratify the Meech Lake Accord died on the order paper in the provincial legislature.

In Ottawa, the federal government scrambled to extend the ratification deadline. But with no vote in Manitoba by June 23, Clyde Wells decided not to schedule a vote in Newfoundland. The divisive Meech Lake Accord was dead. The consequences of that death would be even more controversial.

IN THE IMMEDIATE aftermath, the fallout from the failure of the Meech Lake Accord in 1990 was hard to measure. On the day of the deadline in Calgary, Jean Chrétien won the national Liberal Party leadership. Chrétien had been true to his Trudeau roots and opposed Meech Lake. Politically, he would be the major beneficiary of its failure.

The following day, June 24, in a forecast of what was to come in the province, angry and disillusioned Quebecers poured out into the streets of Montreal in the largest parade in memory, celebrating the Quebec major holiday St. Jean Baptiste Day.

But as Canadians got ready for their summer holidays, other stories quickly filled the news. Most dramatic was a standoff between Mohawk Indians and the Quebec Provincial Police near Oka, just outside of Montreal, that escalated into a confrontation with the army. Throughout the summer, images of a face-to-face showdown between masked Indian "warriors" and Canadian soldiers, and of the Mercier Bridge across the St. Lawrence blockaded by Mohawks, filled the airwaves and the newspapers until, in September, the army moved in force to end the uprising.

Internationally, attention was drawn to the Middle East, but not by the usual Arab–Israeli confrontation. On August 2, Iraqi dictator Saddam Hussein invaded the neighbouring, and much smaller, country of Kuwait, prompting international outrage. It would be February of the next year before an American-led, United Nations–sanctioned force threw the Iraqis out.

In the fall, the Constitution and the fallout from the Meech Lake failure moved back onto the national agenda. Responding to criticism that Meech was the product of closed-door, elitist negotiations by eleven white men, Prime Minister Mulroney created a so-called Citizens Forum on National Unity. It was chaired by my former *Globe and Mail* colleague Keith Spicer, who stepped away from his job as chairman of the CRTC to lead the six-month project. It appeared to go everywhere and hear everyone, but when its report was presented, the aspect that attracted attention was Spicer's bold essay on how unpopular Mulroney was with Canadians in every part of the country.

By the summer of 1991, Mulroney was ready to re-engage politically on constitutional change. He appointed his erstwhile rival Joe Clark as minister of constitutional affairs, and Clark set off on a new process to try and find a formula that Quebec—and just about anyone else you could think of—would approve. The process involved the federal and provincial governments and aboriginal leaders, but through a series of conferences in January and February of 1992, held in Halifax, Montreal, Toronto, Calgary and Vancouver, regional input was obtained from virtually every group imaginable. Through the spring and summer, Clark and his colleagues worked diligently to try and put all the square pegs into round holes. Finally, at a meeting in Charlottetown—where the initial meeting leading to Confederation was held in 1864—agreement was reached on what became known as the Charlottetown Accord.

Where Meech Lake had been spare, Charlottetown was the opposite. In addition to recognizing Quebec as a distinct society, it would also further limit the powers of the federal government, while expanding those of the provinces. It promised an undefined form of aboriginal self-government, an elected Senate with each of the provinces having six seats, and special seats set aside for aboriginal senators.

While the Quebec government took part in the Charlottetown negotiations, Robert Bourassa had also launched two separate processes after the failure of Meech to discuss his province's future within Canada. One, headed by Jean Allaire, was an internal report commissioned for the Quebec Liberal Party. The other, the Belanger-Campeau Commission, had a federalist and a separatist co-chair and held hearings around the province. Both produced reports recommending a long list of "demands" Quebec should make from the rest of Canada. After the Meech failure, Bourassa had also promised a referendum in Quebec by the end of 1992, either on a new constitutional deal with the rest of the country or on Quebec independence. That put pressure on Joe Clark and the Charlottetown negotiators to get a new deal in place. And because British Columbia and Alberta also had laws saying constitutional changes had to be approved by referendum, the Charlottetown Accord was put to a vote in every province on October 26, 1992.

I had been following the process throughout the year, from live coverage of the weekend conferences in January and February, through the ongoing negotiating sessions leading up to the final talks in Charlottetown. When the referendum campaign was launched, my *Capital Report* program was replaced by an hour-long *Referendum Report* that Wendy Mesley and I co-hosted five nights a week. It was only a matter of weeks, not years, but the accord named after Charlottetown seemed to follow a similar trajectory to the one named after Meech Lake.

At first, there seemed to be general acceptance that the deal was a good thing for national unity, if not that great a deal in and of itself. But as opponents started attacking the accord, doubts began to form and the polls started to shift; supporters of Charlottetown were on the defensive. Even Pierre Trudeau was back in the debate, delivering a blistering attack on the accord and its proposals during a speech in Montreal. Later, I interviewed Trudeau, where again he listed his complaints and bristled when I asked him why there was so little support for his view among French-speaking Quebecers.

"Twenty-five years after his death, there are still Gaullists in France, a very important political group representing the views of General de Gaulle. In Quebec, there doesn't seem to be any Trudeauism among French-speaking Quebecers. Why do you think that is?" I asked him.

Trudeau's eyes flashed. "That's because they're cowards. They're afraid of being attacked by the separatists."

As support in Quebec and English Canada turned away, Mulroney resorted to calling opponents of the accord "enemies of Canada." All of this was reflected in our nightly coverage, and we could at first sense and then see that support for Charlottetown, as it was generically known, was ebbing.

On the evening of October 26, as the returns came in, I was at the CBC anchor desk along with Peter Mansbridge and Nancy Wilson. I had mixed views covering the whole negotiation process. I thought the accord was a mishmash of ideas and compromises that probably was almost impossible to implement. Even if it took effect, no one had any idea what Canada would be like or how it would function. On the other side of the argument, a second rejection in just over two years of a constitutional agreement with the primary objective of getting Quebec to sign the Constitution could have catastrophic effects and lead to the breakup of the country.

I had those same views as we watched the vote count. Apparently, so did most other Canadians. Across the country, four provinces and one territory voted in favour of Charlottetown. Six provinces and one territory voted against. Nationally, the No side took 50.4 per cent of the vote, the Yes side 49.6 per cent. In the short term at least, it was fortunate that Quebec was with the majority in rejecting the deal.

What was also recognized, but perhaps not entirely understood, was what a shot across the bow the results had been to "elite" Canada. The federal government and all the provinces, the major political parties and the national business community had all endorsed and campaigned for the passage of the accord. But in a way unlikely even a decade earlier, a majority of Canadians had not been impressed.

On the other side, opposing the Charlottetown Accord were the two parties created by the fallout from Meech. Preston Manning had created the Reform Party in 1987, but it took the Meech Lake Accord and western Canadian anger at the special treatment for Quebec they believed it represented to make Reform into a full-fledged force west of the Manitoba–Ontario boundary. The Bloc Québécois was Lucien Bouchard's creation a month before Meech collapsed. The strength of his personality had already made the Bloc a force to be reckoned with two years later. At the time of the Charlottetown referendum, Bouchard and the Bloc were firmly on the No side against its passage. Manning at first equivocated before also joining the opponents. The results of the federal election one year later would prove that each had made a wise choice.

34

"I Just Spoke to Gorby"

O<small>N</small> A<small>UGUST</small> 16, 1991, an international event suddenly attracted domestic interest in Newsworld's coverage. Soviet President Mikhail Gorbachev was on vacation when he was kidnapped as part of a coup to overthrow his government. No one was entirely sure what was happening, but at Foreign Affairs people following the events decided that the coup had succeeded. I invited External Affairs Minister Barbara McDougall on TV to talk about the change in power in Moscow. Based on her officials' briefing, McDougall said the coup seemed to be a success and that Canada would work with whoever turned out to be in charge.

No sooner than McDougall left the studio than the light on my phone was blinking. The reception asked if I would speak to Lloyd Axworthy, the Liberals' foreign affairs critic. He came on the line steaming. Why had McDougall and the government written off Gorbachev, who by Soviet standards had assumed power legitimately, in favour of a bunch of unknown communist hardliners who had staged a coup? Axworthy was calling from home but he wanted to come to the studio and make his point on television. I told him to come quickly.

In this case Axworthy was right. In relatively short order, the coup collapsed and Gorbachev returned to Moscow to take up the reins of power. Upon his return everyone was cheering that the coup had been aborted, including of course the Canadian government, and from all over the world, leaders were trying to speak with Gorbachev by phone, including Brian Mulroney.

In the early days of Newsworld, technical facilities and experienced people were both in limited supply. Ironically the Parliamentary bureau had been almost overlooked when the network was being planned, but it had a rather rudimentary studio available all day and a crew of keen young technicians who had come mainly from cable television broadcasters and were excited to be working on Parliament Hill for the CBC. And I was there—former foreign correspondent, national reporter, senior parliamentary editor and program host. Our bureau was where the network would go to cover major breaking news.

The Gorbachev story was one example. I was on the air conducting a morning news special following the different developments and speaking with Peter Roberts, who was sitting in the studio with me. Roberts had had a sterling diplomatic career, including as Canadian ambassador to the Soviet Union in the 1980s. We were speculating what might happen next in Moscow when I received the signal to take a commercial break.

No sooner were we off the air and the commercials on than the light on the desk phone flashed. I picked it up.

"I've just talked to Gorby!" said an excited voice that I immediately recognized as belonging to Brian Mulroney.

"Really, how did that happen?" I asked the prime minister.

"We've been in contact with Moscow and they said he would phone me at around 3 a.m. our time. So I got up and sat by the phone. But by

4 p.m. nothing had happened and Mila said I might as well come back to bed because he wasn't going to call. But then this morning, just a few minutes ago, he did call."

"How is he?" I asked.

"He said he is fine."

I was getting a cue to go back on the air. Roberts was staring at me. He could only hear my side of the conversation and had no idea with whom I was speaking.

"What are you going to do now?" I asked the prime minister.

"I'm going down to the caucus meeting to tell them what I just told you."

"Are you looking at your TV right now?"

"Yes."

"Then you'll know why I have to hang up. Goodbye."

The show's introductory music was playing as I hung up.

"Here we go," I told Roberts, who still had no idea who had been on the other end of the phone. As I came up on camera I said: "I can now report that there has been a telephone conversation between President Gorbachev and Prime Minister Mulroney."

Roberts's jaw dropped and his eyes shot wide open as he realized I had been talking to Mulroney on the commercial break.

"The Soviet president is calling world leaders to thank them for their support. The conversation was originally meant to have taken place with Mr. Mulroney very early today but it did not happen immediately. However, they have now spoken and Mr. Gorbachev reported that he is fine. The prime minister is now on his way to the Conservative caucus meeting going on this morning to tell his MPs and senators what I have just told you."

...

AFTER THE COLLAPSE of Meech Lake and the return of Mikhail Gorbachev, the phone calls from the prime minister became less frequent but they did not dry up. He would occasionally call just before I was to go to air or even on a commercial break to pass some tidbit along. Not surprisingly the information usually showed him or the government in a favourable light. Then out of the blue in late August, I had a less direct form of contact with him.

Bill Fox called and invited me to dinner at Hy's Restaurant. Bill had left Mulroney's office in early 1986 but he had not strayed very far. He had developed a successful career as a consultant, stayed active in Conservative politics and kept up socially with the Mulroneys. His wife, Bonnie Brownlee, was executive assistant to Mila Mulroney.

At first we gossiped about politics the way people around Parliament Hill do. Then Bill got to the point.

"You know the prime minister has great respect for you. He would like you to come and work for him and take over responsibility for communications."

I was stunned. Never had such a thought crossed my mind.

Bill said I could take on the job in one of two ways. If I came in as communications director just before the next election, Mulroney would arrange for me to join a major Canadian corporation as a vice-president of communications at a generous private sector salary. If I preferred the security of the public sector he would open up the position of cabinet assistant secretary for communications in the Privy Council office and I would work from there. Before the next election I would move at a senior level from the Privy Council office to a government department I found interesting.

I must admit I felt a certain satisfaction at the offer. It was just three years after Liberal Opposition leader John Turner in had tried to recruit me as his communications director. Mulroney was offering me the same title but a much bigger job. But as flattered as I was, I wasn't interested. I asked Bill to thank the prime minister for thinking of me and making such a generous offer, but that journalism not government communications was what I knew and what I liked.

Bill said he would pass that on but then added: "He'll be disappointed—and he doesn't like taking no for an answer."

Two days later Bill called me again. "I told you he doesn't like taking no for an answer," he said.

He proceeded to tell me that if I came on board through the Privy Council he would upgrade the communications job to a full cabinet secretary. That would mean more money, and when I left for another job in the public service I would be at a level where I could become a deputy minister.

Again I thanked Bill and told him to thank his former boss, but I was staying put. I knew a good many people in the public service including deputy ministers. I thought them smart and hardworking, but I never considered such a career for myself.

35

Tragedy Strikes

A T AROUND EIGHT o'clock on the morning of February 17, 1992, I was standing near a boarding lounge in the Vancouver International Airport, waiting to board a direct flight to Ottawa.

I had been in Vancouver over the weekend with a fairly large team of CBC journalists and technicians, covering the fifth in a series of conferences on proposed changes to the Constitution, organized around the country following the failure of the Meech Lake Accord. I had used an upgrade certificate and was going to fly in business class, and was looking forward to enjoying a smooth flight across the country, a dinner that night with Audrey-Ann and, as a bonus, a visit with Linc. I hadn't seen him since he returned to Kingston after Christmas to resume his second-year classes at Queen's University. This third week in February was reading week, and he was home to have his wisdom teeth out, see his friends and perhaps even do a little reading.

As I waited for the plane to be called, Elly Alboim approached me with a piece of paper in his hand.

"You have to call this number at the Civic Hospital. It's about Linc," he said, concern in his voice.

Civic Hospital? Linc? What was that all about? Linc was having his teeth out at a dental surgeon's office downtown, recommended by his orthodontist. What had happened?

I quickly called the number. The emergency room doctor came on the line.

"You had better get here right away. Your son is not good," he told me.

"What's happened?" I demanded.

"He went into cardiac arrest at the dentist while under the general anaesthetic. The 911 crew revived him, but there has been a lot of damage. You better hurry."

"Well, I'm on a plane from Vancouver to Ottawa. I can't get there any quicker than that," I told him.

I hung up and walked away from the phone, stunned. Elly came over and asked me for details. When I told him, he had just one word.

"Shit!"

On the plane to Ottawa, I sat by myself, trying to understand what was happening. Slowly, the word was filtering back through the cabin to the other CBC people on the plane and some of the politicians and conference officials travelling with us.

Although I didn't know it at the time, Elly had been on the phone to Ottawa on the plane. About an hour before landing, he came to my seat.

"It's all arranged, and when the plane lands, they will get you off first. Nancy Swetnam will be at the airport. The bureau has arranged for a police car to take you and her from the airport to the hospital. Don't worry about your bag. Denise Harrington says she lives near you and she will take it to her house."

And this is the way it happened. Nancy raced me down to the police car waiting outside, jumped in the back seat with me and, with two detectives up front, we hurried to the emergency entrance at the Civic Hospital. Audrey-Ann was there, looking as though she had been hit by a truck, which figuratively she had been. Linc had been moved from emergency to the intensive care ward. We hurried up, and I saw just how serious his condition was. He was heaving and gasping for breath, eyes staring straight ahead, with no sign he was either hearing or seeing us.

We staggered from his bedside to the intensive care waiting room. A kindly critical care doctor named Ruaraidh McIntyre came into see us and explained that Linc had been without oxygen at the dentist long enough that most of his brain had shut down and died. Only the part in the stem of the brain that controlled breathing was still alive, but in cases like this, that usually shut down within twenty-four hours. However, Dr. McIntyre said he had put Linc on a respirator so that he would breathe normally and appear to be only asleep. That way, it would be easier to visit with him, but his brain activity would be monitored and if his natural breathing stopped, he would be declared dead.

Somehow, word was spreading about what had happened. I was called to the waiting room phone. It was the prime minister.

"What has happened?" Brian Mulroney asked.

I told him, and the prognosis.

"God love him. God love him," was the reply.

Deputy Prime Minister Don Mazankowski also called. So did Trina McQueen, by now the head of CBC News. Claudia Millman, my sister-in-law, and her son, my nephew Ted, appeared in the hallway outside the waiting room door. So did Andrew Lay, Linc's friend from Hillcrest High School, and Linc's high school girlfriend, Debbie Brooks, and her mother.

We went down and sat with Linc. He was breathing easily and appeared to be having a deep sleep. We talked to him, but there was no indication he could hear us. Finally, after midnight, assured by the nurses that nothing was going to change overnight, we went back to the waiting room to go home. Waiting for us was Alec Jason, one of the producers from *Capital Report*. He had come to drive us home whenever we wanted to leave and was prepared to stay all night if necessary.

Back at the hospital the next day, things unfolded as Dr. McIntyre had predicted. Linc was still on the respirator, but at around two in the afternoon he appeared to become restless. He was moving in his bed. Then he became still. The doctors brought in a new machine and did tests. Linc, lying on his back, was apparently breathing peacefully as he had been before the restless period. But it was just the machine working. The tests showed he was brain dead.

I knew it was true, but asked for a second opinion. While we waited, Audrey-Ann and I agreed that his organs should be donated for transplant to people that needed them. If there is anything good that has come out of this horrific event, it is that decision. I know that his eyes, kidneys and heart have all brought life and hope to others.

On the day Linc died, my cousin Sheldon Bowles and his wife, Penny, arrived unannounced from Winnipeg. They were a tower of strength. A year earlier, Sheldon had taken charge of the funeral of his brother-in-law, and he stepped into that same role as I sat by, semi-stunned. On the advice of Audrey-Ann's friend Carol Henderson, we held the funeral at St. Bartholomew's Anglican Church. Since we were Anglicans and Linc had been baptized at the National Cathedral in Washington, it seemed a logical choice. Beyond that, I vaguely knew the minister, Desmond Kimmitt, who had worked for the auditor general at one point during a break from his vocation as a clergyman.

Linc died on Wednesday. We wanted a memorial service on Saturday. That way, his friends still home for reading week would be able to attend before going back to their different universities. Because of the unusual way in which he died, and because of my apparent name recognition, news of his death travelled far and wide, on television, radio and by Canadian Press to newspapers around the country. In Ottawa, there was a big story in the *Citizen* with a colour picture of Linc in his high school graduation robes that I gave to the reporter who came to my home to do an interview.

The calls continued the next day. Jean Chrétien reached me at home to give his condolences. He told me he couldn't forget that a young man in Shawinigan had died under similar unexplained circumstances at the dentist.

Devastated as we were, there was a glimmer when we received a phone call from Elly that Peter Mansbridge had come up with a great idea: that we set up a memorial bursary in Linc's name. We quickly made arrangements and were able to mention this in his obituary. The Lincoln Taylor Newman Bursary at Queen's University would be established to assist students in their first year of Arts on the basis of financial need. Decades later, the bursary, thanks to the initial support of so many and donations since that time, helps keep Linc's name and his legacy alive in a small way, and students who are grateful send inspiring letters of its importance to them.

Following a committal service on Saturday morning, when we arrived at St. Bartholomew's for the memorial service that afternoon we could see there were a lot of people going into the church. We knew that both Prime Minister Brian Mulroney and his wife, Mila, and Governor General Ray Hnatyshyn and his wife, Gerda, were going to attend. After their security details had informed Desmond Kimmitt, he phoned to tell us. The church is across the street from the grounds of the Governor General's residence, Rideau Hall, and on the front right-hand side of the church is the "Governor General's pew." It is usually used by families at funeral services, but on any occasion when the Governor General is in the church, it is meant for him and his party.

The Hnatyshyns offered to sit elsewhere, and it was into the special seats at the front that Audrey-Ann and I; her sister Barbara and partner, Brian Erb, from Regina; and from Winnipeg, my brother, Roger; my mother; Sheldon and Penny Bowles and his mother; my mother's sister, my aunt Frances; and other cousins Bill Bowles and Shirley Newman all squeezed in. As we came through a side door to our seats, we could see the church was crowded.

We had planned to have our friend Dick Irvin do the eulogy. As the broadcaster for the Montreal Canadiens and through his work on *Hockey Night in Canada,* he had seen us in both Washington and Edmonton during the years we lived there and had visited us with his wife, Wilma, in Ottawa. Wilma and Dick were from Regina. Wilma, Audrey-Ann and I had all worked either in Winnipeg or Regina in radio together. Their children called me Uncle Don and to Linc, the voice of the Canadiens was Uncle Dick.

Normally, Dick would have been in Montreal for a Saturday night hockey game and could have come to Ottawa for the memorial service and made it back for the broadcast. But that Saturday night there was no hockey game in Montreal, and knowing that well in advance, Dick and Wilma were in Edmonton, where their daughter Nancy was being married. Faced with those facts and urged on by Desmond Kimmitt, I decided I would deliver the eulogy myself.

Andrew Lay and Paul Shone, one of the people Linc shared a house with at Queen's, each talked briefly about him and then read a piece of scripture. When it was my turn to speak, suddenly I realized just how crowded the church was.

Every pew was packed. The centre aisle of the church was filled with young people, many of them girls, sitting on the floor all the way to the back wall. The passage at the back into the church hall was packed with people who had neither seats nor floor space.

While preparing his obituary for the papers, my aunt Frances had suggested that Linc, in his natural, easy-going way, had left us a "legacy of love and laughter." I picked up on that theme for my remarks, talking about how he enjoyed life, loved sports and music, could get mad but never hold a grudge and how that, after his voice changed, he loved to do impersonations—including me, with his "Don Newman voice," which he would use to try and trick people calling our home into believing it was me who had answered. I allowed, though, that I thought his impersonation of comedian Eddie Murphy was better. And I concluded by saying how much Audrey-Ann and I wanted everyone to remember him, for the love and for the laughter.

The ladies of the May Court Club, a women's volunteer service organization on whose executive Audrey-Ann served, catered the reception in the church hall. The line was so long it lasted for two hours. It included the Governor General and Gerda Hnatyshyn; the prime minister and Mila Mulroney; many CBC colleagues from the bureau and from Toronto, like Peter, Wendy and Trina, and from the press gallery; and many politicians like Don Johnston and his wife, Heather, and diplomats. Don, who would later become secretary general of the Organization for Economic Co-operation and Development and one of my closest friends, left a Liberal Party conference where he was running for president of the party to attend. There were many of our friends and Linc's, including the young people who earlier had been sitting on the church floor.

The memorial service and all the people who came were a wonderful tribute to our son. We were touched and grateful for the friendship and support we felt. Since then, I have gone to many funerals of people I did not know well but with whom I was acquainted. I know it probably makes no difference to them, but I now know how much it can mean to their families.

When people had left and we were alone, the reality set in. We had lost our son, our only child. We were so pleased when he was born that we hardly thought about having more children. Over the years, we had wonderful times together. Sometimes I thought it was almost magic. Now the bitter reality sank in: we would never be a family again. I thought that things could not get worse. But I was wrong.

THREE WEEKS AFTER Linc died, I went back to work. My colleagues were kind and supportive. Above and beyond the call of duty, Kathleen Hunt, who was a producer on *Capital Report,* volunteered to manage the non-stop flow of mail that flooded my office. All offered condolences. In a way even more touching, most letters were from people I had never met.

As soon as I was back, I was again into the middle of the meetings, conferences and speeches as the government tried for constitutional renewal after the failure of the Meech Lake Accord. I found it difficult to concentrate, particularly when I was not on the air. Once, during a program, I lost track of what I was talking about during an interview. To the surprise of the guest, the control room and network control in Toronto, I suddenly called for a commercial while I figured out what was going on. Still, I was lucky to have so much work to do. It forced me to concentrate on things other than the hole I felt inside of me at the terrible loss of Linc.

As duty called and I kept going, I worried about Audrey-Ann. She didn't have the same pressing duties that I did as she tried to carry on. However, she and Carol Henderson kept their business going, making and selling high-end note cards with beautiful colour photographs of Ottawa that Carol had taken. And Carol and her Ottawa friends rallied around, including Janet McLaine, Joan Boswell, Liz Ostiguy, and Dannie Stevens.

The news rolled along and I rolled along with it, like the negotiations on the new multifaceted agreement that would become the Charlottetown Accord and then the referendum that would reject it; the Mulroney resignation; and the selection of Kim Campbell to replace him. By then, it was June 1993, a year and two months after Linc had died. Sunday, June 20 would have been Linc's twenty-second birthday. I was out all day at a CBC conference, and when I returned home for dinner, it was as though the other shoe had dropped.

"I was having a shower. I have found a lump," Audrey-Ann told me in a very matter-of-fact way.

It turned out to be much more than matter-of-fact. She was soon diagnosed with stage four breast cancer that had spread to her liver. We were both floored, but then galvanized into action. Unlike Linc's passing, where there was nothing to be done, at least with this terrible news there was still the possibility for hope and action. Audrey-Ann began chemotherapy in August 1993. She had several rounds on and off for over a year and was able to maintain something close to a normal life. On the mornings when she had her chemo and medical appointments, I would go with her and then go on to the CBC to broadcast.

Then, around Thanksgiving in 1994, she became very tired. She stayed home most of the time, and then started taking her meals in her room. Her friends came over often with meals for us. Eventually, she became so weak and unable to help herself that we had a nurse with her Monday through Friday, and over nights and weekends I filled in for the nurse.

But there was nothing anyone could do. She became weaker and weaker until, on December 12, she was slipping in and out of a coma. She died on December 13, two years and ten months after Linc. Family, friends, colleagues and, again, various dignitaries, like the Hnatyshyns, rallied around for her memorial service on Saturday, December 17.

Brian Mulroney called me before the service from Montreal, where he was attending Céline Dion's wedding, to offer his condolences. Close friends Wilma Irvin, Dannie Stevens and Dr. Peter McLaine spoke touchingly of her.

As I listened, sitting in the same pew where Audrey-Ann and I had sat in grief for Linc less than three years earlier, I couldn't believe this had happened again. And yet I knew it had. I felt very much alone.

36

The Liberals Back In
and the Quebec Referendum

Getting the first interview with a new prime minister is always a bit of a trophy—a good "get," as we say in television. I was on the phone with Peter Donolo right after the swearing-in of the new Liberal government on November 3, 1993, asking for an interview with Jean Chrétien. His communications director drove a hard bargain.

"You can be first if you come to Seattle," Donolo said.

Going to the northwestern United States to interview a Canadian prime minister was not a usual way to operate, but then I realized that it would be a great place for a first Chrétien interview. He was attending a meeting of the Asia-Pacific Economic Co-operation forum on Blake Island in Puget Sound, near Seattle, with the twenty other heads of government in the group, including U.S. president Bill Clinton.

In Seattle, Chrétien would also have a one-on-one bilateral meeting with Clinton. It would be the first time they had been together and would yield an additional dimension to an interview with the prime minister, since Chrétien had made much in past years about Brian

Mulroney being too friendly with presidents Ronald Reagan and George H.W. Bush. In the election campaign just past, the Liberals had also been critical of NAFTA, the North American Free Trade Agreement that was bringing Mexico into the free trade agreement between Canada and the United States.

"I'll come if we have the interview after the Clinton meeting," I said.

"Done," Donolo agreed.

I went to Seattle via Vancouver. It was a good way to kill two birds with one stone. Terry and Brian McKenna had produced a biographical film with Pierre Trudeau that was to run on CBC Television, and McClelland and Stewart (then a fully Canadian-owned publishing house) had taken the transcript of their interviews with the former prime minister to produce a companion book. Trudeau was in Vancouver to promote the TV program and the book and take part in a conference at the University of British Columbia. Avie Bennett, the head of McClelland and Stewart, was travelling with him and had talked Trudeau into an interview with me as part of the TV and book promotion.

I hadn't seen Trudeau since our conversation on the Charlottetown Accord. By contrast, this time he seemed a bit disinterested and bored talking about himself. The only time he got agitated was when I suggested that, since he had been so close to and admiring of his father, he might have followed his father's example and become a businessman and owner of sports teams if his father had not died young. Trudeau said he would have turned out to be who he was anyway. I was travelling with producer Edith Champagne, who managed to take his remarks from the interview and some of the footage of the biographical feature and turn it into an interesting program.

But the more interesting interview by far was the one two days later with Chrétien. We set up in a room in the prime minister's suite in one of the big downtown hotels. He was meeting with Clinton at another hotel when we arrived. However, his daughter France and her husband, André Desmarais, were in the suite, and I visited with them while waiting for the prime minister. When Chrétien came in, he was in a good mood, almost bouncy as he walked over to shake hands. It was obvious that he liked Clinton, although, remembering his campaign rhetoric, Chrétien tried not to show it while the cameras were rolling.

When we had finished the taping, I thanked him and said I hoped he would come on my program regularly now that he was in office.

"Don't expect that of me," he replied. "I watched Trudeau and Mulroney and they were always up talking, always in the middle of things and they ended up being hated. I'm going to be less in the spotlight."

I was rather disappointed when I heard that, although I shouldn't have been. Over the next ten years, Chrétien was on television with me at least twice a year and sometimes more. He was on more than any prime minister before or after, including his last interview as prime minister in Toronto at the convention where he stepped down almost ten years to the day after our first talk in Seattle.

During the election, I had done a special hour-long program five nights a week. After the election, I went back to the half-hour *Capital Report*. But in the early months of the Chrétien government, I often did a live program on Saturday as well. As finance minister, Paul Martin was going around the country each weekend, holding conferences on getting the deficit under control. Just as I had covered the constitutional conferences when the Conservatives were in office, I covered the economic ones in 1993. We arrived at an arrangement that I would interview Martin each week at the conference location. After a few of the conferences, which were pretty much the same every week, I was ready for them to end. I think Martin felt the same way. A few weeks in, I was in my studio in Ottawa and he was at the conference in Toronto. Watching him being hooked for our talk, I heard him say wearily, without knowing I could hear, "Oh well, if I am talking to Don Newman, it must be Saturday."

In Ottawa, most of the news was economic, but it had to compete for attention with what was happening in Quebec. There would be a general election in 1994, and after the failure of Meech and the defeat of the Charlottetown Accord, it appeared the separatist Parti Québécois led by Jacques Parizeau was looking ahead to the election so it could take power. And that is exactly what happened on September 12, 1994: the Parti Québécois won seventy-seven seats, the Liberals went into opposition with just forty-seven and the newly formed Action Démocratique Québec party won one.

The next day was a beautiful late summer day in Montreal, warm but the light slightly diffused as the sun was close to the fall equinox and its rays hit the earth at a slightly different slant. That afternoon and into the evening, Montrealers were sitting out on terraces around the city, enjoying the weather along with a glass of wine or a cold beer. There was a feeling of tranquility. But it was misleading, and listening to the conversations in both French and English, it was clear people knew that calm was about to dissipate. The election of the separatists meant that another vote was coming, and this one would be about taking Quebec out of Canada.

In the summer of 1995, the person running Newsworld was a clever producer and executive named Slawko Klymkiw. He asked me how I would feel about making a few changes. First, he wanted me to be on the air in the late afternoon rather than in the evening. Right away, I jumped at the chance. Since the launch of the network, I had been appearing twice—once between four and five, and once again between five and six, on a daily program hosted from Toronto by Alison Smith called *This Day*. I interviewed politicians, taped the interviews while they were on live, and then recycled them for *Capital Report* later in the evening. It was much easier to get people for interviews between four and six than after dinner, and I knew more people were actually seeing me on *This Day* than on *Capital Report,* which I did by myself.

When I quickly agreed, he moved on to what could have been a more sensitive question. He said I could be on from five to six by myself, or from four to six with a co-host in Toronto. By and large, people on television don't like co-hosts, and co-hosting can be fraught with problems.

"Who's the co-host?" I asked.

"It would be Nancy Wilson."

"Okay. I'll do four to six."

I had known Nancy when she was a reporter in the Parliamentary Press Gallery with Global Television. She had been a host on *Canada AM* on CTV and at the CBC had filled in for Barbara Frum on *The Journal.* She was a real professional and had a great laugh. It was agreed we would team up together starting in September, and the program would be called *Politics.*

Changing time slots brought me two other good things in addition to Nancy. A new, expanded studio was built over the summer for the debut of the new show, and having two hours a day to fill meant I needed more help getting things on the air, both for the program and for all the other live broadcasts I was doing.

Klymkiw told me to look around for someone we could bring on board as a senior producer who was already at the CBC. If I couldn't find someone, he said he had some candidates he could move from Toronto.

I knew exactly who I wanted. Dave Mathews had come to the Ottawa bureau as a field producer in the mid-eighties. In a bureau of good field producers, he was superior. When I became senior parliamentary editor

Mike Duffy, me, Peter Mansbridge and David Halton as we congratulate ourselves and each other after our Liberal leadership convention coverage in June 1984.

In a scrum with Liberal Opposition leader John Turner in 1985.

As president of the Parliamentary Press Gallery, I welcome Governor General Jeanne Sauvé to the Gallery dinner on the Hill in 1987. To the back right of Sauvé is John Turner.

My son, Linc, in his high school graduation photo, June 1990. Linc died in February 1992 and Audrey-Ann in December 1994.

rondevries.com

Leading the scrum of Prime Minister Brian Mulroney outside the conference centre during week-long Meech Lake negotiations in June 1990.

Ken Ginn/PMO

In Vancouver with CBC executive producer Arnold Amber during the Clinton-Yeltsin Summit in April 1993. I'd just interviewed Prime Minister Mulroney.

In 1997 after my receiving the first Charles Lynch Award for outstanding coverage of national affairs, with Peter Mansbridge and former Ottawa bureau chief Elly Alboim.

Receiving the Order of Canada from Governor General Roméo LeBlanc at Rideau Hall in September 1999.

Year-end interview in December 1999 with Prime Minister Jean Chrétien at Rideau Gate.

With Washington colleague Henry Champ at the Summit of the Americas in Quebec City in 2001. As police tear-gassed rioting protestors, the smell wafted into the press centre.

Ken Furness

Stephen Harper and Stockwell Day face off in the *Politics* studio during a Canadian Alliance leadership debate I moderated on March 7, 2002.

The Canadian Press/Tom Hanson

At a first ministers meeting in 2003 with Dave Mathews and Sharon Musgrave, senior producers of *Politics*, live coverage and special events.

Bev Chappell

The *Politics* team in December 2004, on the last day in our
National Press Building studio.

With Major George Pearce (Ret.) on November 11, 2004, at the National War
Memorial. George was with me for twenty-one Remembrance Day broadcasts.

Dave Chan/PMO

Interviewing Prime
Minister Paul Martin
the new studio in Ap
2005. He was trying
avoid defeat on a bu
vote, which would ha
triggered an election

Deb Ransom / PMO

Year-end interview with Prime Minister Stephen Harper, who was leading his first
minority government, in 2006.

Receiving an honorary Doctorate of Laws in September 2007 from University of Winnipeg president Lloyd Axworthy. The honour was worth wearing the hat.

With Finance Minister Jim Flaherty and Rick Mercer, Canada's hilarious political satirist, in October 2007 at a CBC reception for parliamentarians.

My wife, Shannon, in September 2008. We were married in November 1997.

Dyanne Wilson

House of Commons Photography

Thanking the House of Commons for its tributes and standing ovations on my last day of broadcasting *Politics*, on June 19, 2009.

In November 2011, with Governor General David Johnston at a Canada–U.S. innovation conference I chaired in Ottawa for public policy group Canada 2020.

Jake Wright

Waltzing it up with Shannon at the Viennese Opera Ball held at the National Art Gallery, in February 2013.

Caroline Phillips/*Ottawa Citizen*

in 1988, Elly Alboim told me that one person I would never have to worry about was Dave. We didn't work much together, but I got to know him indirectly when I gave the toast to the bride at his wedding. He and my colleague from *This Week in Parliament*, Nancy Swetnam, were married in 1989.

And it is a good thing that they were. When I first approached Dave in the summer of 1995, he was the assignment editor for *The National* in the bureau and was reluctant to leave that job. I was thinking about who might be a good second choice when I got a phone call at home that evening from Dave.

"Nancy tells me I'm crazy. She says she loved working with you and I will too."

So Dave came on board as the senior producer on the Ottawa end of *Politics* and live specials. And it couldn't have been better timing. Dave's father was an American who had come to Quebec to work, married a woman born and bred in Quebec and raised a family. When Dave spoke English, you thought he was an anglophone. When he spoke French, you would swear he was francophone. He started at the CBC at Radio-Canada in Montreal, then switched to the English television side and ended up as a producer for *The National* at the Quebec National Assembly before coming to the Parliamentary bureau.

As assignment editor, he had dealt every day with CBC people in Toronto, and was now producing a daily show with half of it coming from there. Dave was skilled at working with colleagues at the centre of the CBC universe. Even more important, when we started working together, he had invaluable experience no one else at the CBC had outside of Quebec. He had worked at the National Assembly, knew the politicians and the journalists and all the other players. Who better to have as a producer and a colleague to cover the most crucial story of 1995 and beyond: the Quebec referendum.

...

Jacques Parizeau's government spent the first half of 1995 trying to soften up Quebecers so that it could hold a referendum to take the province out of Canada. The target, of course, was the eighty per cent of the Quebec population who were French-speaking. Given that almost all the other twenty per cent would be certain to vote no, the battle was on for the hearts and minds of the people who considered themselves vrais *québécois*, French-speaking Quebecers born in the province and whose families had been in Quebec since before the Conquest in 1759.

The date of the referendum was set for October 30, 1995. The question was less ambiguous than the one used by René Lévesque and his government in 1980. That question was over one hundred words long and talked about negotiating "sovereignty-association" with Canada. The question put forward by Parizeau talked about "sovereignty" and negotiation of a new arrangement with Canada, although no one in Canada was talking about negotiating a new arrangement with Quebec after a yes/oui vote. Even more disinguous were the signs and billboards the Quebec government produced to promote support for sovereignty, which used the ultimate Canadian symbol. On billboards across Quebec, the letter *O* in the word *oui* was a Canadian one-dollar coin, a loonie. Jacques Parizeau and his separatist friends wanted to go; they just didn't want to go too far.

Fifteen years earlier, during the first referendum in 1980, there were only three parties in the House of Commons: the governing Liberals, the Progressive Conservatives and the NDP. All opposed sovereignty-association or anything like it for Quebec. In 1995, the political landscape was entirely different in Ottawa. The Official Opposition was the Bloc Québécois, formed after the failure of the Meech Lake Accord and dedicated to taking Quebec out of Canada. And its leader was the charismatic Lucien Bouchard, now an even more dramatic personality following emergency surgery in late 1994 to amputate his left leg after he was attacked by flesh-eating disease. Bouchard walked with a limp and used a cane. He was a moving symbol of determination and courage.

At the start of the referendum campaign, I invited Bouchard onto *Politics* for an interview. Polls showed he was the most admired politician in Quebec, and I asked him if he would be taking a leave from Ottawa to campaign for the Yes side. He told me he would stay in Ottawa each day for Question Period and then fly by chartered plane from the small Gatineau airport on the Quebec side of the Ottawa River for a campaign appearance that evening in Quebec. Then he would fly back and be ready to repeat the process the next day. The strategy was obvious and, from the separatist point of view, a good one: he would get television coverage from Question Period that would help the Yes campaign, and then that evening would make an appearance to fire up the supporters on the ground.

The only problem from the Yes side's point of view was that the plan, along with the rest of its campaign, wasn't working. Despite Bouchard's fly-in appearances, the central figure in the separatist campaign was Premier Jacques Parizeau. Parizeau was smart and articulate. But he had the look and manner of a banker in the City of London before the Second World War and was about as far as could be imagined from the way most francophone Quebecers thought of themselves. So, like a football team at halftime whose starting quarterback isn't scoring any points, the Yes team made a change. For the second half, Parizeau was out and Bouchard was in. The Bloc leader left Ottawa to head up the campaign in Quebec, leaving a Montreal MP named Gilles Duceppe—the first person elected as a member of the Bloc in the summer of 1990—to lead the party in the House.

The first day Duceppe was in charge, I invited him onto the program. He was sitting in the foyer of the House of Commons in front of a camera, an earpiece in his ear so he could hear my questions. He couldn't see me, but I could see him. The Bloc Québécois and other separatists were spinning the move to have Bouchard replace Parizeau as though it were something that had been planned from the beginning of the campaign. I was to interview Gilles Duceppe right after a commercial break, so to start the segment, before I actually spoke to him, I played the tape of Bouchard a few weeks earlier saying that he would not leave Ottawa to campaign full time in Quebec. Since the Bloc didn't usually watch English-language television, I don't think Duceppe had heard Bouchard say he was staying in place to lead the Bloc. The look on his face as I watched him listening was worth the trouble of playing the clip.

However, that was just an aside to the campaign. The change at the top of the Yes campaign worked in spectacular fashion. Bouchard brought a passion and energy to the separatist message as he hobbled with his cane from meeting to meeting. The polls flipped around. With about a week to go until voting day, the Yes side was ahead by about five points in the polls.

The CBC had purchased a rolling poll that took a sample each evening and tracked public opinion on the sovereignty question. Early on in the campaign, I checked it every few days, but since the No side was well ahead I didn't follow it closely. However, once Bouchard took over, within three days you could see opinion changing, and with one week to go it looked like a clear separatist win. The federal cabinet was seeing similar polls, and panic was setting in. About a week before the vote, Fisheries Minister Brian Tobin was in my studio for an interview. Afterwards, in the hall outside the makeup room, he told me something had to be done and done quickly. His plan was to bring people from all across Canada and stage a large unity rally in downtown Montreal on the Friday before the vote. The idea was to show and convince Quebecers they were wanted in Canada. There was just over a week to organize it, and he was trying to get the go-ahead to plan for it. What did I think?

I knew the rally would get huge publicity outside of Quebec. I didn't know quite how it would be perceived within the province, but I thought it was better to try it than not. Even if the Yes side ended up winning, outside of Quebec the government and the other parties would have been seen to have tried everything to prevent it. Within a day, Tobin had received approval and planning began in earnest. At the CBC, as I suspected, the rally would be carried live across Canada on Newsworld. I would go to Montreal to anchor, and Alison Smith would fly in from Toronto join me in the booth.

The rally was on Friday, October 27. That afternoon, I would do my end of *Politics* from the special newsroom set up at Radio-Canada headquarters in Montreal for the English coverage of the referendum. By the time I was on the air, the rally would have been over for at least two hours, the speeches and anything else already boiled down into news reports, so I needed something big that no one else in the media would have to make the show stand out. The question was, what could that be?

Then I had an idea. I thought back to 1990 and the week before the Meech Lake deadline, when the Newfoundland House of Assembly was debating whether the province should ratify the agreement. In a very unusual manoeuvre as prime minister, Brian Mulroney had gone to St. John's to speak to the assembly. I remembered he had urged its members to consider how they would feel if they voted against Meech Lake and then, watching the returns on television in a future Quebec referendum on separation, saw the province was going to leave Canada.

At the time, he seemed rather melodramatic. In October 1995, it had the ring of prophecy. Since leaving office, Mulroney had been low-key and largely out of sight, particularly after the disastrous results for his party in the 1993 election. To have him on television on this issue right before the referendum, I thought, would be important. I called him at his Montreal office and told him my plan. I would play the bit of his Newfoundland speech from 1990 where he talked about a future referendum and then cut directly to our interview on the current situation. Mulroney seemed interested, said he would think about it for a day, and we agreed to talk before the rally.

The morning of the twenty-seventh, I arrived at his office on McGill College Avenue with Dave Mathews and a camera crew. He was the Brian Mulroney of old—in good spirits, talkative and with plenty to say. He stopped to take a call from Paul Desmarais Sr. to discuss the early voting turnout and the lines at the polls, and then we did the interview where he recorded his reflections and views.

From his office, I had to hurry to Place du Canada. When I was in school in Montreal, the two-block park was at the corner of Peel Street and Dorchester Boulevard and called Dominion Square. It hadn't moved, but reflecting the changes in Quebec and Canada, it was now at the corner of Rue Peel and Boulevard René-Lévesque. The Canadian Imperial Bank of Commerce had an office tower on the corner, and next to it, the main branch of its retail bank in the city. The CBC and Radio-Canada had secured access to the flat roof of that building, about four storeys above the ground. There was an anchor desk for me and Alison, and another about thirty feet away for the anchor team that would do the broadcast in French for Radio-Canada.

Two things stand out from the broadcast that day. The first is the iconic shot from our helicopter of the Canadian flag being carried through the streets of Montreal amongst the throngs of people on their way to the rally. We didn't know that was going to happen, and when we saw the picture a couple of minutes before airtime, we knew it was the shot we'd use to begin the program. The other memory is less pleasant. Both we and Radio-Canada signed on at noon, just as the rally began. Alison and I spoke for a moment. We could see the Radio-Canada anchors doing the same thing. Then the crowd began to sing "O Canada." Alison and I immediately stopped talking. Not our Radio-Canada colleagues; they kept speaking as though nothing was happening and denying their audience listening the knowledge that the Canadian national anthem was being sung.

Frankly, I was appalled, although I guess I shouldn't have been. The French-language version of Newsworld, Réseau de l'information, has the abbreviation RDI. In French, it is pronounced "air day ee." During the referendum campaign, federalists in Quebec felt the coverage of RDI was so biased in favour of the separatists that they jokingly referred to the network as "air day oui." The joke was a bitter one.

The day of the vote, I was in Ottawa, doing a variety of lead-up programs to the coverage of the results that night. I was keeping things on an even keel even though the rolling poll that morning had predicted a narrow win for the separatists. That evening, as the count came in, I was situated in the foyer of the House of Commons with a camera and microphones to interview Ottawa politicians on their reaction. But no one was ready to react. The count was slow in coming in, particularly from the Montreal area, where the turnout was extremely heavy and the counting took a long time.

The early returns from the heavily French-speaking areas outside of Montreal seemed to confirm the morning poll prediction. At one point, the Yes side had collected about sixty per cent of the vote. But then, slowly, things changed. As the no votes piled up, the bar we were using at the bottom of the screen to track the vote percentage began moving from the Yes side on the right towards the centre. Finally, as the No side eked out a lead, and with only Montreal votes still to count, Jacques Parizeau bitterly acknowledged defeat and Jean Chrétien happily claimed victory.

The prime minister had been watching the results at his residence at 24 Sussex Drive. A camera had been set up in his office, and he would come to Parliament Hill to make his comments when the results were known. With the results in and Canada held together by one per cent of the total of 4.7 million votes cast, Chrétien arrived to make his remarks. He came through the west door of the Centre Block, up the wide stairs towards the foyer of the House of Commons, where I was sitting on a stool. He looked tired, relieved and excited all at once. As he turned the corner to go up to his office, our eyes met. He smiled and gave me the thumbs-up.

37

Televising the Supreme Court

THE QUEBEC REFERENDUM was a huge political issue between the separatist Parti Québécois and the federal Liberal government. Given the razor-thin margin of the outcome, after the close call for Canada, Ottawa decided a legal framework was needed around the issue.

Enter the Supreme Court of Canada. In 1998, the federal government placed the question of Quebec independence and how it might be achieved before the court for its opinion. And thanks to more than a decade of behind-the-scenes work, what happened when the court heard this most important of all national issues was seen across Canada on television.

In March of 1982, Bertha Wilson was sworn in as the first woman judge to sit as a justice on the bench of the Supreme Court of Canada. It was an event of historic significance, so much so that the doors of the courtroom were thrown open to the prying eyes of television cameras so that her swearing-in could be broadcast by the CBC and seen across Canada. My role that day was to be in the splendid lobby of the court, interviewing the great and the good as they came to witness history.

The swearing-in of Madame Justice Wilson preceded by about a month the patriation of the Constitution, and with it the launching of the Charter of Rights and Freedoms. The Charter soon became the legal touchstone against which laws limiting rights were measured. Interest groups seeking inclusion and freedoms began using the Charter to challenge restrictive legislation that had been passed over a long period of time by the federal Parliament and provincial legislatures.

These "Charter challenges" were starting to end up being brought for final resolution before the Supreme Court. Suddenly, the potential arose that laws that had been the bedrock of some of the Canadian social fabric might either be changed or thrown out by the courts. Reporters were suddenly taking a greater interest in the court and its justices as cases on abortion, aboriginal issues, assisted suicide and other contentious matters began winding their way up through the judicial system, ultimately to be resolved by the Supreme Court.

Since it was commissioned in 1875, the Supreme Court had been open to the press. Print reporters could sit in the courtroom and listen to the arguments of opposing counsel as the justices heard an appeal. The court did not directly explain its decisions. Instead, it announced when its decisions were to be made public. By tradition and courtesy, counsel for the disputants in a case got a short heads-up about the decision. Lawyers involved in a case, as well as other interested parties, would sometimes comment, but in truth, before the Charter cases began, the decisions of the Supreme Court, aside from constitutional matters, were often both arcane and narrow.

But all of that changed with the arrival of the Charter. Now there was widespread interest in some of the matters coming before the court, and the rules governing how they were reported were, from journalists' point of view, inadequate. Especially glaring for the media was the absence of television in the court. Now that the House of Commons was on television, there was a feeling amongst both television and print reporters that everything else should be on television too. However, if that was the inclination of the Parliamentary Press Gallery, there was no indication that it was shared by the nine justices on the Supreme Court, as I was soon to find out.

In early 1986, I was approached by two of the best reporters in the press gallery, David Vienneau of the *Toronto Star* and Stephen Bindman of Southam News. Each covered justice and legal matters and, more regularly, the Supreme Court. They asked me to join them as a member of the liaison committee between the Parliamentary press gallery and the court—three members from each side—to discuss matters of mutual interest and concern. (Later I became the gallery's president.) For the gallery, the major issue then was getting the proceedings of the court televised, and as print reporters Vienneau and Bindman felt they needed an established television journalist to help them make their case.

I hadn't thought much about the issue, but how could I be against televising Supreme Court proceedings? I signed on as a committee member, little realizing just what I had committed to or how long and difficult it would be to achieve our goal. However, I soon got an early indication at the first meeting of the liaison committee.

Vienneau and I were invited to lunch with the three justices on the committee: Mr. Justice William McIntyre, Mr. Justice Gerald Le Dain and Madam Justice Bertha Wilson. One end of the justices' library serves as the court dining room, and we were ushered in for a glass of wine before sitting down to lunch. Quickly, the discussion turned into a debate between me and Justice McIntyre. I argued that television in the Supreme Court would do no more than make available to people all across the country, including in his hometown of Vancouver, what people in Ottawa could see by coming to the court and sitting in the public gallery. However, Justice

McIntyre seemed to view television the way some primitive tribesmen had viewed cameras when someone tried to take their photograph—as if allowing one to be pointed at you to collect or transmit your image somehow captured your soul and you never got it back.

Arguments that TV in the court would turn proceedings into something like Question Period in the House of Commons were easy to refute. The justices—particularly the chief justice—controlled behaviour in the court. No lawyer hoping to convince the court of an argument could begin by annoying the justices by grandstanding.

It seemed to me that Mr. Justice Le Dain appeared to take very little interest in the discussion. A few months later, I found out why, when he resigned from the court well in advance of the mandatory retirement age of seventy-five. Justice Wilson didn't say much, but whenever I glanced her way while McIntyre was shooting down the idea of televising court proceedings, she would smile at me.

Well, I thought, I may not be getting anywhere with McIntyre or Le Dain, but I at least have one member of the court on my side. Oh, how wrong could I be. Lunch ended, and on the way out, I stopped to say goodbye to Justice Wilson.

"Mr. Newman," she said, "my husband and I love your program, *This Week in Parliament*. We watch it every week. But I would never agree to television in the Supreme Court."

And that, for the moment, was it. It would take a number of years, changes in the composition of the court and the importance of some of the cases being heard before the first live telecast would originate from the courtroom. And it would be almost another decade before hearings and decisions of the Supreme Court would be covered in the same manner as most news in Ottawa.

The first important change was the retirement at seventy-five of Justice McIntyre and then of Chief Justice Brian Dickson. McIntyre was replaced by Beverley McLachlin and Dickson by Antonio Lamer, who had been on the court since 1980 and had been a member of the press gallery-Supreme Court liaison committee. Other retirements brought on John Sopinka, Peter Cory, Frank Iacobucci and John Major. All brought more contemporary attitudes than the people they replaced, but even then, getting television into the court was no easy matter.

In 1989 it was Newsworld and a case that wasn't directly televised that got the ball rolling. A little over a month after Newsworld went on the air, the court heard a case around the explosive issue of abortion. A woman in Quebec named Chantal Daigle became pregnant by her boyfriend, a man named Jean-Guy Tremblay. The pair then had a falling-out, Tremblay allegedly became abusive, and Daigle didn't want to see him and didn't want to have his baby.

But he went to court. Among other things, his lawyers claimed the fetus was a person and that Daigle was trying to deny the father parental rights to an unborn child. The case triggered a huge sensation. Abortion was an even bigger political issue than it remains today, and the case made headlines beyond Canada. In our CBC bureau, a team from NBC in the United States set up shop to cover the story. There were no cameras in the courtroom when, on a hot August morning, lawyers for both Daigle and Tremblay argued before the justices. But there were certainly cameras in the lobby of the court. Wisely, it had been decided to set up an area for cameras and another for spectators. Reporters sat inside, listened to the arguments and then hurried outside with running updates; meanwhile, people from organized groups on both sides of the issue kept popping up before the cameras to give their views. Tremblay was at the court, but Daigle wasn't. Then, after lunch, Daigle's lawyer explained why: she had left the country, gone to Boston and had an abortion.

Neil Macdonald was covering the case for the CBC. He ran out of the court, to our studio down the street in the Parliamentary bureau, to breathlessly tell me the news as we were on live. It was dramatic, though not as dramatic as a few minutes earlier, when Daigle's lawyer had stood up in court to tell the justices.

In the weeks and months that followed, I was able to use that case to urge the justices to experiment with cameras in the court. After all, everything about the Daigle case had been on TV except the people deciding it, the arguments they had to consider and the probing questions they asked. Over a period of time, my points seemed to register. Led mainly by Justice Sopinka, the court bought and installed its own remote-controlled, sound-activated camera system and then, on a trial basis, allowed coverage of an appeal to the court as long as the entire case was carried. At first, that worked fine, but some cases weren't worth carrying in their entirety. The next test between the court and the gallery was how to air packaged reports of cases using video from the court without actually broadcasting the entire proceedings. It shouldn't have been that hard, because even when Newsworld was carrying entire cases, *The National* and newscasts on other networks were editing the taped coverage and producing packaged stories from the court, just as they all did from the House of Commons.

Still, to convince the justices they could rely on the packaged stories without a complete broadcast took a lot of work. I had all of the networks provide me with copies of packaged stories they had run from various Supreme Court cases, and then took them to the justices on the liaison committee for their examination. The justices seemed convinced, but with a proviso: there had to be, within some reasonable time frame, a full broadcast of the entire court proceeding.

How to manage that? Luckily, CPAC, the Parliamentary channel owned by the cable companies, was recording the entire court proceedings, and they promised a full replay within a reasonable time frame.

That made the justices happy, even though the full replay was often around midnight on Saturdays.

Beyond the Daigle abortion story, three others stand out in the early coverage of the court. First among these was the case of Robert Latimer, a farmer from Wilkie, Saskatchewan, who admitted he killed his twelve-year-old daughter Tracy by carbon monoxide poisoning in the family pickup truck. She was severely handicapped with cerebral palsy. Latimer even showed the RCMP how he did it. It was, he claimed, a mercy killing.

Twice he was tried in Saskatchewan. The first time, he was convicted of first-degree murder, but the case was overturned after it was shown that, at the request of the prosecution, there had been jury tampering by the RCMP. The next time, Latimer was convicted of second-degree murder, but a judge in his home province dramatically reduced his sentence, calling the crime "compassionate murder." That finding was appealed all the way to the Supreme Court, and the second-degree murder conviction was reinstated. The day the decision was handed down, groups supporting Latimer and the rights of the handicapped were at the court for the verdict. We also had a satellite truck at the Latimer farm for his reaction. It was compelling television around a very emotional issue.

The second case that carried a heavy emotional wallop involved Sue Rodriguez, a forty-three-year-old woman in Victoria living with ALS, the degenerative disease for which there is no cure. She wanted a doctor to help her end her life at a time of her own choosing, but assisted suicide is illegal in Canada. She had the support of New Democrat MP Svend Robinson when she launched a Charter challenge that went all the way to the Supreme Court. The court ruled against assisted suicide. Despite the court's decision, someone helped her end her life shortly after it. No charges were brought against anyone.

There had been no television cameras in the court in 1980, when arguments were presented over whether or not the federal government could unilaterally ask the British Parliament to pass legislation to patriate the Canadian Constitution. But there were cameras and hours of coverage when the next great constitutional issue was argued before the court.

The narrow federalist victory in the 1995 Quebec referendum traumatized much of English-speaking Canada. Particularly after Quebec premier Jacques Parizeau said that if the separatists won, he was going to unilaterally declare Quebec independent from Canada the day after the vote. And this was going to happen despite the ambiguity of the question that was asked and the narrowness of any separatist victory. Almost two years after the federalist victory by less than one per cent of the vote, the Chrétien government referred three questions about possible Quebec independence to the Supreme Court for an opinion. The questions were:

Under Canadian law, did the National Assembly of Quebec have the right to unilaterally declare Quebec independent from Canada, either following a referendum or at any other time?

Was there a basis in international law for a unilateral declaration of independence by Quebec?

If there was a conflict between Canadian law and international law, which law held precedence?

The court set aside the better part of a week in January of 1998 to hear the arguments. The Parti Québécois government of Premier Lucien Bouchard refused to take part in the case, maintaining that, as a "people," Québécois had a right to determine their own future. To argue the separatist case, the court appointed an *amicus curiae,* a "friend of the court," a lawyer charged with arguing the separatist case.

There were fifteen intervenors in the reference case. We set up an anchor desk in the lobby of the court, were able to mix the pictures from the court with the broadcast from the desk and from our studios in the Parliamentary bureau, cameras in the foyer of the House of Commons and our studios in Toronto, where we had various constitutional experts on hand to provide commentary. We had only been on the air about an hour when my cellphone rang. It was Tony Burman, the head of Newsworld. He liked what he was seeing so much that he wanted an hour-long wrap-up program at 7 pm. That was after a full day of live coverage and our regular *Politics* program between five and six. It was a lot of work and a lot of airtime, but I was glad to do it. This was Canadian history in progress.

After hearing the arguments, the court took eight months to consider its findings on a series of questions momentous to the future of the country. In August, the court announced its decision would be handed down on August 20. I was on holiday, but I made sure to return for what indeed would be historic. Again we were set up in the foyer of the Supreme Court. Other television networks had anchor desks and camera positions nearby. The public area was packed with spectators. The court's opinion was handed to reporters at nine forty-five. One of our producers was quick to note that the court had decided Quebec did not have the right to unilaterally declare its independence from Canada, either under Canadian law or international law. My colleague in the Parliamentary bureau, Debra Brown, stayed in the briefing room to get more details.

We had gone live on the air fifteen minutes before the opinion was released. We were planning to stay on until 10 a.m. With confirmation that Quebec had no unilateral right to secede, our commentary and comments were focused on that fact, including reaction from Parliament Hill and from the National Assembly in Quebec. I was starting to play in my mind with what I would say at the sign-off when, suddenly, breathless from the briefing, Debra Brown was standing behind the cameras, trying to get my attention.

"There's more," she said loudly enough for me to hear, something you wouldn't normally do during a live broadcast. She certainly looked as though what she had to say was urgent, so on the air, I said, "Debra Brown was in the briefing on the opinion and she's going to come in here and give us some more details."

We pushed the guest we had in the chair next to me out of his seat, and Debra, holding the microphone rather than pinning it on her jacket, gave us the blockbuster news. While Quebec had no unilateral right to declare its independence, if a clear majority of Quebecers voted yes to a clear question on separating from Canada, Ottawa and the other provinces would have to negotiate Quebec leaving the country.

That changed everything. The opinion was as cleverly crafted as the ruling eighteen years earlier on the federal government's ability to unilaterally return the Constitution from Britain. Obviously, there was a lot more to this story, and just in the nick of time, Debra had been able to get it to us.

We stayed on the air all day and did another special program in the evening. By the time I left, I was exhausted but exhilarated. Canadian history had been made right before our eyes, and at CBC Newsworld we had been a part of it.

The just-in-time delivery by Debra of the second part of the opinion also gave me an opportunity to resume discussions with the court about providing lockup briefings for reporters before decisions were released, instead of at the same time.

The justices on the court were delighted with the way the coverage had played out, but I pointed out that a couple of minutes later and we would have missed the qualifier about Quebec being able to negotiate its way out of Canada under the Constitution. The justices listened, but were not convinced. It took another case, a couple of years later, before the lockup concept finally made sense to the court.

In 1999, the court ruled that an aboriginal fisherman named Donald Marshall had the right to fish for eels on the Bay of Fundy, outside of the commercial fishing season, because of rights assigned the Mi'kmaq people in a treaty with the British Crown in 1760.

The court ruling was unpopular with the non-aboriginal commercial fishermen on the Bay of Fundy, all the more so when aboriginal leaders interpreted the court ruling to mean Mi'kmaq people also had rights to catch lobster and harvest trees on Crown land.

Tensions mounted around Burnt Church, New Brunswick. The RCMP was trying to keep the peace. While this was developing, a non-aboriginal fishermen's group, the West Nova Fishermen's Coalition, asked the court to rehear the case. Whether the group asked on its own initiative or was prompted to make the request has never been clear, but either way it gave the court the out it needed. A rehearing was unnecessary, it said, because the ruling applied specifically to catching eels out of season and nothing else. Things quieted down in New Brunswick, but I was able to convince a couple of the justices that a lockup before the ruling was handed down might have headed off the reaction to the decision.

Lockups were subsequently tried. At first, briefing officers from the court were very cautious—they didn't always achieve the clarity reporters needed. But over the more recent past, things have improved and now things seem to be working well for everyone.

It is interesting how things evolve. In February of 2011, I was invited to lunch with the justices of the court, some of whom I had met, but at least three of whom I had not. I suddenly realized, sitting at the table with all nine, that only Chief Justice Beverley McLachlin, who succeeded Lamer in 2000, had been on the court when television first began broadcasting the proceedings. So I told the assembled members of the country's top court in the '90s of my first lunch in their dining room twenty-four years earlier, and my exchanges with Justices McIntyre and Wilson.

To the present court, it seemed like something out of the dark ages. They thought it hilarious.

38

Shannon

IT WASN'T IMMEDIATELY clear as the returns came in on election night, but the results of the 1997 election set in motion a chain of events that ultimately transformed both the two major parties in Parliament and the country itself.

Those changes were slow to unfold. But when they culminated almost nine years later, Canada had a new government and a changed political landscape.

Now, years later, it is clear to see how events unfolded as they did. But after the June election in 1997, I was not thinking much about the unfolding of the political landscape. I was thinking of getting married.

Shannon Day was the national director of media relations for a consortium of the major telephone companies created in the 1990s with the deregulation of long distance and the emergence of new entrants. I had first been briefly introduced to her in the National Press Club when she was working for *The Globe and Mail* in its publishing division. She was then the senior editor of a newsletter created to monitor the implementation of the Canada–U.S. Free Trade Agreement.

She was certainly attractive and intelligent, but not very talkative. I put that down to her being shy or not being too impressed by television journalists. Although I never met her in Alberta, she had worked in the office of Peter Lougheed and then moved to Ottawa to earn a journalism degree.

After experiencing so much loss in my life, the tide turned. My friends and colleagues had been so supportive. I dated some nice ladies, but by 1996, Shannon and I began to see each other exclusively and by 1997 we had decided to marry.

The question then became where and when. Between us we seemed to know half the people in Ottawa. A small, private wedding in Ottawa seemed impossible to arrange.

Finally, we decided to be married in Vancouver. Desmond Kimmitt, who had been so helpful to me when Linc and Audrey-Ann died, had retired there and we thought that to include him in the ceremony would add a nice continuity. We had a few close friends in Vancouver. More importantly, Shannon's family was in Edmonton, and my family in Winnipeg, and since they would have to travel if we married in Ottawa, travelling west instead of east didn't seem any great hardship.

The next question was when. I would be broadcasting from Vancouver the third week in November as Canada hosted the Asia-Pacific Economic Co-operation (APEC) conference. The week following did not look busy, so we decided to get married on the last Thursday of November and have a brief honeymoon on Vancouver Island.

I was in Vancouver the week before to cover APEC, and for the "pepper spray" incident for which it would become famous. An RCMP officer, providing security for Indonesian dictator Suharto, used pepper spray without warning on a group of protesters and a television camera-man covering the protest. Suharto was staying in a suite at the top of the Fairmont Hotel Vancouver, and there were police ringing the hotel as I went in to check on our reservation for rooms for both us and our guests, as well as a dining room we had reserved for dinner after the wedding ceremony.

I was informed there was no problem with the guest rooms and that the hotel would be pleased to offer Shannon and me the bedroom and sitting room in a suite with a dining room.

"That sounds very nice," I told the assistant manager. "Could I see it?"

"I'm afraid not," she replied. "President Suharto is using it now, and there are guards with machine guns in the halls and all the rooms."

Since Desmond Kimmitt did not have a licence to perform mar-riages in British Columbia, he arranged with Dean Peter Elliott of Christ Church Cathedral in the heart of Vancouver to make the cere-mony legal. The Anglican cathedral is right across the street from the Hotel Vancouver. We were a small, happy group of family and a few west coast friends gathered before the large cathedral altar at twi-light for the wedding ceremony. And equally happy across the street, as we took our places around the candlelit dinner tables and drinks were served next to rooms vacated by the dictator of Indonesia and Chinese president Jiang Zemin, who came to power in 1989 after the Tiananmen Square revolt.

We had told no one in Ottawa of our wedding plans, and we were not quite sure how to break it to all our friends when we returned. It turned out to be easier than we'd thought. We arrived back from the west coast and went immediately to a dinner party given by the minister of foreign affairs, Lloyd Axworthy, and his wife, Denise, for U.S. senator Patrick Leahy of Vermont and his wife, to celebrate the Ottawa signing of the treaty banning the use of landmines. Shannon and I came directly from the airport and arrived before anyone else at Rideau Gate, the government guest house where the dinner was being held.

People around Ottawa were used to seeing Shannon and me together, and as the other guests began to arrive, we chatted as though nothing had happened. We were standing with David Collenette, the defence minister, and his wife, Penny, when the Axworthys and Leahys arrived. Lloyd started taking the Leahys around the room, introducing them to the Collenettes and then turning to me.

"This is Don Newman. He is with the CBC," he said as Leahy and I shook hands.

"And this is my wife, Shannon," I said, introducing her to the senator.

There was a pause of perhaps a second. Then both Penny Collenette and Denise Axworthy said loudly in unison: "Your wife!"

And so the word was out, at least in official Ottawa. The American ambassador, Gordon Giffin, and his wife, Patti, were at the dinner party. Just in case someone had missed the news, the next week at their Christmas season party, Patti called everyone to attention and announced that Shannon and I were married and presented a porcelain bowl as a wedding gift. We think of them every time we see it in our home.

I don't know if Jean Chrétien was thinking of it as a wedding gift, but early in the New Year I was at my desk in the CBC Parliamentary bureau when the telephone rang. It was Percy Downe, the director of appointments in the Prime Minister's Office.

"The information commissioner's job is coming open, and so is the privacy commissioner's. The prime minister would like you to consider filling either of them."

I was surprised. "There has been a rumour that the two jobs are going to be combined into one," I said. "I take it that's not true."

"No, they are staying separate," said Percy, "so take your choice."

I was amazed by the offer, said I would think about it and get back to him. That evening, Shannon and I talked it over. It was again pleasant to know that a prime minister—this time from a different party—had the confidence to offer me an important job. But as before, I enjoyed what I was doing and thought it a useful role that I could play.

The next day, I called Downe and thanked him for the offer but declined it. I got down to planning that day's broadcast, because after the 1997 election there was a lot of news to report.

39

The Liberals: Civil War

$\mathbf{T}$HE TRANSITION SEEMED miraculous. After bringing down four budgets in less than four years in office, the Liberals and Finance Minister Paul Martin had produced a budget with a surplus. Many of the reporters in the pre-budget lockup to read the documents before they were presented in the House of Commons had no frame of reference from which to work. The last balanced federal budget was more than twenty-five years earlier, and few of the journalists currently in the press gallery had been there at the time.

Of course, the balanced budget had not been achieved without pain. The 1995 budget slashed government spending, particularly the transfer from Ottawa to the provinces. But while the spending cuts were bringing down outlays, the recovering U.S. economy, fuelled by the tech boom, was pulling the Canadian economy, now even more closely linked through the free trade agreement, along with it, boosting Ottawa's revenues.

With the good economic news, and having survived the near-death experience of the Quebec referendum, Jean Chrétien decided it was time to sell his story to the Canadian electorate. He called a general election for June 2, seeking his second straight majority. In the end, that's what he got. But it was a close call: the Liberals returned to office with 155 seats, just three above the threshold needed to maintain a majority government. Still, they were well ahead of the Reform Party, which was now the Official Opposition with 60 seats, eight more than in the previous Parliament. The Bloc Québécois had dropped 10 seats, down to 44, and was in third place, but the election also produced the first Parliament in which five parties had official status, each with more than 12 members. The NDP had rebounded to 21 seats from just nine, and the Progressive Conservatives were back with 20, from just two.

It wasn't that clear on election night, but the 1997 election turned out to be a seminal event. It was the departure point for a circuitous seven-year journey to the unification of the Reform Party and the Progressive Conservatives—and, over the same time frame, to the unpredicted demise of the Liberals.

In 1990, Jean Chrétien had won the Liberal leadership on the first ballot. Paul Martin was a distant second. The scale of Chrétien's victory should have insulated him from any criticism or challenge from within the party, but Martin had a devoted group of followers in the party who were already looking to the next time the leadership changed and the chance for their man to take the top job. The stunning majority in the 1993 election shut down any early Martin hopes, and the co-operation between the Martin and Chrétien teams in slaying the deficit and balancing the budget over the next few years is a model of political and parliamentary co-operation. After that, though, things cooled and communication between the two men was often done by trusted members of their office staffs: Terrie O'Leary in Martin's office and Peter Donolo in Chrétien's.

After the 1997 election, tension in the Liberal Party started to heat up, moving from warm to a slow boil. Chrétien's decision to call an early election had almost cost the party its majority. He no longer looked invincible. Beyond that, the clock was running. In a normal election cycle for a majority government, the next general election would come in 2001. As a rule, party leaders are good for about ten years after they take on the job, whether they are prime minister or not. In 2001, Chrétien would be Liberal leader for eleven years, and prime minister for eight. And by the calendar, he would have his sixty-seventh birthday in 2001.

Paul Martin seemed in a better place. If Chrétien's stature had been diminished by the election call, Martin's had been enhanced by the deficit elimination. But his many supporters also were aware that time was not a great ally of their man. In 2001, Martin would celebrate his sixty-third birthday, and while he was younger than Chrétien, and seemed more so because of his shorter political career, by the likely date of the next election he would be just two years shy of the age at which many Canadians leave their jobs and retire.

So as the Liberals began their second term with a majority government, they were not all sailing in a happy ship. There was a general assumption that Chrétien would step down before the calling of the next election, but not everyone agreed. And some of those closest to Paul Martin believed it was unlikely unless pressure was applied to make him step aside.

Paul Martin and his supporters weren't the only ones interested in Chrétien's plans. Other members of the cabinet, current and past, and at least one recent provincial premier were also considering planning for a succession.

In the fall of 1997, Nancy Wilson and I began our third year of co-hosting the two-hour *Politics*. The next year she moved to the morning program and we began a new one-hour *Politics* originating just from Ottawa. By 1997, we were well established as the top-rated program on Newsworld. During that season, I also hosted—alone—an hour-long program called *Politics This Week,* which appeared on Newsworld on Sunday afternoon at 5 p.m. The idea was to record that show on Fridays, leaving my weekends free, but that didn't always work if news was breaking. But when it was possible to plan out a whole show, we took the opportunity to explore different issues that didn't often get an in-depth airing on daily television.

In the spring of 1998, we decided to do a program on the Liberals after Chrétien. I asked Neil Macdonald to prepare a piece on the possible contenders to succeed the prime minister. Then I interviewed people who had run successful leadership campaigns in other political parties, asking them to handicap and describe the tactics they would use if, hypothetically, they were involved in a future Liberal leadership campaign.

Television isn't about foretelling the future. But if any program I have done was prophetic, that one was. Neil correctly identified the other possible contenders, beyond the clear front-runner Martin, as cabinet ministers Allan Rock, John Manley and Sheila Copps, and former minister Brian Tobin, who had become premier of Newfoundland and Labrador. Frank McKenna, who had recently stepped down as premier of New Brunswick, was the other possible contender we considered. I then asked John Laschinger, who managed a number of Progressive Conservative leadership campaigns, and Gerry Caplan, who had done the same for the New Democrats, to tell us how they would manage front-runner Martin's campaign and the bids of the longer shots. Much of what they predicted came to pass. Still, early in 1998, there were very few who thought a change in leadership for the Liberals was over five years away or that the battle to arrive at that change would be as bloody and damaging for the party as it turned out to be.

Covering Parliament in the late 1990s was like covering an increas-ingly bitter civil war. The Martin camp was watching Chrétien for signs that he would leave and the Chrétien camp was growing increasingly resentful of the pressure to go. The disagreements were often played out behind closed doors, but they periodically flared in the open. One of those outbursts was over the Clarity Act, the legislation the prime min-ister decided to introduce putting into law the Supreme Court's decision that Quebec could only leave Canada after a clear majority of Quebecers voted in favour of a clear question on seceding.

Many in Chrétien's cabinet advised against it. They thought it pro-vocative, that it would create a backlash and make relations with a sep-aratist Quebec government headed by Lucien Bouchard even more strained. Even Stéphane Dion, brought in as constitutional affairs min-ister after the close call in the 1995 referendum, advised that while the idea was a good one, the timing was wrong. For Quebec federal Liberals who didn't like Chrétien, anything he proposed on the national unity file was wrong, and those Quebec Liberals supported Paul Martin to replace the party leader. So Martin was in a spot. His Quebec supporters were opposed to the Clarity Act, but as a cabinet minister, he was committed to supporting the government. Word started circulated that Martin was privately opposed to the Clarity Act, and at one point he basically ran away from reporters to avoid discussing it. However, when the matter came to a vote, he and the other Liberals ministers voted for it.

As the century turned and the new millennium began, there was still no sign Chrétien was thinking of leaving. Instead, there were rumours that Martin might quit if Chrétien didn't go. A week before the federal Liberal policy convention in Ottawa, a group of MPs backing Martin met with the finance minister's advisers and campaign strategists at the Regal Constellation Hotel, near the Toronto airport. The meeting dis-cussed ways of further positioning Martin as the inevitable heir apparent to Chrétien and of persuading the prime minister to retire. The following week, Jason Moscovitz broke the story on CBC that the meeting had taken place just as the party convention was about to start. The Martin team had thought the meeting would remain secret; it didn't. They and Martin were caught flat-footed. The finance minister was pursued down an escalator by reporters and cameras, at first denying knowledge of the Toronto meeting and then reappearing to confirm it had taken place.

In the short term, the results of the meeting and the initial denial that it had taken place, followed by the confirmation that it had, made the Martin team look like the gang that couldn't shoot straight. But the longer-term effects were devastating. As had been widely reported, Chrétien and his wife, Aline, were watching the news when the report of the meeting at the airport hotel aired. It was then that they agreed that Jean Chrétien would seek another term as prime minister.

40

Harper Gets on *Politics*

O N A COLD winter morning early in 1998, I was sitting in my office on the top floor of the old National Press Building, daydreaming and looking out the window at the bright winter sunshine falling on the Peace Tower on Parliament Hill.

The phone rang. When I picked it up, the voice at the other end said, "Hi, Don, this is Stephen."

My mind raced. The call sounded like long distance, and the voice did sound familiar, but who was calling? Time to use an old trick and narrow the possibilities. "It's cold today here in Ottawa," I said. "How is it where you are?"

"Pretty cold here in Calgary, too," came the reply.

Aha! Calgary . . . Stephen. The mystery solved.

"Well, Stephen Harper," I said, "what can I do for you?"

"I want to stay politically relevant, so I want to be on your show," he replied. "I want to be on your Monday panel and I will be the best panellist you have."

I had met Harper after he came to Ottawa as one of the fifty-two new MPs in the Reform Party wave in 1993. But he was no ordinary neophyte member. Along with Tom Flanagan, he was one of Reform leader Preston Manning's top advisers. And he was used to playing political hardball.

He had first come to Ottawa to work in the office of Progressive Conservative MP Jim Hawkes. But as the PCs under Brian Mulroney became more Quebec-centric with the Meech Lake Accord and continued to run higher and higher annual deficits, the Reform Party under Manning's leadership was gaining strength in western Canada and particularly in Alberta. That was good enough for Harper. He quit his job in Jim Hawkes's office and went home to run for Parliament. He won the Reform Party nomination to run in Calgary West against his former benefactor, Hawkes, whom he then handily defeated in the general election.

But now, five years later, he was looking for a way to keep his name in the game. Harper had had a falling-out with Manning over the future direction of Reform and did not run in the 1997 general election. Instead, he took a job as president of the National Citizens Coalition, a small right-wing protest group with a name more impressive than the influence it carried.

Reform had done marginally better in the 1997 election, winning a few more seats in western Canada and becoming the Official Opposition. But the party actually lost the one seat it had in Ontario, which meant new scenarios would be unfolding around the party's future, and Harper wanted to be on TV to have a voice in them.

But there was one other wrinkle I wanted to iron out, before agreeing to give him a tryout. The 1997 election had brought the Progressive Conservative Party back to official party status with twenty seats, after the humiliation of winning only two in 1993. But after that relatively modest accomplishment, national PC leader Jean Charest had been lured back to Quebec to become leader of the federalist forces grouped in the Quebec Liberal Party to try and hold off the Parti Québécois, led by the "sainted" Lucien Bouchard. And that meant the federal leadership of the Progressive Conservative Party was open.

And who was one of the people rumoured to be considering a run for that job?

"Listen, Stephen," I said, "I am willing to give you a try, but I want you to come clean with me. If you want to come on the program for five or six weeks to raise your profile, and then announce you are leaving to run for the PC leadership, forget it. I am not going to be used as part of your leadership campaign."

Without a pause, Harper replied, "Don, don't worry. There is no point in running for the leadership of the PCs or the Reform until somebody puts those parties together."

So with that assurance, I put Harper on the program. And he was good—cool, never losing his temper, but always coming at every issue with a right-wing perspective. Generally, he crossed rhetorical swords with Gerry Caplan, the former national secretary of the NDP. Both were smart, articulate and ideological. Clearly, they didn't like each other, but while their clashes were spirited and lively, they didn't degenerate into the kind of talking-point, faux-angry banality that has taken over much of the so-called commentary on television.

Harper and Caplan were particularly heated during the 2000 election, the election in which Reform, now renamed the Canadian Alliance, won ten additional seats, but Jean Chrétien's Liberals won an additional twenty to form a third straight—and stronger—majority government. So distraught was Harper with the results that he, along with nineteen other Albertans, signed a letter to the provincial government calling for a "firewall" to be erected around the province to protect Albertans from the federal government.

When I saw the letter, I called Harper immediately.

"Stephen, I am looking at this letter you have signed, and I guess you have given up any idea of federal politics and now want to be the premier of Alberta."

"Why would you say that?" he asked.

"Well, how can you hope to be prime minister when you sign a letter saying a province should put a firewall around it to protect it from Ottawa? Didn't you read the letter before you signed it?"

"Of course I read it," he said testily. "Don, when I am prime minister, no province will need a firewall around it."

"Well," I told him, "get ready for Monday. The others are going to go after you."

"Bring it on."

I didn't have another important conversation with him about being on the *Politics* program for another year, when Harper again called me. This time, I knew who it was.

"I won't be on the program this Monday," he told me.

That wasn't a big surprise. People often took a week or two off, and there were always people willing to fill in.

"Are you going on a holiday?" I asked.

"Actually, I won't be on any more Mondays."

"What? You're not sick or anything, are you?"

"No, I'm fine."

"Well, then, why won't you be on the program anymore?"

"I can't tell you."

"Bull. You called me lobbying to get on, and now you want to leave me high and dry. I want to know what's happening."

"Well, if I do, you can't tell anybody."

"I don't know if you watch the rest of the program, Stephen, but a lot of it is me telling people what I know. But you owe me an explanation."

"Okay. You're right. I am going to challenge Stockwell Day for the leadership of the Canadian Alliance."

"Stephen, you told me a few years ago it wasn't worth running for either the PC leadership or the Reform leadership until someone put the two parties together. The Reform Party is now the Alliance, but nothing else has changed."

"I did tell you that, Don," he said. "I thought that would have happened by now, but I guess I will have to do it myself."

Which, of course, Stephen Harper did.

After he became prime minister and tried to bully the Parliamentary Press Gallery, including declining to attend the annual press gallery dinner, I stopped going to his annual Christmas and summer parties. It seemed inappropriate to accept his hospitality if he wouldn't accept ours. But before we stopped communicating directly, he did appear with me on television a couple of times as prime minister. As usual, he was all business—no small talk.

As a small joke, before one interview began, I said laughingly, "I tell everyone you are prime minister because you were on my program."

Short pause. No smile. "Well, I was on your program."

41

Order of Canada

ONE EVENING WHEN we came home in April 1999, there was a card in our mailbox from Canada Post. We had been out when a postal employee tried to deliver a registered letter to our home, and now the letter was waiting to be picked up at the local postal outlet in a nearby strip mall.

Neither Shannon nor I were expecting anything. Occasionally, we receive registered letters containing tax receipts, and since it was near the filing deadline at the end of the month, we assumed that was what this registered letter contained. We put the notice on a table in the hall and promptly forgot about it. On a Sunday afternoon over a week later, as we were getting ready to go grocery shopping, Shannon picked up the card and put it in her purse.

"We had better go by and pick this up," she said.

At the postal outlet, I went in with the card, handed it to the clerk and was given a brown, eight-by-ten manila envelope that was addressed to me. On the top left-hand corner was stamped RIDEAU HALL. I could feel a piece of cardboard inside the envelope to keep it stiff. At events in Ottawa where the Governor General is in attendance, the official photographer at Rideau Hall usually accompanies His or Her Excellency and shoots pictures of the Governor General shaking hands with various people. Without opening the envelope, I thought, "A picture of me with Roméo LeBlanc."

I returned to the car with the envelope unopened. I started driving to our shopping destination while Shannon made a grocery list. When she finished, she asked if she could look at the picture. She opened the envelope and looked in.

"There is no picture here," she said. "It is a letter about the Order of Canada. Maybe they want you to emcee the Order of Canada ceremony," she suggested. Then she paused. "Oh, no . . . they want to give you the Order of Canada!"

Receiving the Order of Canada had never been on my horizon. I knew some people lobbied and campaigned for the recognition, but it had never been in my frame of reference to be a recipient. Obviously, Shannon's suggestion that I might be asked to emcee an honours ceremony meant she too had no concept that I might be receiving the honour. Since I had not been seeking it, I was probably even more pleased that I was to receive it. I called to accept and was asked to keep the information secret until the official announcement was made around the first of July.

Shannon and I were on holiday at the end of June. Suddenly, I realized that if the announcement was made while we were away, my mother in Winnipeg would not realize I was being recognized.

"She will think there is another Don Newman," I said.

"Well, call her, but tell her to keep it a secret," Shannon said.

I called and immediately knew it was the right thing to do.

"You can't tell anyone, not even family, but it will be announced soon that I am receiving the Order of Canada," I told my mother.

There was a short pause on her end of the phone.

"That's nice, dear," she said, as only a mother could. "But why are they giving it to you?"

42

Bush and Gore 2000

"FIRST WITH THE NEWS" is a motto than many organizations have adopted and that some of them try to live up to. Certainly, a scoop is something that every reporter relishes. What you don't want to be is last with the news, although in November 2000, that is what happened to me.

The United States presidential election was held on Tuesday, November 7. The candidates were Democrat Al Gore, who had served two terms as president Bill Clinton's vice-president and was now trying to succeed him in the Oval Office. The Republican candidate was George W. Bush, the governor of Texas and the son of former president George H.W. Bush, the man Clinton had defeated in the 1992 presidential election.

Still a relative infant, Newsworld had no special coverage of the 1992 presidential election. In 1996, a program was mounted from Toronto, with me and Alison Smith as the co-hosts. It was serviceable, but a relatively modest affair. By 2000, the network was ready for a more ambitious undertaking, and we had committed resources to make the program work. An election night set was built in one of the large studios in Toronto, and I anchored the program from there. Most of the other resources were in the CBC's Washington bureau. Henry Champ and I had been colleagues at CTV almost twenty years earlier. He had gone on to a career at NBC News in London and then in Washington before joining CBC Newsworld. For a couple of years, when the program originated in Halifax, Henry was one of the anchors of the morning show, but he wanted to move to Washington, where his family lived, and he became the first dedicated Newsworld reporter in the CBC's Washington bureau.

And *dedicated* was the word. Up early doing hits into the morning program. On throughout the day. At about three every afternoon, he would phone me if I hadn't already called him, asking if he could be of service to *Politics*. And almost always, he could. Around 1998, Henry's empire expanded when Jennifer Brown moved from our *Politics* program in Ottawa to work with him in Washington. She could work as hard as Henry—she was about thirty-five years younger—and together they fed the network with news, interviews and commentary, and I was lucky that my program was their main target.

For the 2000 presidential election, Jennifer had created a card for each of the fifty states and the number of votes it had in the electoral college that actually elects the president. Each card was taped on the wall just off-camera from where Henry was sitting. As either Bush or Gore won the greater share of the popular vote in a state, Jennifer would take the card down and add the electoral votes to the total of the candidate who had won. From where Henry was sitting, he could see at a glance each candidate's total as they worked to collect the 270 electoral votes need to become president. By counting the cards on the wall, he could keep track of the states still to report and the number of electoral votes outstanding.

The process worked like a charm in an election that was painfully close. We had gone on the air at 8 p.m. and were still broadcasting at

2 a.m. After Gore narrowly lost his home state of Tennessee and failed to lock down the presidency, it was clear the whole election would come down to the last state to report: Florida. The race there was incredibly tight, although Bush was very narrowly ahead. Finally, with all of the polls reporting, Bush was on top and word came that Gore was conceding. Our producer, Mark Bulgutch, decided we were already way over budget and that the concessions and victory speeches were pro forma, and the word came from the control room to sign off. I thanked Henry for his major contribution to the program, declared George W. Bush the next president of the United States, said good night to whatever viewers had stayed with us and signed off.

Dave Mathews and I were staying at a hotel across the street from the CBC. We had to be on the first plane from Toronto to Ottawa the next morning to do a show from our bureau at nine-thirty. After two hours' sleep, my wake-up call roused me. I glanced at an early edition of *The Globe and Mail* at my hotel room door, which confirmed Bush had won, went downstairs, met Dave, who was looking at the same edition of the paper, and hurried to catch our plane. We arrived in Ottawa, jumped into a cab and went directly to the Parliamentary bureau.

That's where we learned the real news from colleagues who hadn't been covering the election. After we signed off and left the studio, Gore had withdrawn his concession. He had learned there were enough irregularities in the vote count in at least one heavily populated county to put the results for the entire state of Florida in doubt. To say we were embarrassed would be putting it mildly.

Of course, after the election ended up in the Supreme Court and the Republican-appointed justices decided in Bush's favour, he did become president. I tried to tell my colleagues I was just ahead of the curve and was breaking news. No one believed me.

43

Canadian Alliance

R ANDY WHITE WAS sitting with me in the anchor booth at the second Think Big conference that Preston Manning and the Reform Party had organized in Ottawa in 2000. White was House leader of the Reform Party in the Commons, the man who helped plan the business of the House along with the government House leader, and one of the originals who had come to Ottawa with Manning in the Reform breakthrough of 1993. On the floor below us, Reformers were about to vote themselves out of existence and rename their party the Canadian Conservative Reform Alliance.

To help fill the airwaves and make conversation while we waited for the results of the vote on the name change, I suggested to White that if Reformers really wanted Canadians to think that what they were creating was a new political party—not just Reform by another name—they would have to choose a new leader.

"Yes," White speculated in response to my question, "that might have to be the case."

We wound up our conversation, White left the booth and the vote results were announced. No more Reform. Welcome Canadian Alliance.

As I was preparing to leave the conference, my cellphone rang. It was Randy White.

"Well, these guys play for keeps," he said. "After I left you, I had a call. I am no longer the House leader."

That confirmed what I already knew. No matter how political parties try to portray themselves as being different and doing politics differently, at its essence politics is politics, no matter the ideology of the people who practise it. If you are not clearly for me, then you are against me and I will treat you as an enemy. That is why politicians usually see reporters as their enemies. Highly partisan people cannot believe that everyone isn't like them, and if you are reporting something that hurts a politician or helps one of their opponents, it is not seen as just the facts, it is seen as taking sides. As the saga of the Canadian Alliance unfolded, I would have to directly explain that to one of the people involved.

The first order of business for the Canadian Alliance was to select a leader. Preston Manning was the early favourite to stay in the job he had held since creating the Reform Party. But suddenly the Alliance leadership race got interesting when a *bona fide* challenger emerged. Stockwell Day, Alberta's finance minister, announced he was a candidate. To add heft to his entry into the race, he was nominated by Alberta premier Ralph Klein. Two other candidates rounded out the field: Keith Martin, a medical doctor and Reform MP from Victoria, and Tom Long, who had worked closely with Ontario premier Mike Harris. In his early forties, Long was handsome and articulate and was particularly interesting because he was from Ontario, the province that had been hostile to Reform and whose voters were the main target of the rebranding exercise.

To put some focus on the leadership race, CBC Newsworld partnered with the *National Post* to stage three debates amongst the four candidates—one in Vancouver, one in Halifax and the third in Toronto. I hosted the debates and, along with *Post* columnist Andrew Coyne, asked questions of the leadership hopefuls. Surprisingly, Manning did not overwhelm his three challengers. Perhaps because of his total command of the Reform Party, he seemed unsettled by having to deal with people critical of his ideas for taking the new party forward. Day, on the other hand, seemed to bask in the national attention. Tom Long also acquitted himself well for a person who, until then, had been in the political back-rooms and not centre stage.

Rather than limiting the vote to convention delegates, the election of the leader was conducted on a one-member, one-vote basis. The first ballot was held on June 24, and the results were tabulated at a big party rally, with the candidates present, in Calgary. As the returns came in, they reflected what we had seen in the debates: Preston Manning was the choice of 36 per cent of the party members who voted, but that put him eight points behind Stockwell Day. Tom Long was third at 18 per cent, and Keith Martin the low man with just over one per cent.

It was a stunning setback for Manning. He came to the stage looking as though he couldn't believe what hit him. The gap was so wide that those of us on the air found ourselves trying to make sense of it. Would Manning bother going to a second ballot, or would he concede that to continue didn't make sense? However, Manning made it clear he would fight to the end. He noted that the total votes cast were significantly lower than the total membership of the party. He publicly reasoned that a lot of people hadn't bothered to vote because they assumed he would win. Now he asked them to realize that was wrong and to turn out and vote for him in the final runoff two weeks later.

After some negotiating, Tom Long endorsed Manning, and together they flew around southwestern Ontario in a helicopter in the days leading up to the second ballot on July 8, trying to transfer Long's mainly Ontario support to Manning's total. But it didn't work. On a hot summer Saturday evening in a big hotel ballroom near the Toronto airport, the votes from Canadian Alliance members around the country were tallied. The final results still had Manning at 36 per cent support. Day had 64 per cent and was the new leader of the new party.

As I came down from the platform where I had been broadcasting the results, I bumped into Randy White. He was beaming and gave me the thumbs-up. After being fired by Manning from his job as House leader, there was no doubt as to how he had voted.

Day's victory would turn out to be the high point of his leadership of the Canadian Alliance. He got off to a bad start when, in September, he appeared in a wetsuit on a Sea-Doo in his new riding near Kelowna in the interior of British Columbia, proclaiming to reporters and Canadians across the country, as we broadcast his press conference, that there was "a new sheriff in town." Sensing the Alliance was unready and Day a weaker candidate than many had thought, Jean Chrétien went against the advice of most of the members in his Parliamentary caucus and called a snap election for November 27, 2000.

Chrétien's instincts were right. On election night, the Liberals gained seats in Quebec and held on to their dominance in Ontario. The Alliance also had more seats than Reform had won in 1997, but only six more. Their total of 66 was far short of the Liberals' 172. That was the beginning of the end for Day. Led by Chuck Strahl and Diane Ablonczy, 13 Alliance MPs loyal to Manning or who didn't like Day for other reasons left the Alliance to sit in the Commons as the Democratic Representative Caucus. To increase their clout in the Commons, they then aligned themselves with Joe Clark's Progressive Conservatives, who were down to just twelve members and barely holding official party status in the Commons after the 2000 election. For a brief moment,

Clark held out the hope that this was the beginning of the right uniting under his leadership, a hope that was to be subsequently dashed.

After the 1988 election, when Manning decided to try and expand the base of Reform beyond the western provinces, he enlisted the help of a man named Rick Anderson. Anderson had been a Liberal, but he wandered from the party because he felt it was too "top down" and moved to Reform because he believed it would be more "grassroots." Anderson quickly became one of Manning's closest advisers, and one not from Alberta. Now he was around the dissident Alliance members of the Democratic Representative Caucus, and Day was convinced it was Anderson—and through him, Manning—who was working to undermine his leadership.

Because I had known Anderson since the early 1980s, when he was still a Liberal, and because he was articulate and I put him on television from time to time, Day became convinced I was part of the "Get Stockwell" campaign. I wasn't, of course; I was just covering the developments around a mutiny against his leadership. I thought it an important story to be told, but I had no investment one way or another in whether it would be successful.

As the pressure mounted, Day declined our invitations to come on *Politics* for an interview. One afternoon, I heard he was going to CTV for an interview there. Obviously, this was meant to be a message to me. I called one of the people who worked in his communications office, a woman named Line Maheux, who had originally come to Ottawa from Granby, Quebec, to work for Manning and Reform.

"I guess Stock doesn't want too many people to see him," I needled, knowing that she knew our ratings were at least double our competitors', and sometimes higher. "That's why he is going to CTV instead of me."

"He knows you are helping Rick Anderson and he doesn't want to see you," she replied.

"Do you think that?" I asked.

"No. But he does."

"Well, you tell him that if he wants me to be his enemy, I will be. If you treat someone as your enemy, sooner or later that is what they will become. But you tell him I'm not his enemy and he should be getting over here."

We hung up. I didn't think there would be much follow-up. But I was wrong. Line was back on the phone in a few minutes.

"Okay, he going to come, but only for five minutes," she said.

"Once he's on, he's on. Five minutes isn't time to talk about anything," I replied. On our *Politics* program interview segments were seven minutes each. And sometimes, for a political panel or some other special interview, we would do two segments together. However, if I went much over the seven-minute window on a regular program, I was seriously altering the rest of the lineup that followed.

Day showed up and came right into the studio without saying much. I greeted him, but didn't chat as we went to air. Once on the air, he opened up, answering questions, making points covering off the different questions I challenged him with. As we approached seven minutes on the air, senior producer Dave Mathews warned me in my earpiece that time was about up. But we were just getting rolling and I decided to carry on. After I had gone two minutes over, Dave was back in my ear again.

"Either stop right now or go another five minutes and we will kill another section of the program," he said.

I decided to carry on. After all, I wasn't sure that Day was ever coming back again. After we had done thirteen minutes, Dave was back with the warning.

"You have to end it now or this will be three-quarters of the broadcast."

I knew the interview was good, but it wasn't *that* good. I thanked Stockwell Day and said I hoped he would come back. He thanked me and said he would.

And he did, most dramatically after the pressure forced him to step down and defend his Alliance leadership in a vote in Calgary in 2002. Day's main challenger was Stephen Harper, who had informed me of his intentions in his phone call telling me he was leaving *Politics*. Two other MPs, Grant Hill and Diane Ablonczy, were also candidates.

At *Politics*, we decided to stage a debate between Harper and Day. To our delight, both sides agreed. We asked viewers to send in the questions they wanted the candidates to answer. Then we sifted out the ones that had been most often asked and formulated those topics into tight questions we could put up on the screen and have the candidates answer. Questions would go to the candidates by lot in alternating order, and so would their opening and closing statements. The person answering the question had one minute to give his answer. The other candidate had thirty seconds to reply. At my discretion, if I felt there was more to say, each candidate could have an extra thirty seconds and then we moved on to the next question.

On the day of the debate, everyone on our staff was nervous. To be a success, the questions and answers would have to be tight and the clock followed closely. For my part, I had to be scrupulously fair so that time and opportunity were equally distributed.

Our studio was small, located then on the ninth floor of the National Press Building across from Parliament Hill. Since this was the only nationally televised debate between the two top candidates, we wanted them to be as comfortable as possible. Before the broadcast, we put Day and his people in the staff lounge and the Harper team across the hall in a suite of offices. Makeup artist Joan Hodgins went to each of them in their holding areas to get them ready for the cameras so they wouldn't have to meet in the makeup room.

The atmosphere was like the seventh game of a Stanley Cup final, the Grey Cup just before kickoff or the Queen's Plate when the horses are in the starting gate. Day and Harper came into the studio, barely acknowledging each other, sat down, and we were off. Harper came out swinging, attacking Day in his opening statement, staying aggressive in his early answers. He seemed to catch Day off guard—I know he surprised me. But before long, Day was giving as good as he got. As the debate went on, the air was electric. It was a real debate—forceful, often angry, and cutting. A number of times, the exchanges were so strong I let them go on for the extra thirty seconds allowed.

The time flew by, and then I thanked them both and signed off. We all stood up to take off our microphones as I congratulated them both. Almost out of character, Harper tried a little small talk.

"Is this the last time I will see you until Calgary?" he asked Day, referring to the meeting where the first-ballot results would be announced.

"It is unless you start following me around," said Day as he walked out of the studio.

The debate was a big success for our program. It generated what you can usually only hope for: coverage and comment in other media, both print and electronic. Most people couldn't decide who had won. Many thought it was a draw. I agreed, but I believed a tie was a win for Harper. As Joe Clark had found out, and so had Margaret Thatcher, once a weakened leader is forced to defend their job, the end is usually near. At that point, people in a political party are looking for change and a credible replacement can win by looking capable of doing the job. Clearly, Harper had shown in the debate that he was the equal of Day, which is why I started telling colleagues not to underestimate the chance of a first-ballot lead for Harper—which, because it was essentially a two-man race, amounted to a first-ballot victory.

And that is what it turned out to be. On March 20, 2002, Harper won 55 per cent of the vote to become the second leader of the Canadian Alliance.

A few months earlier, Stephen Harper had told me he was seeking the Alliance leadership as the first step towards uniting the right and putting that party together with the Progressive Conservatives. And now he was halfway there.

44

Unity

THE FIRST THING Stephen Harper did after becoming leader of the Canadian Alliance was offer an amnesty and tight timeline to the renegade members of the Democratic Representative Caucus to return to the party. All but one accepted. Inky Mark from Manitoba stayed with the PCs. Controversial Jim Pankiw of Saskatchewan was denied readmission to the party. Harper's move accomplished two things in one quick stroke: it reunited the former Reformers under one political tent, and it left the Progressive Conservatives and Joe Clark barely hanging on to official party status in the House of Commons.

Effectively, it also killed any hope of the PCs under Clark becoming the vehicle for reuniting the right. And it spelled the end of Clark's come-back and his active political career. In August of 2002, three months after Harper took over the Alliance, Clark announced he would step down.

It then took nine months for the flagging Tory party to select a new leader. Two members of the Parliamentary caucus were the front-runners for the job, each of them young, both of them from Nova Scotia, reflecting the Atlantic redoubt into which the party had been driven. Peter MacKay was the son of former Mulroney cabinet minister Elmer MacKay. Scott Brison was quick on his feet and confident, and was only the second openly gay person to sit as a member of the Commons. Joining them in the race was David Orchard, the Saskatchewan grain farmer opposed to free trade and a merger with the Canadian Alliance, who had also run for the leadership in 1998, when Jean Charest left the party to become Quebec Liberal leader and Joe Clark returned to lead the PCs.

A new name joined the race: a Calgary lawyer named Jim Prentice who was largely unknown when he launched his campaign but made a strong impression as it unfolded. Unlike Orchard, he was open to merger talks. Just as the 1998 leadership race had shown how far the party had shrunken from the lavish convention that selected Kim Campbell in 1993, so too did the convention of 2003 graphically illustrate the continued decline of the Tory party. It was held at the Metropolitan Toronto Convention Centre, and only a relatively small portion of the huge convention space was needed. Other things had changed as well. In 2002, Brian Mulroney had derided Stockwell Day as "Preston Manning in pantyhose." In 2003, he was talking about the need to bring the Conservative "family" back together.

Also illustrative was the impact of David Orchard. His followers seemed like a cult in 1998 and they did again five years later. Their total numbers had not grown significantly, but on the first ballot in 1998 they made up 16 per cent of the vote. In 2003, that same total number represented 24 per cent. Clearly, the PC Party was shrinking away right before everyone's eyes. On voting day in 1998, Orchard had been in third place after the first ballot; in 2003, he was second. Prentice was third and Brison came last. Dropped from the ballot, Brison then endorsed Prentice, and on the third ballot Prentice moved ahead of Orchard into second place. That eliminated Orchard. He was going to be the kingmaker, since his loyal followers would do as he instructed.

With his view of the world and the party, which were reminiscent of John Diefenbaker, Orchard was opposed to any deal to join the Canadian Alliance. Maybe he calculated that, as the PCs continued to shrink, his followers would soon constitute a majority in the party—although, by the time that happened, the party would be so small that the value of being leader was hard to imagine. Nevertheless, as the price of his backing on the final ballot, Orchard demanded a signed statement from the person he supported that there would be no negotiations to unite the Alliance and the PCs. Prentice refused to sign; MacKay agreed and signed a hastily drafted agreement. On the final ballot, Peter MacKay became the new leader of the Progressive Conservatives.

There is a saying that a verbal agreement is not worth the paper it is written on. In David Orchard's case, it turned out a written agreement wasn't worth anything, either. A few months after becoming leader, MacKay agreed to talks between representatives of the PCs and the Alliance. By early fall, the party leaders were involved, and by October a deal was close to being struck. The amalgamated group would be called the Conservative Party. The last stumbling block was the question of how the leader would be selected. The Alliance wanted the one-person, one-vote method for every party member. The Progressive Conservatives realized they would be overwhelmed by the much larger Alliance membership. They held out for a different formula where every riding association would have the same number of votes in the leadership selection process, no matter how many members the riding association actually had. Support for leadership candidates would be divided on a percentage basis. A candidate that received half of the votes in a particular riding would get fifty points towards the leadership. A candidate getting a fifth would get twenty. When Stephen Harper agreed to that last point, the deal was done and the new Conservative Party finally came into being in December 2003.

With the leadership selection process in place, a leadership race was on. Harper immediately announced he would run; MacKay announced he wouldn't. Prentice said he would, and set a date to formally declare he was a candidate. Then, on that day, said he would not be running. Lack of funds to mount an effective campaign was the reason he gave. In Calgary, the rumour circulated that Harper's backers had made it clear to potential Prentice contributors that leadership favourite Harper would not be pleased with another candidate from their city in the race.

After some manoeuvring, only two other candidates joined the race: former Ontario cabinet minister Tony Clement, who went into opposition at Queen's Park when the PCs lost the 2003 Ontario election, and auto-parts heiress and businesswoman Belinda Stronach. As a politician, Clement had lots of experience but not a lot of money; Stronach had the opposite, plus by far the greater aura, the most celebrity appeal, of all the contenders. She also seemed to be following a family political strategy. Her father, Frank Stronach, had run in the 1988 general election as a Liberal. By then, he was already hugely successful and wealthy, but the feeling was that if he became an MP and the Liberals were to lose the election, Frank Stronach could be a leadership candidate to succeed John Turner. The Liberals did lose, and Turner stepped down, but Stronach lost too and didn't become publicly involved in Canadian politics again.

To some, it appeared that Stronach was following her father's earlier game plan, adjusted to conditions in 2003. She was trying to become the leader of the biggest opposition party with an eye towards becoming prime minister. The fact that it was another party, that its policies were quite different from those of the party her father had joined, and that her own political views were still largely unformulated, didn't seem to matter. To counter her lack of experience, Stronach hired some of the top organizers in Conservative politics. John Laschinger was her campaign manager; Geoff Norquay and Jaime Watt were also on her team as communications advisors. As we had during the Canadian Alliance leadership race, *Politics* organized a debate of the Conservative Party contenders. Harper and Clement quickly accepted. The Stronach campaign delayed, and then turned us down. Team Stronach's immediate spin line was not only that she was too busy, but that she felt she should only take part in party-sponsored debates, two considerations that didn't cross the mind of either Harper or Clement. Some commentators and a couple of newspaper editorials took up the issue and said it was clear Stronach wasn't ready for big-time politics. I had hoped she would take part. I had only met her once, briefly, and thought she would be an interesting participant. However, I wasn't upset that she had dodged us, although a couple of weeks later, before the leadership race was over, I had a call to set up a meeting between me and her campaign manager, John Laschinger. I had known "Lash," as everyone called him, for years and liked him. He just wanted to make sure I wasn't mad at him for Stronach having ducked the debate. I assured him I wasn't.

You may have noticed that political parties like to choose their leaders on Saturday afternoons, particularly during hockey season. There is a reason for this. At six-thirty on Saturday, *Hockey Night in Canada* begins; it's the top-rated show on the CBC and one of the most-watched shows in the country on any network. The Conservatives decided their leader would be declared in Toronto on Saturday, March 20, 2004. As was my custom, on voting day I was wandering the floor with a battery-operated remote microphone and a crew with a portable camera, gathering information and looking for people to interview. Everyone believed the outcome to be a foregone conclusion: Stephen Harper on the first ballot. In the convention hall, there were boards electronically displaying vote totals as they were calculated from every riding across the country. Fairly early on, Harper had a lead, but not enough to go over the top. Then numbers stopped being added to the totals. It was pretty clear the party was holding back the results until closer to the hockey game.

When the parties merged and the leadership race was set up, Harper asked John Lynch-Staunton to be the interim (and, on paper, first) leader of the party until one was chosen in the leadership race. Lynch-Staunton was a longtime colleague and friend of Brian Mulroney, who appointed him to the Senate in 1990, and was leader of the Opposition in the Upper Chamber. He was also a good friend of mine, a friendship formed in a very bipartisan way and with a thespian touch. We were introduced by a mutual friend, Donald Johnston, who had been a Trudeau cabinet minister. When Parliament was in session, until he retired from the Senate in 2005, "Lynch" and I had a standing Monday lunch date to gossip and joust about politics. Lynch, his wife, Juliana, Shannon and I enjoyed times in Montreal and at their country home in the Eastern Townships, and on various occasions in Ottawa, Stratford, Toronto and New York, with Lynch's childhood friend actor Chris Plummer and his wife, Elaine. Sadly, Lynch died suddenly in August of 2012.

On March 20, 2003, Lynch-Staunton had earlier been back in the counting room watching the results when I ran into him on the convention floor. He thought the delays the party was orchestrating were silly, and so he gave me the final results and what was happening next with the Conservatives, and then walked away, knowing I would soon have it on television.

At the CBC, people were starting to wonder whether the Conservatives would push their convention into hockey game time. Now that I knew the answer, I too decided to have a little fun. I told the producers I had all the results and asked for airtime. In the anchor booth,

Peter Mansbridge was killing time talking to Peter MacKay, who was a guest commentator for our coverage. Mansbridge sounded relieved he could hand off for a couple of minutes.

"Peter," I said to Mansbridge, "these are the official results that are about to be released. Stephen Harper has fifty-six-per-cent support, Belinda Stronach has around thirty-five and the rest—around 10 per cent—is Tony Clement's. These results are going to be announced officially in a couple of minutes. Now, you can tell Peter MacKay that there is going to be a special party caucus meeting in Ottawa on Monday morning, and Belinda Stronach and Tony Clement will also be there, so he will have to be there too. And Ron MacLean (the host of *Hockey Night in Canada*), if you are watching, you will have to be at work on time this evening."

Mansbridge was laughing as I sent it back to him.

"I just want to thank Don for doing all our work," he said.

Since the results were already out on the air, a few minutes later they were announced to the convention, and Stephen Harper was the leader of the united Conservative Party. Two years before, the former self-described loner had told me that he had hoped someone else would have done the job, but since they hadn't, he would have to tackle it himself, and he did.

45

Chrétien Goes

WHEN JEAN CHRÉTIEN decided in March of 2000 that he would lead the Liberal Party into another general election, he didn't know when that election would come or against whom he would be running. As prime minister, he could control the timing of an election, but he couldn't control the leadership of the Official Opposition, the Canadian Alliance. When the Alliance chose Stockwell Day to replace Preston Manning as its leader in the summer of 2000, Chrétien decided an early election would be better than letting the parliamentary timetable run closer to the usual four- or four-and-a-half-year cycle.

It was a gutsy decision. At least half of the Liberal MPs in the Parliamentary caucus didn't want Chrétien to lead the party into an election. Even those who supported him thought the timing was wrong, just under three and a half years after the June 1997 election, which in turn had been called just three and a half years after the Liberals took power in 1993. But Chrétien trusted his political gut. When thirty-one Liberal MPs went to the microphone at a Liberal caucus meeting in early October, thirty of them spoke against the wisdom of an election call. Chrétien demurred, sided with the one MP who spoke in favour of going to the polls and asked Governor General Adrienne Clarkson to dissolve Parliament and set November 27 as election day.

And what a strange election campaign it was. The Martin and Chrétien camps were barely speaking to each other. The bad blood had not cooled from the meeting of Martin loyalists at the Toronto airport hotel in March, although the Liberals tried to counter media reports on the true state of the party by running television ads showing the two men apparently chatting amicably as they walked together through a park. As they campaigned in their ridings, Liberal candidates received so many complaints about the state of the party leadership that campaign co-chair David Smith had to call a meeting in Toronto to calm some candidates down.

Still, in the final week of the race, most observers expected the results to be much like the election three and a half years earlier: a small Liberal majority and a stronger Alliance Opposition with the Progressive Conservatives and NDP losing some seats. Quebec . . . well, Quebec was Quebec and the Bloc would still own most of the seats there.

That is certainly what I thought, and it's what most journalists in Ottawa lacking close connections in Quebec thought. But some people knew better. On the Saturday evening before election day, Shannon and I were out at a popular Ottawa restaurant. Pollster Frank Graves was sitting at a nearby table. As Frank got up to leave, he stopped at our table to talk.

"What do you think?" he asked.

"About like last time," I said.

"Which last time?" he pressed.

"Nineteen ninety-seven," I replied.

"More like '93," he said.

"Really?" I said incredulously.

"Watch Quebec," was his advice.

And Graves was right. Chrétien's political instincts had been correct. New Alliance leader Stockwell Day was not ready for a big-time national campaign, nor were a lot of the members of the team he had brought with him from the one-party rule of Alberta. A number of mistakes on the campaign trail, plus a stunt where he pulled out a sign reading NO 2-TIER HEALTH CARE during the leaders' English television debate sealed his fate. Day and the Alliance won sixty-six seats, six more than they had going into the election, and just two in Ontario, but the party was still way back in second place and still just the Official Opposition.

But as Graves predicted, the big surprise was in Quebec, and there again Chrétien's political instincts had been right. The Clarity Act setting out federal terms for negotiating Quebec independence had been law for less than a year, but the predicted backlash in Quebec against the law didn't happen. In fact, just the opposite occurred: the Bloc Québécois lost six seats to the Liberals. Consequently, on election night the Liberals strengthened their majority and held 172 seats. The Canadian Alliance had 66, the Bloc Québécois 38, the New Democrats 13 and the Progressive Conservatives 12.

So on the evening of November 27, Jean Chrétien emerged with his political instincts confirmed, a larger majority in the House of Commons and a party more determined than ever that he would have to retire.

However, in the short term, things seemed quiet amidst the Liberal Party. The rumblings on the right and the attack on Stockwell Day by the dissident MPs in the Democratic Representative Caucus attracted the attention of most political journalists. But less noisily, the Paul Martin machine was in high gear, and in 2001 it started taking over the Liberal Party. In each province and on the national executive, people who supported Martin's leadership aspirations were running for and winning executive positions in the party apparatus. It seemed that each time

I stopped in at Darcy McGee's, a pub on the Sparks Street Mall near Parliament Hill and one block away from Earnscliffe, the lobbying and communications company that was the epicentre of Martin support, someone working either directly for Martin or at the firm would introduce me to someone as Paul Martin's person in this or that province. It would turn out that person was also on the provincial executive of the federal Liberals.

Through 2001 and 2002, Martin collected more supporters, IOUs and money for a leadership run. So too were other cabinet ministers with hopes of succeeding Chrétien, although not as successfully. All of this was making the prime minister extremely uncomfortable. In two different interviews I had with him over ten months, his eroding position atop his party and the government were starkly evident.

On Thursday, September 6, 2001, we sat down in his office to talk about his plans as Parliament was getting ready to return. The interview set off a furor both within the Liberal Party and across Canadian politics generally. I led Chrétien through a series of dates that would mark significant political anniversaries, as well as his birthday, and suggested that as prime minister he would want to be in office to celebrate each of them. Chrétien agreed that he would, which meant that he was planning to stay in office for some time to come and not contemplating getting out of the way anytime soon.

News organizations usually try to ignore when someone else has a big story, particularly if it comes from an interview. But after that interview, no one covering politics could ignore what Chrétien had said. His remarks were discussed on other television programs, were news in the papers the next morning and the subject of a Jeffrey Simpson column in the weekend *Globe and Mail*. In political circles, people were still taking about what Chrétien had said the following Monday. But they stopped the next day. It was September 11.

The pressure continued to build through the first half of 2002, and at the end of May, Chrétien brought the matter to a head. He told his cabinet that no one in it could continue organizing and raising money for a leadership campaign to replace him. Others, including Industry Minister Allan Rock and Heritage Minister Sheila Copps, were affected by the order, but clearly it was aimed at Paul Martin and everyone knew it. That was the straw that broke the camel's back. Martin told reporters he was "reviewing his options," then went on a Friday evening to speak at a union hall in Toronto while Chrétien addressed another meeting nearby. We sent the Newsworld cameras to the Martin speech, and afterward he came out to repeat what sounded very close to a resignation. Broadcasting live, I speculated that he couldn't stay in the Chrétien cabinet and then reasoned that, before long, John Manley would be the finance minister.

That turned out to be just what happened. From home on Sunday afternoon, I called David Herle to find out the state of play.

"I am surprised you are not on the air already," David told me.

So I called Toronto and raced to the CBC bureau. The program in Toronto was already on the air, speculating about what might happen. Dave Mathews called in the crew, and as soon as we were ready we took over the network. While we were waiting to get on, I called Francie Ducros, Chrétien's press secretary, for her take on what was happening. She told me Martin had quit. What about his replacement at Finance? She said my speculation about Manley on Friday was correct.

As we went on the air, we had duelling versions of what had happened. David Herle came on, insisting that Chrétien had fired Martin as finance minister. We were no sooner off the air with Herle than Eddie Goldenberg, Chrétien's longest-serving loyal staffer, was coming into the studio. He insisted Martin had not been fired; rather, he had quit. Soon everyone was getting in on the act. Opposition leader Stephen Harper, looking very much like he had been enjoying a Sunday afternoon in the backyard, came on to weigh in. I got the sense he didn't want the Chrétien–Martin fight to ever end.

As June began, Paul Martin was out, the Liberal Party was in a state of ferment and Jean Chrétien was getting ready to host the G8 summit in Kananaskis, Alberta. This was the second time Chrétien was to be the host of the club of the leading industrial democracies in the world, the first having been in Halifax in 1995. In addition to the leaders of the United States, the United Kingdom, France, Germany, Japan, Italy and Russia, Chrétien wanted the meeting to focus on Africa, and he had invited a number of leaders from that continent to join in the talks at the resort on the edge of the Rocky Mountains, west of Calgary.

The meetings were scheduled on June 26 and 27. I had scheduled an interview with Chrétien in the middle of the week before. I told Ducros I would talk about the upcoming meeting, but I would also ask about the state of the Liberal Party. She was initially reluctant to talk about Canadian politics, but I insisted it would look stupid if we didn't, and I would not do the interview unless we did. After thinking about it and perhaps discussing it elsewhere, Francie called me back and agreed.

However, I am not sure Chrétien was ready for questions about his increasingly shaky position atop the Liberal Party. After running through what he hoped to achieve in his talks with the other leaders, I asked him if he felt confident in his own leadership. He seemed to recoil as he heard the question.

"Hey, guy! Why are you asking me that?" he demanded in response.

"Because the Canadian people want to know your thoughts and how you feel, given the recent developments and the departure of Paul Martin," I replied.

Chrétien steadied himself and repeated that he felt fine, planned to continue and would face a review of his leadership at a party convention in the spring of 2003.

"Aren't you worried that you won't get through the leadership review, that you will be forced to resign?" I asked.

"Liberals don't do that to their leaders," he replied.

But it turned out Liberals did, and faster than Chrétien could ever have imagined possible. By the time he arrived at a caucus meeting of Liberal MPs and senators in Chicoutimi, Quebec, at the end of the summer, Chrétien realized he would not survive a party vote on his leadership, so he pulled another grand manoeuvre: he announced he would step down and not lead the party in the next election, but he wouldn't leave until the spring of 2004. As a fallback strategy, it was very clever. He would avoid a vote on his leadership, but stay in power for another year and a half.

It might have seemed like a great idea at the time, but I wasn't sure. I had come to embrace the philosophy of Dick Goodwin, who was the managing editor of the *Winnipeg Tribune* when I resigned to go to *The Globe and Mail*. I had offered the customary two weeks' notice, but he declined.

"I'll pay you for two weeks, but you should leave right away. You won't be thinking much about what you can do here and you will just be in the way of the others who will have to take over."

It wasn't exactly that way for Chrétien, Martin and the Liberals, but almost. For the next year, while Stephen Harper and then Peter MacKay were pulling together the Conservative Party into a united political machine, the Martin and Chrétien wings of the Liberal Party were tearing apart what had been one of the great political operations of the twentieth century. It would have been hard to imagine a few years earlier, but as Martin and Harper squared off for a general election in 2004, it was Harper who was leading the united party and Martin who was trying to manage a party split in two.

46

Paul Martin to PM

THE CONVENTION AT the Air Canada Centre in Toronto where Paul Martin succeeded Jean Chrétien as leader of the Liberal Party in November of 2003 told the story. As the party gathered on the evening of Thursday the 13th to say goodbye to Chrétien, the VIP seats around the lower bowl closest to the retiring prime minister's box were filled with his longtime loyalists, cabinet ministers, party officials and friends. Ottawa-born singer Paul Anka, who had vaulted to international fame in the late 1950s, sang a version of "My Way," the song he had originally written for Frank Sinatra, with special lyrics honouring Chrétien, just as he had for Pierre Trudeau when he retired in 1984.

I was standing on the convention floor with my senior producer, Sharon Musgrave, just in front of where Chrétien was sitting. Earlier in the day, I had interviewed Chrétien for the last time on the CBC in his role as prime minister. It felt like brackets around an era as I recalled that I had done the first interview with him on the network, back in Seattle when he initially took office. That evening, we were inviting people who had been a part of that era to share a few thoughts before a tribute to Chrétien got underway.

The next evening, Sharon and I were standing in the same place. We were still at the Liberal Party leadership convention, but looking around, we could just as easily have been at the convention of another political party. Paul Martin was sitting where Chrétien had been the night before, but around him were none of the same people who had surrounded Chrétien. Instead, there was a whole new group, just as large, some of the faces just as familiar. Martin had become leader of the Liberals by taking over and replacing the whole infrastructure of the party.

There have always been two wings of the Liberal Party, the pro-business wing and the more progressive wing. Until now, they had coexisted and kept the party in power. But this was different. Now there were two Liberal Parties at war with each other. As developments would later show, it was a war neither of them could win.

People will argue for years to come over where the blame really lies. There is probably enough to go around for everyone to have a share. But clearly, sometime after the 1997 election, without a sign from Jean Chrétien that he was prepared to leave, the Martin camp began thinking about how he could be replaced. Ironically, the ill-advised meeting at the Regal Constellation in Toronto in early 2000 to talk about advancing Martin's leadership cause and speed up its timing had the opposite effect. It hardened Chrétien's resolve to stay on and try to prevent Martin from ever becoming leader. That in turn backfired on Chrétien. He slowed down Martin's ascent but created the circumstances where, even as a sitting prime minister, he was forced to quit. The man he was trying to block then replaced him with an even greater amount of support than he otherwise would have had.

Not everyone in politics realized how bad things had become in the Liberal Party. In 2001, I was discussing the strained relations among the Liberal leadership with my pundits' panel on the *Politics* program. After the program ended, I was at my desk in my office when the telephone rang. It was retired Progressive Conservative senator Finlay MacDonald, calling from his home in Halifax.

"You guys in the press gallery are just falling for a trick," he admonished me. "The Liberals aren't that stupid. Chrétien and Martin have it all worked out. They are just letting you think there is a fight to get some attention, but that is not the way Liberals operate."

I tried to convince him that, strange as it might seem, it *was* the way Liberals were operating. And they continued to operate that way. In fact, it got worse. After Martin left the cabinet in the summer of 2002, the entire efforts of his team were directed to stepping up Chrétien's departure and getting as many potential candidates who might run against Martin as possible to stay out of the race. Ultimately, both Brian Tobin and Allan Rock decided not to declare. John Manley declared and tried to challenge Martin on the names of people who were giving him money. But Martin already had so many supporters, there was no traction for his attack, and Manley dropped out of the competition. Only Sheila Copps stayed on to the end. The day before the leadership vote at the Toronto convention, she spoke to the delegates. At that point, she had no hope of even a strong showing, but she seemed to be looking for a role in a Martin government despite her loyalty to Jean Chrétien.

"My father worked with your father, Paul," she said, apparently recollecting some cooperation between her father, when he was mayor of Hamilton, and Martin's father, who was a Liberal cabinet minister. But it was to no avail. Not only was she omitted from the Martin ministry, she was denied a Liberal nomination in the next election when she lost to Martin supporter and new cabinet minister Tony Valeri.

Martin was equally rough on other leadership aspirants and Chrétien ministers and supporters, excluding all but a few of his friends from the former prime minister's cabinet in his own. He did offer John Manley the job of Canadian ambassador to Washington, but after thinking about it for a few days, Manley turned him down. Only one of his former challengers ended up with a good job. Allan Rock, who had been justice minister, industry minister and health minister in the Chrétien government, had hoped to stay in a Martin cabinet. After Martin told him that wasn't going to happen, Rock had an even better idea. He told Martin he would like to be Canadian ambassador to the United Nations, and after thinking about it for a day, Martin agreed.

Martin was sworn in as prime minister and unveiled his cabinet on December 13, 2003. The sniping started immediately.

"After you have seen most of these guys in action in his cabinet, you will understand why they weren't in our cabinet," Eddie Goldenberg, Chrétien's chief adviser, told reporters.

Martin celebrated Christmas 2003 as prime minister. It seemed as though he had received all the presents on his list. Finally, he was prime minister, holding the office that had twice eluded his father, Paul Sr. He was heading a majority government riding high in the polls, and the path looked open to an election in the coming year that would confirm his government with a big majority. However, the New Year brought a big problem that was not of his making. But how he decided to handle it made the problem much worse and ultimately led to his downfall.

The issue had begun in Quebec, and it was the Bloc Québécois that originally made the most of it. The Bloc repeated allegations that, following the incredibly tight results in the 1995 sovereignty referendum, the federal government had launched an advertising campaign in Quebec that was designed to raise the profile and underline the brand of Canada in the province. No one disputed that fact. What was in dispute was what happened to some of the money paid to the advertising and communications companies that conducted the campaign. Did it, as alleged by both separatists and others, end up being kicked back to the coffers of the federal Liberal Party in Quebec?

When the allegation first arose, Chrétien instructed Auditor General Sheila Fraser to investigate. By the time she reported, it was January 2004 and Martin was prime minister. When she released her report, Fraser told reporters that her mandate did not allow her to investigate the advertising companies in Montreal that had run the campaigns on the ground. She could only investigate the procedure followed in Ottawa to award the contracts. As for that process, "They broke every rule in the book," Fraser said, without saying initially who "they" were.

The opposition parties seized on the report, and particularly Fraser's comments, using their parliamentary immunity to allege corruption at the highest levels of the Liberal government. The Martin people were thrown on the defensive. In their mind, it was all very unfair. An apparent scandal from when Chrétien was prime minister was now spoiling their opportunity to run the country. And so, fixated by their huge rift with the Chrétien people who had denied them power, the Martin team now committed a fundamental misunderstanding of how most Canadians did not differentiate one Liberal from another.

In early February of 2004, I was at my desk when the phone rang. It was Jamie Deacey, a longtime friend, a Liberal organizer and a fervent Martin loyalist.

"I just want to give you a heads-up," he said. "We are going to appoint a royal commission to look into the sponsorship scandal."

"You're doing what?" I asked in amazement.

"We're having a commission to investigate sponsorships," he replied.

"You're having a royal commission to investigate the Liberal Party," I said.

"Didn't happen on our watch," he replied.

"Do you think most people in Canada will look at it that way?" I asked. "To them, a Liberal is a Liberal and Paul Martin was finance minister for most of that time. Most people think that, after Question Period, the finance minister goes up to his office and writes cheques for the government out of a big ledger."

"Didn't happen on our watch," Deacey repeated.

In the short term, the appointment of a royal commission headed by Mr. Justice John Gomery did help deflect some of the initial criticism triggered by the auditor general's report. However, over the next two years, testimony before the inquiry would prove fatal to the Martin government, even if, as its members believed, it didn't happen on their watch.

The sponsorship issue was just one in the election Martin called for June 28 in search of his own majority government. But from the beginning of the campaign, the Liberals seemed strangely unprepared, while the newly amalgamated Conservative Party under Stephen Harper seemed to have all its ducks in a row. Going into the last week of the campaign, some people were predicting the unthinkable when the election was called: that Stephen Harper would have more seats than Paul Martin when the votes were counted and the Conservatives would have a minority government.

However, in the fifth and final week of the campaign, a remarkable reversal of form took place. The Harper Conservatives seemed to have no final-week strategy. The leader spent the last weekend of the campaign in Alberta, where his party already had every seat, strangely proclaiming to the faithful Conservative voters that "the West wants in." Martin's Liberals suddenly had a plan: they organized a last-ditch cross-Canada campaign dash that started with Martin dipping his foot in the Atlantic Ocean in Halifax and ended with a foot dip in the Pacific in Vancouver. It wasn't enough to save a majority government, but the Liberals emerged with a minority on election night. Martin had 135 seats, thirty-three fewer than when the election was called. Harper and the Conservatives had added twenty-seven seats for a total of ninety-nine. The Bloc Québécois had bounced back up to fifty-four and the NDP had nineteen.

When he became leader of the Liberals in November of 2003, Martin had seemed unbeatable. Seven months later, the 2004 election signalled that was not necessarily so.

47

Martin in Power

EVEN THOUGH THEIR string of three consecutive majority governments had been broken and they were left in office with a minority
government, in the immediate aftermath of the June 2004 election, the
Liberals were elated. A week before, there had been a real chance they
might lose the election and be out of office for the first time in more than
a decade.

The Conservatives were of two views. Some, like leader Stephen
Harper, seemed in a funk. He dropped out of sight, and some rumours
wrongly had him contemplating resigning. A week before the vote, it
looked as though a minority Conservative government was a likely
outcome, and remaining in opposition was consequently seen as a failure. But others had a more optimistic view. In its first electoral run as
a united party, the Conservatives had won ninety-nine seats, including
twenty-four in Ontario, had proven that the once-invincible Paul Martin
was indeed vulnerable, and that with a minority government, the opposition could trigger another election the first time it looked like the government could be replaced.

By summer's end, Harper had come around to this view. In fact, he organized a letter co-signed by NDP leader Jack Layton and Bloc Québécois leader Gilles Duceppe that he sent to Governor General Adrienne Clarkson. The letter reminded the Governor General that, under the parliamentary system, if a minority government is defeated on a confidence vote in the House of Commons, there need not be an election called if there are other parties in the House ready to co-operate and form a new government of their own. The letter from Harper, Layton and Duceppe said if the Martin Liberal government were to be defeated in the House, they all were willing to co-operate to create just such a government.

(The fact that he was the author of that letter in 2004 did not stop Harper and the Conservatives, in power with a minority government elected in the fall of 2008, from attacking the Liberals, NDP and Bloc for signing a similar letter to Governor General Michaëlle Jean. The three opposition parties wanted to replace the Conservatives after a pending confidence vote, held right after the election, when the government signalled in an economic statement it would cancel public funding of political parties. At that point, Harper and the Conservatives did what they had done before, and what they have done since: ignore the inconvenient facts and go aggressively on the attack.)

The election of 2004 swept a number of familiar Liberal faces from the House of Commons and brought in close to thirty new Conservative ones. Among the most interesting new Conservatives were four rookie women MPs: Rona Ambrose from Alberta, and from Ontario, Diane Finley, Helena Guergis and, the most interesting of all, Belinda Stronach.

Although she failed to win the Conservative Party leadership, Stronach's political appetite had been whetted. She won in a tight race in the Newmarket–Aurora riding against Liberal Martha Hall Findlay, who would later go on to make a name for herself as a two-time contender for the Liberal leadership. Stronach had a talent for attracting attention, and Harper seemed threatened by her, so she wound up in Ottawa in a Conservative caucus where the party leader didn't want her and she felt uncomfortable with many of the party's social positions.

Stronach had avoided the debate I organized for the Conservative Party leadership candidates, and I had barely said hello to her before she became an MP. But shortly after Parliament resumed in September of 2004, I was involved in an event with the National Arts Centre in Ottawa and approached her to take part. We met for drinks at Zoé's Lounge in the Château Laurier to talk about her participation, and I found her well informed, funny and quick. After she quickly agreed to be part of the NAC event, talk drifted to politics.

"You are going to have to take it easy with Harper or he will see you as a threat," I suggested.

"I know," she replied. "Brian said the same thing."

For a moment, I thought she was talking about Brian Tobin, the former Liberal cabinet minister and premier of Newfoundland and Labrador, who after politics had worked for her father, Frank Stronach, at Magna International. Then, as the conversation unfolded, I realized she meant Brian Mulroney. Clearly, Belinda knew *everybody*.

While fate had given her fame and fortune, as I watched her on Parliament Hill I began to admire how she was prepared, at least up to a point, to put up with the natural indignities that elected office visits on everyone who holds it, and that jealous colleagues and opponents who are more than willing to heap upon the favoured. Usually, people with enough money that they don't have to worry are unwilling to be subjected to that kind of treatment, so they stay away from politics or other venues where that is part of the regular scene. I also observed what I had noticed in her leadership campaign. She had a gift politicians long for: she was a public figure upon whom some people would cast their own hopes and aspirations. In the leadership campaign, it was generally women around her age who fit that category. Wherever she went as an MP, it was usually young people.

Still, Belinda Stronach didn't—and doesn't now—lead an ordinary life. With her connections, she lived a life far beyond the imagination of ordinary mortals. Ironically, the most introspective conversation I had with her was when she was enjoying one of those perks. On January 19, 2005, I was flying with my producer, Dave Mathews, on the Toronto-to-Washington flight to broadcast the second inauguration of President George W. Bush. Belinda was on the plane, and since there was no first class on the flight, she and I were in the same cabin. Belinda was going to the inauguration as the guest of a California fundraiser for Bush. And not only would she be up close at the inauguration, but there would be a party in her honour in Washington the evening after the swearing-in.

But on the flight to the U.S. capital, we talked Canadian politics. In particular, we talked about same-sex marriage, which was then the big issue of the day. To almost all of the ninety-nine members of the Conservative caucus, same-sex marriage was a huge negative. A few MPs, like Belinda and Jim Prentice, had voted with almost all the Liberals and the NDP in support of expanding the definition of marriage to people of the same sex.

We also talked about how Stronach had different positions on gun control and abortion than most of her Conservative colleagues. Being more flippant than thoughtful, I suggested that maybe she was in the wrong political party.

The last time I spoke to Belinda when she was a Conservative was at the party's policy convention in Montreal a few months later. On the Friday evening, Belinda had taken over the bar of a chic boutique hotel, had special Conservative-blue cocktails prepared for the convention-goers, and provided name entertainers to perform. It was just the sort of thing that Stephen Harper and the Alliance members of the new Conservative Party would neither think of nor countenance. It wasn't long before Harper was accusing her of trying to undermine him and was trying to minimize her role in the party.

WHILE BELINDA STRONACH's unhappiness with the Conservatives was growing, Paul Martin's need for more Liberal supporters was increasing too. Not far down the political road, those needs would meet.

Martin's term as a minority prime minister had begun well. He had to make the most minor of adjustments to his throne speech, which opened the first session of the new minority Parliament, to get it passed on a vote of confidence. Around the same time, he was meeting with the provincial premiers, trying to make good on his election campaign promise to "fix health care for a generation." Jean Chrétien had shunned the kind of first ministers' conferences that had been favoured by Pierre Trudeau and Brian Mulroney. Martin decided he wanted Canadians to see their governments at work and opted for the kind of gathering that the Government Conference Centre not seen since the days of Meech Lake.

It soon became apparent that Chrétien had been right to avoid these types of meetings. After arguing publicly without reaching agreement, the conference went behind closed doors, and on its final day and well into the evening, the premiers would pass before the cameras on their way to meet the prime minister as they traded offers and counteroffers.

I was sitting in the anchor booth above the main conference hall, ready to go on the air should an agreement be reached. With me was former Saskatchewan premier Roy Romanow, who would be our commentator if the conference ever publicly resumed. A few years earlier, Romanow had led a royal commission on health care appointed by Jean

Chrétien, and in those heady days of big federal surpluses, he had recommended very few changes to the health-care system, but proposed spending an additional $9 billion a year from a projected $13 billion government surplus to improve care and waiting times for Canadians.

While the premiers were off working on their counteroffers to the federal proposals, Romanow would get calls on his cellphone from the prime minister. Martin wanted to be sure Romanow was onside and would say so publicly when the deal—whatever it turned out to be—was announced.

When the deal to fix health care for a generation was finally reached, it involved $41 billion in federal spending over ten years, with payments to the provinces increasing by six per cent a year for the life of the deal. Much of the money would go to improving wait times for heart disease, cancer, cataracts, diagnostics and joint replacement. The provinces— except Quebec—would agree to try and meet national standards and would report annually on how they were doing.

Despite their minority status, the Liberals seemed in control of the agenda. On February 23, Finance Minister Ralph Goodale brought down his budget, and any thoughts that the government would be defeated on confidence votes around the budget quickly disappeared. Goodale was still on his feet in the House of Commons when Harper came out to the reporters and camera crews packed into the foyer of the House of Commons to say that the Conservatives would support the government.

"There is nothing in this budget," he said, "to defeat the government on."

As the budget was being brought down, the Gomery Commission was resuming its hearings in Montreal. Near the end of the first phase, the high point had been a bravura performance by Jean Chrétien, displaying golf balls he had been given by President Bill Clinton and others, inscribed with the names of the people who had given them to him. Chrétien was responding to an ill-advised interview Gomery had given before Christmas, in which he suggested that Chrétien was, in his words, "small-town cheap," for having golf balls with his name on them that he gave out as souvenirs.

In Montreal, the inquiry took a different turn. Now the executives of the advertising and communications companies that had raised the profile of the federal government by putting the "Canada brand" on events all over the province were called to testify. These were people beyond the reach of the auditor general's investigation. Under examination by commission counsel, they tended to appear suspect, some sleazy, as they admitted ties and donations to the Quebec arm of the federal Liberal Party.

The appearance of one man in particular was damaging. Jean Brault was head of a Montreal public relations firm called Groupaction, and after his testimony, public opinion turned against the Liberals. The view of the Martin group, that the sponsorship problems had "not happened on our watch," was not embraced by most ordinary Canadians. Suddenly, the Liberals were falling in the polls and Stephen Harper reversed his decision to support the Liberals' budget. Confidence motions to support the Liberal budget had passed in the Commons with Conservative support, but now the pieces of legislation to implement the budget proposals had to be passed, too, and the votes on them were also confidence votes. If the Liberals lost any of them, the government would be defeated and an election called. Paul Martin and his team would have to campaign with the damaging sponsorship testimony on everyone's mind.

It was around this point that the needs of Paul Martin and Belinda Stronach started to coalesce. But it took the help of others for their collaboration to work. Faced with plummeting support in the polls after Jean Brault's testimony, Martin went on television on April 21. He made the case that he had established the Gomery inquiry, so he had nothing to hide, and that an immediate election was not necessary because he would call an election for Canadians to decide thirty days after the commission's first report in the late fall.

The next day, he came on television with me to try and sell his idea. I wasn't overly convinced of his plan.

"Desperate men do desperate things. Are you a desperate man?" I began the interview.

"No, I am not," he replied.

But it appeared he was. With the Conservatives and the Bloc Québécois committed to voting to bring the government down, Martin and the Liberals needed the support of the NDP and the three independents sitting in the House if they were to avoid defeat. Even then, they would need a parliamentary first to survive: if the NDP and independents voted with the government, it would create a tie vote on a confidence motion, forcing Speaker Peter Milliken to cast a vote to break the deadlock. No speaker had ever been required to break a tie vote on a confidence motion, but the practice and tradition in the Commons was that, when a speaker had to vote, it was a vote to keep the debate going. Obviously, support of a motion that would defeat the government and force an election would not keep the debate going, and all parties realized that if the House were tied, Milliken would support the government and an election would be avoided.

After his promise of an election thirty days after the Gomery Commission's report, Martin and the Liberals went about trying to round up support. On the morning of April 26, I was in Toronto to speak at a breakfast meeting of the Young Presidents' Organization. The meeting was held at the National Club on Bay Street in the heart of Toronto's financial district, and most of the under-forty executives who comprised its membership worked nearby. When I walked through the door, most of the audience was milling around, apoplectic. The big headline in *The Globe and Mail* reported that the Liberals had made a deal with the NDP for support on the budget votes. The Martin government would cancel $4.6 billion in tax cuts for businesses and increase social spending instead.

Suddenly, the topic of my speech had changed before my eyes. I had everyone's attention while I explained that this was a perfect example of how politics makes for strange bedfellows. In the short term, the Liberals survived and the NDP got bragging rights that it had opposed business and supported the less affluent, a big part of the New Democrats' natural constituency. In the longer term, if the Liberals survived, the tax cuts would be back and the NDP could say they tried.

Getting the New Democrats onside was a big step in saving his government, but Martin still needed the support of all three independents in the Commons. And that became impossible on May 15, when David Kilgour said he would vote against the budget bill. Kilgour was a former Progressive Conservative MP who had left that party over the goods and services tax in 1990 and become a Liberal. He quit the Liberals in April of 2005 in response to testimony from the Gomery Inquiry and now was going all the way and voting to bring down the government.

Carolyn Parrish, another former Liberal MP, was ready to back the government. The plans of Chuck Cadman were unknown. All of this seemed problematic until the dramatic developments of May 17. With his government apparently on the brink of defeat, the Prime Minister's Office announced that Paul Martin would be holding a morning press conference. I had gone on the air at the scheduled time, but Martin wasn't in the Press Gallery Theatre eight floors below me in the National Press Building. Producer Kathleen Hunt was on the sidewalk by the front door of the building, connected via cellphone with senior producer Sharon Musgrave in the control room. Sharon could talk to me through my earpiece while I was on the air.

"Kathleen says Martin is on the sidewalk with Belinda Stronach," Sharon suddenly reported rather quizzically. I let the information pass.

It didn't make much sense. Maybe they had just run into each other passing on the street.

"Take a look at this," Sharon suddenly shouted as the picture changed to a shot of Martin and Stronach walking through the door together into the Press Theatre. In an instant, all was clear.

"Holy mackerel—Belinda Stronach is becoming a Liberal," I said in a loud and surprised voice.

And she had, leaving behind the new Conservative Party she had helped bring together and had made a bid to lead. Leaving behind Stephen Harper, who was trying to undermine and diminish her, making her feel unwelcome in the party.

Stronach became the minister of human resources development, with the added responsibility of implementing the recommendations of the Gomery Inquiry when the commission reported. To the loud guffaws of the press gallery reporters at the news conference, she and Martin claimed her crossing the floor had nothing to do with the confidence vote scheduled to take place in the Commons two days later. Neither she nor Martin could keep a straight face, because, of course, it had every-thing to do with the vote. By joining the Liberals, Stronach had cancelled out the vote withheld by David Kilgour. There was once again a strong possibility of a tie that the speaker would break in favour of the Liberals. It would all come down to the vote of Independent Chuck Cadman.

On the face of it, Cadman would seem to be an unlikely government supporter. First elected as a Reform Party candidate from Surrey, British Columbia, near Vancouver, in 1997, he was re-elected as a member of the Canadian Alliance in 2000. In 2004, he was out-organized for the Conservative Party nomination in his riding, but ran as an independent and won the seat. He resisted invitations to join the Conservative caucus and sat in the back row on the opposition side, voting as he pleased. By 2005, his health kept him away from the Commons a good deal. As the decisive May 19 confidence vote approached, he was taking chemo-therapy treatments in British Columbia for terminal melanoma, but he flew back to Ottawa a few days early to rest up so that he could go to the Commons and be counted.

There were two budget-related votes late on the afternoon of May 19. Cadman had given a few interviews, including one with me on the *Politics* broadcast when we sent a camera to his apartment in the south end of Ottawa. But he had said to me and everyone else that his mind was still not made up. He would decide on the day whether to prop up the Martin government or bring it down.

On CBC Newsworld, we pulled out all the stops. It was the first time since 1979, when Joe Clark's minority government had been defeated on a budget vote, that the country had faced this situation. In December 1979, the CBC, along with everyone else, had been surprised by the out-come. We weren't going to be caught short this time.

In the run-up to the votes on *Politics,* we had Robert Marleau, a former clerk of the House of Commons who, back in 1979, was a junior table offi-cer whose job was to stand behind the curtains next to the speaker's chair and keep a separate tally of the vote from the one taken at the table in the Commons. He said he was so surprised that the Clark government had fallen, he added up the total again before reporting it to the clerk.

We also had New Democrat MP Bill Blaikie. He had just been elected to Parliament in the 1979 spring election and suddenly found himself, seven months later, going back to the polls again. He was the only member of the House in 2005 who had been there for the last con-fidence vote on a minority government's budget. And we had the sole member of the CBC Parliamentary bureau in 1979 who was still broad-casting. Peter Mansbridge had been a young reporter on Parliament Hill when the Clark government fell. This time, he had come to Ottawa to anchor *The National* in case the government fell, and in a reversal of roles that we found rather funny, I was the anchor and he was the commentator as we watched the votes unfold.

The first vote was to implement the budget. As Harper had said back in February, the Conservatives supported that bill and it passed easily. Then came the real test: the vote on the legislation implementing the deal the Liberals and the NDP had made in April to cancel $4.6 billion of business tax cuts. It was a government bill, and those supporting it voted first, which meant the Liberals—led by Martin and his cabinet, including new member Belinda Stronach—and then the NDP, led by Jack Layton, voted in support as their names were called out. As the cameras went up and down the rows of voting MPs, Carolyn Parrish was visible sitting in the last row on the government side, waiting her turn to vote. After the last New Democrat, she stood up.

"Miss Parrish, aye," said the table officer taking the count.

There was a pause. Parrish was standing directly behind Andy Savoy, the MP from New Brunswick who was chair of the Liberal caucus and who was staring across the chamber. A second later, his face split into a huge grin as the camera cut to the other side of the House to show Chuck Cadman on his feet, voting with the government.

"Mr. Cadman, aye," the counter said over the Liberals cheers.

The Conservatives, Bloc Québécois and Kilgour then voted against the bill, creating a deadlock of 152–152. As past practice dictated, Speaker Milliken then voted in favour, and the government lived to fight again.

In the short term, Paul Martin and Belinda Stronach had won. But the victory was short-lived. Seven months later, the government would again face a confidence motion in the Commons. This time, the result would be different.

48

Lockout

IT WAS IMPOSSIBLE to cover all the events as they unfolded in 2005. That is because, through a massive miscalculation on both sides, the CBC was virtually shut down for two months when its unionized employees were locked out of their jobs by senior management.

The dispute was over a new labour contract and the changes in hiring and work practices that management wanted incorporated into it. The union resisted, fearing that permanent employees would be replaced by temporary workers.

CBC employees who appear regularly, either on radio or television, are union members. Most of the locked-out employees took it personally. I was no different. As a public figure on the CBC, wherever I went, I had to deal with audience and taxpayer reaction—none of it good. And most people thought it was a strike, not a lockout. I also wondered if somehow I could have done something to help prevent it.

The CBC lockout was the strategy of president Robert Rabinovitch; the executive vice-president of English broadcasting, Richard Stursberg;

and George Smith, the vice-president of human resources. They claimed concessions from the union were necessary to keep the CBC afloat in an ever-changing world of media technology, shrinking advertising revenues and no new support from the government.

The union argued that it is the permanent employees who are the true guardians of the CBC and public broadcasting. There was already a strong feeling before the lockout that the president, the board of the CBC and perhaps other executives should be making the case to government for restoring and increasing funding to the CBC, rather than trying to cover costs on the backs of employees who were highly committed to the Corporation and had to make do with fewer resources than they once had.

By 2005, this argument had widespread currency, particularly in the Parliamentary bureau. During the cutbacks of the 1990s, the CBC had lost funding, just like every other government agency and department except for Indian Affairs and Northern Development. But since budgets had come into balance and then into surplus, virtually every department, agency and Crown corporation had seen its funding restored and sometimes enhanced. The CBC had not. Starting in 2000, an additional $60 million annually had been added to the Corporation's budget, but it was done only on a year-to-year basis and could not be counted on for planning purposes. It was also less than the original budget cuts.

There was also a new element complicating this showdown. In the years leading up to the confrontation, there had been a consolidation of the three major unions at the CBC into one. For the first time, journalists, technicians and production workers were all represented by the Canadian Media Guild. Originally, the guild represented just the journalists working at the Corporation, but through a series of elections it had emerged as the sole bargaining agent for all the unionized workers.

Arnold Amber retained his position as president of the union in a vote of both old and new guild members.

As the summer of 2005 approached, the lack of progress in the on-again, off-again negotiations was making Rabinovitch and his managers nervous. They were afraid that, to gain leverage, the union would set a strike date for the beginning of October, just as the new hockey season was about to begin. Or, if the National Hockey League's lockout of its players was not yet over, the union would wait until the start of the Winter Olympics, to which the CBC had the broadcast rights, to exert maximum leverage.

In late May, I had lunch with a friend in senior management at the CBC who must remain nameless. That friend told me that Rabinovitch and his team were planning to lock the staff out over the summer to force a contract before the start of the NHL season. Everyone in management had been told there could be no holidays after the end of July and groups of managers from around the country were being brought to Toronto on weekends to train on operating the equipment, so some broadcasting could continue while the staff were on the street. A few days later, in Toronto, I passed on the news to Arnold Amber. I liked Arnold, had worked with him on many programs over the years, and when he ran for the presidency of the union I had sent out a systemwide email endorsing his candidacy, something I had never done before and didn't do again. Arnold didn't believe the warning.

"They can't lock us out. We are all in the same union. It would shut down the place," was his assessment.

The next time I had lunch with my management friend, I made a point I asked him to pass along to the president—a point I had not personally experienced, but that I had observed over the years while covering labour disputes.

"Robert should understand that there is a big difference between a strike and a lockout," I said. "When workers go on strike, they feel they are in control. They are the ones that withdrew their services and they can restore them and return to work if that is what they feel like doing.

"When they are locked out, they are really offended. It takes a lot more to get them to come back to work. They will like to see a little crawling from management."

When the lockout began on August 15, I wished I had passed on that warning to Rabinovitch personally, particularly after my friend told me management had calculated that the whole affair would be over right after Labour Day. I am sure Rabinovitch would not have paid any particular attention to me, although he and I had a decent relationship. In fact, without him or many others knowing, I had something to do with him still being the president of the CBC.

That happened the year before the lockout. The Martin government had been re-elected with a minority. It wasn't clear how long the government would last or when the next election would come. One warm September evening, I went for dinner with Tim Murphy, Prime Minister Martin's chief of staff. I was well acquainted with Murphy from covering Liberal politics, liked him and knew I could trust him—and he could trust me. We talked about the government's agenda and the chances of surviving in a minority Parliament. Then, over coffee, I brought up another topic in which I had a personal interest, though not a particularly large stake.

"What are you going to do about Rabinovitch?" I asked. His term as CBC president was coming to an end, and it was widely rumoured that he hoped to be reappointed, at least until close to his sixty-fifth birthday in 2008.

"Well, Frulla wants to get rid of him," Murphy said, referring to Heritage Minister Liza Frulla. "She's been told she can if she comes up with a credible replacement."

Rabinovitch, a former deputy minister, had been appointed by Jean Chrétien and was a good friend of Chrétien's chief adviser, Eddie Goldenberg. The Martin people didn't seem to mind him, but they had nothing invested in him, either.

"Has Frulla come up with a replacement?" I asked.

"What would you think of Francis Fox?" was the reply.

My chin almost hit my chest. Francis Fox was a former cabinet minister from the Trudeau era. Flawlessly bilingual, clever, a bit controversial early in his career, but rehabilitated by further cabinet performance, he had once been considered a potential prime minister. I liked Fox, and recently he had been telling me he wanted to have lunch. I was looking forward to doing that—after all, he was Prime Minister Martin's principal secretary.

Now I realized why he wanted to have lunch. Fox wanted to see what the reaction would be to his being named CBC president. He wasn't there to tell that evening, so I told Murphy.

"It won't fly," I told him. "You can't take someone who is the prime minister's principal secretary and make him president of the CBC. The fact that he is Frulla's friend would make it even worse. I have always stayed out of who is president of the CBC, and I have nothing against Francis personally, but if he is named and I am asked by the media what I think about it, I will say it is inappropriate."

"Well, that's good to know," Tim replied.

A couple of weeks later, the announcement came from the Prime Minister's Office: Robert Rabinovitch had been extended for two years as president of the CBC. Francis Fox was appointed to the Senate shortly after. He has not invited me to lunch since.

I didn't share my information about Rabinovitch's job situation with colleagues on the picket line. I didn't think they would appreciate my efforts, although with Francis Fox as CBC president, the government might have ordered the lockout ended and allowed us back into the studios, which was the main goal of the union. Instead, as I predicted, the lockout stretched through September and into the beginning of October. The hockey lockout had ended and the season was about to begin. The government did get involved, with Labour Minister Joe Fontana ordering mediated around-the-clock negotiations, and quickly, the deal was done. Having forced the lockout to avoid facing a strike when the hockey season began, CBC management was nonetheless forced to negotiate in the looming shadow of the puck being dropped. Everyone knew hockey was the driver that got the government involved, although I enjoyed a tongue-in-cheek line in a *Globe and Mail* editorial that said it wasn't hockey but the MPs' no longer seeing themselves on *Politics* that finally broke the logjam.

Many CBC employees thought Rabinovitch a good example of a CBC president who didn't do enough publicly to defend the Corporation or work to have its funding restored and expanded. A former bureaucrat, he was risk-averse and counted on past relationships within the PCO and PMO. Perrin Beatty, who preceded Rabinovitch, bore the same criticism for not doing enough, and so has current president Hubert Lacroix, who succeeded Rabinovitch.

When the Broadcasting Act was rewritten in 1991, the term of the CBC president was shortened from seven years to five. That made being reappointed to a second term as president attractive, and some argue it has changed the behaviour of the person at the top. Certainly, Beatty was quoted as saying that if he were offered a second term, he would seriously consider it. The former Conservative cabinet minister had done what he had been mandated to do by the Liberal government: implement massive cuts without complaint. Rabinovitch had wanted his term extended and it was. Lacroix was eventually reappointed and is now serving his second term.

49

A Most Unusual Election

NOVEMBER 2005 IS a month for the history books. Three events that month triggered the election that would end twelve years of Liberal governments.

On November 1, Justice John Gomery brought down the first of his two reports on the sponsorship scandal that arose out of federal government spending in Quebec after the close call in the province's 1995 referendum on separation. Gomery said he found that a "culture of entitlement" existed in the Liberal government of former prime minister Jean Chrétien. The opposition parties quickly moved to try and tie the accusation to Chrétien's successor, Paul Martin, and had some success doing so.

On November 23, Finance Minister Ralph Goodale surprised many people when he announced that the government would not be taxing income trusts. Shortly before the announcement, the stock market began to rally, creating speculation that there might have been a leak from Ottawa to Bay Street before the decision was announced. New Democrat member of Parliament Judy Wasylycia-Leis sent a letter to the

RCMP, asking them to investigate whether there had been any insider tips from the government to any stockbroker friends.

The Gomery Report and the income-trust allegations triggered the decisive event. On November 28, all three opposition parties voted together to defeat the government by supporting a non-confidence motion claiming the Liberal government was corrupt. The next day, Governor General Michaëlle Jean dissolved Parliament and set January 23 as election day. The campaign would be longer than the usual thirty-five days—there would be a break in the campaign between the Christmas and New Year's holidays.

As it turned out, the most decisive event of the election occurred during the campaign break. Right after Christmas, the RCMP replied to Wasylycia-Leis. They faxed a letter to her parliamentary office, telling her they would launch a criminal investigation into possible leaks around the income trust decision. Everyone in the office was on holidays when the fax came. When RCMP officers saw no reaction from the New Democrats, they got in touch to let them know they should check their faxes. Wasylycia-Leis did, and immediately went public. Liberal Party poll numbers started falling.

Spooked by the slippage and plagued by bad luck, Martin could not recover. On election night, the results of the RCMP actions showed up in the seat count. The Liberals had lost 30 seats and were down to 103, while the Conservatives had gained 26 to end up with 124. Paul Martin, who had been a golden boy of Canadian politics for at least a decade, was now out of office. Conceding on election night, he said he would step down from the Liberal leadership he had wanted for so long. Stephen Harper, who had dropped out of electoral politics after disagreeing with Reform leader Preston Manning and then returned to unite the right, was now the prime minister.

Right after the election, a lot of people were wondering how big an impact the RCMP actions over Christmas had played and what was behind it. Certainly, Liberal polling numbers had dropped almost immediately, and the further behind he got, the worse Martin campaigned. A lot of people wondered why, shortly after he was sworn in as prime minister, Stephen Harper played a public courtesy call on RCMP commissioner Giuliano Zaccardelli. Whether inadvertent or purposeful, the so-called "Zack attack" had helped the Conservatives get in, but if the RCMP was acting too independently, it could also mean that one day the Conservatives too might be the target.

Less than two months after the election, my wife, Shannon, and I were part of the large crowd that is invited each year to celebrate St. Patrick's Day at the home of the Irish ambassador to Canada. Two things stand out from that evening: a brief conversation with Finance Minister Jim Flaherty, in which he told us he'd found there was a lot more work to be done and that things were much more complicated as federal finance minister than when he was finance minister of Ontario; and I had a chance to ask Zaccardelli why the force had been so insistent on getting out the reply to the NDP's call for an investigation.

The central part of the ambassador's home was packed. Shannon and I had stepped away from the main party and, looking into an alcove, I saw Zaccardelli standing by himself. He was smiling as we walked over, but turned serious when I said, "Zack, you were really out there in the campaign with that letter to Wasylycia-Leis. What was that all about?"

He looked down, then back up. Then he walked away.

Over the next few days, whenever I had time, which wasn't often, I tried to pursue the story. But at that time Zaccardelli wasn't talking to anyone. Even with good producers and writers, putting together and hosting a daily political program is full-time journalism and doesn't leave much time for enterprise reporting.

However, Zaccardelli's action during this election campaign was the start of a downward spiral to the end of his time as commissioner. First the Maher Arar case and then a controversy over RCMP pension funds found him without any friends in parliament, and a House of Commons committee ripped into him. Opposition parties demanded his resignation and even the Conservatives were less than supportive. Zaccardelli submitted his resignation and Harper accepted it.

After he retired, Zaccardelli spoke occasionally about the election and his letter to Wasylycia-Leis. Rather than being political in the middle of the campaign, he said, he was just the opposite. That by acting the way he did, he was preserving the political independence of the RCMP by not letting an election campaign change the way he would otherwise have behaved.

In Lyon, France, while he was winding up an appointment with Interpol, the international police agency, Zaccardelli maintained that even if he had realized that publicity around the Mounties' letter that they were conducting a criminal investigation into possible income trust leaks would have an impact on the election, he'd had "no choice" but to do his "duty" and respond to a request from a Member of Parliament and let Canadians know what the RCMP was doing about a matter of great public concern.

Others aren't so sure. People, particularly Liberals, point out that the course of justice could just as easily have been served without public knowledge of the investigation. They became even more convinced of this after the investigation led to one person being charged with leaking information ahead of the income trust decision. That person turned out to be a public servant in the Department of Finance with no political affiliation.

What the RCMP did and why they did it might have been improper and inappropriate, but it wasn't illegal. What the Conservatives did was.

The Conservatives moved money around between their national campaign and various constituency associations running the campaigns of more than sixty Conservative candidates. In the process, they were trying to spend more than the amount—just over $18 million—the party was allowed by law to spend on its national campaign. They also tried to have the local candidates involved in the scheme improperly reimbursed by Elections Canada for money they didn't actually spend on their own behalf.

It was the so-called "in and out" scheme. To be fair, the Conservatives apparently didn't think they were breaking the law. They thought they had found a loophole they could exploit, and one of them even bragged about it in a book. Tom Flanagan spelled out some details of the plan is his book *Harper's Team*. And for six years the Conservatives denied any wrongdoing and sued Elections Canada for money the party claimed it was owed.

The scheme worked this way. When the main Conservative campaign hit the ceiling for national spending in the election, they began transferring thousands of dollars to the campaigns of local candidates who had yet to reach the spending limits on their individual election efforts. This was the "in" part of the scheme. However, as soon as the money arrived in the local Conservative campaign's bank account, it was immediately transferred back to the national campaign office. This was the "out" part of the scheme. Back at national headquarters, the money was spent to buy national advertising for the overall campaign.

Because the money had briefly been in a local campaign account, the Conservatives did not count it against their legal ceiling for national election spending. What's more, because the money had been transferred from a local campaign, they characterized it as local spending and, as such, eligible for a partial rebate from Elections Canada to any candidate who received 10 per cent of the vote in his or her riding. It was when Elections Canada processed the local requests for rebates that they realized the money hadn't gone to directly benefit the local campaigns. By the time officials figured that out, more than $230,000 had been paid out. Elections Canada wanted that money back and refused to honour any more claims for rebates. The Conservatives sued for that money.

Elections Canada refused to pay the rebates beginning in April of 2007, but it took another year before it acted on what it then believed was a criminal matter. In April 2008, RCMP officers, acting on behalf of Elections Canada, raided Conservative Party offices in downtown Ottawa, taking with them computers and other records. The "raid" attracted a lot of attention and put a lot of pressure on the minority government in the House of Commons, where the opposition parties had majorities on the committees and wanted to investigate the in-and-out scheme. So the Conservatives decided to "blow up" the committees, making it impossible for them to meet, call witnesses or conduct any kind of parliamentary inquiry.

When Parliament adjourned for the summer, Prime Minister Harper turned the Conservatives' disadvantage into an advantage. In the same way the Conservatives portrayed the in-and-out controversy as a disagreement over accounting between the Harper government and Elections Canada, the fact that the Conservatives were a minority government somehow seemed to be irrelevant. Harper started complaining that it was the opposition parties that had made it impossible for Parliament to work, rather than the other way around. He wanted a pledge of co-operation, without which he said he would call an election. Then he called an election that gave the Conservatives another minority government. As Harper hoped, the in-and-out scandal was not much of an issue.

The politics of "in and out" would come and go, and so would another election, but the legal process ground on. At one point, tensions flared between Elections Canada and the public prosecutor responsible for pursuing the case in court after charges were laid against four Conservative officials from the 2006 campaign, two of whom Harper had put in the Senate after the party took power.

The public prosecutor wanted to wait until the Conservatives' civil suit against Elections Canada for its candidate refunds was completed. Elections Canada thought that if the criminal charges led to convictions, the civil suit would be moot. It was only after the Conservatives' civil suit was overturned by the Federal Court of Appeal and the Supreme Court refused to take the case in 2012 that both sides got down to serious plea bargaining. The result: the Conservatives paid two fines totalling $52,000; charges against the senators and the other officials were dropped; the Conservatives paid back $230,000 they had received in illegal in-and-out rebates, and the case was closed.

The final settlement came six years after the election in which the in-and-out scheme had been deployed. Two more elections had been held in the intervening period, the first giving the Conservatives a second, albeit larger minority government in 2008, and then a majority in 2011. The 2011 election even had echoes of the in and out. In the spring of 2013 a federal court judge ruled that automated robocalls misdirecting young voters away from their polling stations was the work of someone with access to the Conservative Party's database. The judge said he could not identify who was directly responsible and did not have evidence that the calls had affected the outcome of the election. He did comment that the Conservative MPs involved in the case engaged in "trench warfare" in trying to prevent the case from proceeding.

By the date of the next election, tentatively scheduled for October 2015, the Harper government will have been in office for almost a decade. That's a pretty impressive run. It is a bit longer than Brian Mulroney from 1984 to 1993, and a year less than Pierre Trudeau in his first run as prime minister between 1968 and 1979. By that time, it is unlikely that many Canadians will remember that it all started with the campaign of 2006, when the Conservatives won after the RCMP became inappropriately involved and the party ended up paying big fines for breaking the spending rules.

50

Harper and the Media

For a man who wanted me to put him on TV so he could stay politically viable, once in office, Stephen Harper showed no respect
for the media in general or the CBC in particular. All prime ministers
manage their time and try to manage their media exposure, but Harper
tries to control it the way he controls his cabinet, caucus, party and just
about everything else that comes across his path.

But when he quit being a panelist on my program, jumped back
into politics, became leader first of the Canadian Alliance and then the
Conservative Party, Harper seemed as accessible as any other leader of the
Opposition trying to get rid of a sitting government and get into power. At
the beginning of the Conservative Party leadership race, he and Laureen
Harper invited me and Shannon to dinner at Stornoway, the official residence of the leader of the Opposition. There were just the four of us for a
pleasant dinner. As I recall, Harper's main point of interest was my view
of Larry Smith, the former Canadian Football League commissioner who

was flirting with the idea of running against Harper for the leadership of the newly amalgamated Conservatives. Nor was he sure it was a good idea to plan an editorial board meeting with the Montreal *Gazette* when Smith was the publisher. I didn't know Smith, but I told Harper not to worry. With its suicidal plan to expand into Shreveport, Sacramento, Las Vegas and other minor-league American cities during Smith's time as commissioner, the CFL had appeared to be on the ropes. I said I would be surprised if Smith actually ran, and he didn't.

In 2011, when he had been prime minister for five years, Harper put Smith in the Senate. Smith then ran as a Conservative candidate in the next election, lost, and was reappointed a senator by Harper.

In opposition, Harper was always looking for television opportunities, and he often came on with me. In the *Politics* studio, people entered through a door behind the main set, and I could not see them until they walked around in front of the anchor desk. When he came into the studio, Harper would flash back to the *Seinfeld* television program, on which a recurring character with the same last name as mine made a regular appearance.

"Hellooow, Newman," he would call out from behind me with a laugh.

"Hellooow, Harper," I would reply without turning around.

When he became prime minister, Harper said that he would not use the theatre in the National Press Building where prime ministers since 1967 had held their press conferences. Instead, he would hold them in the foyer of the House of Commons, with the doors open into the chamber and the flag beside him. There, he would be able to control the questioners in a way he couldn't in the Press Gallery Theatre, by taking questions from a list of reporters whose names were chosen by his press secretary in advance. He would look more "presidential" on TV. The Press Gallery protested, but at the same time, a few reporters warmed up to his handlers to get on the list. Harper and his media handlers dug in.

Harper also stopped coming to the annual press gallery dinner, a tradition where journalists, politicians, lobbyists and diplomats gather, either on or near Parliament Hill, for an evening of drinks, dinner, speeches and fun. The first year Harper declined to attend, the Conservative members of Parliament stayed away too, except the ten from Quebec. I guess there were so few of them that they figured there was nothing Harper could do to them.

Harper's first director of communications was a woman named Sandra Buckler. She was a public relations and government relations professional working in an Ottawa firm that also had offices in Toronto. Buckler was a committed Conservative, but in Ottawa in the early-to-mid-2000s, when there were a lot more Liberals than Conservatives, she was well liked. After the election in 2004, whenever I would run into her, Buckler would lobby me to be on television. In 2005, when the Martin government, fell I put her on a panel with Brad Lavigne of the NDP and Susan Murray of the Liberals on a morning version of *Politics* we aired during the campaign. She and Murray went after each other like hockey players in the playoffs. I think Lavigne felt a bit like the third wheel. As the Conservatives started to pull ahead, the more she could dominate the panel. And the more she could, the more she did.

In fact, when the Conservatives won their minority government she was a bit of a star in party circles. A few days after the election, Buckler called me and said we had to have lunch. Across the table, I found out why. Her employers wanted to make her a vice-president of the company and send her the next day to Toronto where, with her new profile, new title and better salary, she would explain to both current and prospective clients what to expect from a Harper government. Countering that offer, she said, was the opportunity to stay in Ottawa and be the new prime minister's deputy director of communications.

"I don't see why this is a hard decision," I said. "If you worked for the prime minister, after a couple of years you would want to leave, get a job as a vice-president in a company like the one where you now work and go to Toronto to tell clients about the government. With the offer you have, you can do this now. Besides, when the Accountability Act you people are talking about goes into effect, you might have trouble accepting a job like the one being offered now. Besides, just as a point of general principle, you never want to be a 'deputy' anything."

"Good advice," Sandra said.

That evening, I had just arrived home from the CBC when my cellphone rang. It was Sandra Buckler. I quickly realized she had only heard the part of my advice that she wanted to hear.

"I'm it," she said, the excitement in her voice rising through the phone. "I'm it, I'm not the deputy, I am the main communications director."

"Congratulations, Sandra," I said.

Unfortunately, Sandra's warm good nature did not transfer to her boss. If anything, the opposite occurred. As Harper's efforts to control the press gallery generated pushback and resentment, sunny Sandra became cloudy and sometimes reclusive. In April of 2008, with the government getting a particular going-over in the media, I suddenly realized Sandra was in danger. When prime ministers can't get their message out, they blame the people in their office who deal with the messengers. Brian Mulroney had done it more than once, and had even replaced his good friend Bill Fox as his press secretary. Now, I felt, Sandra was in danger of being dropped by Harper, so this time I invited her to lunch.

She wasn't very happy when I told her of my concerns. In fact, she said I was upsetting her and she was already concerned about her health.

"You have to plan it so you get another job, either somewhere in the government or in the private sector, before they decide to move you. Believe me, it always happens," I told her.

"No, you're wrong," she said. "I am going to stay and help him get the majority."

That was the end of the conversation. Two months later, it was announced that Sandra Buckler was no longer the prime minister's communications director, although she did get subsequent jobs in the cabinet ministers' offices. When I occasionally saw her after she left the PMO, her sunny self had re-emerged.

Buckler was replaced in the Prime Minister's Office by Kory Teneycke. Tall, thin and articulate, I first met him in Toronto at the Liberal convention where Paul Martin became party leader. Why Teneycke was there, I have no idea, although he seemed to be with Conservative lobbyist Tim Powers. Teneycke got off to a bad start with me after he credited the re-election of the NDP government in Saskatchewan to what he called the biases of the CBC. What Canada needed, he told me, was a television network like the right-wing Fox News Channel in the United States. I thought this was a bad idea; politics there is highly polarized, and the media has lost some of its impartiality and rigour.

But to his credit, Teneycke is now the head of Sun News Network, the even-further-to-the-right cable channel that spins nonstop praise for Stephen Harper and his government and relentlessly attacks the CBC. For Teneycke, nothing much else seems to have changed since 2003 except the reach of his message and the size of his paycheque. However, for a free marketer like Teneycke, it must have been galling to go before the CRTC, the national broadcast regulator, as he did in the spring of 2013, to ask for guaranteed carriage on the nation's cable systems and the subscriber fees that status brings. Otherwise, he said, Sun News wouldn't survive without what amounts to a subsidy (despite the channel being owned by a large Quebec-based private-sector media company that has the ability to raise its own money in the markets, from the banks, or by digging into its own capital). The request was subsequently turned down by the CRTC.

Between leaving Prime Minister Harper's office and the appearance of Sun News on the country's cable systems, Teneycke did some work at the home of the Great Satan, the CBC. In one of the embarrassing, periodic "if we play up to them, they will be nice to us" episodes, the CBC paid Teneycke a reported $75,000 a year to appear as a right-wing commentator. While he was doing that, he was laying the groundwork for Sun News. Perhaps he thought he was doing research for the attacks that are now a constant on Sun News, but if he was, he isn't a very good student. Most of what appears on Sun should be better researched. On the other hand, maybe he just enjoyed collecting some CBC money while he was planning his attacks against the Corporation.

When it is not a hallelujah chorus for the government in general and Prime Minister Harper in particular, Sun News spends most of its time attacking the CBC. Some of the attacks say the CBC wastes money. Most are pathetic but I can think of two instances when Sun News was right.

In 2004, Richard Stursberg was hired as head of English services at the CBC. Robert Rabinovitch decided he had to shake things up at the Corporation and that Stursberg was the man to do it. And shake up things Stursberg did. He wanted the English service on TV to be more about entertainment than about news, and he wanted the news to be the same—more about entertainment and less about news. To that end, he hired an American consultancy called Frank N. Magid Associates to give him ideas for improving the news, particularly local news. "Improving" in this context is a relative concept, although Stursberg thought it meant adding viewers, and in and of itself, a larger audience is a good thing. But the Magid company has been know for years as the consultants who favour the philosophy "If it bleeds, it leads," which is synonymous with dumbing down the news. But while Stursberg wanted more people watching the news, he didn't want to spend more money to attract them. In fact, he attacked news budgets and poured the money into entertainment programming. That led to chief news editor Tony Burman resigning in 2007, and to his replacement, John Cruickshank, resigning a year later.

In the summer of 2008, I called Cruickshank to talk about budget cuts he was imposing on all programs on Newsworld.

"I can't do anything about it," he said. "Richard is taking my money."

From my perspective, the other waste of money was the hiring in 2010 of the American management consultancy Bain Capital. It is the company 2012 Republican president candidate Mitt Romney made his fortune before going into politics, although he was long gone before the firm was hired by the CBC. Bain was to provide the CBC with a strategic plan, and it was paid five million dollars to do so. Sadly, the Americans at Bain had difficulty getting their heads around the concept of the Canadian Crown corporation. By law, Crown corporations are not allowed to borrow money because the government is ultimately responsible for the debts. A major recommendation from Bain to the CBC: get the right to borrow money. That, of course, was a nonstarter.

But aside from hiring Americans who don't know about Canada, it is hard to point to any wasted money at the CBC. It would have been harder to make that case when I first joined in 1976, but even then it would depend on your definition of waste. After all, is it a waste if the people producing and reporting an election night program, who are on the air for six or more hours, have a few drinks and nibbles after the program? Until the 1990s, they had dinner before the broadcast too. Is that a waste? I think not.

Now, when people at the CBC seek to curry favour by saying there is still some "fat at the CBC," I believe the fat they are talking about is between their ears.

51

Liberals in Opposition

EVERY ELECTION IS a matter of choice. Undecided voters without a close attachment to a political party have to choose between the parties, their platforms and their candidates. As a general rule, the party with the best candidates, the best platform and the best advertising wins, but it is also a matter of luck and how good your opponents are.

There is no doubt that the luck of having a divided opposition played a big role in the three majority governments that Jean Chrétien and his Liberals achieved between 1993 and 2000. And there is no doubt that the luck of having a divided Liberal Party, which led to the Gomery Inquiry that influenced the outcome of the election in 2006, played an important role in making Stephen Harper prime minister. Harper has also been lucky that, following the 2006 election, the Liberals could only remember back to 1984, when their party had been hammered down to just forty seats and a major rebuilding job was required. Had they been able to remember back another five years, to 1979, how different recent Canadian history might have been different.

In 1979, after nine years in power, the Liberals lost a close election that gave Joe Clark and the Progressive Conservatives a strong minority government. But nine months later, after the Clark government was defeated on a confidence vote, a new election put the Liberals back in power for another four years.

In 2006, Harper won the smallest minority government since Confederation. With 124 seats, the Conservatives were 30 short of a majority, and with 103, the Liberals were only 19 behind. Still, on election night, Paul Martin appeared on camera from his campaign headquarters to concede defeat and announce he would not lead the party into another election. In other words, he was quitting, even though the weakest minority government in history, led by an untried and inexperienced leader, was about to take office. It was a scenario where another election could be triggered at any time.

Instead, the only Liberal memories were apparently of 1984, when voters thoroughly rejected the party and it took two elections and a leadership change to get back into power. Martin's decision to step down had a ripple effect. Most of the people who had spent the previous fifteen years taking over the Liberal Party and making Martin the leader left too. What had been a formidable political machine was suddenly hollowed out, along with most of the experienced people interested in becoming leader.

After dropping out of the contest against Martin in 2003, John Manley was now working at a Bay Street law firm, and the appeal of being leader of the Opposition was not strong enough to get him back into politics. Former New Brunswick premier Frank McKenna had been appointed by Martin as Canada's ambassador in Washington. McKenna quit diplomatic work following the election defeat. He opted to become a vice-chairman of the TD Financial Group rather than seek the Liberal leadership. Allan Rock was at his post in New York as

Canadian ambassador to the United Nations, and he decided to stay there until his term drew to a close.

Bill Graham, who had been minister of foreign affairs and then of defence, was named the interim Liberal leader and the leader of the Opposition in the House of Commons. He did a good job, but he wasn't interested in defeating the government and leading the Liberals into an election and Liberals weren't that interested in following him. So instead of looking for a way to capitalize on Harper's early mistakes, the Liberals instead found themselves making sure the government wasn't defeated. It gave both the prime minister and the Conservatives a huge opportunity to learn on the job, to "govern as though they had a majority," when in fact they were nowhere close to having one.

So when the race to succeed Martin got underway the three top prospects were not among the candidates. Instead, the field was led by two people with impressive credentials, except that they had not been earned within the Liberal Party.

Bob Rae had been premier of Ontario. But in the leadership race, he had two strikes against him: he had led the Ontario NDP, and was premier during the tough first half of the 1990s, when the economy was in recession and his government was unpopular. Rae's brother John had been an adviser to Jean Chrétien when Chrétien was in the Trudeau cabinet. Chrétien invited Bob Rae to run as a Liberal in the 2000 election, but he declined. In fact, Rae did not officially join the Liberals until he decided to run for the leadership. The big knock on him was he was "out of the party."

Michael Ignatieff had been recruited by a group of Toronto Liberals to run for the party in the 2006 election. Part of their pitch was that one day he could be leader, a sort of latter-day Pierre Trudeau. The problem was that the Liberals had to go to Boston to meet with him. Ignatieff was a Canadian who had developed an international career as a public intellectual and university professor, better known in England or at Harvard than in his native land. The big knock on him was that he was "out of the country."

By the time the leadership convention opened in Montreal on November 29, these two candidates with their big "out" issues were running first and second in support for the leadership. Ignatieff was about ten percentage points ahead. Not only did their race strain a friendship that went back to their fathers and through their own university days, but each became the surrogate for the ongoing split in the Liberal Party between the Martin and Chrétien wings, with Ignatieff representing the former and Rae the latter.

Six other candidates were on the ballot when the voting began at the Palais des Congrès on the morning of Saturday, December 2. On the first ballot, Ignatieff and Rae were running one-two with six others trailing them. But as other candidates were dropped from the first two ballots, Stéphane Dion, whom many had considered a longshot, kept picking up support. After the third ballot, on which three names remained, he was leading the race. That dropped Rae down to third place, eliminating him. On the fourth ballot, Dion captured 54 per cent of the vote and was the new Liberal leader.

Winning the leadership was the high point of Dion's time in the job. Even with a permanent leader in place, the Liberals were unwilling to challenge the Harper government on confidence votes and allowed the Conservatives to remain in office. Soon it became a running joke on how the party would find new and ingenious ways to avoid voting on confidence motions. In the summer of 2008, a year and a half after taking over the leadership, Dion unveiled his major policy initiative. He had been environment minister in the Martin government and was a strong supporter of measures to limit greenhouse gases that contribute to global warming. He wanted that to be the centrepiece of the Liberal campaign platform, and in the early summer he unveiled what he called a "green shift" that would cut income and other taxes while putting a tax on carbon.

Dion had been a university professor and there was no doubt he was clever. But in English, that cleverness did not come through. The Conservatives immediately fixed on the new tax on carbon and railed against it as a tax on virtually everything. And Harper took the initiative. Instead of waiting to be defeated in the House of Commons, he ignored the new fixed-date election law he had supported and asked for an October election. When that election produced another Conservative minority government, Harper decided to try a new tactic: cutting all public funding for political parties, which he knew would hurt the Liberals, NDP and Bloc Québécois much more than it would penalize his own party, with its larger donor base. It was a surprise move that was not fully consulted with his cabinet and that would nearly cost him power.

The recent election had left the Liberals with only 77 seats and the party wanted Dion out. So, against his own wishes, Dion had already agreed to step down as Liberal leader and the race was forming to replace him when the Conservatives put their plan to stop public funding for political parties into the economic update that Finance Minister Jim Flaherty delivered in the House of Commons in late November. The update was a curious statement indeed. Not only did it have the funding announcement in it, but the finance minister's report seemed oblivious to the economic carnage then enveloping Wall Street, Europe and much of the rest of the world, with no plans to stimulate what was obviously a slowing Canadian economy.

The opposition parties publicly staked out the economic high ground rather than their own funding dilemma as the basis of their attempt to defeat the economic statement on a vote in the House of Commons. That meant the government would lose a vote of confidence, triggering another election. To try and prevent an election so soon—less than two months— after the last, the opposition parties proposed that a Liberal–NDP coalition govern the country with the support of the Bloc Québécois on all confidence votes over the next eighteen months. They hoped that the proposal, similar to the one Harper had pushed when he was Opposition leader in 2004, would convince Governor General Michaëlle Jean not to agree to the election that Harper would certainly ask her for after the Conservatives lost the confidence vote on the fiscal update.

The Liberals held a special meeting of all MPs and senators to confirm support for the coalition plan. With a leadership race already planned to replace Dion the next spring, the party had to decide who would in fact lead the party and be prime minister if the deal with the NDP and the Bloc went ahead. Both Bob Rae and Michael Ignatieff were planning to run again, and so was Dominic LeBlanc, a young MP from New Brunswick. The short-term answer to this leadership vacuum was to let Dion serve as interim leader, while the others would campaign towards a leadership vote to replace him early the next year.

I was standing in the rotunda of the Centre Block, just down the hall from where the Liberals were meeting, when that decision was made. I understood their leadership issues, but it seemed to me a bad idea to let Dion front the proposed coalition government. Canadians had decided decisively a month and a half earlier that they didn't want Dion as prime minister. I put that idea to Liberal MP Pablo Rodriguez as he emerged from the caucus.

"You are probably right," he said, "but what could we do?"

Conservative cabinet ministers were giving interviews ignoring the fact they had a minority government, claiming a coalition would be some-how illegal and stating that the separatist Bloc Québécois would be a part of the government when they knew that would not in fact be the case.

But the real test came when all the party leaders were given public airtime to make their arguments. And it was then that the weakness of keeping Dion as Liberal leader became apparent. The Liberals taped Dion's statement in his office, but then couldn't get the tape to the central broadcast point in time to be part of the main telecast. Whether the late tape was Dion's fault or not, it was to many Liberals just another example of a failure of leadership. The next morning, Harper was at Government House, asking the Governor General to prorogue the House, enabling the government to dodge the confidence vote, while in the foyer environment minister John Baird was on live television with me saying they wanted a "time-out," and if Michaëlle Jean didn't agree, they'd "go over the head of the Governor General."

The Governor General gave Harper his prorogation and the Conservatives got the time-out, which saved their government. A week later, the late Dion tape came home to roost. The Liberal caucus and party executive pushed him from the leadership and installed Michael Ignatieff as interim leader, clearing the way for him to be unopposed at a convention in Vancouver in May.

The timing of the Liberals' leadership move turned out to be no better than with Dion. The Conservatives were worried that, from the convention that confirmed him as leader, Ignatieff would come out running, defeat the government on a confidence vote and jump into an election campaign. That's why, in early June, the Conservatives began negotiating with the Liberals to avoid a defeat on a confidence vote, something they hadn't bothered to do before and didn't bother with after.

Instead of taking their chances right away, the Liberals fell back into the old practice of propping up the Conservatives on confidence votes so there wouldn't be an election. It took almost two years after he became leader for Ignatieff to bring the government down, and when he did, he brought himself down as well. In May of 2011, the Liberals suffered their worst defeat in party history, dropping to third in the House of Commons. Ignatieff lost his own seat, along with forty-two other Liberals. He retired from politics and returned to academic life.

With circumstances in Quebec that no one has completely explained, Jack Layton led the New Democrats to their best showing ever, and they became the Official Opposition. Layton died not long after, from the cancer he had been fighting for the previous three years, before he had a chance to enjoy his great success.

But the biggest winner of all was Stephen Harper. Nine years after he had called me to leave the *Politics* program with his plan to unite the right-wing parties, he had achieved his ultimate triumph. He was prime minister of a majority Conservative government.

52

Remembrance Ceremonies and Canada's Veterans

AROUND THE BEGINNING of November 1987, I received a call from Hans Pohl, a producer who worked in the CBC's news specials unit with Arnold Amber. Since Larry Stout had left the CBC earlier that year, would I like to take his place anchoring the network's Remembrance Day broadcast from the National War Memorial in Ottawa on November 11? Yes, indeed I would, I told him.

The war had been over for forty-two years; I had just turned forty-seven. But with my boyhood in England right after the war, the bomb sites all around London still dotting the city like open sores waiting to be healed, and the air raid shelter in the park not far from our home, I had a closer sense of the Second World War than many Canadians my age.

Canada's National War Memorial was just two blocks from the CBC's Parliamentary bureau, where I worked. During the time I lived in Ottawa, I would sometimes walk down to witness the wreath-laying ceremony. More often, I would watch on TV. However, the year before, in 1986, I decided to do a story around the National Remembrance Day ceremony for *This Week in Parliament,* featuring George Hees, the minister of veterans affairs.

On a cold November 11 morning, with an early snow on the ground, my camera crew and I accompanied the minister down from Parliament Hill, through the crowd, and onto the parade square in front of the War Memorial.

Hees was seventy-seven and a bit of a war hero—also why I was doing a story about him on Remembrance Day. As a major in the Fifth Infantry Brigade, he had been wounded in Holland in the final weeks of World War II. His life had been saved only because he broke the rules: he had drawn his revolver and, when no longer in use, instead of returning to its holster as required by regulation, he stuck it in his belt. A minute later, he took a direct hit. But instead of the German bullet passing into his body, it hit the handle of the revolver and ricocheted across his stomach. He was wounded, but not dead, as he would have been had he put the revolver away properly. Hees liked to tell that story, adding colour and bolstering his reputation as a bit of an adventurer.

A former linebacker with a Grey Cup–winning Toronto Argonauts team, tall, dark and handsome, the consummate charmer, Hees earned a reputation with the ladies. When his name got embroiled in the Gerda Munsinger political sex scandal (though he was later cleared of misconduct), it was enough of a problem that he did not contest the 1963 federal election. Two years later, he was back, running in a rural riding east of Toronto, and in 1967 he sought but failed to win the federal Progressive Conservative leadership.

He stayed on, working away among the backbenches of the House of Commons, and was bitter when Joe Clark left him out of his minority government's cabinet in 1979. When Brian Mulroney challenged and defeated Clark in 1983, Hees was understandably one of Mulroney's most vocal supporters. In fact, I was standing next to Hees on the convention floor when the final results were announced, declaring Mulroney the victor.

"We got him!" Hees exulted at Clark's defeat. Mulroney didn't make Clark's mistake. Hees became his minister of veterans affairs in 1984.

As fate would have it, it was lucky I was standing there with him in Confederation Square in 1986. I got a close-up look at Prime Minister Mulroney arriving before Governor General Jeanne Sauvé, and each of them being greeted by the president of the Royal Canadian Legion. I also followed closely the ceremonial laying of wreaths, something I hadn't watched as intently on TV or from the crowd in prior years.

The Governor General, as Canada's head of state, lays a wreath first on behalf of the people of Canada. Next comes the Silver Cross Mother, on behalf of the mothers of Canada who have lost children in the country's wars, followed by the prime minister, the minister of veterans affairs, and the chief of the defence staff. Next are four young people, winners of contests run in schools across the country by the Legion for the best posters and essays or poems commemorating fallen soldiers. The final wreath of the official viceregal party is laid by the longest-serving foreign diplomat, the dean of the diplomatic corps.

A year later, this turned out to be very important information when I was part of the live coverage. Although the program was produced by the network's news specials unit based in Toronto, for a number of years it had been anchored by a man named Brian Smith, who worked as a television announcer with the local CBC station in Ottawa. Larry Stout, based in Toronto, appeared beside Smith to add colour and say things about the importance of remembering. When I was asked to join the broadcast, Stout had just left the CBC; I naturally assumed I was to fill his role. It turned out I was wrong. When I turned up to meet with

Arnold Amber about half an hour before going on air, he quickly sensed I didn't understand my assignment.

"You know you are the anchor?" he asked.

"No," I said, amazed. "Hans Pohl didn't say anything about that. He said I was on because Larry was gone, and I assumed I was playing his role."

"It should have been explained properly to you. With Larry gone, I want to make some changes. I've told Smith he is not the anchor, and so I hope you feel you can handle it, as I don't want to now go back to him."

I thought I could do it, particularly since I had seen it all up close the year before. Besides, I knew if I didn't try, I wouldn't be getting any more work from Amber. There really wasn't a choice—there were just minutes to go till airtime.

"Okay," I said, "I'm fine with it."

It was cold outside that November morning, but it was even colder inside our broadcast booth. Because of the new assignments, there was very little interplay between the two CBC broadcasters. I could only hope that people watching at home thought the periods of silence between me and Smith were because of the solemnity of the occasion.

As it turned out, Amber was happy with the changes he had made, and he told me to be ready to do the broadcast again the next year. Remembrance Day in 1988 fell in the middle of the election campaign. I had been in Toronto, working on preparations for the election-night broadcast, and returned to Ottawa on the evening of November 10 to find that I had a new partner for the morning of November 11.

George Pearce had retired from the Canadian army with the rank of major. He had his paratroop wings, and he also had an amazing knowledge of Canadian military history, the badges of every regiment and the medals and decorations of every campaign. He knew the date of practically every major battle on land, sea and in the air. He was a walking military encyclopedia, and even more important, as far as I was concerned, he wanted to be on the program. In fact, despite having no broadcasting experience, he had called the producers in Toronto to tell them what he thought was needed, and so impressed them with his knowledge that they brought him in.

The 1988 broadcast was only my second, and I was still getting my feet wet when it came to handling the program. Intuitively, George just followed along. Not only did he add interesting and often important insights into the coverage, but like a pro, he slipped into an easy change of gears that occurs in every Remembrance Day broadcast when the silent solemnity of the wreath-laying in the first half of the program subtly takes on the up-tempo feel of a reunion as the vets, units and military bands parade around Confederation Square and the Governor General takes the salute.

We would do twenty more Remembrance Day telecasts in the following years. Over time, George's role expanded to bring more information and feeling into the remarks he would deliver near the beginning of the broadcast. Always he talked about an anniversary being recognized that year, and always he tied it together with feeling and sincerity and the themes by which he lived his own life: honour, duty, courage and respect. If it had been a religious broadcast, his remarks would have been the homily.

As the years clicked by, George was a treasure trove of information on anniversaries and dates Canadians should be remembering. In later years, Mark Bulgutch became the executive producer of the program and Dave Knapp was the producer who was in charge of the facilities and technical arrangements. It was Mark who asked George to be the CBC's liaison with the Royal Canadian Legion, which organized the national observance. Soon he became an authority not just on the combat decorations veterans were wearing and the regiments marching past; he knew the names of the sentries on the War Memorial, the names of the hymns being played during the wreath-laying, and the music being played during the march past.

Our second or third year together, we almost came a cropper. A cold, hard rain that had started two days earlier continued the morning of the eleventh. The booth used for the broadcast was known as the "Pope booth," having been built for the coverage of the tour of Pope John Paul II in 1984. It had a wooden floor raised on stilts about five feet off the ground. The walls and the roof were made of heavy canvas. It had a horseshoe-shaped desk for the anchors, and the window behind the desk was heavy plastic. No matter how cold it was on Remembrance Day, the plastic was always taken out so that the camera shot of the War Memorial behind us was clear and crisp.

The rain this year had begun to collect on the roof of the booth, and while we were on the air, the roof began to sag noticeably. I checked it a couple of times as the bulge got bigger, but thought we would make it to the end of the broadcast at noon without any untoward occurrence. Most of the time, George and I were not on camera. The pictures from the wreath-laying or the veterans' parade were telling the visual story. We didn't talk much during the laying of the wreaths—nor should one, given the solemnity—but we chatted away during the parade as George identified the various components of the parade marching by and sometimes commenting on their uniforms as well. As we kept talking, the time was ticking by and the bulge of water was getting bigger. Then I got the cue that it was time to sign off, which I did. George and I stood up, took off our microphones, laid them on the desk, picked up our notes, walked around to the front of the desk, and then continued behind the cameras. It was a good thing we did, because suddenly—*whoosh!* The bulge of water above our seats gave way, and gallons of water poured down on the desk and chairs.

We were just out of range and didn't even get splashed. But if the roof had given out two minutes earlier, we would both have been on camera when the water came cascading down. We would have ended the program sitting there, staring at the camera, completely drenched. Not a way to look on TV on Remembrance Day—or any other time, for that matter.

ATTENDANCE AT THE National Act of Remembrance at the War Memorial, as well as the television audiences, began to grow after 1994 and the celebration of the fiftieth anniversary of the successful D-Day landing in Normandy on June 6, 1944, that marked the beginning of the end of the Second World War.

The CBC mounted massive coverage of the events, the kind of coverage that budget cuts would make it impossible to do now. My assignments were all in England: at Green Park, across from Buckingham Palace, where the Queen dedicated a memorial to Canadians who fought in both world wars, and then down in Portsmouth for the embarkation ceremonies.

I left London on the afternoon of Friday, June 3, right after the dedication ceremony with the Queen in Green Park. Producer Tom Dinsmore and I boarded a train jammed with people who, like us, were heading for the south coast and the weekend celebration. Our tickets had been delivered to the CBC's London offices from a travel agency, but on the train the conductor said he had never seen tickets like them before and threatened to throw us off. We talked him into letting us stay on the train, then asked him for directions to the car selling sandwiches and drinks.

"It's two cars up," he said, pointing. "But there is no point going there. It's sold out. In fact, there isn't a sandwich anywhere south of London."

That was just the beginning of our adventure. Hotel space was so tight that all the CBC had been able to obtain for our crew were rooms above a pub on a road on the outskirts of Portsmouth. The rooms had not been used in years—perhaps since the embarkation in 1944, or so it looked—but had been pressed into service to make a few quick pounds during the celebrations. The water and toilet facilities were suspect. It reminded me of the American Enterprise Hotel the CBC people were stuck staying at when we covered the 1980 Republican convention in Detroit.

Still, it was all that was available. The way we survived the next three days was to use the room only for sleeping. We used the lavatories in the pub or the porta-potties near our broadcast location, and hoped there was enough hot water for shaving in the morning.

Fortunately, the broadcast location and the emotional story we had to tell were so compelling we could forget our accommodations. On the final day, the Queen attended a "drumhead" religious ceremony, with an oil drum used as an altar, positioned almost directly below our broadcast booth. She then sailed through a huge fleet of ships from the allied countries during the war and took the salute from each, before boarding the large American aircraft carrier USS *George Washington,* where she joined President Bill Clinton for the same crossing to Normandy that Canadian, British and American troops had made fifty years before.

The service, the sail past and the departure of the fleet were all very impressive. But I found an event the day before the most moving. The fifteen thousand Canadians who sailed out onto uncertain seas in June of 1944 had been based at, and embarked from, the small town of Gosport, just west of Portsmouth. Fifty years later, on Saturday, June 4, 1994, there was an event to commemorate them. Prime Minister Chrétien was there, as were other civilian and military figures. The mayor of Gosport was a woman who, as a little girl, had remembered the Canadians in her town until, one morning, they had all gone. She said at the time that she didn't know what was happening. But by now, she had known for many years and was grateful. It was moving and made you proud to be a Canadian.

The next year was the fiftieth anniversary of the end of the war. I was again in London, this time broadcasting from Hyde Park, St. Paul's Cathedral and in front of Buckingham Palace. I was there when the Queen, the Queen Mother and Princess Margaret came out onto the balcony, as they had fifty years earlier with King George VI and Winston Churchill. The Queen, her mother and her sister joined the crowd in celebratory singing of "The White Cliffs of Dover," the song that kept spirits high during dark times of the war.

That evening, I was in the CBC bureau near Oxford Circus when the final events were wrapping up. All the televisions were tuned to the BBC coverage, and when the ceremonies concluded with the playing of Elgar's "Land of Hope and Glory," the English staff hired to work with the Canadians in the bureau stood on their desks and sang the words.

Remembering those historic milestones, despite the veterans of both wars dwindling over the years, created more interest in Remembrance Day. But the numbers really grew in 2002, after Canada committed troops to Afghanistan and we had already taken casualties. As the years progressed and the number of Canadians killed increased, appropriately, the crowds did as well. The fighting in Afghanistan brought another change in our coverage. The day before the ceremony, we would interview the Silver Cross Mother and play her reminiscences during the broadcast before the wreath-laying ceremony began.

By the end of the nineties, old age had exhausted the pool of women to serve in that role. Suddenly, with the fighting and casualties in Afghanistan, there were mothers in their late thirties and early forties whose sons had been killed halfway around the world. These losses were very recent and very raw. I felt it gave a whole new meaning to the sacrifice of war. I made sure I had watched the tapes of these mothers talking about their sons and their deaths a number of times before we played them on air, so I knew and was used to the anguish we were going to see and hear. I am sure many people at home, seeing them for the first time, had more than one tear in their eyes. I felt that would be entirely appropriate at home, but not in the anchor booth.

That experience also gave me a tremendous respect for the young soldiers in the field and the officers who have the responsibility of leading them. It also sometimes made me wonder, when I listened to some politicians talking about the wars they were willing to send the soldiers to fight in, whether they had even the slightest idea of what they were really talking about.

As Canadians were overseas serving in harm's way, our Remembrance Day coverage changed to reflect that. Because of time differences, we had tape available of Canadian troops observing the Act of Remembrance at military camps in Afghanistan, Bosnia and on ships at sea. One year, we had video of Prime Minister Chrétien at a Commonwealth War Graves ceremony in the Far East, and another year tapes of aging veterans remembering their fallen colleagues at the Canadian cemetery at Pusan, Korea. In 2008, we went live, by satellite, to the Canadian base in Kandahar for a report on Remembrance Day observances by the Canadian troops inside the wire there. Dave Knapp and Fred Parker also played major roles improving the broadcasts and getting the programs to air.

I did twenty-two Remembrance Day broadcasts. Each was on the air for only ninety minutes, one day a year. The longer I did them, the more I realized how important the ceremonies and anniversaries were in bringing Canadians together, and to Canada as a whole.

53

Leaving the CBC

IN THE SPRING of 2007, I went to Toronto to have dinner with Tony Burman, the head of news at the CBC. Tony was one of the first people I met when I joined the Corporation in 1976, and while we didn't always agree, I liked him and felt the news was in good hands as long as he was in charge.

Four years earlier, we'd had a dinner in Ottawa at which I told him that in two years I would be sixty-five and was thinking about what I would do at that time. Don't do anything, was his advice; stay on as long as I was enjoying the work. I knew, without his saying as much, that he also meant I could stay as long as my audience was holding up. Now I wanted to give him a heads-up that, in 2009, I would have contributed as much to my pension as I could and I had tentatively selected that date to leave the CBC.

"Here's the deal," he said. "Instead of two more years, give me three and I will Brokaw you."

You had to be in television—and probably more specifically, television news—to know what that meant. But if you did, you knew it was a good deal. When Tom Brokaw was retiring as the anchorman of the *NBC Nightly News*, during his final year he shared his job with his successor, a man named Brian Williams. After twelve months, Brokaw was no longer there, but the transition was seamless and the broadcast kept its high ratings.

"After two years, I will have settled on your successor. The third year, you can share the program and I'll pay you as though you were still doing it full time."

"Sounds like a deal to me," I said, and we shook hands on it.

There turned out to be a problem, though: two weeks later, Tony had his final falling-out with Richard Stursberg and resigned from the CBC. I was back to figuring out when and how I would make my own exit.

Tony was replaced by John Cruickshank, a Canadian with a great journalistic reputation, experience at *The Globe and Mail* and who, for obvious reasons, was looking to return to Canada after being publisher at Conrad Black's *Chicago Sun-Times*. I didn't know John, but when I met him in October of 2007 we got along well and I looked forward to working with him.

However, John soon fell victim to the same problem Tony had. Stursberg wanted to divert money from CBC News and put it into entertainment programming, and he did. The difference between the resources we were given to cover the Canadian and American elections in 2004 and 2008 was, for me at least, a dramatic example of how budgets were being cut. If I needed any further confirmation, it was quick in coming. After a year on the job, John Cruickshank quit and moved to the *Toronto Star*, where he remains as publisher.

I had my birthday right after the 2008 election and realized that I was in the last year where I could keep improving my pension. I was already disappointed with the declining resources we were faced with in the Ottawa bureau, but I was still enjoying most of my work, and a big event like the prorogation crisis, where our *Politics* program was able to dominate the coverage and our ratings swamped CTV's, generated a good deal of pleasure.

At Christmas, Shannon and I went to New York. Walking in Central Park, we discussed whether I should make the television season we were then halfway through my last. Shannon advised me to think more about it; I might miss the CBC if I left. We agreed we would both think about it and discuss it again at Easter. By then, I was certain I would be leaving, but when I told the CBC, there was more than a suggestion that I had not given them enough notice to find a replacement. I had to get my agent to negotiate my way out. In the end, though, I left on good terms. Before I had time to let any of my colleagues or friends know, it had leaked to the media. Part of my arrangement in leaving was to promise to appear on CBC if there was an election in the fall after I had signed off.

The last big story I covered before I left the CBC was the public inquiry into the business dealings of former prime minister Brian Mulroney and German-Canadian businessman Karlheinz Schreiber, in May 2009. Justice Jeffrey Oliphant tried to get to the bottom of the three packages of thousand-dollar bills Schreiber had given to Mulroney after he had left office. But the justice didn't have a lot of success.

Schreiber said the money was to build a factory in Montreal that would produce light armoured military vehicles.

Mulroney said the money was to be used to lobby G8 countries to purchase the vehicles for their militaries. Either way, no factory was built and there were no vehicles made in Montreal for anyone to buy.

Mulroney didn't pay tax on the money until a number of years after he received it. Schreiber is now in jail in Germany for tax evasion, which is not connected to his dealings with Mulroney.

To use a Mulroneyism, the inquiry found that the former prime minister had been less than "fulsome" in detailing his business dealings with Schreiber when he sued the federal government for damages in 1995 and 1996. An official in the Department of Justice had written a letter to authorities in Switzerland saying the Canadian government was investigating Mulroney and others on possible kickbacks from the Air Canada purchase of Airbus aircraft, and Mulroney had gone to court to defend his reputation.

In discovery in his court case, Mulroney said that after he was prime minister he had had a cup of coffee a couple of times with Schreiber, but he never mentioned the payments in thousand dollar bills. Even more mysteriously, Mulroney had kept two of the payments of the money in a safe in his basement in Montreal and the other, which he received in the United States, in a safety deposit box in a New York bank.

In what might have been meant as either an understatement or irony, Oliphant found Mulroney's dealings with Schreiber "inappropriate." However, there were no recommendations of charges or other legal action against Mulroney in the Oliphant report. Nor were there any against Schreiber.

After the inquiry's public hearings ended, and ten months before the final report was issued, German agents whisked Schreiber out of the country on an extradition order over the August holiday long weekend in 2009. That happened just two days after Schreiber had told me in a private meeting, immediately after I left the CBC, that he and his lawyers had enough legal motions to file before the courts to keep him in Canada indefinitely.

After the first wave of bad publicity when the Oliphant report was issued in 2010, Mulroney shrugged off the hit to his reputation and re-emerged more or less as his old self. In October 2012, a dinner was organized in Toronto marking the twenty-fifth anniversary of the signing of the Canada–U.S. Free Trade Agreement. I was invited to attend by a corporate sponsor. Mulroney was there speaking to the who's who of the Toronto elite and business establishment. He received a standing ovation. It was as though nothing had happened.

On June 19, my colleagues on *Politics* took over the broadcast and created a tribute program for me that was way over the top but greatly appreciated. Earlier in the day, the speaker of the House of Commons, Peter Milliken, had arranged for me to be recognized from the floor of the House, and I was shocked when I received a standing ovation from the MPs. It too was greatly appreciated.

Although it sounded like I was retiring, I wasn't planning to do so in the traditional sense. Shannon and I had earlier formed a company called the Day-Newman Network Inc. to handle her consulting jobs and my non-CBC work, and now everything we both do is done through the company. I spend time working as an adviser with the Bluesky Strategy Group, an Ottawa communications and government relations company founded by Tim Barber and Susan Smith, two very bright, energetic, hard-working professionals with a great deal of experience in Ottawa and Queen's Park in Toronto. I am also chairman of the advisory board of Canada 2020, a public policy group they formed in 2005 along with Eugene Lang and Tom Pitfield. Canada 2020 puts on events and dinners, publishes policy papers and has great success in pushing forward debate on a number of policy areas, including health care, Asia-Pacific issues, competitiveness and innovation, energy and the environment and income inequality.

When I'm not at Bluesky or Canada 2020, I am often in Toronto or Ottawa, speaking to industry associations, at meetings of boards of directors or moderating panels at conventions. As the 2015 election approaches, I expect the pace will pick up even more. But at the same time, it is important to give back—which I try to do through involvement with various nonprofit groups and charities—and to do the things I want to do and enjoy the good times with Shannon, family, friends and colleagues.

Everything I am doing now draws on the experience of the more than forty wonderful years I had working as a daily journalist. The skills I was able to develop through the patience of the many people who employed and helped me continue to stand me in good stead. I wouldn't have missed a day of it, and I now miss the colleagues, but not the grind, of a daily program. Nor do I miss the repetition of political spinners who began to aggravate me and who lower the level of discussion and impede efforts to bring forward the truth that Canadians—whom I sought at all times to serve, without fear or favour—deserve to have. And I always relish the enjoyment of someone I have never met before seeing me on the street, in a taxi or in a restaurant, smiling with a look of recognition and saying, "Welcome to the broadcast!"

Acknowledgements

I T DOESN'T MATTER what is on the air at any given moment. It could be a hockey game, it could be a comedy, it could be a documentary or it could be the news. For the people who worked on it—writing it, producing it, taking it to air or broadcasting it—the product they have created is a show.

Maybe it was my background in newspapers, or maybe I'm just a stick in the mud, but I was never comfortable with the idea that information programming was in fact a show. I knew, of course, that for viewers to watch, it had to be interesting, convey information that people wanted or needed to know, and have a pace and rhythm that attracted viewers and then got them to stay. Still, I never liked calling what I did a show. In my mind, that implied something lighthearted and purely entertaining.

But if you don't call it a show, what do you call it? In the fall of 1998, when *Politics* was shortened to an hour and I became the sole host, that became a question I had to answer. At 5 p.m. Eastern time an opening rolled across the network. It featured distinctive music and shots from the House of Commons, and my picture appeared briefly. But there was no voice on the opening, just the music, so I decided I should introduce myself and then welcome viewers to what they were watching.

I thought about saying, "Welcome to the program," but that to me sounded more suitable for introducing serious music. Besides, "program" had another meaning, as in, "You can't tell the players without a program."

Now, what we were doing each day was clearly broadcasting, and what we were putting on the air was a broadcast. There was the answer: "Welcome to the broadcast."

Over the years the greeting became better known and, along with my voice and my emphasis, arguably became as well known as the name of the broadcast—which is why this book has my greeting for a title.

I didn't decide to write a book until 2011, although when I left the CBC I received plenty of encouragement to do so. Only when two women who knew a lot of about books suggested I try did I seriously consider it.

My friend Charlotte Gray, the award-winning biographer and my colleague from the board of Canada's National History Society, urged me to try my hand. When supported by Charlotte's editor Phyllis Bruce, whom I got to know as a contributor to the Society's book, *100 Photos That Changed Canada*, my course was set. Charlotte went a step further and introduced me to her agent at Westwood Creative Artists. Hilary McMahon then became my agent and steered the project to a home with HarperCollins. I thank Charlotte, Phyllis and Hilary for getting me and the book going!

I realized as I wrote what I already knew: though I was fortunate to have had the colleagues I had and stories to cover wherever I worked, I could not have enjoyed my career without spending most of it at the CBC. Not only with *The National*, then both a weekly program and a daily program on the political life of our country, but also the many live specials, leadership conventions, elections and policy debates. I also had the opportunity to work, over the years, with talented people both on and off camera. Some are mentioned earlier; others in the Ottawa bureau include Keith Boag, Julie Van Dusen, Alvin Cador, Jerry Beauchamp, David McCormick, Heather Spiller, Chris Hall and Chris Waddell, and from Radio-Canada, Daniel L'Heureux.

A lot of talented CBC people across Canada helped put our hundreds of live specials and programs on the air, but I owe particular thanks to the group in Ottawa that worked closely with me over the final few years I anchored, including the senior producers, Dave Mathews and Sharon Musgrave, who are part of some of the stories in this book. Like Dave, Sharon was invaluable. She continues to work at the CBC in charge of live broadcasts from Ottawa and runs the election night decision desks across Canada. Others I wish to thank and acknowledge include Kathleen Hunt, Jackie Melville, Janyce McGregor, Paul Bisson, Chris Rands and Hannah Thibedeau, as well as Susan Bonner, who often filled in for me as anchor when I was away, and Rosemary Barton, who is now playing a big role on *Power and Politics* with Evan Solomon.

In the control room the team was led by director Gerry Buffett, switcher Rob Scott, resources producer Kent Richardson and audio man Henri Poirier. On the studio floor Mike Suzuki was the cameraman who worked with me the longest, and Tommy Sharina I first met in Edmonton. Of the many technicians, a special place in my heart for Moira Alfers for her good humour. Also, production assistant Nancy Attfield kept us all on time, unit manager Brenda Levy made sure we stayed close to the budget and Ken Furness, the bureau's chief engineer, performed technical wizardry. I owe special thanks to Joan Hodgins, who in 1993 began working her makeup magic on me. All of these people played an important part in the broadcasts.

I also realized how fortunate I was, over the years, to have been a member of the Canadian Parliamentary Press Gallery. To have been friends, colleagues and competitors with some of the best journalists from around the country, all of us focused on the issues and people who defined the political life of our country, and to have worked with the staff of the gallery, led by the outstanding chief clerk, Terry Guillon, has been a real privilege. A gallery director in the 1980s and president in 1987, I now derive one of my great pleasures from my life membership to the gallery, which I received for over thirty years of reporting from Parliament Hill.

To my surprise, I came to realize that writing a book and appearing on television have a lot in common. The writer or the person on camera is ultimately responsible for the words or the performance, yet neither can happen without the efforts of many other talented people.

That was certainly true at the CBC, and it is true as well at HarperCollins, where my editor, Jim Gifford, deserves my complete gratitude for his patience, wisdom and good humour towards a neophyte author who had trouble meeting a deadline. Thanks to copy editor Lloyd Davis for turning my sow's ear into a silk purse, and to production editor Kelly Hope. As well, recognition is due to all of the other smart, creative people involved, from art, marketing and publicity divisions. Thanks, too, to those who gave legal advice.

My friends, relatives and colleagues also patiently heard my excuses and kept interested, even though it meant postponing our time together.

In addition to walking down memory lane, I also began to realize that some of my experiences could be encouraging to young journalists. Whatever the technology we use, whatever happens to the industry I started in and however it evolves in the future, we should all remember that a functioning democracy is essential to a free society, and that fearless, fair journalism that reports, explains and analyzes is essential to a functioning democracy.

I hope what I have written here explains how I have tried to be a part of that. And while that sounds serious and self- important, I hope it also captures what a good time I have had doing it all. As I was writing I more than once thought of the adage, "Find a job that you love and you will never work a day in your life." By that standard I have never done a lick of work.

The dedication of this book is "For Shannon." That is because without my wife, with whom I also work on other projects, there would have been no book. Shannon's personal and professional background added weight to her thoughts, recommendations and ideas as she tirelessly read every word that I wrote, offered considered opinions and editorial improvements, checked names and dates, did research, organized pictures and kept the author focused.

I am responsible for any errors and omissions.

But in every other way the book is just as much Shannon's as it is mine.

Index